Political Corruption in America

Political Corruption in America

George C. S. Benson
The Henry Salvatori Center
Claremont Men's College

with the assistance of

Steven A. Maaranen
Alan Heslop
Claremont Men's College

Lexington Books
D.C. Heath and Company
Lexington, Massachusetts
Toronto

ST. PHILIPS COLLEGE LIBRARY

Library of Congress Cataloging in Publication Data

Benson, George Charles Sumner, 1908-
   Political corruption in America.

   Bibliography: p.
   Includes index.
   1. Corruption (in politics)—United States—History. I. Maaranen, Steven A., joint author. II. Heslop, Alan, joint author. III. Title.
JK2249.B46   320.9'73   77-88815
ISBN 0-669-02008-7

Copyright © 1978 by D.C. Heath and Company.

All rights reserved. No part of this publication may be reproduced or transmitted in any form or by any means, electronic or mechanical, including photocopy, recording, or any information storage or retrieval system, without permission in writing from the publisher.

Published simultaneously in Canada.

Printed in the United States of America.

International Standard Book Number: 0-669-02008-7

Library of Congress Catalog Card Number: 77-88815

Contents

	Preface	xi
	Introduction	xiii
Chapter 1	**The Nature of Corruption**	1
	Corruption in Foreign Countries	3
	How Important Is Corruption?	5
	Techniques of Graft	5
	Fields of Graft	9
	Fighting Anticorruption Measures	15
Chapter 2	**The Origins of Municipal Corruption**	17
	Colonial Traditions of City Government	17
	Changing Municipal Conditions and the Origins of Corruption	19
	New-Style Urban Politics: New York and Philadelphia	22
	Role of the State and Federal Governments	24
	Foreign Immigration Augments the Urban Machines	24
	The Immigrant and the Urban Machine	27
	Nonimmigrant Corruption	31
	Conclusions	32
Chapter 3	**The Politics of Municipal Corruption**	33
	Patterns of Political Corruption	33
	Organization and Politics of the Municipal Machine	34
	The Party Machine and Political Corruption	48
	Nonmachine Political Corruption	49
	Effect of Corruption on Local Government	51
	The Origins of Municipal Reform	51
	Conclusions	54
Chapter 4	**State Corruption in the Nineteenth Century**	57
	The Course of Political Corruption in New York State	58
	Big Business and Political Corruption in Ohio	63
	Corruption in the West and South	65
	Land Corruption	68
	Railroad Corruption	70
	Influence of Immigration	72

	Influence of States on Local Government	72
	Conclusions	72
Chapter 5	**Federal Corruption in the Nineteenth Century**	**73**
	The Federalists and the Jeffersonians	73
	The Jackson Era and the New Politics of the Democracy	75
	The Lincoln Administration	79
	Corruption and Reform in the Postbellum Years	80
	Reform and Relapse from Hayes to Roosevelt	83
	Conclusions	86
Chapter 6	**Local Corruption since World War I**	**89**
	Introduction	89
	Political Machine to Organized Crime	90
	A Study of Four Cities	93
	The Present State of Municipal Corruption	113
	Geographical Considerations	114
	Conclusions	116
Chapter 7	**State Corruption since World War I**	**119**
	Role of the States	119
	Corrupt States	121
	State Police	129
	Reformed States	130
	Conclusions	135
Chapter 8	**Federal Corruption from World War I to 1969**	**137**
	Congress	137
	Congressional Investigation	142
	Corruption in the Administration	145
	The Federal Government and Organized Crime	161
	Administrative Tribunals	164
	Conclusions	166
Chapter 9	**Corruption in American Elections**	**169**
	The Administration of Elections	169
	The Conduct of Campaigns	174
	Money in Elections	177
	Conclusions	183

Chapter 10	**Costs of Corruption**	187
	Intellectual Arguments for Corrupt Machines	187
	Development of Cynicism	189
	The Costs of "Honest" Graft	190
	Effect of Corruption on Governmental Finance	191
	Quality of Administration	193
	Effect of Corruption on Crime	195
	Effect of Corruption on People, Especially the Poor	199
	Is Corruption Needed to Secure Citizen Participation?	205
	Conclusions	208
	Summary and Analysis	208
Chapter 11	**Theories of Corruption**	211
	Benevolence of the Machine	211
	The Modernization and Economic Development Theory of Corruption	212
	Sociological Theory of Unfulfilled Needs	216
	Class against Corruption	218
	Overemphasis on Business Values	221
	The Party Dominance Theory	221
	Weakness in Forms of Governments	223
	Money in Elections	227
	Unnecessary Legislation	228
	Demographic Factors	230
	Poorly Paid Public Employees	231
	Overdecentralization	232
	Ethical Standards	233
	Faulty Administrative Tradition, Especially in Police	234
	Organized Crime	236
	Why Is America So Corrupt?	237
Chapter 12	**Levels of Government and Corruption Control**	239
	Change and Suggestions of Change	239
	Arguments for Greater Federal and State Responsibility in Corruption Control	239
	Arguments for Anticentralists	242
	State Efforts against Corruption	243
	More Party Opposition to Keep Law Enforcement Alert	246
	How Administrators May Combat Corruption	247
	Police Reform	247

	Present Federal Efforts against Corruption	249
	An Alternative Approach for Federal Action	251
Chapter 13	**Business, Labor, and Political Corruption**	255
	Introduction	255
	Is Business to Blame for Corruption?	255
	Business Corruption of Government in the Nineteenth Century	256
	Business Corruption of Government in the Twentieth Century	259
	Business-Government Corruption as a Two-Way Relationship	260
	Business Sponsors Government Reform	262
	Other Ethical Questions about Business and Government	263
	Conclusions on Business-Government Relationships	264
	Organized Labor and Political Corruption	265
	A Brief History of Organized Labor and Political Corruption	266
	Attempts at Union Reform	269
	Conclusions	271
Chapter 14	**Improvement of Political Ethics**	273
	Community Ethical Standards	273
	Corrupt Educated Individuals	274
	Men Who Looked the Other Way	277
	Inadequate Ethical Education	278
	Civic Education and Corruption	279
	Ineffectiveness of Civic Education	280
	Can Civic Ethics Be Taught?	280
	The Churches	282
	The Press and Television	285
	Professions and Their Standards	287
	Citizen Associations and Individual Reformers	288
	Summary and Conclusions	290
Chapter 15	**The Way Out of Corruption**	293
	Recommendations	295

Notes	297
Bibliography	317
Index	331
About the Authors	341

Preface

This book is a product of the Henry T. Salvatori Center for the Study of Individual Freedom in the Modern World. The three faculty members who have worked on this book, Professors Heslop and Maaranen and myself, all wish to express their gratitude to Mr. Salvatori for the opportunity to undertake the study.

I am responsible for most of the work. Professor Maaranen wrote Chapters 2, 3, 4, and 5; Professor Heslop wrote Chapter 9. However, several people have helped us in numerous respects.

I am grateful to Tyler Draa and Tom Kunkel, Claremont Men's College undergraduates, for extensive help in editing the manuscript and in checking on facts, footnotes, and bibliography. My 1977 class "Ethics in Business and Politics" gave very useful comments on an early draft of the book. The secretary of the Center, Donna Marleau, has worked hard and shown much patience on several drafts of the manuscript.

George C. S. Benson

Introduction

The publication of this study of political corruption in the United States should not be misconstrued as an attack on American constitutional democracy. The authors are proud of the United States. They respect its representative system of government, its democratic way of life, and its free economic system. The book grew out of the authors' belief in this country and their hope for its future.

Some critics of our approach may note that it is only in comparison with a few other constitutional democracies that the United States may be said to suffer seriously from a problem of political corruption. Other critics may say that we exaggerate the harm done by corruption or overlook the "functional advantages" of some kinds of political corruption. Our view is that the United States cannot afford the loss in moral authority that results from corruption. Leadership of the free world requires us to offer an example of constitutionalism at its best.

Definition of Corruption

The term *corruption* has a variety of meanings. Its basic physical meaning of putrefaction has been carried over by analogy to a variety of political definitions, a number of which are well presented by Heidenheimer.[1] After Heidenheimer's array of definitions had been considered, a modified version of a definition devised by David H. Bayley appeared to be even more applicable to the subject at hand: "Corruption, while being tied to the act of bribery, is a general term covering misuse of authority as a result of considerations of personal gain, which need not be monetary."[2]

In this book, Bayley's definition will be used in a somewhat altered form. *Political corruption* is a general term covering all illegal or unethical use of governmental authority as a result of considerations of personal or political gain. This modified version of Bayley's definition was chosen in part because of the belief that phenomena like Watergate, which had little to do with bribery or monetary gain, should be discussed in this book, although they will not be discussed in detail for reasons given below. The term *illegality in government* would have included not only Watergate but also many problems of constitutional or statutory authority, which would greatly extend the length and alter the nature of this book.

The word *corruption* flows naturally from its biological origin, which ultimately means the complete putrefaction of a society. Robert Payne has written a book, *The Corrupt Society,* which gives examples of such complete corruption as Hitler's Germany, China under the Hsin Dynasty, Stalin's Russia, and more recently the Nixon administration.[3]

xiii

Apart from the question as to whether these regimes are actually comparable, the authors simply do not believe that corruption in American politics has descended to such a level. America has allowed corruption to go much further than it should; however, America could reduce the amount of corruption greatly if it should seriously undertake the task. Numbers of modern countries have improved their ethical standards.

Another difficulty in definition stems from the use of the term *corruption* to include any financial gifts or offers to candidates or to their campaign funds. It is true that such gifts can be employed for ends similar to those intended for the bribes discussed throughout this book. If legislation makes such gifts illegal, they would then become corruption under the definition used here. But discussion here is limited to actual illegalities, which are themselves a large enough problem for us to handle. The best method of representing the viewpoints of unions, corporations, or other economic groups to government officials is another problem, calling for another book.

Advocates of Common Cause, to which the senior writer belongs, have said that their proposals (for example, Proposition 9 on the California ballot in 1974) would "end corruption in California." Such statements are misleading. The activities of state legislators and a few other officials were affected greatly by passage of the act, but the bribery of local officials (especially police), which constitutes the largest part of corruption, might not be affected at all.

Political Corruption and Machine Politics

Political machines in America have been so likely to be corrupt that many Americans tend to use the terms *machines* and *corruption* interchangeably. However, they are not always synonymous. Not all political machines are equally corrupt, or indeed corrupt at all. For instance, the Byrd machine in Virginia had an above-average record of honesty. Some non-machine-controlled cities and states have bad records of corruption, usually on the part of lower-ranking officials, but sometimes including higher officials. Similarly, the formal termination of machine control in large cities like New York, Philadelphia, and Boston has not eliminated corruption, as a number of recent investigations indicate. In fact, some persons trying to conduct legitimate businesses in these cities have indicated that one payment to a given machine was a cheaper, easier way to operate than several payments to different individuals in several municipal departments of a non-machine-controlled city.

In general, however, there has been a substantial correlation between machine politics and political corruption. Tightly controlled political machines tended to use corruption as a major source of revenue for payment of machine officials and such fractions of the population as seem likely to replay the machine's bounty with votes. The fact that lower-ranking officials are aware of misdeeds of machine leaders means that these officials are less deterred by the threat of discipline and, hence, are more likely to become corrupt themselves. The political impregnability of many machine bosses has led them to conduct corrupt activities with little regard for attacks by good-government proponents. It is one of the disappointing conclusions of this book, however, that the fall of the traditional, nineteenth-century style, centralized machine has not eliminated political corruption in America's state and local governments. A few jurisdictions are even worse than they were in the nineteenth century. To some extent, contemporary political corruption is a continuation of traditions established by the machine. But there seem to be other factors which help to keep political corruption alive. In the rest of this book, an effort will be made to appraise these factors, as well as to assess the amount and significance of the corruption which has transpired at various levels of government.

Often Exaggerated Corruption

Care must be taken to avoid taking unproved charges too seriously. The media as well as individual writers often make charges of corruption too hastily and too easily. Supreme Court decisions have removed much of the protection of action for libel from public officials. For example, the Harding, Truman, and Nixon administrations have been accused of being "full" of corruption; yet this charge is untrue in all three cases. All three administrations had department heads of unquestioned honesty who ran good administrative operations in sharp contrast to other bad spots of corruption in all three. The exaggeration of writers who charge overall corruption is frequently followed by citizens who should know better. The authors have often heard unusually honest city administrations accused of being "corrupt" by citizens angered by a presumably unjust traffic ticket or by being overlooked by the garbage collector.

This book attempts to confine itself to proved corruption. There are enough examples of this to be a cause of real concern to thoughtful Americans. There is also a danger that exaggeration of corruption may lead to overcorrection. Irving Kristol has written that the attempts to improve public morality by statute after Watergate may damage democratic government more than they help it. He is concerned about the effect of "sunshine" laws in keeping distinguished men and women out of politics, ridiculously sharp enforcement of laws against "price fixing" and international payoffs, and the reduction of reasonable representation of interests before legislative bodies.[4]

In addition to exaggerating corruption, many people often oversimplify the causes. Well-educated people frequently try to explain America's ongoing corruption problem with one reason. Even thoughtful writers have exaggerated the importance of single explanations. For instance, some of Professor Huntington's followers have overused his economic development theory. Robert H.

Williams, investigative reporter, in his thoughtful *Vice Squad,* has implied that "victimless crime" laws are the main reason for police corruption; yet he fails to explain why other modern countries with similar laws have much less corruption. Berg, Hahn, and Schmidhauser in *Corruption in the American Political System* seem to ascribe corruption to excessive campaign expenditures; many of the examples in this book are quite unrelated to campaign funds. Other writers ascribe corruption to immigrants, although "older stock" Americans started and controlled many corrupt machines.

A conclusion of this book is that political corruption has taken root in several areas of American local government and remained there for various reasons, only some of which we can hope to control. Chapter 11 has a full discussion of most of the suggested causes; as far as we can tell, the basis of corruption is not confined to any one.

Plan of the Book

The first chapter defines some of the methods of corruption and very briefly lists various reasons given for corruption by a number of academic and political commentators. Then Chapters 2 through 5 deal with corruption at different levels of government. To keep the chapters shorter and to simplify the research assignments, there are discussions of corruption on each level of government before and after World War I (Chapters 6 through 8); this division was chosen because of the reform movement which began about 1890 and had substantial impact by the time of the war. Chapters 9 through 13 deal with various topical aspects of corruption. The last two chapters include recommendations for reform. The topical chapters and the reform chapters are the ones in which this book differs most sharply from other writings on corruption.

Omission of Watergate

Watergate has largely been omitted, primarily as a matter of reducing the book's length, not because of a lack of concern about its importance. It would be difficult in a single chapter to add anything significant to the two score or more books published on Watergate. Also Watergate is in most ways completely out of the mainstream of American corruption. No bribes or kickbacks were accepted by the principal conspirators; no machine-type politicians were involved. However, it is necessary to point out here that Watergate was in part a result of previous corruption. The Watergate conspirators were undoubtedly influenced by doubts regarding the validity of the 1960 Presidential election results in Chicago and the knowledge that they were struggling against some potent, corrupt forces. Victor Lasky has listed previous presidential aberrations in *It Didn't*

Start with Watergate.[5] The decision of the Watergaters to fight corrupt fire with corrupt fire is, of course, not excusable. On a more cheerful note, the large amount of reform legislation supported by Common Cause as a preventive measure against further Watergates may have some beneficial effect, even if most of the legislation bears little relation to specific Watergate events. Progress toward better political ethics is to be commended, even if its raison d'être is difficult to follow.

Unusual Theses

In an historical sense, this book is not original. Although several years of research have gone into it, it has not been possible to review the files of all important newspapers or to pursue every depository of local history. Several hundred books and many scores of articles have been used; but often the books were written by reporters or other nonhistorians and are agonizingly devoid of footnotes, indexes, dates, or bibliographies. Fortunately, enough material exists for cities such as New York, Chicago, Kansas City, and San Francisco to permit double and triple checking of data. Most of the reporter-authors have tried to be objective. The reasons that this "rehash" of materials is being published are twofold. The authors have tried to present a thoughtful, chronological history of corruption in America in order to lend weight to the concluding analysis and recommendations as well as to supplement the sorely inadequate material currently available in historical literature. The book contains several theses which differ sharply from much of the existing literature about political corruption in America.

First, the book is written on the assumption that there are ethical standards in various American societies, and that departure from these standards is, over time, bad for American society as a whole. If ethical standards of political life have fallen lower among the politicians and citizens of New York and Chicago than among those of Los Angeles and Dallas, this results in poorer government in the former cities and eventually in all four. A large number of writers on political corruption and law enforcement ignore ethical standards, often to the detriment of otherwise thoughtful studies. This book identifies the standards and even suggests means of improving ethical instruction.

Second, the unhappy administrative effects of corruption are mentioned in many chapters and are summarized in Chapter 10. Much recent literature on corruption, authored by distinguished social scientists, tends to ignore the administrative consequences of corruption and to limit comments to an assumed sociological or psychological benefit of corruption. Without denying the possibility of some of these positive effects, the authors of this book are concerned that the extent and significance of the unhappy social and administrative consequences of corruption should also be considered.

Third, this book is unusual in that it attempts to appraise most of the reasons for corruption advanced by observers. More than a dozen "reasons" for corruption are fully discussed in Chapter 11, on the basis of the evidence given in the preceding chapters. Many readers will disagree with the emphasis given to one or another reason in this book. We hope that such readers will at least agree that this book has tried to sort out all the reasons acknowledged, rather than riding on one or two as many previous analyses of political corruption have done.

Fourth, as a result of the breadth of analysis of reasons for ongoing corruption in America, the list of remedial measures is broader here than in most writing on this subject. A host of well-meaning changes in structure of government have been proposed as reforms to end corruption. The thesis of this book is that, while some structural reforms are important, the most important reform is to educate and select better people for public office. A good sense of ethics in public servants is as important as constitutional government, the rule of law, free enterprise, or widespread public education in the maintenance of a free society.

Fifth, there has been impressive evidence that American government needs to use higher levels of government to help enforce honesty at local levels.

Many readers will note how much these theses differ from those of Common Cause. Much Common Cause-sponsored legislation has been, and will be, beneficial. But Common Cause and related reform groups seem to have overlooked the corruption which this book finds most frequent and most damaging to American values of life—the ongoing corruption of state and local government, especially that which is associated with organized crime and concentrated in law enforcement agencies. If any Common Cause recommendation has a real impact on this kind of corruption, the authors are not aware of it.

1

The Nature of Corruption

Leonard White, in his series on the administrative history of the United States, has suggested that the first third of a century of the republic was relatively corruption-free. The "leading citizens" whom both Federalists and Republicans tended to appoint to office were likely to be fairly honest. America was still largely an agricultural country, which reduced the resources and opportunities for corruption. In addition, we still maintained a degree of revolutionary pride in our democratic institutions. However, the Yazoo land frauds in Georgia and other isolated examples of bribery and fraud showed that Americans were not unacquainted with corruption in this period.

Alexis de Tocqueville, young French judicial official and budding author, traveling in America in 1831-1832 and writing his classic *Democracy in America* in the 1830s, mentions no specific corruption but clearly identifies corruption as a danger of and to democracy, as well as a potential component of it. While he admires Americans and their governments greatly, he notes that he found "so much distinguished talent among the citizens and so little among the heads of government." The quality of American political leadership seemed to him to be declining. He was concerned that the rulers of a democracy were suspected of corruption by private citizens and that "an odious connection" was thus formed "between the ideas of turpitude and power, unworthiness and success, utility and dishonor."[1] de Tocqueville was not very clear about why democracy is more subject to this danger than aristocracy, except that "there is a kind of aristocratic refinement and an air of grandeur by the depravity of the great, which frequently prevent it from spreading abroad," and which democracy lacks.

With the election of President Andrew Jackson in 1828 and the corresponding acceptance of the theory of rotation in office, attitudes began to change. Almost at the same time, the arrival of masses of immigrants, who were unused to American institutions of democracy, and the irresponsible type of city charters adopted in the nineteenth century aided the rise of the urban political machine.[2] The machine almost invariably brought with it a high degree of political corruption. There were occasional reform mayors, but cities like New York, Philadelphia, and Chicago probably had substantial ongoing corruption, especially in the police departments, from 1850 to date. The city machines' political power made it possible to extend some of this corruption to state governments and to a limited extent to the federal government. The latter had perhaps its worst scandals in the Buchanan (1857-1861) and Grant administrations (1869-1877), but serious scandals also appeared in the Harding, Truman, and Nixon administrations.

Reform movements have often appeared. At the turn of the century, under the prodding of the muckrakers (reform journalists), there were signs of a general reform movement. Since then, cities like Milwaukee (reformed by socialists), Los Angeles, Cincinnati, and Kansas City (reformed by upper-middle-class citizen groups) have had continuous records of relative honesty for some decades. Some states have had excellent records, such as California since 1910 (except for the Samish regime in the state legislature in the 1940s and 1950s). Wisconsin since La Follette's time, New York since 1920, and Michigan since the 1930s. In general, reform has been more frequent and more continuous in the West and South than in the Northeast.

All city machine politics have been declining virtually everywhere except in Chicago, and that machine shows signs of weakening. Higher levels of education have liberated many people from the umbrella of machine politics. Ethnic groups have attained improved status in American life. Federally sponsored welfare programs have made the machine, and its shallow benevolences, less useful. However, there has been a continuation of large amounts of corruption after the political machine disappeared. In 1970 New York's Mayor John Lindsay was forced to investigate a police department which was still over a quarter corrupt. In a study of Boston, Chicago, and Washington in the late 1960s, "excluding any participation in syndicated crime, roughly 1 in 5 officers was observed in criminal violation of the law."[3] And this observation was made by observers who had little time to be acquainted with the police officers. The incidents observed were almost always acceptance of money or merchandise. A. J. Reichley writes, in *Fortune:*

The last two years alone have seen: the conviction of Federal Judge Otto Kerner for taking a bribe in the form of race track stock while he was Governor of Illinois; the conviction of Attorney General of Louisiana Jack Gremillion for perjury; the conviction of Gus Mutscher, former Speaker of the Texas House of Representatives, for participation in a stock swindle; the conviction of former U.S. Senator Daniel Brewster for taking a bribe; the indictment of close associates of Governor William Cahill of New Jersey for promoting a scheme to evade income tax laws covering campaign contributions. None of these deeds approached Watergate in seriousness, but all are evidences of the low level to which ethical standards have fallen in many areas of government.[4]

Undoubtedly the most publicity ever given to political corruption in this country is that given to the Watergate episodes, in which a President of the United States quite deliberately assisted in the coverup of two illegal burglaries. The complex of causes leading to President Nixon's breakdown in administrative integrity may never be fully explained. Of more importance to this book is the question of what the intense publicity on Watergate will do to political corruption in this country.

Today it is probably fair to say that America has as much corruption, both absolutely and proportionately, as any other modern constitutional democracy. There are no international indices of corruption, but the available data indicate that corruption here is at least as severe and extensive as in other modern democracies. American idealism does not appear to be reflected in our political ethos.

Corruption in Foreign Countries

Corruption occurs infrequently in the British national and local government. Britain did have a great deal of corruption in the first quarter of the nineteenth century—probably more than occurred in the United States at that time. But a reform effort that Professor Friedrich describes as a "little short of miraculous" overcame this corruption and incompetence.[5] Later in the century, the British central government succeeded in helping local government eliminate most of its corruption. The late Hiram Stout, in his book *British Government,* says, "On the score of integrity, no major scandal has touched the Civil Service in recent years."[6] A 1972 article in *The New York Times* indicates that corruption is negligible in the British judiciary, as well as being low in the courts of France and West Germany.[7] Attesting to the contrast bewteen England and the United States, the Royal Commission on Standards of Conduct in Public Life (Salmon Commission) in 1976 reported a yearly average of 1.4 convictions for failure to disclose an interest in local government and 16.5 convictions under the Prevention of Corruption acts in local government; civil servants' convictions for bribes and gifts were slightly over 4 per year. In contrast, in the Chicago area alone, U.S. Attorney Thompson secured convictions of 47 precinct captains and judges of election, 35 police officers, and 22 other public officials in a period from November 1971 to the end of 1973.[8] Recent investigations have shown a surprising amount of corruption among Scotland Yard detectives, but the number involved is still small in contrast to American big city forces.

Roland Huntford, although sharply critical of Swedish governmental policies, comments: "It is vital for an understanding of Swedish society to realize that public corruption, in the form of personal bribery, does not exist."[9]

Professor Heidenheimer states that the German civil service experienced a minor wave of corruption in the 1950s, but that the German public official is still widely admired.[10] Hans Rosenberg gives some background of the more than century-old Prussian bureaucratic efforts to maintain honesty.[11] Holland, after a good deal of effort, has succeeded in setting high standards prohibiting the corruption of government officials,[12] although Prince Bernard has been an unhappy exception. Switzerland seems to maintain consistently high standards of honesty in its government.[13] The only modern democracy which may have had amounts of corruption parallel to ours was France under the Third Republic.[14] However, it is our impression that France now has less corruption than the United States.

While there is political corruption in Japan, there is much less than in the United States. In 1973, 863 Japanese officials at all levels of government were suspected of bribery; half of them were tried, and 95 percent had their sentences suspended.[15] In the early 1970s, Lockheed Aircraft spent $12 million bribing Japanese political figures to secure use of Lockheed aircraft on Japanese airlines. However, when the bribes were revealed in 1976, the Japanese reaction was spectacular, including an effect on a general election and the jailing of a former premier.

These figures are small compared to the large numbers of police believed to be guilty of corruption in our Northeastern cities.[16] The countries listed above were not always ahead of the United States in political rectitude. Several of them were probably worse off in 1800. The authors have not been able to determine how all these countries were reformed, but there are considerable data on the nineteenth-century reform of Great Britain, which coincided with the decline in American political ethics.

Several writers agree that Britain's reform was at least in part a result of an evangelical religious movement started by John Wesley in the eighteenth century. This movement, which reformed churches, schools, universities, business, and other institutions besides government, included more emphasis on individual ethical standards than did most religious movements. Since Wesley never dropped his Church of England priesthood, it was a movement which went forward in the poorer, evangelical, and established Anglican classes.

Factors other than the religious movement have been said to cause Britain's reform. These include the acceptance of the responsibilities of running an empire, responsibilities which required an ethical, educated group of public officials; the increased recognition of the necessity of fair treatment for each individual; the evolution of the doctrine of democracy in Britain; and the contributions of Utilitarian philosophy.

Wraith and Simpkins, two Englishmen who became interested in the amount of corruption in Nigeria and other countries of Africa formerly ruled by Britain, examined the reform of their own country carefully, to see what patterns it revealed for the future elimination of corruption in Africa. In addition to the reasons suggested above, they also gave a score or more of other reasons. The Corrupt and Illegal Practices bill of 1883 ended corruption of the electorate. The growth of responsible political parties made it important for parties to appear virtuous. Bribery of members of Parliament stopped in the 1780s, because the American victory at Yorktown in 1781 ended Lord North's government, because King George III gave up efforts to control parties, because members of Parliament were becoming more wealthy and less bribable, and because of a freer press. Reform in the civil service occurred in part because business has expanded its power and wanted more efficiency in government. New schools for the middle and upper classes produced a more highly educated constituency. Local government was improved by the Municipal Corporations Act of 1835, but bribery was not stopped unitl the Public Bodies Corrupt Practices Act of 1889. Enfranchisement of middle-class citizens brought support for the auditing of local government accounts by the central government. Law enforcement was improved by a system of Home Office inspection. The armed forces were reformed in the 1870s partly in response to the German danger, partly because of nationalist imperialism. Education was reformed largely through central inspections.

The authors suspect that few of these reforms would have occurred had Britain not been moved by the Evangelical movement and by the rise of more efficient business classes. The nineteenth-century development of more efficient and responsible bureaucracies in Central and Western European countries seems also to have been correlated with economic and educational advancement of the population.[17]

In spite of the good record of modern democracies, there is still much corruption in world governments of today. If we can draw conclusions from publications of English scholars, political corruption seems to be widely present in the new African states. Several books attest to political corruption as a major factor in the life of India. Although it is sharply punished, corruption constantly reappears in the political life of the Union of Soviet Socialist Republics. In Latin America corruption appears to be widely present. In countries like Thailand and the Philippine republic, corruption is recognized as a major difficulty which the government may encounter.

How Important Is Corruption?

Political corruption has become a serious liability to American life. An acute observer believes that the union corruption which Senator McClelland and Counsel Robert Kennedy valiantly tried to explore could have been cured if government had been honest.[18] It is hard to know how much union corruption has added to costs of production or reduced benefits to workers. The Watergate aberration of the Nixon administration cost the country much in the seeming progress in foreign policy and in domestic legislation.[19] Corruption is essential to organized crime[20] and is probably an important cause of ongoing crime (an area in which America unfortunately leads advanced modern democracies), at great cost to our economy. But the financial detriment of corruption may ultimately be outweighed by what Friedrich calls the damage to our "ideatic core."[21]

Chapter 10 illustrates the importance of the impact of corruption of the effectiveness of American government.

Techniques of Graft

There really is much variety in the methods employed to cheat the government or the taxpayer, but there are more areas of exploitation. This section will review techniques of bribery (or extortion), security buying and selling, the "kickback," one-handed or "honest" graft, and patronage. Then we will indicate how these techniques are employed in such fields as bidding for contracts with the government; the collection and maintenance of public funds; the buying, selling, and use of public property tax assessments; the legislative process; law enforcement; and public services.

As American public administration standards have slowly improved, techniques of graft have become more subtle, more easily concealed, and harder for the prosecutor to prove to judge and jury. The old emphasis on bribes and kickbacks has recently moved toward "honest" graft, which includes payment to political bosses through large legal fees or insurance charges or architects' fees or awarding of contracts. All forms of graft, however, still occur extensively. George Amick points out that if the law were to authorize judges to fine grafters up to the amount extorted, the bribe recipient would not be able to look forward to enjoying his or her "boodle" upon leaving prison, as was the case in New Jersey when he was writing.[22]

Bribery or Extortion

The most common technique of political corruption, at least until this century, has been bribery, which is the offering of money or other inducements to secure the desired action from government officials. Bribes have been offered and taken many times in all the areas of public policy discussed below. Bribes may be paid before the needed action or after it; sometimes part of the payment is made before and the balance upon completion of the action.

If the individual or corporation or union or other group offers the funds to the public official, the money is a *bribe*. If the government official demands money, whether before or after payment, the transaction becomes *extortion*. There are clearly cases in which a willing briber meets a willing official that might be described as either bribery or extortion.

Successful prosecution of the initiators or recipients of bribes usually requires a witness to the transaction or the testimony of either briber or bribee. Since such transactions are usually made without witnesses (in some states, like New York, accomplices can act as witnesses only in connection with corroborative evidence), it is frequently impossible to secure convictions of both briber and bribee unless one of the parties turns "state's evidence" against the other. The bribee is convicted more often than the briber, perhaps because the official can more easily be forced to turn state's evidence or perhaps because it is harder to secure jury decisions against bribers. In the prosecution of the Ruef-Schmitz machine in San Francisco (1906-1908), it proved impossible to secure conviction of the bribers (company officials) in spite of the evidence secured from the bribees (San Francisco supervisors). Acceptance of unreported bribes, of course, also opens the recipient to prosecution for failure to report income for taxation.

A fairly simple way to discover bribing practices is for a person from outside to offer to buy a brothel or a gambling den, at which time one quickly becomes acquainted with the bribes needed for protection. In both Clark County (Las Vegas), Nevada, and the Miami area this technique has been used by newspaper investigators.

A device which has been successfully employed on some police forces to reduce bribes or extortions is the financial questionnaire. If police officers have rapidly accumulated several hundred thousand dollars from an annual pay range of $10,000 to $20,000, questions may reasonably be raised as to the source of such income. Frequently the answers to the questions justify retirement, if not prosecution. When President Truman was planning a general checkup on the federal government and brought Newbold Morris, a La Guardia associate, to Washington to do this, Morris planned a general questionnaire on income and assets for federal employees. Department-head opposition led to Morris's removal, but the questionnaire is published in his book *Let the Chips Fall*.[23]

Selling and Buying Securities

Sometimes the briber offers the bribee an opportunity to buy securities at a low price, later perhaps buying back the securities at a much higher price. The most publicized recent example was that of Governor Otto Kerner of Illinois who paid $18,000 for racetrack securities which he later sold for $116,000. This transaction was a disguised bribe for Governor Kerner's help in securing legislation and administrative regulations favorable to the racetracks owned by the donor of the securities.

If, as is usually the case, the purchase and sale of the securities must be recorded by the company, this method of corrupting officials is more easily traced than a strictly cash transaction.

The Kickback

In place of direct bribes, but no different in actual result, is the "kickback." Favored contractors', engineering, architectural, or other firms are given contracts for rendering services to the government, upon condition that a percentage of the contract be paid by the firm to one or more favored politicians who saw to it that the contract was awarded to the "right" contractor. Kickbacks may range up and down from 10 percent of the cost of the contract. Frequently the department head or committee concerned has authority to select the architectural or engineering firm which receives the contract. If the law requires competitive bidding, the official may have the power to reject all bids. If he or she does so often enough, the favored bidder may soon become the low bidder or the only bidder, since bidding is an expensive process.

The Tweed Ring secured much of its personal income from kickbacks on New York City contracts. Most widely publicized of kickbacks in recent years were the payments made to Spiro T. Agnew as manager of Baltimore County, governor of Maryland, and Vice President by engineering firms which received substantial contracts from Baltimore County and Maryland. The kickback has been widely used by other Maryland officials and has been even more generally employed in northern New Jersey and elsewhere.

The technique employed by federal officials to discover the kickback should be more widely used. Financial records of architectural or engineering firms which had received substantial payments from Baltimore County were subpoenaed. Checks, both incoming and outgoing, were carefully reviewed to discover any payment of large sums of cash. When it was found that one firm paid one of its financial officers 5 percent of every payment received from the county, and the officer cashed each of these checks, it was probable that the officer was paying a kickback. This and other such discoveries were followed by further investigation and interviews.

"Honest" Graft

This term has been used in several different ways. The classic definition by George Washington Plunkitt of Tammany Hall[24] was a situation in which the official, because of his government position, knows of land or materials that are to be bought or sold. The official buys the land or the goods and later sells them to the government at a much higher price. Or he may use his knowledge of future government plans to buy land which he later sells to other private parties at a much higher price. Robert Brooks, writing in 1910, described similar situations and called them "auto corruption."[25] The term is used in other ways. A New York police captain used it to his staff to indicate that they might take free meals and services or funds for cooperation, but not if they were required to do illegal things. One writer, George Amick, has used the term *one-handed graft* to describe a basically similar situation.[26] The chairman of the Delaware Port Authority owned a sub-subcontractor which did extensive business with a subcontractor. This chairman regularly voted for contracts. His position as chairman of the Port Authority surely helped to determine the frequent selection of his firm as sub-subcontractor. Thomas Keane, Mayor Daley's floor leader on the Chicago City Council, had friends in a real estate trust who bought tax titles on Keane's advice and sold the land to the Chicago Housing Authority on Keane's urging. Keane was sentenced to a moderate jail term. In New Jersey up to 1971, municipal engineers were allowed to approve plans which they had drawn up as private businessmen. Obviously, the client was more likely to secure approval of his plans, regardless of their legality. The ease of concealment of "honest" graft and the difficulty of securing convictions have made this an increasingly important method of corruption in recent decades. Honest graft may be used for political as well as pecuniary gain. Edward N. Costikyan, a reformed Tammany leader writing in 1966,[27] recognizes that most graft had become "honest" graft and ascribes it to the higher ranks of civil servants, rather than to political leaders. He doubts that it ever can be eliminated. He notes that there was a great deal of such graft in Robert Moses' administration of various public authorities, not for Moses' personal gain, but for the political power which Moses gained by awarding contracts to firms with important friends.

Robert Caro's book on Moses confirms this judgment. The Triborough Bridge and Tunnel Authority (Robert Moses was chairman) insurance went to one of Impellitteri's backers when "Impy" was mayor. When de Sapio brought Wagner into the mayoralty, the insurance shifted to a de Sapio associate.[28]

Honest graft frequently involves what lawyers call "conflict of intest." If an official owns stock in a corporation, it is a conflict of interest for him to be negotiating any arrangements on behalf of the government between that corporation and the government. Conflict of interest frequently exists but is fairly easily recognized. There may be times when unimportant conflicts of interest are exaggerated for political purposes. Ironically, conflict of interest is a concept well recognized by lawyers, who constitute too large a fraction of those interested in American politics.

Patronage

Patronage, the assignment of government positions to political supporters, may be a very legitimate political activity. Even a country as honestly run as Great Britain recognizes that some positions should be viewed as political appointments in order to carry out the program of the victorious party, or to reward some of its more active members. But patronage can easily become a means of corruption. If appointees must pay for their jobs, as Tammany Hall required its judicial appointees to pay, the action becomes corrupt. Laws of most states and the federal government prohibit the collection of political assessments from civil service employees, but such collection undoubtedly continues. Patronage employees are more easily forced into corrupt actions.

Fields of Graft

There are various activities of government in which the above techniques can be used. This section will review some of the activities most prone to corrupt action: bidding on public contracts, the use of public funds, the handling of public property, tax assessment and collection, zoning and land use, the legislative process, law enforcement, and the administration of public services.

Bidding for Contracts

Governmental purchases of goods and services in 1974 totaled $308 billion, or almost a quarter of the GNP.[29] Usually, competitive bidding is required for negotiation of contracts above a certain limit, frequently set at $5000. There are important exceptions; for example, the professional services of engineering or architectural firms are often exempted. Huge contracts for new weapons systems in the Department of Defense are exempted so that the armed services may select the technically superior rather than the most economical system. In many cases where there is no competitive bidding requirement, political pressures are soon generated. Whether or not these pressures are corrupt depends on how they are applied and the law of the government concerned. Usually, the federal pressures are confined to political ones; this is bad for the public but not necessarily illegal.

Where bidding is required to be competitive, resourceful graft seekers have found means of evasion. In one instance, the Jersey City Incinerator Authority, forced to go through competitive bidding, required that firms be "qualified" by providing a letter from a surety company guaranteeing a 17-year bond covering 100 percent of the bid price; the company was also required to put up a $100,000 bid deposit, maintain a 17-year land fill site, and employ an engineer with 10 years' experience. These conditions could be met only by a favored company, North Jersey Incineration, incorporated in 1967. One other bidder was disqualified for failing to meet the time requirement; a second was forced out by threats to cancel his other business. So the favored contractor was awarded the bid subsequently, and the difficult hurdles were eliminated by administrative action. Fortunately for Jersey City, the next reform administration was able to reverse the contract in 1975.

Another device is to hold up a payment to a contractor on a legitimate operation until he makes a payoff to the favored officials. A contractor may also subcontract to a politically favored company. Services below the minimum for competitive bidding ($2500 in New Jersey) may also be bought. Another procedure is to inflate the contract (for a consideration to certain officials) after the contract has been let to the lowest bidder. Commissioner James Marcus of New York City used an "emergency" provision to award a reservoir cleaning contract to a firm which had agreed to pay a kickback.[30] Professional service contracts are almost unbiddable, since the quality of the service is much more important than the price.

Government purchasing offices are, of course, widely approached with individuals offering kickbacks to the purchasing staff or to others. Most of the West Virginia scandals of the 1960s were of this nature. Two of the governor's friends established dummy corporations in other states which were to be "a conduit for payoffs from businessmen favored with state contracts."[31] Commissioners of roads, and of finance and administration, were appointed to "deliver the contracts." Later the payoffs were all routed to a single corporation in Florida. Maryland's widespread scandals have largely been kickbacks from engineers, architects, contractors, and suppliers.[32]

Amick notes that West Virginia tried to prevent repetition of the Barron scandals by setting requirements for buyers in the state purchasing office—college graduation or two years' purchasing experience. Such requirements are not unreasonable, but they certainly are not complete in the sophisticated cities of the Northeast.

Other suggestions may be more useful. Amick's include detailed rules and policies to govern discretionary actions, specification writing by the central agency, local government use of central purchasing, and auditing by truly outside auditors. Others have suggested improvement of professional standards of engineers and architects to exclude paying bribes or kickbacks, a suggestion more fully discussed in Chapter 14.

Public Funds

Collection and deposit of public funds have long provided an opportunity for political favoritism and corruption. In fairly recent years in states like Georgia, public funds were generally deposited in the banks which had given support to the "right" candidate. In Chicago two members of the city council were indicted for voting to put city funds in a bank of which they were shareholders; but then they were acquitted by a machine judge. In New Jersey banks were offered public funds if they would buy securities through a bonding house which employed the brother of a New Jersey state official.[33]

V. O. Key lists three places where graft can occur: fund collection, fund custody, and fund disbursement. Interest on bank deposits was long considered a perquisite of treasurers; however, in many jurisdictions little effort was made to collect it. In Cook County interest has been received by the government only since 1902, and no public report was made on it up until 1934 when Key wrote his thesis. In Pennsylvania under the Quay machine, 2 or 3 percent on state deposits was paid to the Republican committee. When it was established that interest belonged to the public treasury, the treasurer of Chicago still took a part of it. In the 1920s treasurer Len Small of Illinois used an imaginary bank to make loans from the state treasury to commercial companies.[34] Sometimes public funds have been deposited in a bank on the condition that the bank make loans to the treasurer or to his political associate. The Quay machine in Pennsylvania used this method. Other cases were reported in Michigan and Texas. Interest-free deposits were given by New York City politicians as late as the 1960s.

Treasurers have at times converted public funds to their own use, customarily with some effort at concealment. The amounts of vouchers have often been raised; payrolls have often been padded (a major example being the Chicago Sanitary District).

Public Property

Public property can be misused by corrupt politicians in many ways. The Tweed Ring actually sold New York's City Hall, and later had the city buy it back. Much more recently, Thomas E. Keane, Mayor Daley's floor leader in the Chicago City Council, organized a secret land trust which bought and sold Chicago city property for its own financial advantage. Property bought at tax sales for low prices might then be resold to a city department at high prices.[35]

V. O. Key gives examples of fraudulent and corrupt appropriation of public lands and of public timber in the Western states in the last half of the nineteenth century. Dummy entrymen secured rights to property which were turned over to large corporations. Fraudulent entries were frequently made. A Minnesota lumber company filed as applicants for homesteads the names of people found in the St. Paul and Chicago directories.[36] The Teapot Dome and Elk Hills oil reserves were examples of a high official accepting bribes for permitting exploitation of government oil resources.

Tax Assessment and Collection

Tax assessment by ill-trained and unprofessional local assessors in some districts is easily subject to corrupting pressure. The tax assessor of Calumet Township, Lake County, Indiana, made a great deal of money while subjecting people to excessive abuses.[37] A number of California assessors were bribed to reduce assessment in the 1960s. In Illinois much of the process has long been capricious.[38]

Such situations are worse in a city like Chicago where, as Key pointed out in the 1920s, individual members of the board of review could raise, lower, or wipe out assessments made by the board of assessors. Assessors operated in secrecy. Professional tax "fixers" flourished. As in other fields of corruption, the line between bribes and campaign contributions was hard to find.

In Chicago workers in the machine were rewarded by ridiculously low assessments, a precinct captain's house being assessed at one-fifteenth the value of a similar house next door. In the customs service, import duties were lowered for favorite customers over several decades.[39] The Bureau of Internal Revenue has had similar charges against it.

Annual publication of assessed valuations is one safeguard against such action. Assessment should be centralized, to secure professional workers as well as to secure more honesty, and should be regulated under state guidelines.

Ratios of assessment to market values should be published. Direct appeal should be allowed to a state tax court.

Zoning and Land Use

Local governments often have extensive powers of determining the use of land (for residential, business, industrial, or agricultural use) and the conditions under which land may be developed. A great many opportunities for corruption appear in this area. Even in relatively honest areas like Los Angeles County, supervisorial campaign funds tend to come from large developers and from building trades.[40] Campaign gifts may be legal, but beyond them are the possibility of bribes or kickbacks, in return for a favorable vote for zoning or rezoning or land use or construction variation on a given property. This is not just a West Coast possibility; Amick mentions examples from New Jersey, Maryland, and Florida.[41]

Aspects of zoning, planning, subdivision approval, and building codes may also raise questions of conflict of interest, if any official concerned has any financial interest in the project. A column by Alfred Balk in *Harper's*, October 1966, discusses zoning as an "Invitation to Bribery."

The Legislative Process

The process of lawmaking is obviously one which involves many opportunities for corruption, as the discussion of Congress in Chapter 7 or the states in Chapter 6 indicates. It is perfectly possible to have substantial legislative corruption next door to a relatively honest administrative machinery. Legislative bodies have been much speedier in enacting reform legislation for the administration than for themselves.

Key, writing in 1934,[42] gives a broad picture of the varieties of corruption in Congress, several state legislatures, and city councils. Wisconsin found bribes in the distribution of public lands in the 1850s. The U.S. Senate investigated the bribery of senators for votes on tariffs in the 1890s. Bribes have been used to keep legislators from investigating. In cities, permits to construct switch tracks or bay windows or to vacate streets have provided a basis for bribery. General Brayton, the blind boss of Rhode Island in the 1890s and early 1900s, did business for any corporation which hired him and rewarded legislators with campaign funds. Committees or chairmen have often been bribed to pigeonhole undesired legislation. The American Bridge Company in 1910 passed out bribes to New York legislators in order to defeat a bill which would have improved the procedure for construction of town bridges by requiring a referendum and approval of a state engineer. New York Life Insurance Company gave its legislative agent in Albany $1,312,197 between 1895 and 1905 to secure favorable and defeat unfavorable legislation.

Sometimes campaign contributions were used rather than bribes. The line between the two was often hard to find. Artie Samish's control of the California legislature in the 1940s was based on campaign contributions, some of which were not spent for campaigns.

Railroad passes were generally given to legislators until World War I. The presence of many lawyers in state legislatures made it possible to reward legislators for their votes by giving legal business to their law firms—a practice which has not completely disappeared from the U.S. Congress. Patronage is also used to control legislative votes. In the late 1920s, fifteen Illinois state senators had been on the payroll of the Chicago Sanitary District. In recent times the racetracks have employed a number of members of the New Hampshire, Massachusetts, and Maryland legislatures.

There is, of course, a great deal of logrolling (we will support your bill if you support ours) in state legislatures. This process may be legal but is frequently made illegal by bribery. "Strike legislation" was often used by corrupt legislators to extort funds from corporations.

It is still not clear how corruption in the lawmaking process can be stopped. Most states have quite inadequate legislation. Congress is now beginning to try to legislate some ethical standards, and does give legislators a chance to plead conflict of interest. This is one field in which Common Cause-sponsored legislation may be helpful.

Law Enforcement

Police corruption is the most persistent form of corruption, but since so much about it will be dealt with elsewhere in this book, it is not necessary to review the whole field in detail. It has a pervasive effect on other government departments, because police must be used to enforce legal provisions against corruption elsewhere. Bribery (or extortion) is most widely used, but other favors may also be given to corrupt police.

Other portions of law enforcement are also corrupted quite widely. Organized crime usually has influence on some judges in cities like New York and Chicago. In one blatant instance, a New York State Supreme Court judge thanked gangster Frank Costello for his appointment. Prosecutor's offices are often infiltrated, although the higher educational requirement makes assistant prosecuting attorneys somewhat less vulnerable than police officers. It is interesting that for several decades the New York County prosecutor's office has been generally respected while the police were not so esteemed.

Public Services

As government goes into broader activities, increased opportunities for graft become evident. In both Boston and New York, the right to use stalls in a public market has been sold by officials or used as party favors. In New York City work relief has been confined to deserving Democrats, contrary to law.[43] Welfare institution inmates have had their funds exploited by machine appointments in New York City. Other examples could be found.

There are no special corrective measures offered for these fields. An audit and constant administrative supervision are essential.

Fighting Anticorruption Measures

This review of techniques and fields of corruption has included discussion of a number of anticorruption measures. Some of these are quite honestly suggested, and may give some degree of partial protection against corruption. But they do not seem to have stopped the semicontinuous corruption of certain cities and certain states. It is hard for the authors to avoid the conclusion that the election or appointment of better officials is the one relatively secure method of eliminating corruption. The three concluding chapters of this book give further recommendations for fighting corruption.

In a chapter entitled "Beating the Rap,"[44] Key discusses methods used by political machines to defeat investigations and prosecutions. Machines like to control the vantage point from which an investigation may be prevented or throttled. The prosecutor's office is an important vantage point. Judges are instrumental figures to control; they may limit investigations or kill off prosecutions. In Atlantic City, Boss Kuehnle worked out a system by which the sheriff drew grand juries with a few distinguished citizens and a majority of pressureable persons. Legislative committees of inquiry are controlled by political pressures. The Illinois legislature does not investigate Chicago affairs because both parties may be involved. Dual inquiries are frequently employed to cloud the issues. Critical newspapers may be controlled by offices for the publisher or through expensive official advertising. Bribes to the press may also be used, as in the historic case of the Tweed Ring or the Southern Pacific machine. Litigation may be brought against the investigating agency; or its budget may be reduced or eliminated (a method tried by Tammany Hall against the Seabury investigation). A counterinvestigation may be brought against personnel of the investigating agency. A counterpropaganda campaign may be started against the investigators.

Evidence is often destroyed. Potential witnesses go off on trips. A procedure described by Key which is even more prevalent today is the killing of informers or other potential witnesses. Witnesses may also be intimidated, a standard procedure of organized crime. Ordinances may be passed to deprive a witness of his or her livelihood. Records of the investigating body may be altered. Minority members can constantly hold up an investigation.

All these counterattacks can be met by strong prosecutors, judges, and investigators. The FBI has a witness protection service. Strong judges can sidestep delaying actions.

But sometimes the criminals' countercampaign is effective. As one example, although organized crime has been expanding, there has been no full congressional investigation of it since the McClelland committee of 1959-1960 in which Robert Kennedy starred as counsel. The machine or other corrupting groups like organized crime have been able to kill many state and local investigations. Prosecutions are often ineffective.

2 The Origins of Municipal Corruption

James Bryce's 1893 examination of the American Commonwealth concluded that "the government of cities is the one conspicuous failure of the United States.... The faults of the State governments are insignificant compared with the extravagance, corruption, and mismanagement which have marked the administrations of most of the great cities."[1] This condemnation, intensified by the turn-of-the-century political reformers, influences the prevailing perception of American city government. Yet corruption was not always a feature of municipal government.

Colonial Traditions of City Government

City governments in the American colonial era and during the early years of the Republic were, by all accounts, public-spirited, honest, and efficient; the corruption that did exist never approached in incidence or in magnitude that which has prevailed since the mid-nineteenth century. The quality of municipal government in the Colonies on the eve of the Revolution was decidedly higher than in England. In the words of the municipal historian Ernest S. Griffith:

The American cities were English in many of their traditions, in their legal status, and in their framework . . . but the Colonists themselves, through their own initiative, must be credited with the really remarkable achievements in democracy, standard of public service, and local self-government. These marked most of their cities and towns of a genius already distinct from that of the English towns of their day. Corruption, use for partisan and parliamentary ends, and much of the oligarchic character of the English towns of the Stuarts and the Georges, had no place in the freer atmosphere of the New World.[2]

The reasons why this should occur becomes clear when it is remembered that the moral, intellectual, and political principles of Anglo-Americans were largely supplied by men and women alienated from the government and religion in England. They were determined to surpass the Old World by creating a "City on the Hill" in the new one, which would be based on higher ethical principles. Since the New England colonists established control over their political institutions from the bottom up, their township governments first displayed the new principles. There the townspeople were the source of power; they exercised control over their affairs as though this were the natural course of events.

The traditions of English local government in the seventeenth and eighteenth centuries were quite different from New England ideals. English municipalities had been largely reduced to vassalage for national and parliamentary purposes. The powers of the municipal corporation were severely restricted, and those that they did have were frequently exercised by petty oligarchs. Since chartered towns (boroughs) were allotted members of Parliament, it was important which towns were allowed charters and which persons in the chartered towns made up the corporation. The established interest (whether this be the Crown, the aristocracy, or the party) used its charter-granting authority to gain parliamentary advantage. Charters were granted either to specific bodies of officials or to officials and a specific group of freemen-voters, who were sure to be favorable to the granting interest. When James II came to the throne in 1685, he revoked a large number of charters and granted new ones to corporations more favorable to the royal interests.[3] The political usefulness of the borough was its preeminent value; municipal functions were accordingly weakened. The powers of the corporation usually extended no further than the control of municipal property and the promulgation of local police ordinances. Other governmental functions were jealously retained by the national government or the local aristocracy.[4] Local government as a responsible civic function at this time was illusory.[5]

In addition to the general subordination of English local government to partisan purposes, and the withholding from it of real responsibility, the selling of municipal offices was an accepted practice. Certain offices, such as that of the town clerk, could be financially profitable. Hence, the corporation officials who controlled the offices frequently sold the privilege of exercising the lucrative posts. The purchaser would recoup his expenses and more by levying charges on anyone who needed his services.[6]

Both the proprietary system and its abuses, such as the sale of offices, extended to the American Colonies. The proprietor, as representative of either the Crown or the commercial company, exerted a wide influence over local government in America as in England. Where colonial towns were incorporated (mainly in the middle colonies), their charters were granted by the royal governor of the colony. Freeholders were usually given the right to elect the city council, but a representative of the proprietor (e.g., in Maryland Lord Baltimore's representative) was frequently appointed mayor, retaining close control of the town for the proprietor and controlling the disposition of the municipal patronage. The revenue at the disposal of the proprietor was considerable and was allocated to secure his interest as he deemed fit.

—what evidence, if any, was there of an essential "civic mindedness" springing from a sense of community obligation or from an inner urge to see things done better and more efficiently? Not a great deal, as yet, for only here and there—most frequently in the larger New England towns—did evidence of this kind of civic spirit crop out.[7]

The effects of rank and prerogative on the quality of local government were not, however, entirely negative. They certainly allowed the unconscious abuses associated with privilege, but they also ensured that the best citizens would concern themselves with public affairs and either stand for office or accept appointments to office. Public service was of a high level, but it was understood as an attribute of rank. "The English traditions of a governing class and of public service were interlocked inextricably; and, where one weakened, so did the other—in America as well as in England."[8]

Despite these forces for good government and the generally ethical government that characterized the colonial and immediate postcolonial years, there were a few instances of blatant corruption of kinds familiar today. The aldermen of Philadelphia awarded themselves leases on the city's wharves, and New York aldermen did the same with that city's waterfront lots; but these actions were considered appropriate perquisites for the unpaid service of these municipal officials. In 1731, however, Philadelphia's Mayor Fishbourne was found £2000 short on his accounts and consequently was denied further public office. The mishandling of public monies occurred in several other colonial cities, including Annapolis, New York, and Philadelphia. Several instances of those practices, and of bribery and fraud in voting, which came later to characterize city government, were noted elsewhere. By 1752 a Pennsylvania act warned against the practice of "engaging persons to vote . . . by giving them strong drink. . . ." The same practice was denounced in New York in 1753 and 1768, resulting in electoral reforms in 1771 which tried to eliminate vote buying.[9]

Such activities, however, were rare. They could easily be explained away as carryovers of English corruption. Departures from disinterested government which accompanied the prerogative, although commonplace in English towns and well established in the Colonies, were viewed as abuses. The selling of municipal offices, which had spread to the Colonies in the eighteenth century, was cited as a source of grievance with England by North and South Carolina, Maryland, and Virginia.[10] The whole system of proprietary rights and its attendant privileges was increasingly criticized as being offensive to the colonists as English subjects.[11]

Changing Municipal Conditions and the Origins of Corruption

The success of the Revolution and the great experiment in free government that it inaugurated set the tone of municipal government in the United States for the next 20 or 30 years. The determination to make the experiment work and to repudiate all the abuses associated with English monarchical rule was a powerful incentive for responsible, honest local government during these years. The waning influence of rank, and of the assumption that public service was a duty devolving from rank, remained as an influence on American local government until the 1820s.

The smallness of American cities and close familiarity among their inhabitants contributed further to the high quality of local government. Estimates indicate that only four cities in the Colonies at the time of the Revolution contained over 10,000 inhabitants.

The tradition inherited from England limited the range of municipal functions that American city governments were expected to perform. As in England, they carried out limited police and judicial activities, but had few administrative functions. Until well into the nineteenth century, even the police forces of American cities were not professional, uniformed services, but the voluntary, citizens' "night watch."[12] Paving and repairing streets, maintaining security, and regulating commerce were almost the only functions expected from local government. Not until 1774 did the first city—Albany, New York—attempt to provide a municipal water supply.[13]

The burgeoning growth of the American city ensured that its administrative structure would change; several factors during the nineteenth century determined the direction of that change. Equality, the main principle of American democracy, altered the nature of municipal government. With the election of Andrew Jackson in 1828, entrenched privilege and its accompanying justification for the rule of the fittest were supplanted by a more egalitarian creed. By 1830, the principle of rotation in office was an established feature of city government as well.[14] It became the means by which rewarding political supporters with offices was justified. Thus patronage, which traditionally had been in the hands of public officials, became a regular method of maintaining political parties. As early as 1828, this system had implanted itself in Pennsylvania:

The immediate effect of the doctrine was to awaken the cupidity of the idle and ambitious, to make useless every consideration of principle in the formation of party attachments and to substitute for it a blind devotion to powerful leaders. It held out the idea that all men were qualified for all offices, decried the value of experience, faithfulness and skill, and invited the momentary incumbent to fraud and negligence.[15]

This was not, however, a new practice. The colonial governors had also used their patronage to secure their political positions.

The ability of these circumstances to contribute to large-scale political corruption would have been negligible in cities like those of eighteenth-century America. A vast and rapid growth, however, occurred in American cities during the nineteenth century. The larger population demanded new or enlarged services. Each new service created new jobs; each new job added to the patronage available to elected officials. Within this framework, "regular party usage" came to dominate American municipal government throughout the nineteenth century.

The bulk of the growth of American cities prior to 1815 must be attributed to natural increase and migration from rural to urban areas; immigration from Europe amounted to only 4000 to 6000 people per year. Not until 1825 did the immigration commission register over 10,000 immigrants in a single year.[16] Peace brought a revival of commercial activity in the United States, and greater opportunities drew an increasing number of men and women from the countryside to the city. A large portion of the small but steady stream of foreign immigrants also took up residence in the cities of the Eastern seaboard. The Irish, in particular, tended to select Boston, New York, and Philadelphia for their homes.

From a town of 23,000 in 1776, New York had grown to 60,000 in 1800 and to over 112,000 by 1820. The growth of other cities, though not so dramatic, was considerable. The larger cities were the leaders in the provision of municipal services, because of their early introduction to the problems of growth. In Philadelphia, for example, the yellow fever epidemic of 1793 demonstrated the need for a clean and uncontaminated water supply. This led to the development of the Schuylkill water system that began to supply clear water to the city in 1801. As the century progressed, the provision of police, fire protection, paving and sewering, public education, parks, health and welfare services, traction, power, and lighting fell within the domain of the municipal government as it attempted to adapt itself to the new conditions.

By the 1830s, the governing institutions designed for simpler times had become inadequate to deal with these large and variegated tasks. The most capable citizens and most adept merchants were avoiding politics, because of either the degradation that was prominent there or the greater opportunities in business. City government was coming to be regarded as a political, rather than an administrative, affair just at the time that it was taking on more administrative functions. The men chosen for office were likely to be able politicians but incompetent administrators. They were also more prone to be involved in corrupt activities. In addition, the typical local government structure was too cumbersome to allow for effective administration. The early American city was usually presided over by an elected council, which elected one of its own members to act as mayor. There were sometimes bicameral councils, and by the mid-1830s the mayor was frequently elected by the people. These councils were ineffective bodies for supervising the activities of public service departments, so the practice evolved of entrusting these duties to supervisory commissions. The supervisory boards were "elected by the people, appointed by the mayor, or, in some cases, designated by the governor of the state."[17] Power over city functions, therefore, was diffuse and fragmented. Even if commissioners were elected by the people, this was by means of the "long ballot," which had the tendency of making all the candidates anonymous.

During the 1820s and 1830s, a variety of circumstances contributed to the growth of corruption in American cities. As the cities expanded in population and services, their existing political institutions proved unable to satsify the new demands; this vacuum was filled by the "new" political parties, built on the spoils system. Moreover, constantly growing municipal services provided the parties with expanding resources of spoils. Party organizations depended on poor immigrants and other voters, newly arrived from Europe and the countryside. This combination first appeared in the great cities of the Eastern seaboard, notably New York and Philadelphia in the late 1820s. Similarly, later in the century, cities in the South and the West experienced the impact of later waves of migration and immigration.

New-Style Urban Politics: New York and Philadelphia

The early appearance of widespread political corruption and nascent political machines in New York and Philadelphia foreshadowed trouble for American city government. The Tammany Society was founded in New York City in 1789 as a social organization roughly representing the antimonarchist middle class and offering an alternative to the more aristocratic Cincinnati Society. The Tammany Society's members were rapidly molded by Aaron Burr into a following that assisted him in winning the vote of the pivotal city in state and national elections. "Although rigid restrictions on suffrage limited the Society's leverage in this first political contest [1792], the braves [Tammany members] were effective in mobilizing small merchants and property owners...."[18] The nativist, rather genteel character of Tammany was altered when, in 1817, a large crowd of Irishmen descended upon a meeting of the Society, demanding that it nominate a notable Irish politician for the United States Congress. The vehemence of their argument terminated in a brawl that reduced the Tammany meetinghouse to a shambles. Irish immigrants and their descendants rapidly found a political home within the Democratic organization at Tammany Hall. Mindful of where its potential voting strength lay, Tammany became one of the keenest supporters of an enlarged franchise at the New York state constitutional convention which, in 1821, removed the property qualification for voting, thereby widely extending the franchise. By 1828 Tammany's leaders were pressing for the reduction of the 5-year waiting period for the naturalization of immigrants. They had discovered a potent and growing constituency.

During the 1820s and 1830s, the leaders of Tammany did not engage in excessively corrupt political practices. The focus of Tammany's political activities was still on state and national offices. State and national jobs in the city were treated as patronage and were distributed to reward the services of Tammany's minions. General Jackson, following his victory in 1828, awarded the bulk of federal jobs in New York to Tammany for services rendered. Burr's lieutenant, Sam Swartwout, was given the tempting post of collector of the port of New York, from which he later absconded to Europe with some $1.25 million of public money.[19] His example, although widely condemned, apparently fired the imagination of succeeding generations of New York public officials. In addition to this theft, and a few others of lesser proportions, there continued those voting improprieties that had long been noted in New York. As the size of the city's operations grew relentlessly, the possibilities for obtaining loot became more evident and the means of controlling city elections more ready. The attention of Tammany began to center on city government.

While Tammany was largely politicized for national purposes, only later turning its attention to local politics, the local organization of Philadelphia appears to have begun at the lowest level, for local purposes. In Philadelphia the tradition that the best citizens were obliged to participate in politics had lasted well into the nineteenth century. By the 1820s and 1830s, however, such men were devoting themselves strictly to business.

A new type of politician, the boss, took a place in Philadelphia's pre-Civil War municipal politics.[20] Joel B. Sutherland, the son of a Scotch immigrant, emerged as Philadelphia's first political boss by creating a political machine on the South Side in the late 1820s. Since Sutherland held both city and national offices, he was able to add federal jobs to the limited patronage available through city departments. Support for his local machine was further augmented by members of fire companies and their associated gangs, who provided votes to Sutherland and the Democratic party in his district.

In both Philadelphia and New York, the fire companies proved early to be highly useful tools for a local politician. Until the Civil War, most fire companies were strictly volunteer organizations. They frequently developed a strong political complexion and, after the large-scale arrival of immigrants, usually had an ethnic bias. Ward politicians worked to gain the allegiance of their local fire companies, which could deliver a compact and reliable set of votes and could also be used for more vigorous electioneering activities. Frequently, politicians first rose to prominence through their ability to deliver the votes and support of a fire company to a particular party or candidate.

The political allegiances of fire companies in Philadelphia's South Side have been carefully investigated. This study shows that fire companies came to represent different social and ethnic groups; each allied itself with the major party organization that most nearly represented its views. In one ward, the Weccacoe Engine Company was predominantly native American and supported the American Republicans. The Weccacoe Hose Company was largely Irish and allied itself with the local Democratic organization.[21] Until municipal services expanded later in the century, thereby providing ample resources of patronage for the party machines, the fire companies provided much of the organizational basis, the men and muscle, of the local machine.[22] The fire companies, and the gangs that ran with them, proved their worth to the local machine by voting loyally, patrolling the voting places, and, if necessary, intimidating opposition voters, fighting the rival fire companies that attempted to intimidate voters, or acting as "repeaters" (multiple voters) if the electoral results were likely to be close.

Learning quickly from the example of Sutherland, other machine politicians took control of several portions of Philadelphia. As immigrants began to arrive and join the city's voting population, they were attracted to the Democratic party. But unlike their domination of other large cities, the Democrats in Philadelphia remained the minority party. The Republican party, which forged a coalition of native Americans, Protestants, and middle- and upper-class voters, as well as significant factions of the immigrant communities, controlled the city throughout the nineteenth century.[23]

Role of the State and Federal Governments

The corrupt machine came to America by way of the city. But what was the role of states, which create, control, empower, finance, and may supervise cities in preventing corruption?

Unfortunately, in the first 125 years of the Republic, the states' responsibility for local government was misunderstood and poorly managed. There is no record of a state bureau of local affairs helping localities with their pressing problems. Frequently, state legislatures passed "ripper" legislation to help some political friend win a position or gain some funds from a city. State appointment of big city police boards was generally a failure. The state was inclined to view city problems only from the political viewpoint of the state official concerned.

The federal government had even less responsibility for local governments. In fact, after Jackson's era the patronage of the U.S. Customs Office and U.S. Post Office in New York was used to build support for local machines.

Some of these difficulties arose from the very causes of municipal corruption. Lack of appreciation of the importance of city government was a major factor; so were the corrupt machine, the misunderstanding of immigrant attitudes, and the general misunderstanding of governmental problems.

Foreign Immigration Augments the Urban Machines

Prior to the beginning of the great Atlantic migration, manifestations of ward-level machine politics had already appeared, along with the rapid growth of opportunities for municipal politicians to exploit their offices. It was not, however, until many immigrants began to arrive from Europe and settle in American cities that the corrupt character of political machines appeared. The coincidence of the eruption of municipal corruption on a gigantic scale, and the Atlantic migration, led many to suppose that the immigrants were substantially responsible for that corruption

Migration from Europe to America was divided into two distinct periods. The first began in the mid-1840s and comprised Western European nationalities. The dominant immigrant nationalities, in numbers of arrivals, were German, Irish, English and Scot, Norwegian and Swede, and French. This wave reached a peak in the 1850s and again in the 1880s. The second migration was predominantly from Southern and Eastern Europe. It began in the 1880s and grew rapidly until it was shut off by the outbreak of war in 1914. By 1890 there was a marked decline in the arrivals from Germany and Ireland and a large increase in those from Italy, Austria-Hungary, Russia, and Poland.

Between 1820 and 1890, over 4.5 million Germans, 3.8 million Irish, 2.8 million English and Scots, and 1 million Swedes and Norwegians had entered the United States.[24]

Patterns of National Immigration

The Irish were the first to arrive in American cities in large numbers; they were best suited of the immigrant nationalities (except the English and Scots) to enter into political life, and they were well convinced that government ought to benefit those who governed. Unlike the Germans and Scandinavians, the Irish spoke and understood English. The English and Scotch immigrants also enjoyed this advantage and undoubtedly used it to facilitate their entry into the social and political life of America. But this group seems to have scattered itself widely and evenly throughout the United States, and it did not make up large, recognizable communities in many large cities.[25] Whether because of their smooth assimilation or because of their unrecognizability, the British immigrants did not play the visible role or arouse the same resentments as did the other immigrant groups.[26]

The situation of the German immigrants was markedly different from that of the Irish. As with the Irish, the German migration of the 1850s was preceded by many years of limited migration to the United States. Germans were second only to the Irish in numbers of immigrants between 1830 and 1845. The Germans who immigrated during this period were mainly small farmers, independent shopkeepers, and artisans—members of the lower middle class. "They were people who had something to lose, and who were losing it, squeezed out by interacting social and economic forces."[27] The same potato disease that caused the Irish famine struck Germany in 1846 and stimulated emigration as did the revolution of 1848. The German farmer, unlike the Irish refugee from the famine, did not emigrate in desperation, with scarcely enough money to pay his passage. There were, during the 1850s, more poor Germans among the immigrants, but the bulk were still from the lower middle class.[28] They had enough money to reach the interior of America and to purchase land when they got there. They also possessed the experience and knowledge to bring a large farm under cultivation.[29]

Many Germans were, therefore, isolated on the farms and small towns of mid-America and unlikely to become involved in political corruption. In some cities, though, large numbers of Germans did gather, especially in the Midwest.

Even then, their entry into political life was delayed by their ignorance of English. Moreover, the Germans did not seem to have the instinctive and pressing interest in politics that characterized the Irish.

The underlying cause of emigration from Scandinavia was the same as from Ireland and Germany: the population was increasing faster than the productivity of the still-intact agrarian economy. There seemed no choice but emigration or a reduction in standard of living. In general, however, this pressure in Scandinavia operated upon a fairly prosperous rural economy. The emigration occurred later than in Ireland, it was more similar in social characteristics, purpose, and destination to German emigration. From 1840 to 1860 these pressures accumulated, setting in motion a small but steady train of emigrants from Sweden, Norway, and Denmark. This number was considerably augmented by religious dissenters from the state churches of Sweden and Norway, who sought the religious freedom of the United States, and by a smaller number motivated by general political discontent.[30]

Integration into Urban America

Immigrants of all nationalities had to make similar adjustments to American life. A portion of the immigrants, especially in the early years, fled to the United States from religious or political persecution. For them, the toleration they found was sufficient return. The vast majority, however, were set in motion by vaguer yearnings for freedom from economic deprivation or a restrictive social order, by the prospect of a better and more prosperous way of life.[31] While seeking out the economic means to retain the life they knew, they jealously guarded those traditional patterns which gave that life meaning. The difficulties of doing this on alien and polyglot land were enormous. So they clung to their fellow nationals whose ways were familiar and who could help them get what they needed from the new environment.

Partly as a consequence of their own clannishness, the immigrants faced a series of obstacles to the fulfillment of their aspirations. They had few of the social and political skills needed in order to prosper in American society. The ethnocentricity of their communities; their competition with "natives" for jobs; and their odd manners, speech, habits, ideas, and religions aroused the suspicion and hostility of established residents. These sentiments gave rise to the Know-Nothing party, which flourished briefly from 1854 to 1858. Accusations against the immigrants did not end then, however. The growing foreign-born population was soon popularly associated with the deteriorating quality of city government. In 1866 E. L. Godkin expressed the accumulated observations of the nativists in the pages of *The Nation:*

What is our [New York's] shame and misfortune to-day will, if some remedy is not applied, be in a very few years the shame and misfortune of Boston, of Philadelphia, of New Haven, of Rochester, of Cincinnati, and San Francisco. The canker is at work everywhere. The purses of the rich are everywhere passing into the hands of the ignorant, the vicious, and the depraved, and are being used by them for the spread of political corruption, for the promotion of debauchery and idleness among the young men of the poorer classes, for the destruction of our system of education....

We all know what the source of evil is. In all our large towns a swarm of foreigners have alighted, ignorant, credulous, newly emancipated, brutalized by oppression, and bred in the habit of regarding the law as their enemy, the rich as their tyrants, and a longed-for but unattainable prey.[32]

Yet these obstacles to the success of the immigrants were balanced by other, favorable conditions. The factories that were growing up in the cities and the numerous new municipal projects and services all required large quantities of unskilled labor. The immigrant was usually willing to work for low wages. There were men near at hand, either friends of fellow nationals, who had contacts with employers and would for a price help the immigrant find a job. Finally, and most important, the immigrant was a potential voter, and municipal politicians recognized that an immigrant's vote was as valuable as any other. There were those around the city who were anxious to exchange favors which they had at their disposal from the government for the vote of the immigrant. In this way the path was prepared for the integration of the immigrant into the political community and the dark world of machine politics.

The Immigrant and the Urban Machine

It may be seen, in retrospect, that American city politics by 1850 was ripe for the establishment of machine politics and that the immigrants and other poor people just then beginning to throng America's cities were the ingredient necessary to guarantee the machine's success. By the time of the great migration, "native" Americans and earlier immigrants had already cleared the path for political machines. The new immigrants simply followed in the footsteps of these trailblazers. The opportunity was open for immigrants to participate in machine politics, which they readily proceeded to do. Ever since, immigrant groups and especially the Irish have been popularly associated with political machines and all the corruption they spawned.

The immediae link between the immigrants and the machine was a group of middlemen—labor bosses, ward heelers, saloonkeepers, fire captains, police officers—all of whom served as contact points between the immigrants and the established authorities of the city. The intermediary spoke the immigrant's language, understood his needs and wants, and provided a personal, readily accessible alternative to the impersonal, too often inflexible, or even hostile formal authority. Each could offer the immigrant personal service and access to those things the immigrant needed in order to accomplish his aspirations— access based on friendship and persuasion rather than the formal rules and regulations which seemed designed to frustrate him. The labor boss could find him a job. The ward healer could help him if he got in trouble with the law, provide a job from the city patronage that he controlled, or turn out mourners for a family funeral. The saloonkeeper often arranged loans where banks refused and could perhaps be prevailed upon to exert his political influence on behalf of a distressed client. The fire company offered a social outlet and a means of gaining prestige in the community. As the volunteer fire companies were superseded by professional ones, they became a fund of jobs for the politically trustworthy and useful. The policeman dispensed justice according to his own lights. He might turn a blind eye to the frailties of his friends. He was an effective buffer between the immigrant and the unknown authorities. Like the fire companies, the police forces offered large and attractive pools of patronage jobs, often under the control of the local captain. All these facilitators of socialization became woven into politics, because their friendship with and influence over the immigrants resulted in an ability to deliver votes.

Oscar Handlin's description of the labor boss's automatic political importance is revealing. A typical example was that of a well-liked Irish lad who was taken on by the Brooklyn Naval Yard in 1855, placed in charge of a gang of workers, and given the title "Labor Boss."

To hold his own position it was necessary that he retain the favor of the political authority that appointed him. He did so by the ability to deliver a certain numberber of votes. And he was able to deliver those votes because he controlled a fund of desirable jobs. . . .
Throughout the country in the great cities, other bosses became the heads of other gangs. Everywhere the connection bewteen these allegiances and the opportunity to work was plain. . . . The available jobs were directly or indirectly dependent upon political favor.[33]

The manner by which the volunteer fire companies exercised a hold over the allegiances of the immigrant and the opportunities that this offered to the leaders of the fire companies have been described above. As time went by, shrewd politicians began to organize these controllers of votes, and dispensers of favors, into political organizations capable of delivering vast numbers of votes at any given election and to whatever candidate the machine offered. Here are found the origin and source of political power of the nineteenth-century machine, as well as the reasons for its ultimate reliance upon foreign immigrant communities. Certain aspects of the relationship of immigrants to organized political corruption, however, remain to be considered, before the particular occupations of the machine are examined. The close association of urban immigrants with machine politics has been accounted for. But why was there a wide variation in the success of different ethnic groups in American politics? Why were some seemingly more prone to participate in urban political corruption?

The Irish and Machine Politics

The most visibly successful of the immigrant nationalities in penetrating American municipal politics were the Irish. Their deep involvement in political machines and political corruption was notorious and undeniable.

The Irish enjoyed social advantages which assisted their entry into municipal politics. They spoke English. They were familiar with the operations of a democracy, even if their relations with it had not been rewarding. The Irish character is credited by many writers with giving them a unique aptitude for personalized politics.

The same genius for organization which made the Irish so successful as leaders in the Church and in the field of labor helps account for their success in politics. To all three fields, warmhearted, sociable Irishmen brought a human touch that proved most important. In Ireland, politics had been a struggle, with not too much concern for the rules of the game, and the Irishman had few, if any ethical scruples about the machine politics of American cities a century ago. Their wit, their flexibility in dealing with people, and their oratorical gifts made them natural leaders for a turbulent urban democracy which had neither accepted nor mastered the techniques of orderly, honest, and efficient government.[34]

The Irish were, perhaps, less likely to scruple at the dishonest tactics of the political machine than were their fellow immigrants or native American city dwellers. From years of subjection in Ireland, they had developed a sovereign disdain for the forms of democracy under which they had been ruled by the Anglo-Protestant minority. Many had, during the struggle, developed the skills necessary for carrying on politics in a democratic framework.

By the time of the great migration of 1848, the Irish Catholics had endured over two centuries of subjection to laws which they thought unjust and to a political order over which they had little control. Cromwell, following his victory in England, mercilessly extirpated resistance to his Roundhead regime in Ireland. In 1652 he parcelled out 11 of Ireland's 20 million acres to his officers and followers, creating an alien landlord class and dispossessing the Irish. In 1688 the English Parliament passed the Penal Laws to finally end the Irish threat to England. The restrictions placed on Irish Catholics by these laws were extensive and severe.

No Irish Catholic could vote, serve on a jury, enter the army or navy, teach school, carry a gun, or own a horse of the value of more than five guineas. No

Irish Catholic could enter a university, become a lawyer, or work for the government. Those few Irish who clung to sizable pieces of land did so at the price of swearing allegiance to the Anglican Church. When an Irish Catholic died, his estate was divided among his sons unless the eldest became a Protestant, in which event all of it went to him. Priests were subject to arrest and deportation. The Irish language was forbidden, and schools became almost unknown.[35]

The Penal Laws were not rigorously enforced, and by 1780 the "purely penal part" of the code was abandoned, but the Irish people had by then become accustomed to political persecution and economic deprivation.

The Penal Laws, intended to destroy Catholicism, actually entrenched the position of the priest. The dogged persistence of the priests in continuing their ministry despite the penalties of the Penal Laws gave them an unrivaled respect among the Irish Catholics.

Living under the sway of the Penal Laws, the Irish developed an equal contempt for the law and for government. These were perceived as methods by which the possessors of power subjected and punished them. Levine concludes that the Irish Catholic's experiences with English law and justice had a decisive effect on his political behavior as an immigrant in America. By the time of the migration,

. . . the Irish were a thoroughly politicized people. . . . They had known approximately two centuries of close personal experience with Anglo-Saxon Protestant government, having witnessed how an alien landlord class through its control of government made a mockery of law and a chimera of justice. The Irish disdain of law was probably as important to their future in American politics as was their knowledge of the ways in which the institutions of Anglo-Saxon government functioned.

This experience encouraged specific attitudes toward government:

The sum of their political experiences forced them to adopt the view that political power was to be sought by all conceivable means, and that it was to be used only in the interests of those who possessed it.[36]

That American democracy did not have this character, and therefore need not be approached with these preconceptions, was a fact that only slowly penetrated the Irish immigrant community. In some ways, the retention of these views was encouraged by the American environment. The established political and social authority in the Eastern cities was, as in Ireland, predominantly Anglo-Protestant. It was infused with a vague but noticeable hostility to the strange foreigner, and not least to the Irish Catholic, and this hostility did not disappear with the demise of the Know-Nothing party. The Irish immigrants responded to this hostility, and reinforced it, by their clannishness, isolation, and sense of difference. To the extent that the city environment fortified the impression that life in America should proceed upon the same rules as in Ireland, it intensified and prolonged the Irishman's willingness to condone political corruption. The Catholic Church, despite its dominant role in the lives of the Irish immigrants, was less successful in proscribing political corruption than in imposing its ethical teachings in matters of morals, censorship, drinking, and sex. The Catholic clergy in Ireland, at least from the time of the Penal Laws, had been leaders of the resistance against the political system operated by their enemies and the enemies of their faith. During the political activism of the 1820s, priests were among the forefront of the party pressing for Irish representation in Parliament. "Every priest was ex-officio a member of O'Connell's political organization, the Catholic Association."[37] Having so long urged with their very action the propriety of resisting the political order, and evading its injustices, the Catholic clergy in America were not immediately able, if they were willing, to reverse the attitudes of their flock.

Very rapidly the Irish rose into positions of prominence in many city governments. Before the 1848 immigration, earlier arrivals had filled many places as policemen, firemen, and in public works; these were jobs that offered genuine security. Many soon rose to positions where they could control jobs, and hence votes, thereby gaining prominence in the emerging political machines. As the Irish communities grew, the importance of these key Irish intermediaries grew; as they rose higher in the political organization, they could command even more jobs on behalf of more recent arrivals from the *Auld Sod*. The hold of the Irish on the political organization quickly became self-perpetuating.

Once the Irish, with their favored position, had ensconced themselves in positions of political power, other immigrant groups found it difficult to supplant them. In time, numbers of German and Scandinavian newcomers accumulated in cities, familiarized themselves with the language and the political system, and began to demand a voice in the policies of government, as well as a share in the goods at its disposal. But although they could not be denied positions of political leadership in their own communities, they found the higher positions in the political organizations already stubbornly held by Irish-Americans.

Nonimmigrant Corruption

It has been noted that municipal political corruption and the machine were actually originated by "native" Americans. Foreign immigrants, especially the Irish, were well placed by historical circumstances and attitudes to be recruited into these activities, and in time to become widely involved in corruption and machine politics. Urban immigrants did not originate corruption, nor were they the only ones to carry on corrupt practices after their arrival. A study of rural Connecticut found a great deal of corruption among Yankees. Aaron Burr, of distinguished New England ancestry, helped found Tammany and turned it to political purposes. Throughout their history, many of the state political machines were consistently dominated by nonimmigrants. In the early 1900s Lincoln Steffens found that the "old American stock" of Rhode Island was easily corrupted, and the old American stock elsewhere was not incorruptible.[38]

Nor was there anything like unanimity among the urban immigrants in support of corrupt politics. There were numbers of immigrants among many of the political reform groups of the later nineteenth century. Griffith, for example, lists several German-Americans who were leaders of civic reform in Brooklyn, New York, St. Louis, San Antonio, Wichita, and Paducah.[39] Southern cities had very few immigrants but managed to develop machines, although most of them were more honest than those of the North.

Conclusions

Certain traditions of seventeenth- and eighteenth-century political corruption were transplanted from the old world to the new, particularly in the functioning of local governments and the prerogatives of some colonial governors. A more potent and virulent strain, however, developed after the 1820s with the establishment of partisan political machines in some of the larger cities. When the great numbers of immigrants—some of whom, notably the Irish, were "against the government"—were absorbed into the machine and multiplied its power, political corruption rapidly became a leading problem of American municipal government. The rapid growth of cities during the nineteenth century served to augment opportunities for the misuse of public works, the employment of political hangers-on in patronage jobs, and graft on a large scale. Against these forces the feeble municipal governing structures were helpless. Neither state nor federal governments had begun to develop policies or programs to control dishonesty in local government.

3
The Politics of Municipal Corruption

Corrupt machine politics became the dominant pattern of government for American cities in the last quarter of the nineteenth century. Municipal machines themselves tended almost universally to become corrupt. Moreover, the pattern frequently became linked with political corruption on the state and national levels. State and national corruption prior to World War I was often an extension of municipal machine practices which were designed to gain and keep office in the cities.

The pervasiveness of machine politics and of the accompanying corruption in nineteenth-century America is astounding. In his *American Commonwealth*, James Bryce estimated that the government of every American city with more than 200,000 inhabitants was corrupt during this last quarter-century. Many cities of 50,000 to 200,000 were corrupt, and even several cities smaller than 50,000 were riddled with corruption, although on a less grandiose scale than, say, New York or San Francisco.[1] The findings of the municipal historian Ernest S. Griffith are also grim. He noted that from 1870 to 1900 Newark was the only large city to remain reasonably honest. The New England towns of Cambridge, Worcester, and Springfield were the only medium-sized cities he discovered that were consistently uncorrupt. Every city he examined in the middle states and all the Southern cities except Atlanta, Charleston, and possibly Richmond and Memphis were persistently or intermittently corrupt. In the West only Oakland and in the mid-West only Milwaukee seem to have avoided the corrupting tendency of politics in this era.[2]

In nearly every other city of medium size or larger, evidence of corrupt practices by the elected officers can be discovered. While the depredations of the government of many larger cities are well known, the appearance of similar actions in smaller cities, across the length and breadth of the nation, is less well known. Jersey City, Louisville, Chattanooga, Cincinnati, Columbus, Indianapolis, Omaha, Seattle, and Denver are only a few of the cities which exhibited one or another variety of machine control, and which were later indicted by their own citizens for their wasteful, inefficient, self-serving, or corrupt officials.[3]

Patterns of Political Corruption

Of course, no two cities had identical machines or were corrupt in precisely the same ways, but there were several typical patterns of corruption. Some machines were thoroughly organized in every ward of the city, and they were therefore capable of completely dominating city government for long, unbroken stretches. In other cities, like Boston and Chicago, the machine was incompletely organized. There, rival factions and parties vied for control of the city as a whole. In Cincinnati and San Francisco, only portions of the city were organized by the dominant machine. There the machine was compelled to fight periodically against the "better elements," who sporadically organized to "throw out the rascals" of the political organizations. In some other cities, there was little permanent machine organization in the wards or electoral precincts, but even there the elected officials quickly learned how to profit from the public funds. But without a vote-getting apparatus, tenure in office was more precarious, and opportunities for large-scale peculation more limited. In a few cities, the controlling ring was not even composed of elected officials. The Philadelphia Gas Ring extended its control of the city from the board of the municipal gasworks and the extensive patronage that it supplied to the board members.[4] In Omaha, "franchised corporations, living upon the rights and privileges given by the City Council . . . are the ring."[5] The owners of municipally franchised corporations in many other cities, while usually not comprising the actual political ring, were able to exercise a prodigious influence on the decisions of the city government. In a few places, state legislatures used their power over city charters to influence or alter the political complexion of the city governments, normally to the advantage of the combination that ruled the state legislature.

Organization and Politics of the Municipal Machine

The essential element of every machine was votes; so most of the machine's activities reflected the need to gain and keep the allegiance of voters. Municipal politicians, unable to rely on ideological appeals, found a secure method of cementing a political following by appealing to the voter's self-interest. The enfranchised urban dweller gave the machine politicians his vote. The politician fulfilled his part of the bargain by providing the voter with real or illusory goods, of a kind more immediately useful than the "good and efficient government" which satisfied the needs of the more affluent groups. This exchange of votes for goods relied upon personal contact. At the lowest but most vital level of machine operation was a local agent or intermediary who was able to discern the needs of voters in a given area and distribute the goods available through the political manner. The best machine—in fact, one could say the only machine that really deserved the name—was based on highly organized parties in the smaller electoral divisions (the precincts or wards). The machine qua machine was a hierarchy built up from this broad and firm base.

The local officer of the political machine was the precinct captain or ward leader. He was usually what would be termed a "self-starter" in politics. That is, he organized his own political following and thereby brought himself to the attention of more prominent and powerful politicians. William Marcy "Boss" Tweed first gained entry into New York politics through his ability to deliver the votes of the laddies in his fire company. Chicago's "Bathhouse John" Coughlin rose to his first political office in that city's First Ward as the successful, generous owner of an enterprise that brought him many acquaintances and loyalties. With these connections, Coughlin quickly became an asset to the ward's political leaders.

Joseph "Chesterfield Joe" Mackin, the First Ward's dapper Democratic boss,

. . . often patronized the downtown baths. Mackin liked Coughlin's homely philosophy and enthusiasm for people and urged him to become a member of his organization, the First Ward Democratic Club. Coughlin, pleased at the bid, . . . promptly joined and became an ardent Mackin man. He was soon appointed Democratic captain of the precinct in which his newest bathhouse was situated. It was an honor he prized, above all others, to his death.[6]

The ward or precinct leader, whether a self-starter or selected by the machine hierarchy, was normally a member of the ethnic group dominant in the division, even where the machine as a whole was run by members of some other nationality. In many cities by the late nineteenth century, Irish politicians had captured the highest city offices, but they recognized that the newer immigrant communities preferred as their local agent one of their own, whether he be Polish, Italian, Jew, or Swede. In the larger and ethnically mixed cities, the political machine was often remarkably diversified.[7] The precinct leader was the lowliest, but in many ways the most important (as Coughlin's attachment to that job shows), intermediary between the city's real governors and the urban voter.[8]

As the cities grew, diversified, and assumed new duties, additional functionaries and employees of the city government began to appear in the local districts. Most often these were patronage employees hired on the recommendation of the local captain. They depended for their livelihood on the continued success of the machine and the friendship of the local political operative. In New York, under the 1844 police law, the officers and men of the police force were chosen for one year at a time, on the recommendation of the local politician. Baltimore, Cincinnati, and Boston, among others, followed a similar practice.[9] Control of the police gave the political organization a considerable additional means to influence the lives of the voters in the city. With the police, they could reward the machine's friends and punish its enemies. By skillfull use of the force, they could enrich the machine itself. Under the Tweed Ring (1862-1871) and later Tammany organizations, the police were largely incorporated into the party organization.

Gamblers and criminals were given freedom and immunity from arrest. It was not that every policeman was dishonest; it just seemed to New Yorkers that every time a policeman was seen, "he was browbeating a saloon keeper for a free drink, extorting money from streetwalkers . . . [or] running errands for politicians."[10]

As will be seen, the Tweed Ring, like many other machines, relied on the protection of illegal activities for a portion of its revenue, and was therefore obliged to control the police in order to ensure selective protection. In addition to acting as local agent of the machine, the police department supplied a large fund of patronage appointments, which brought more voters into dependency on the machine. And finally, police officers were frequently employed to manage elections for the party to whom they owed their jobs.

Obstacles in the way of complete dominance by party machines have been overcome by the easy processes of law, and police departments have been revamped, and reshaped, not in the interests of public service, but to facilitate the operation of the spoils system or strengthen the grip of some political machine. . . . The struggle for party dominance, the desire for "jobs" for the faithful, the determination to control the machinery of elections were the contributing motives in the principal alterations.[11]

    In addition to the police, there were other functionaries in the wards. The fire companies served as a source of patronage and of election-day muscle for the machine, but they were generally made professional nonpatronage forces at an earlier date than were the police forces. On the other hand, the army of city inspectors and regulators was always growing, and it could supply the machine with some of the same leverage as the police force. This army, too, was directly in the pay of the dominant combination. The building inspector could ease the problems of a friend by overlooking deficiencies in the safety features of his tenement houses. The same inspector could as easily demonstrate that unknown defects could result in the shutting down of a hostile businessman's enterprise, but that the defect somehow escaped his notice once a contribution had been made to the inspector and the machine.

    Tweed Ring judges were just as venal a part of the machine as any other official, selling writs of habeas corpus, receiverships, and court orders. Judge Cardozo took bribes to release more than 200 clients of one law firm alone before he resigned to escape impeachment in 1872.[12]

    All these agents were regularly employed in bringing the presence of the machine into the local district—all were active agents of the organization. Most of the remaining city employees were more passive operatives. The man who leaned on a city broom very likely had a swarm of relatives who relied on his earnings for their bread. Each had a personal motive for keeping his patron in power.

Every machine organized itself differently to capture the key decision-making positions, but the object was always the same—to control the revenue- and job-producing activities of the city. The special targets of the machine leaders were offices that disposed of large amounts of patronage; those that enforced legal sanctions on gambling, liquor, and prostitution; offices that awarded municipal contracts, franchises, and licenses; offices responsible for criminal prosecutions; and others. Control of all these could be crucial to the success of the machine. In fact, anyone who showed himself capable of impeding the major activities of the machine soon became an object of the ring's attention. If a judge persistently convicted the machine's repeaters, he had to be converted or defeated and replaced. If the state legislature insisted on interfering in the city's police department, the legislature had to be controlled or bought off. If the comptroller questioned the street department's expenditures, he had to be brought around. Not every machine, of course, was able to accomplish all these tasks. They made the attempt when it seemed necessary. Those that failed often fell.

Tammany Hall's New York

Tammany Hall, the Democratic party organization in New York City, provides the best example of continuous machine control in an American city. During the heyday of Boss Tweed, it closely approached the ideal machine. His successes, and ultimate failure, in gaining personal control of the government of New York City illustrate many of the strengths and weaknesses of machine politics.

Even before the rise of Tweed, New York City's government was corrupt. The very character of the city's government seemed conducive to political corruption. It suffered from the major defect of city governments of its day—the decentralization of power and responsibility. The New York charter in operation prior to 1857 was a makeshift of expedients. Each time the city assumed a new responsibility, a new department had been created to direct it.

In 1857 a new charter was passed because of public concern about corruption. However, the new charter only complicated the government and permitted the institution of a more corrupt regime under Tweed. The Republican party had just gained control of the state legislature in 1857, and the modifications they made to the city charter supplied partisan advantage rather than actual reform. Its method for controlling municipal corruption was to transfer a large portion of control over the city's affairs to the state. Several city offices were to be transformed into state offices, to be filled by the appointment of the governor. The immediate effect of the new charter was to hand over to the Republicans a large portion of the city's patronage. The charter did little to organize or centralize the city government.

New York City's government structure remained exceedingly complex, with a decision-making process that was so dispersed as to be largely ineffectual. Three separate bodies could legislate for the citizens. The city's bicameral legislature was composed of a 17-member board of aldermen and a 24-member board of councilmen. Moreover, the county was coterminous with the city, and it sported a separate board of supervisors which disposed of its own budget. The 1857 charter restricted the power and patronage of the mayor, which had not been extensive. The chiefs of nine of the city's departments were independent of the mayor's control, being appointed by the state or directly elected. The departments ran most of the city's programs and spent most of its budget. But the departments "themselves were in administrative shambles, having powers that were either undefined, doubtful, or conflicting. Their executives, being independent of the mayor's control and arrogant and jealous of their power, built private empires." The resulting city government was "a crazy quilt of petty sovereignties, each independent of the other, and all spending money without any accountability to anyone."[13]

With two of his associates, Peter Sweeny and Richard Connolly, Tweed gained control of the Tammany organization in 1863, when his party was suffering from the effects of its latest internal battle. Tweed, who had worked his way into the party's leading circles via his own ward, was already a member of the county board of supervisors and the city's fire commission. In 1863, he was also appointed assistant street commissioner. The commissioner, who had just been elevated to the state senate, delegated full departmental responsibility to Tweed. The street commission became one of the major sources of strength for the Tweed Ring. Tweed's control of this vast patronage gave him unrivaled power in the city's informal hierarchy.

In the state and national elections of 1868, Tweed and his confederates began to close their grip on the government of the city. Tammany mounted a vigorous campaign to elect their candidate, then mayor of New York City, to the governorship (a necessary step to controlling the city under the 1857 Republican charter). The campaign was accompanied by what may have been the most massive voting fraud in the city's history. First was a massive naturalization of immigrants, on Tammany's orders, by judges controlled by the organization. Over 1400 voters were naturalized on each of the days leading up to the election, comprising a goodly portion of the 41,000 who were naturalized in the whole year. This was more tahn 4 times the normal yearly average. In addition to enrolling voters through naturalization, the machines devised an extensive padding of the voting lists. Operatives registered large numbers of fictitious names in the various wards and employed repeaters to vote under these fictitious names. Finally, since more votes were reported than were numbered in the voting population, an even more direct type of election fraud must have been employed. The election produced a Democratic majority of 60,000 in the city, swinging the statewide election to the Democrats by 10,000 votes. The

Democrats captured the governorship and, in the 1869 elections, regained a majority in the state legislature. A close associate of Tweed, A. Oakey Hall, was elected to fill the place vacated by the new governor. At one step, Tweed destroyed the power of the state to interfere with the city's operations, and elevated one of his closest associates to the mayoralty.

With these compliant officers added to the circle of influence that Tweed had already secured, the ring had captured the city government.

The 1st of January, 1869, found it master of every department of the city, and of nearly every department of the State government. It controlled both Legislature and Common Council. Its adviser, Hoffman, sat in the Governor's chair at Albany, and its other adviser, Hall, sat in the Mayor's seat in New York. Sweeny was City Chamberlain; Tweed held the Department of Streets; Connolly had been advanced to the office of Comptroller. Barnard, Cardozo, and McCunn were secure on the bench. . . . Well might the Ring feel secure and prepare to reap the rich harvest of corruption.[14]

In addition, the Tweed Ring had implicated reliable majorities of the board of supervisors and board of aldermen and had reliable agents in the offices of corporation counsel and treasurer of the city and county.[15] With a secure electoral majority through the Tammany organization, and an almost absolute domination of the city government, Tweed and his ring embarked on the career of corruption that was to end in their undoing.

The machine required money to satisfy the demands of those who voted for it and to sustain the numerous employees of the organization. In addition to these costs, which were massive in themselves, was the expense of gratifying the avarice of the ring leaders, which, however, seemed insatiable. It was more the unmistakable greed of the ring leaders, and the vast sums they appropriated to themselves, than the ordinary costs of the machine that eventually eroded the ring's electoral base. Once the ring mastered the government, numerous means of extracting money from the city fell into its hands. The most accessible and secure source of income was from graft on municipal contracts. Before 1869, city contractors expected to pay 10 percent in graft to the machine. Under Tweed this rapidly rose to 65 percent, of which 25 percent went to Tweed, while the remaining 40 percent was distributed among lesser accomplices. The history of the New York Court House is the most familiar and notorious example of the ring's method of operation. Planned in 1868 at a cost not to exceed $250,000, the Court House under Tweed management eventually absorbed over $8 million of city revenue. Many of the contracts were let to friends of the ring or to companies owned by the ring's members at inflated prices. The ring collected its 65 percent from the contract on top of the inflated prices. All the costs were passed along to the taxpayers. Through the control of the Street Department, and later the Department of Public Works, the ring was also able to take advantage of advance knowledge of real estate developments, such as the laying of new streets, to realize immediate cash profits. From the widening of Broadway alone, the well-informed speculators were thought to have realized a profit of $1 million in public compensation.[16]

Boss Tweed and many of his counterparts in other cities were able to turn their influence over municipal contacts into hard cash in another way. Rather than simply bidding for contracts and paying a percentage graft, some companies (either spontaneously or in response to a hint) placed the boss directly on the company's payroll. Tweed was made a director of the Third Avenue Railroad Company, which held a franchise in the city, and he was retained by Jay Gould as legal advisor of the Erie Railroad at an annual salary of $100,000. He was also director of the Brooklyn Bridge Company and part owner of the New York Printing Company (from which the ring ordered all the city's printing). He was part owner of the New York *Transcript*, which was largely supported by city advertising. He was president of the Guardian Savings Bank. Any company doing business with the city knew the advantage of employing Tweed or one of his associates.

The patronage available to the ring was made doubly useful. The machine cemented the loyalty of supporters with patronage jobs, but at the same time it demanded from them in return a payment for the office, which went back into the coffers of the machine. Those seeking offices which could themselves be turned to profit were charged heavily for Tammany's endorsement and support. The Tweed Ring controlled all the city's departments except the board of education, and in 1869 began attempts to include this potent source of patronage and revenue within its regime. This was financially accomplished by a bill forced through the state legislature, which eliminated the sitting independent board and substituted a new commission appointed by the mayor.

Finally, the Tweed Ring secured revenue by the exploitation of "the twilight zone between crimes of violence and illegal practices that had the sanction of community or neighborhood public opinion—such as gambling, brothels, and unregulated liquor sales." Here the systematic selling of legal immunity, enforced by shakedowns of the recalcitrant, "aggregated a very large amount, and filtered down to and up from the patrolman on the beat." The net revenue of the ring was enormous. Depending on how the money is calculated, from $30 to $100 million was obtained by the ring in three years. Some $30 million was stolen directly from the city treasury.[17]

Tammany had been, during the days of Republican ascendancy in Albany, an insistent advocate of home rule for the city of New York and an end to "drynurse and leading string's system of government for New York City." This had, the reformers said, "made New York no better, and Albany a great deal worse."[18] After the Democrats won control of the state government in 1869, the Tweed Ring no longer had strong motive to change the city's charter. But the Young Democracy saw in a call for charter reform a means of amalgamating all the dissatisfied elements in the city, and perhaps of overthrowing the Tweed

Ring. The Tweed group, however, produced a clever plan to undercut the Young Democracy. In 1870 they introduced into the state legislature their own reform charter which was designed to meet almost all the demands of the municipal reformers while still allowing Tweed to retain control.

The Tweed Charter, as it came to be called, was remarkable in that it could accomplish several things with one stroke. First, restore some autonomy to New York, but not enough to incur the wrath of the Republicans. Second, incorporate many of the changes which reformers had for years been demanding. Third, reorganize the government of New York so that those in the Young Democracy who held official positions would soon be put out of office. And last but not least, provide new opportunities for graft.[19]

The Tweed charter took some wind out of the Young Democracy's sails, but the reformers soon countered with their own charter, which would save them from the consequences of Tweed's. The fight between the two factions moved to the floor and committee rooms of the state legislature. The Young Democracy concentrated their efforts on winning the votes of Democrats from outside the city. But power in the legislature was closely balanced. The Democrats had a majority of seven in the Assembly, and of only one in the Senate. The ring concentrated its efforts on acquiring the votes of Republicans. For this task the graft from many of the ring's operations was brought to bear, and ring contractors were prevailed upon to contribute $200,000 for the campaign. In all, the ring distributed some $600,000 in bribes, mostly among Republican legislators, while promising them other favors as well, including portions of the city patronage.[20]

The new charter, as the reformers wished, placed clear responsibility for the running of the city's government in a few hands. The mayor was authorized to appoint all the heads of the departments, who were responsible only to him. He could bring any official to trial for corruption, and the aldermen could bring the mayor to trial on that charge. Some departments were consolidated, and their jurisdictions delineated. The state's power to interfere in the day-to-day operation of the government was eliminated.

The corrupt activities of the ring multiplied under the new charter, partly as a result of the need to repay debts incurred in passing the charter. The ring acted as though it felt secure. In 1860 the city debt had been $19 million. At the end of 1870, it exceeded $73 million, and during 1870 alone $25 million had been added.[21] Rumors of the thefts by the ring were rife, but the principals had such thorough control of the government that no real evidence could be obtained. But in July 1871 a disaffected subordinate of the ring managed to reproduce copies of the secret financial transaction of the ring and deliver them to *The New York Times,* whose publication of the accounts precipitated the downfall of the Tweed Ring.

After the fall of the Tweed Ring, New York enjoyed only temporary respite, for Tammany Hall kept returning to power. No reform mayor lasted more than one term until La Guardia's three terms in the 1930s and 1940s.

Richard Croker, Tammany leader from 1885 to 1902, sometimes viewed New York City as one of his business assets. The New York Auto-Truck Company, of which he was a large shareholder, wished to attach its compressed-air pipes to the elevated structures of the Manhattan Elevated Railway Company. When the railway company demurred, a wrathful Croker secured passage of several ordinances which, if enforced, would have put the Elevated Railway out of business. The bonding company of his closest friend bonded all city employees whose jobs required it. Testimony to the Mazet investigation indicated that New York Telephone gave a fraction of its stock to Croker's close associate, in return for a contract for street lamps.

Croker's use of city authority for his own business reasons supplies evidence against the theory of some political scientists that corruption aids the development of business. For several years after London's successful operation of subways, New York City delayed construction because Croker and others had an interest in Manhattan Elevated Railway Company and feared competition. When construction finally started, Tammany's great interest was how it could make the most money off the contract.[22]

Some portions of the police were corrupt most of the time since establishment of the force, according to a Knapp Commission estimate in 1972. The Lexow committee uncovered a system in which policemen had to pay bribes for every promotion, ranging from $300 to become a patrolman to $15,000 for a captaincy in a lucrative graft district. These police reimbursed themselves by extortion from brothels, saloons, gamblers, and merchants. Methods of extortion countenanced by Tammany were severe. A well-known Captain Alexander William was widely known as "clubber Williams." Machine corruption speedily led to bad treatment of individuals, as the 1894 Lexow committee and 1900 Mazet committee reports indicated—annual bribes of up to $20,000 to $30,000 and, despite the bribes, brutal personal treatment by police.

A part of the Lexow committee report should be quoted:

It has been abundantly proven that bootblacks, pushcart and fruit vendors, as well as keepers of soda water stands, corner grocerymen . . . box-makers, provision dealers, wholesale drygoods merchants and builders, who are compelled at times to use the sidewalk and street, steamboat and steamship companies, who require police service on their docks, those who give public exhibitions, and in fact all persons, and all classes of persons whose business is subject to the observation of the police, or who may be reported as violating ordinances, or who may require the aid of the police, all have to contribute in substantial sums to the vast amounts which flow into the station houses . . .[23]

At times there were outbreaks of rivalry between policemen and machine leaders for payoffs, but in general police followed Tammany leadership. In 1894, a New York grand jury foreman estimated that police protection of all types of vice yielded $7 million in graft per year, much of which was used to maintain the costly life-style to which Dick Croker had become accustomed. Indeed, the tradition of corruption which Tweed had previously established was almost fully renewed by Tammany under Croker's misrule. By 1900, *The New York Times* revealed that a Tammany "commission," comprised of a city official, two state senators, and a gambling syndicate leader, was receiving a monthly stipend of $3,095,000 in graft from gambling interests.[24]

Croker was succeeded as leader of Tammany Hall by Charles F. Murphy in 1902. Murphy, perhaps the most competent of Tammany chieftains, moved corruption into more "respectable" channels. Leaders of Tammany became more interested in water, gas, electricity, or railroads than in prostitution, liquor, gambling, or extortion.[25] However, the police department continued to extort money from prostitution and the other vices. Murphy succeeded in electing Tammany's first governor, William Sulzer, in 1913, but had him impeached because he refused to appoint state officials who would work out corrupt opportunities for Tammany friends. However, Murphy succeeded in 1918 in moving Al Smith to the governorship and had clear ambitions of making him President before Murphy's death in 1924. Murphy increased the ambitions of Tammany and changed its type of corruption, but did not try to make it honest.

Philadelphia's Republican Machine

The New York Democratic machine was the most notorious example of the fully developed political organization. There were others that rivaled it both in degree of organization and control over the electorate and the government. The Republican machine in Philadelphia was organized on a par with Tammany, and it exercised an equally systematic and continuous political mastery. During the 1860s, under the first great Philadelphia boss, James "King" McManes, every one of the city's 700 precincts supported a Republican committee and precinct captain. The captains represented their precincts on the 31 ward committees. The wards in turn sent representatives to the city's central party committeee.[26] McManes initially rose to party prominence through his control of one of the wards, but gained control of the city government through the novel expedient of the city Gas Trust. In 1841, the city of Philadelphia bought out the private company franchised to supply gas to the city. A board of trustees was established to run the company. Like the Department of Streets in New York, the Gas Trust became the largest controller of patronage in the city. The trust itself employed up to 2000 workers. It let contracts for new construction and for repairs, paying for them with bonds of its own issue. These considerable powers could be used by corrupt trustees to distribute favors and collect graft from contractors.[27] McManes, when he won leadership of the Gas Trust in 1865, had a ready pool of resources for his machine. Like Tweed, he found himself offered other employments as well. He became the president and director of street railways (operating on city franchises), the president of a bank, and a stockholder in several other businesses. In 1879 he affirmed that he personally controlled 5630 city jobs—a vast store of patronage and a sure reward for the army of political supporters.[28]

During the 1870s and 1880s, McManes's political control of Philadelphia was pervasive, and his influence extended upward into state and even national politics. He dictated the city's Republican slate of candidates because he controlled the machine that elected delegates to the nominating conventions. He was, in the same manner, able to take a large delegation under his command to the state and national conventions.

The Philadelphia ring obtained its money from most of the same sources as Tweed's. Patronage appointees, from political office holders to policemen and teachers, were regularly assessed a portion of their wages to support the machine. Any official who managed to procure a position which could yield a large profit "was of course required to contribute to the secret party funds in proportion to his income. . . ." Graft and speculation were also widespread, and the cost to the city's taxpayers of supporting the machine and its whole elaborate structure multiplied. In 1860 the city's debt totaled $20 million. By 1881 it was over $70 million, yet municipal services were poor and still deteriorating.[29]

As in New York, the manifest corruption of the machine stimulated a reform movement which, in 1881, temporarily dethroned the "King." But by 1884 McManes was back on the Gas Trust and running the city. The final end of the McManes Ring did not come until 1885. Then the state Republican boss, at odds with the Philadelphia leader, allowed a bill of municipal reform to pass the state legislature which eliminated the Gas Trust and fatally wounded the McManes Ring by eliminating its source of power.

As in New York, however, the fall of the leaders of an organized political machine did not mean that the machine was dead. Many resources of power and voter control remained, and one of McManes's lieutenants quickly replaced him as the reformers redirected their attention to their own affairs. The new boss, "Judge" Israel Durham, retained the extensive political organization, which reached from precinct committee through the wards and into a central campaign committee. Through this organization, he dominated Philadelphia from 1899 to 1903. Durham's operation was not as notorious as McManes's had been, but at one time he spent $5 million of city money on the construction of a water filtration plant. He awarded the contract to the firm of his silent business partner.[30] "Is" Durham's machine relied heavily on ballot stuffing to ensure the election of its candidates. One examination revealed that 63 percent of the voters listed on one division's rosters were actually deceased or had long since moved away. Under Durham, Philadelphia was subjected to the misrule of Mayor Samuel H. Ashbridge who, during his 4-year tenure, was able to eliminate a personal debt of $40,000 and leave office to become a wealthy bank president. Public employees were compelled to kick back a percentage of their income to the machine; even grade school teachers, whose salaries were only $47 per month, were required to purchase their positions for $120. Revenue also came from a number of other sources. In one instance, Ashbridge rejected a legitimate offer of $2.5 million made to the city for a street railroad franchise, awarding it instead to a machine-affiliated concern whose "rakeoff" dwarfed the franchise bid lost by the city.[31] After another bout with reform, the Republican machine produced another boss, Edwin Vare, who attained a higher degree of control than Durham and after 1916 ran a ring almost as thorough as that of McManes himself. The Vare machine in Philadelphia lasted until 1933.

Ruef-Schmitz in San Francisco

San Francisco had corruption from its earliest days. A vigilante group was organized in 1849 and again in 1856 by middle-class businessmen wishing to maintain order and unable to secure it from a corrupt and inefficient city government.[32] San Francisco's most elaborate political machine ruled briefly in the first decade of the century. Directed by Abe Ruef and Eugene Schmitz, this machine displayed many of the same characteristics as its big city counterparts in the East. Abe Ruef entered politics in a city whose control was disputed among petty bosses of the Republican and Democratic parties, none of whom was able to consolidate a complete city machine. Ruef worked his way to control of the North Beach ward. Suddenly, in 1901, he was able to take advantage of a period of labor unrest to create a citywide Union Labor party, which rapidly organized a city-winning plurality. Schmitz, Ruef's candidate for mayor, was installed in offices in 1902, while the boss himself took up a prominent but unofficial position as attorney and advisor to the mayor. Ruef's services as legal advisor were widely in demand among those who had business with the city, particularly as the mayor often suggested that business agents see Ruef about contractual matters. He was hired on a $3000 per year retainer by the Pacific States Telephone and Telegraph Company, which was then resisting efforts by other companies to dispute its monopoly in San Francisco. The new traction company which was working for a franchise in the city, United Railroad, also retained Ruef at $6000 per year to advise them on matters of municipal law.[33] When the United Railroad Company was finally granted a 25-year franchise in the wake of the earthquake of 1906, Ruef, Schmitz, and the supervisors in the ring were paid $200,000 by the company.

The ring also moved into a whole series of graft operations. The San Francisco police commission, which the ring controlled by 1904, was empowered to sell liquor licenses. The liquor dealers jointly employed Ruef as counsel, and the individual saloons also retained him at fees of $50 to $1000 per year. Licenses came up for review every three months, so those who refused to pay the retainer ran a high risk of losing their licenses. There was also graft in street contracts, and the ring was directly involved in prostitution. Crime flourished with a corrupt police department. The use of municipal licensing and regulating to procure revenues for the machine was well developed in the city. Twenty-seven types of businesses needed city licenses to operate, and the 6000 operators of these diverse activities were all assessed a fee, either as a retainer to Ruef or his subordinate or as a bribe to the inspector.

Not one theater in town complied with the fire ordinances, but after the owners had signed over a third of their capital stock to Ruef or his dummies, inspectors from the board of public works were unable to detect any violations. Recalcitrants who declined to be blackmailed found their theaters closed for legitimate reasons. Contractors, butchers, produce dealers were levied upon. The board of health imposed fantastic rules on cleanliness on milkmen, but after these made up a "lawyer fund" and retained a Ruef-selected attorney, they were not incommoded.[34]

Despite its considerable short-term success, the Ruef-Schmitz Ring proved to be less well founded and secure than many of its counterparts. After a persistent prosecution which was supported by federal investigators, the ring collapsed and Ruef was convicted. His machine revealed little of the longevity of other machines which were based on a thorough ward and precinct organization.

Chicago

The Windy City has had troubles with political corruption and vice since its earliest days. In 1855 the first police department was appointed on a strictly political basis. Police and other official corruption reached "scandalous proportions" by the end of the Civil War. Carter Harrison, Sr., was mayor from 1879 to 1887, with support of an alliance between gambling interests and professional politicians. A major gambling figure, "King" Mike MacDonald, ran one of the biggest gambling houses and also controlled mayors, congressmen, and senators. He was a regular political ally of Mayor Carter Harrison (the elder) in the 1870s and 1880s. The alliance between gambling, liquor, and prostitution interests and the political machine in the First Ward under Hinky Dink Kenna and Bathhouse John Coughlin was intimate and easy and lasted for a half-century.

MacDonald and his partners controlled gambling at Chicago and Indiana racetracks; with no danger of Chicago prosecution, they cleared as much as $750,000 in one year in the 1880s. MacDonald began a feature of Chicago public life which has lasted well into the twentieth century: the gamblers and other syndicate leaders have at times had more power than the city government.

In 1884 one of MacDonald's associates was sentenced to prison terms in both federal and state courts for substituting forged ballots and tally sheets in a precinct ballot box. Many similar frauds were undetected.

Following charges by an Englishman, William T. Stead, a reform Civic Federation exposed conditions in Chicago. Twenty-one convictions of vote thieves were secured after the November 1894 election. Bribing of aldermen by street railway magnate Yerkes was demonstrated. In 1911 a Civil Service Commission investigation "revealed a conspiracy between gamblers, politicians, and the police to drive non-syndicate gamblers out of business." In 1888 and 1889 there were charges of bribery against the Chicago police, related to the effort to indicate that the Haymarket riot defendants had not received a fair trial. Aldermen generally were paid, in the guise of legal services, for votes on street car franchises; Jewish peddlers were attacked on the streets, with no police protection. Efforts to sue Union Traction for bribing officials were defeated by bribing the jury.[35]

Chicago's one claim to civic betterment was the Civic Federation, but it confessed in 1896 that it could not drive the bottlers out of Chicago.

The political organization of Chicago was more chaotic and irregular even than Cox's Cincinnati. Lincoln Steffens, in his rather hyperbolic style, described the politics of Chicago in the 1890s:

There were political parties, but the organizations were controlled by rings, which in turn were backed and used by leading business interests through which this corrupt and corrupting system reached with its ramifications far and high and low into the social organization. The grafting was miscellaneous and general; but the most open corruption was that which centered in the City Council. It never was well organized and orderly. The aldermen had "combines" leaders, and prices, but a log of good-natured honest thieves, they were independent of party bosses and "the organizations," which were busy at their own graft.[36]

The city was run by several local machines of both parties. Sometimes the local machines would work together; at other times they competed. The fluidity of the Chicago situation "made it possible for reform organizations to score more frequent victories than they did in most other cities."[37] Nevertheless, Chicago's reputation at that time as a tough, hard frontier town was justified, and its receptivity to organized crime already established.

All the ordinary schemes of extortion were employed in Chicago—holders of patronage jobs were assessed a portion of their wages; graft, especially on municipal franchises, was almost universal, although decentralized to mesh with the city's political decentralization. But in the city's First Ward—and particularly in its notorious Levee district where saloons, gambling halls, and brothels were concentrated—vice operations were conducted on a scale and with a degree of participation by the machine politicians which marked Chicago as a leader in this particular brand of corruption.

Aside from the growth of vice, corruption cost Chicago much in living standards. A 1911-1912 reform commissioner of public buildings, Henry Ericssen, estimated 1800 violations of the building code in 500 buildings. In a one-year period, the city council allowed about 300 violations of codes; in 50 percent of these cases, the violation was not defined, since many violations were permitted. Bribery of inspectors was commonplace. Early in 1914 came reports of illegal extortion of funds from peddlers by the city market master in collaboration with an alderman. In 1914, the council committee on crime, headed by the distinguished political scientist Charles E. Merriam, found extensive evidence of police cooperation with the underworld.

The Party Machine and Political Corruption

The question about these machines, then, is not whether they could be totally honest—every machine, in order to survive, had to partake of actions which would at least now be condemned—but to what degree of corruption were they inevitably committed as a result of the nature of the machine? And how much of this corruption was voluntary, or nonessential? Imperative for the operation of a machine, whether citywide or limited to the ward, were the control of a block of patronage and the disposition of enough money to pay the members of the machine and carry out those welfare activities of the machine while it solidified its hold on the voters.

The machine did perform some social welfare tasks, which were frequently ignored by nineteenth-century reformers. The munificence of the Tweed Ring, for example, was on the scale of its corruption.

It [the Tweed Ring] created a public works program, an extra legal social security plan which was more extensive than anything else offered until the 1930s when Tammany was forced to compete with the New Deal. Nothing seemed to escape the Boss's generosity—hospitals, orphanages, religious schools of various denominations, churches, cultural projects, soldiers' homes—all were grist for his charity mill.[38]

On the other hand, there were two areas of corruption where the descent into undeniably unacceptable behavior was notable: (1) the sale of privileges and immunities, and (2) theft, rakeoff, and kickbacks from municipal contracts. "As regards the sale for cash of privileges and immunities, many politicians and officials did not stop with the twilight zone of liquor violations, gambling, and prostitution, but went on to exploit what would be regarded as crime in any language or society." In New York, Chicago, Denver, and other cities, a close intimacy grew up between criminals, politicians, and the police. In Denver the chief of the underworld had a direct line to the police chief, and he cemented his friendship with the city government by contributing to the campaign funds of both parties.[39] Mike MacDonald, it has been noted, had intimate connections with the leaders of Chicago's political community.

Under Tweed in New York, the practice of using the police to supplement the influence of the ring, which had been practiced for years, was magnified. "The force opened its ranks to Tammany supporters and thieves. Gamblers and criminals were given freedom and immunity from arrest."[40] This immunity was, of course, meted out selectively to the friends and supporters of the machine. After all, one of Tammany's star repeaters might be a petty thief in his spare time. But, the ring reasoned, such a loyal party man ought to have some special consideration, and he was likely to get it. A word from the precinct or ward leader was usually enough to get charges dropped against even the most notorious criminal. A Tammany minion, Patrick Duffy, killed four men between 1857 and 1870, and he was fined 6 cents for punishment. In 1870 he graduated to the general committee of Tammany and the murder of a policeman. He was sentenced to 9½ years in prison, but was granted a pardon less than a year later by the governor, under the suasion of Bill Tweed.

In this ethical climate many members of the community decided that corrupt practices had to be acquiesced in. One businessman argued:

It is quite generally understood that it has to be done; that you have to take those means to accomplish the most beneficial results. We do not feel that we are criminals because we do this.

On the other hand, we are respectable businessmen; and I am satisfied the community would not desire to put us in jail because we did it. The community desires that public utilities shall be put in operation as rapidly as possible ... and probably it would blame us more for failure to provide such utilities than it would for having used some bribery to get officials to do their duty in the matter.[41]

The case was not this simple, however. Bribes were not employed simply to get the politicians to award a contract, but to get the most profitable contract possible. Under such circumstances, the public monies were rarely used efficiently. Still, this businessman's assessment of the reaction of the community to the employment of bribes was not misjudged. Once corruption became the modus operandi of municipal contracting, many citizens were ready to defend those who operated that way. In San Francisco, according to Lately Thomas's *Debonair Scoundrel,* prosecutions against the Ruef-Schmitz ring reached up to the officers of the bribing corporations. In response, "the most corrosive bitterness against the prosecution was observable among the 'better element,' where Heney and Spreckels [the prosecutor and a strong supporter] were denounced as two of 'the greatest rascals that ever forebore to let well enough alone.'"[42]

Nonmachine Political Corruption

Not all nineteenth-century municipal corruption transpired under the auspices of political machines. Indeed, toward the turn of the century as railroads and utilities sought franchises and contracts throughout American cities, "boodle" became increasingly available to individual public servants in exchange for their favorable disposition toward a given business concern. Corruption permeated most areas of municipal government as well as party lines. Detroit's Mayor Hazen Pingree noted:

My experience in fighting monopolistic corporations . . . has further convinced me that they, the corporations, are responsible for nearly all the thieving and boodling with which cities are made to suffer from their servants. They seek almost uniformly to secure what they want by means of bribes, and in this way they corrupt our councils and commissions.[43]

Of Chicago's civil leaders, Ray Ginger suggests: "The Aldermen were all independent entrepreneurs. They paid no heed to party discipline or to anything else. It was strictly each man for himself."[44] Lincoln Steffens cites numerous supportive examples in *The Shame of the Cities*. For instance, in St. Louis (October 1902), Steffens traces the passage of legislation which granted a street franchise establishing new rights of way to an independent promoter that rendered all existing franchises obsolete. For roughly $300,000 in individual bribes, the promoter was able to override an executive veto and successfully guarantee the franchise's passage. He then sold his rights to a group of "Eastern capitalists" for $1.25 million, who in turn proceeded to negotiate mergers and stock transfers with St. Louis' existing street railroads. A grand jury's findings attest to the degree that such activity persisted in St. Louis, as elsewhere, during this period:

Our investigation, covering more or less fully a period of ten years, shows that with few exceptions, no ordinance has been passed wherein valuable privileges or franchises are granted until those interested have paid the legislators the money demanded for action in the particular case.[45]

While a Democratic machine headed by Boss Edward "Colonel" Butler did exist in St. Louis, the evidence suggests that many corrupt activities transpired independently of it. Payoffs for peddlers' licenses, the awarding of municipal contracts to businesses owned by city officials in lieu of competitive bidding, the importing of expensive imported foods and wines in the name of the city's poorhouse, and the loaning of city funds for private profit all supplemented the city's franchise graft and frequently occurred concurrently with machine abuses.[46]

Similarly, during the apex of Tammany's domination of New York, the city's pushcart operators were obliged to pay independent tributes to both the police and Tammany.[47] Even prior to Tammany's control, police systematically received individual payoffs from prostitution and gambling concerns in order to supplement their income.[48]

Effect of Corruption on Local Government

In Chapter 10 an appraisal of the effect of corruption on American government is essayed. Here it is necessary only to list briefly the disastrous effects of corruption on nineteenth-century American local government. That corruption helped America develop one of the most ineffective law enforcement systems of the modern world—one in which the courts are frequently in conflict with the work of prosecutors and police—is, we believe, largely because of the bad habits which nineteenth-century corruption started in prosecution and police officers. Federal aid has helped local public health offices attain better standards, but the bad standards of corrupt localities still leave America behind other countries in many public health standards. The corrupt administration of building inspection developed in cities like nineteenth-century Chicago and New York have helped create our core city problem.

Major economic development has made the high costs of the Tweed Ring's city hall seem relatively unimportant today. But the costs of poor administrative traditions in departments such as police or building inspection and the loss of citizens' confidence in a government which citizens know is cheating have a profound effect on the democratic process. In addition, it was the municipal communities' honest citizens who ultimately had to bear the costs of corruption. Horace Greeley noted: "Every dollar taken from the public treasury, in payment for services not required, is so much money unjustly wrested from private citizens for the aggrandizement of the wielders of power."[49]

The Origins of Municipal Reform

The corruption of the city governments did not proceed without periodic outcries and at least evanescent efforts at reform.

At the base of the municipal reform movement was a perception that the whole principle of democracy was being distorted, producing corrupt partisan rule instead of enlightened, efficient government for the cities. Majoritarian democracy, as interpreted by the party machine, was thought by many to result only in the inefficient, corrupt, and degrading supremacy of the worst elements of the public. As early as 1871, an acute observer noted that "there was little use in denouncing or abolishing the ring if the state of things out of which rings grow was allowed to remain." This root condition can be simply stated: "The city . . . presents the extraordinary paradox of a corporation ruled by those who are not corporators, and of corporate indebtedness incurred by those who are not responsible for its payment."[50] The problem was that propertyless masses of first- and second-generation immigrants and other poor citizens formed a majority or near majority in many large cities. The masses could be appealed to and activated by the machine complex. This army of voters, once mobilized, could carry the city elections. The machine operatives who were thus elected could proceed with impunity to enjoy all the fruits of victory. They could levy taxes on the ratepayers with impunity, since these were usually in the losing minority. And they need give little account of their conduct in office, since it was personal favors rather than effective but impersonal services which tied the voter to the organization.

Most studies of the reform movement indicate that its leaders and most of its rank and file were drawn from groups which were not attracted to the machines. Hofstadter's conclusion that the reform leaders were primarily Protestant and upper middle class has been widely accepted, with the provision that there was also a heavy infusion from the upper class in the leadership as well.[51] Among the leaders of municipal reform, professional people usually were the most active—notably lawyers, clergymen, doctors, and academicians. Small businessmen often were also prominent among the leadership and frequently made up the bulk of the rank and file of the reform committees. The leaders were mostly native-born and members of the prominent Protestant sects. There were many notable exceptions to all these generalizations. A sprinkling of members came from labor leadership. A large portion represented other faiths; Jews sometimes made up a sizable fraction of the reform groups, and Catholics were also found among some of the reform groups. Where immigrant groups had been in residence for longer periods and had had a chance to climb into positions of influence and prominence, they were frequently found on the side of the reformers.

A certain portion of the reformers, notably the urban property holders, only desired a thrifty and efficient government which would provide minimal services at low cost to themselves. The progressive reformers seconded the demand for efficiency, but low cost was not their end. "They believed that the high cost of public service was robbing the urban poor (as well as the middle class) of more than the urban poor was likely to gain from the charity of the political machine that profited from the high cost."[52] During the 1890s and 1900s this latter type of reformer came to predominate more and more.

In these circumstances, the battle for urban reform was waged with fitful but mounting results in the 1870s and 1880s, and then with spectacular success following 1894. From that time on, the efforts for reform profited from better organization, hardening experience, brightened prospects of success, and a greater ability to generate the sustained interest needed to achieve lasting victories. During the 1880s reform groups more permanent than the old ad hoc committee began to be organized. In the early 1890s such groups proliferated. By 1894 there were over 80 in the country.[53] In 1894 the National Conference on Good City Government was convened, and the National Municipal League formed to organize national efforts for municipal reform.

Gradually systematic ideas for modernizing the city charters, for civil service, and for election reform were evolved. These began to show real promise of hobbling the city machines. The Hartranft commission in Pennsylvania and the Tilden commission in New York, in the 1870s, had both called for stronger mayors, along the model of the federal government. Pennsylvania's model, "Bullitt charter," which was inspired by the Hartranft commission's report, took the appointment and control of the administrative heads away from the council, giving them to the mayor. Its purpose was to prevent the blending of legislative and administrative powers which had prevailed under the older charters and allowed the councils to dominate the administrative decisions of the cities. In many respects, the report of New York's Tilden commission was similar, but it included two other significant provisions. The state was to be prevented from enacting special legislation for a single city, thus providing for complete municipal home rule and the removal of state interference from city politics. It also provided that municipal suffrage be limited to city taxpayers, who were a small fraction of most city populations. This, the most blatant of the antimajoritarian measures of the reformers, was apparently responsible for the shelving of the report.[54]

Gradually the Bullitt charter and the Brooklyn charter (another strong mayor charter modeled after the federal system) began to gain in popularity. In 1898 the Municipal Reform League drew up a model charter which incorporated the latest word in theorizing about municipal reform and was designed to be applicable to cities anywhere in the nation. Under the model charter, cities were to be self-governing. A two-thirds vote of the state legislature was needed for any special legislation for a particular city, and that vote could be vetoed by the city council involved. The state would, however, maintain certain supervisory capabilities. The cities were required to make annual financial reports to a state board or commissioner empowered to supervise local expenditure. The commissioner was to check on the veracity of the accounts and see that the city was meeting all legal obligations. The governor also was empowered to remove any mayor for misconduct. The governing structure was on the federal model with a distinct separation of powers and a strong executive. The proposed council was to be unicameral and free from executive interference. The mayor was to be the official head of the administrative offices, with authority to appoint the heads of the departments and full responsibility for their performance.

In 1912 the Municipal Reform League drew up a revised charter, which went far toward removing partisanship from city government. The major provision of this new model charter was the selection of a professional city manager, who would be outside politics and who would run the city on efficient, business principles.[55] None of the structural reforms proposed in the new charters was in itself sufficient to destroy the old system of politics. It is possible to find examples of corrupt machines controlling cities which operated under almost every conceivable type of charter.

Civil service was another reform designed to reduce partisanship and increase professionalism in the increasingly complex and technical undertakings of American governments. Several cities followed close on the heels of the Pendleton Act, instituting municipal civil service programs in the 1880s and 1890s. Like all other measures of reform, civil service could be evaded, for example, by notifying only selected individuals of the location and time of examinations and then grading the papers leniently. Of course, the groups most severely disadvantaged by the successful use of civil service examinations were the poor, foreign-born, and illiterate—precisely those who could qualify for patronage jobs in the machine. Insofar as this reform was successful, it weakened one of the principal props of the machine system.

The introductions of the Australian ballot around 1890 struck a blow at one of the major functions and key vote-ensuring activities of the machine. This is discussed more fully in Chapter 9.

The reformers also agitated for the personal registration of voters. Again, this reform could be shown to be a direct response to electoral fraud, particularly the use of padded voter lists and repeaters. Burnham notes that "Compulsory registration was first required for residents of cities above a certain size, and was only later, if ever, extended to the population of a whole state. In some cases the urge to control the possibly dangerous or subversive potential of mass urban electorates was clearly expressed. . . ."[56] The result of personal registration was to reduce participation because of the greater inconvenience involved. But presumably those more highly motivated would be more likely to register.

The reformers accomplished the adoption, between 1903 and 1913 in most states, of the direct primary in place of the old and corrupt party caucuses. Again this was undoubtedly the eradication of a manifest abuse. But it had the collateral effect of weakening the ability of an organized clique to dominate the nomination procedure and thereby control the outcome of the election.

Conclusions

Municipal corruption became amazingly widespread in the last half of the last century. It was organized sometimes by machines, sometimes by rival factions or parties, sometimes a result of individual effort. The machine was organized to secure support from all the voters, and it did not hesitate to use corrupt means to secure its revenue, police and fire departments being essential. Tammany Hall's Tweed Ring in the late 1860s was an exemplar. Philadelphia's Gas Ring was as bad and kept more continuous control. The short-lived but colorful Ruef-Schmitz machine in San Francisco was based on its own Union Labor party. There were scores of other machines, claiming Republican or Democratic or bipartisan affiliation.

Other machines were less centralized, but almost all were corrupt. Some of this was based on business-offered bribery, but probably more was extortion by local government personnel. Corruption appeared in all possible forms. The "honest" graft emphasis of more recent times was less predominant but appeared often. Bribes and kickbacks in return for governmental favors were widespread. The bad social results of corruption—undisciplined police extorting from and abusing citizens, poor fire protection, unenforced building codes, poor sanitation and health measures, excessive taxes—all fell hardest on the poor.

The reform movement at the end of the century seems to have had wide business support. It was basically a drive for more honest and efficient government. It was usually accompanied by moves to improve the city charter through concentration of executive power. Its progress has been slow.

4

State Corruption in the Nineteenth Century

Corruption in American state governments increased from the early nineteenth century, to a luxuriant flowering from the 1850s to the 1880s, and then diminished gradually with the progressive reform years. The extent and seriousness of political corruption in state governments seem to have been intermediate between the severe and widespread corruption in the cities and the lesser and more intermittent improprieties of the federal level. State offices were more elevated and prestigious than municipal ones, and they often retained this aura while city government fell into disrepute. On the other hand, state offices afforded less honor and prestige than federal ones, and state politicians were more intimately connected with particular interests, with legislation connected to large-scale profit making, and with the influence of big city machines.

In the governments of states, as in the cities, there seems to have been a deepening embroilment in political corruption as the nineteenth century progressed. At least in states dominated by one or two large cities, this can be explained in part by the interrelations which developed between municipal political machines and the state governments. It was noted in Chapter 3 that a principal object of every city machine was to control the revenue- and job-producing activities of the city. These included offices which controlled patronage, construction, enforcement of legal sanctions, and the awarding of franchises and contracts. In many cities a large portion of these jobs were under the control of the state government. Consequently the complete and self-perpetuating machine, whether originating in the city or the state, required elements of control of the other level of government. Lincoln Steffens noted the natural strength of this combination. "City government and state government are of one sovereignty, and, as for corruption, the city and the state are in one system, and the city men and the 'up-state' men have to work together to get what each needs."[1] So, as machine politics and corruption grew at the city level during the 1800s, they penetrated into the governments of the state level. By the 1880s in many places, both the state and city governments were blatantly and notoriously corrupt.

Relatively few accounts have been written of political corruption in the state governments. Corruption there was neither as open nor as well publicized as in the cities, nor was its exposure as newsworthy and politically useful as in the federal government. Still, enough has been written about the course of events in several states to indicate the types of corruption which were practiced, or at least detected, and to give some clues about the extent and causes of this misconduct.

The Course of Political Corruption in New York State

New York State in the nineteenth century shared with New York City the unhappy distinction of maintaining one of the most corrupt governments in the country. The state's problems, like the city's, were intimately interwoven with political machines.

One of the earliest political machines to be established in the United States was Martin Van Buren's Albany Regency, which was the chief political power in New York from 1821 to 1837. But even prior to the creation of the Regency, the basis for the New York political machine had been established by Governor De Witt Clinton. A vast store of state jobs (in 1821, there were 8287 military and 6663 civil appointments) were in the control of the state council of appointment. A fixed term, usually four years, had been imposed on most of these, in conformity with the principle of rotation in office. Consequently, they came open periodically. Even prior to 1820 this system was used to bind together political organizations. Judge Spencer, a prominent local politician of the time, owed his influence "to his manipulation of the appointments of justices of the peace."

In his circuits he would make friends of prominent local politicians, who would recommend to him persons to be appointed justices of the peace. He would obtain the desired commissions at Albany, and this would aid his friends in securing an election to the legislature. Once there, they would vote for a council of appointment which would listen to the suggestions of Judge Spencer.[2]

Eventually Governor Clinton gained control of the state council of appointment and used it to build up his own fledgling state political machine. Clinton's machine was largely a personal rather than a party organization, designed to gain office for him and his associates and to deny political places to the opposing faction led by Aaron Burr. When Martin Van Buren rose to prominence, he seized the rudimentary organization which had been forged by Clinton and turned it into a specifically party machine. Van Buren, in 1821 a United States Senator, joined with several other prominent "Bucktails" (a faction of the Jefferson Republican party in New York). "By bestowing political appointments on friends and turning enemies out of office, the Albany Regency welded the Bucktail party into the most powerful political organization the state had yet seen."[3] The Bucktails had the added advantage of support from Tammany Hall.

In the 1828 election the Regency supported General Jackson, while Van Buren himself stood for governor. Following the success of both candidates, Van Buren was appointed Jackson's secretary of state, and another Regency man filled the vacant governorship. In 1832 Van Buren was Jackson's choice for Vice President, and his fellow Regency chieftain, William Marcy, was elected governor. Thus in that year the Regency firmly controlled both the state and federal patronage in New York, while arranging the New York City patronage with Tammany. In 1836 Van Buren was elected President, and Marcy was reelected governor. The vitality of a well-organized political machine which could dispose of substantial amounts of patronage was thus amply demonstrated.

Following the Civil War, the partisan struggle in New York regularized, while proving a fertile source of misconduct. The Republicans attracted their following from the rural, upstate areas; as a result of electoral districting which favored these constituencies to the disadvantage of urban ones, they were normally able to control the state assembly and senate. The Democrats dominated the great cities of New York and Brooklyn, both of which were becoming well organized by local machines. The massive popular vote which these machines could generate gave the Democrats occasional possession of the governorship.

The Republican legislature jealously maintained the right to pass special legislation for each of the state's cities and rejected periodic Democratic demands for municipal home rule. "This [Republican] policy not only reflected the prejudices of assemblymen and senators from farm districts, but it also enabled the Republicans in the state government to name city officials who otherwise would have been appointed by Democrats in New York City and Brooklyn."[4]

By 1864 the power of the two parties in the state rested firmly upon machine organizations. The bipolarity of Democratic power in New York prevented the establishment of a truly coherent statewide machine, as long as the city machines in New York City and Brooklyn remained antagonistic. The skill and energy of the Brooklyn Democratic boss, Hugh McLaughlin, successfully resisted the encroachments by Tammany from 1870 to 1900, and so the Democrats only sporadically were able to operate together to exert their will on the state government. The most able Democratic bosses, however, were from time to time able to weld together Democratic power; from 1868 to 1871, Tweed and, from 1875 to 1876, Samuel Tilden effectively ruled the state for their party. The Republican machine owed its strength not only to its majority in the state legislature but also to the normal Republican control of the Presidency. Federal patronage in New York was large and could provide jobs for a powerful little army of party workers even in those rare years when the Republicans lost control of the state government.

Following his election to the governorship in 1864, Reuben Fenton was recognized as the state Republican boss, a position he held until Senator Roscoe Conkling assumed the leadership in 1870. During the Fenton ascendancy, the venality of the state legislature was highlighted by the Erie Railroad war. The great railroad magnates, Cornelius Vanderbilt on one side and the triumvirate of Jay Gould, James Fisk, and Daniel Drew on the other, battled for control of the Erie Railroad. A sizable portion of the legislature, called the "Black Horse Cavalry," was known to be for sale to the highest bidder. "The Black Horsemen demanded $1,000 per vote on bills which would decide the contest between

Gould and Vanderbilt for control of the railroad. Vigorous bidding by both camps drove the price as high as $5,000 per vote; until a truce was reached by the magnates and the legislative market collapsed."[5] But if the Black Horse Cavalry lost out on this vote, they were successful in selling their votes on many other occasions, until their activities became notorious. Boss Tweed, a member of the Cavalry in 1867, testified about it after his fall from power:

It was understood in the Lower House that there was an organization formed of men of both parties, Republicans and Democrats, called the Black Horse Cavalry, composed of twenty-eight or thirty persons, who would all be controlled by one man, and vote as he directed them. Sometimes they would be paid for not voting against a bill, and sometimes they would not be desired, if their votes were not necessary.[6]

The corruption epitomized by this group was not machine-related, except that the venal legislators of both parties represented a system in which honesty and the public interest were considerations of little value. One method employed by the Black Horsemen in the 1860s and continued into the early twentieth century was simple but lucrative. A member of the group would introduce a "strike bill," the effect of which, if passed, would be to hinder greatly some wealthy interest or corporation. The legislators then demanded a payment from the threatened interest to kill the bill. Some companies seem, in response, to have created lobbying organizations which purchased the legislation in advance and spared the companies the anxiety of periodic blackmail.[7]

In the lavishly corrupt election of 1868, Tweed and Tammany elected their Democratic candidate, John Hoffman, Governor of New York. In 1869 the Democrats gained a majority of the state legislature and used that opportunity to pass the Tweed "reform" charter at the reputed cost of $600,000 in bribes, mostly to Republican senators and assemblymen.

The eventual fall of the Tweed Ring, and the attendant publicity, allowed the Republicans to regain majorities in the Senate and Assembly and to elect a Republican governor. But while the Republicans retained control of the legislature, the reform Democrats, who had contributed to the destruction of Tweed, gained a longlasting hold on the governorship. Tilden, Grover Cleveland, and David B. Hill, Democratic governors from 1876 to 1895, had strong reform support. In 1875 Tilden appointed a commission, which exposed the "Canal Ring," "a bipartisan alliance whose members illegally pocketed a share of the money appropriated for repairs on the Erie Canal and its feeders."[8] Surprisingly, in light of the partisanship characteristic of the era, all but two members of the ring exposed by the perseverance of the Democratic governor were Democrats.

Dorman B. Eaton in an 1881 book pointed out the conflict between spoils and the public school system:

With a liberality equal to that of any state New York has sustained public schools in which her sons have been fitted for the public service; while in sight of these schools, the federal government has allowed its servants to be selected upon a system which has told every young man that the chances would be far better for him if he would become the first flunkey of a ward politician instead of the first scholar in his school.[9]

Meanwhile, U.S. Senator Roscoe Conkling had wrested control of the New York Republican machine from the Fenton faction. Conkling was an avowed spoilsman and a keen believer in the machine. In 1877 President Hayes began attempts to institute civil service reform. He ordered civil servants not to participate in political activities and forbade the levying of assessments on officeholders. It was clear that several of Conkling's lieutenants, who had received federal appointments in New York (including Chester A. Arthur of the New York Customs House), were in violation of these directives. Conkling repudiated the whole project of reform; Hayes retaliated by attempting to replace Conkling's nominees for federal patronage jobs with others of Hayes's own choosing. Hayes won the first skirmish. But again in 1881 Conkling resisted the new President's nominee for collector of the New York Customs House, ultimately resigning his senate seat when Garfield's choice was confirmed. Conkling's resignation was a miscalculation, however, for he was not victoriously returned to office as he had expected. And after a split in the state Republican party during 1882 which allowed the Democrat, Grover Cleveland, to be returned as governor, Conkling disappeared as a political force. It was ten years before his friend Thomas C. Platt was able to rebuild the state Republican machine into a formidable power.

In the now-dominant party, David Hill succeeded Cleveland as Democratic governor and built up a rival to Cleveland's machine. But in 1894 Hill was defeated by Louis Morton, the candidate of Platt's carefully reconstructed and none-too-honest Republican machine. Platt, by reconciling himself to the national Republican organization, regained the control over the federal patronage that Conkling had lost, and used it as well as state patronage in building up his machine. From 1895 to 1899 Platt's choices filled the governor's chair. By the 1890s large, progressive, reform-minded elements had grown up in both parties, and both machines were forced to make appropriate compromises to retain the support of these factions. Platt's greatest compromise was to accept the nomination of the well-known reformer Theodore Roosevelt for governor in 1898. Roosevelt assumed the distribution of the federal patronage in New York after his election, and Platt was consequently displaced as leader of the Republican machine.

Professor Harold Gosnell, in his thorough *Boss Platt and His New York Machine*, has described corrupt as well as other activities of this machine in the 1890s. Local party caucuses nominated party committee members with little regard to parliamentary rules and often were controlled by bribes. "Strike" bills were killed by party leadership for an appropriate consideration. In 1901 committeeman Aldridge (the semibenevolent boss of Rochester) received $1000 for passage of a bill which removed a tax from certain insurance companies. Patronage—local, state, and federal—was important for the machine; the quality of appointees was relatively unimportant. A Democratic comptroller, elected in 1906, found in twelve counties shortages in accounts of county treasurers; overcharges by county sheriffs; illegal retention of fees by sheriffs, treasurers, and clerks; and numerous similar offenses. In Albany County the Democratic legislators in 1911 uncovered what they charged was a policy of keeping the judiciary under the influence of Republican leaders. Means used to this end included selection of jurors for party reasons and use of indictments for political purposes. Work on the Erie Canal and contracts for state printing were awarded for political reasons. In 1886 a legislator was hired as attorney for the state forestry commission; he was on the assembly committee on public lands and forestry. The New York law firm which included Platt's son was retained in efforts to secure states' privileges for a gas company. The census of 1890, taken largely by Platt's patronage appointees in New York, was used for political purposes. Platt's company became exclusive agent for transporting monies of the United States government.[10]

Believers in the economic development theory of corruption may be puzzled by the Street Railway Association of New York which from 1894 to 1903 spent substantial sums, presumably including payments to legislators, to "put to sleep" legislation against the utilities. The association also gave money to some county Republican committees. Platt himself gave out railway passes to help railroads politically.

Professor Gosnell adds that Platt had learned many of the techniques of corrupt machine control by careful observation of Democratic practice when that party was in power.

In 1905 the state legislature conducted highly publicized inquiries into the gas and insurance companies of New York City. The Gas Trust investigation revealed gross overcharging by the companies. But the insurance investigation revealed an extensive system of corruption, especially of the state legislature, which showed that the system developed by the Black Horse Cavalry still persisted. "A succession of highly paid and hitherto respected insurance exeuctives admitted that they retained control over their companies through extra-legal devices, made regular campaign contributions to the Republican party, bribed legislators of both parties. . . ."[11] Mutual Life Company even maintained a "House of Mirth" in Albany to influence state legislators. The prosecutor of these cases, Charles Evans Hughes, made a great name for himself and used his popularity to secure the governorship in 1906. He was independent of the party's bosses, relying on his popularity with the voters. Hughes was consequently able to enact several reform measures.

At the next election, in 1912, Tammany Hall elected one of its own candidates, William Sulzer, governor. But the reigning Tammany chieftain, Charles Murphy, quickly found Sulzer to be less than the pliant front man he had expected. Instead of appointing Murphy's slate of placemen to state patronage jobs, Sulzer chose men of his own. More importantly, he appointed an investigator to seek out political corruption in all levels of government in New York. The new governor then called a special legislative session to enact a direct primary system which, if enacted, would have severely damaged Tammany's control over Democratic nominations. Murphy responded to the challenge by deadlocking the state legislature and arranging to have a bill of impeachment brought against Sulzer. Eventually Sulzer was convicted of failing to report campaign contributions, and it appeared that in fact at least $15,000 had been given directly to Sulzer for his own use by major contributors. Although Sulzer was probably guilty of a violation of the election laws, his offense was doubtless a trifle compared with those which Murphy and Tammany employed as a matter of course. Sulzer's real crime was defying the organization upon which his political position rested.[12] But the day of unquestioning public acceptance of Tammany's dictates had passed; the dethronement of Sulzer brought a convulsion of public protest which swept out of the legislature nearly everyone who had voted for impeachment. An anti-Tammany Democrat was elected mayor of New York City.

Big Business and Political Corruption in Ohio

State politics in Ohio during the later nineteenth century were neither as well organized nor as corrupt as in New York. However, Ohio gained nationwide infamy at the turn of the century as a prime example of how big business interests could dominate and corrupt local and state politics, and even extend their grasp to the federal administration. This, at least, is the teaching about Ohio politics which was popularized by reformers, and especially by those like Lincoln Steffens with a socialist bent.[13] That there were corrupt dealings between politicians and businessmen in Ohio city and state governments is clear; that the character of these dealings was different from those in other places or showed that business was the ultimate cause of political corruption is, however, disputable.

Despite their formidable supremacy, Ohio Republicans up to 1888 seemed to have little coherent, statewide organization. There were, of course, several urban party organizations, some of which deserve the name *machine* with its worst connotation. The power of the urban machines, on the other hand, was real and persistent. During those years, Cincinnati and Dayton continuously maintained machines, while Toledo, Cleveland, Columbus, Youngstown, Canton, and Fostoria alternated between periods of machine control and intervals of reform.[14] Machine control of Cincinnati was first perfected by John R. McLean, a Democrat, who allied with Republican Tom Campbell. "Under their joint rule, Cincinnati rapidly became one of the worst-governed cities in the nation.... City government was in the hands of committees or boards which were openly corrupt and probably maintained by Democratic planning and frauds."[15] In 1885 a popular reform movement shook off the McLean-Campbell machine and its corrupt practices. But the benefits were short-lived. In its place George B. Cox installed a Republican mastery of Cincinnati politics more secure and more corrupt than the Democratic machine. In alliance with Cox was another Cincinnati resident who aspired to offices of higher dignity, Joseph B. Foraker. Along with Cleveland businessman and politician Marcus O. Hanna, Foraker was credited with creating, maintaining, and regulating the Ohio state Republican machine in the 1890s and 1900s. "Critics of the machine believed that under its control Ohio was ruled not by its people but by banks, railroads, public utilities, and other corporations—and for this, in somewhat different degrees, they blamed Hanna, Foraker, and their associates."[16]

Foraker, the Republican nominee for governor in 1883, had been defeated, losing his home town of Cincinnati to the Democratic candidate. Thereupon he formed an alliance with George "Old Boy" Cox who, it was hoped, could help him carry the city in 1885. Foraker did, indeed, win the 1885 election although Cox was unable to deliver the Queen City. Still, their alliance flourished. In 1886 Foraker influenced the state legislature to abolish Cincinnati's Board of Public Works (the old Democratic board) and substitute for it a new Board of Public Affairs. Cox was given the distribution of the nearly 2000 state patronage jobs which this board disposed of; with this patronage deal Cox secured his hold on the city; Foraker in turn could rely on the Cox machine for his own statewide political activities.[17]

Up to 1888, Foraker also had friendly relations with Marcus Hanna, the newly emergent boss of Cleveland. That city had been run by a Republican organization since the Civil War. During the late 1860s, Hanna's public-spiritedness or his business needs had led him into local ward politics. In 1869 he was elected to the local board of education. A few years later, in 1875, Hanna inherited an interest in a street railroad company to go along with his other sizable business interests. Since the city council was responsible for granting franchises for these railroads, Hanna's contact with Cleveland city politics became more intimate. Under his direction the streetcar company expanded and flourished.[18] Up to 1880, however, involvement in politics was only incidental to Hanna's business interest.

Politics were to reinforce and strengthen and protect his business investments. When Hanna controlled the City Council, he did so because he was primarily interested in the protection of street-railway franchises, not because he wanted to control Cleveland politics. Nevertheless, in doing the former he succeeded, to a large degree, in accomplishing the latter.[19]

Hanna's method of securing the business opportunities he required was the popular one: "As a businessman in politics he corrupted politics. Mr. Hanna boodled," Lincoln Steffens charged. Certainly Hanna contributed largely to the campaign funds of local Republican bosses, who in turn arranged favorable legislation. But such relations between business and the machine were prevalent in most American cities and states. The reformer Frederick Howe commented that the ethics of businessmen like Hanna were the same as those of the East Side politician of New York, the only motivation being a lust for power.[20]

As a result, there did in fact grow up in places an alliance between businessmen and political machines which corresponded to the friendship between the political organizers and criminals. The Ohio Republican machine was seen as a prime example of this sort of alliance. Progressive and socialist reformers, pointing to this relationship, concluded that businessmen, big business, and the capitalist spirit were the root cause of political corruption. This unholy alliance, they asserted, was impoverishing the little man while lining the pockets of the rich. At the same time, it deprived the inherently honest majority of their democratic right to elect their own leaders. Steffens charged that Marcus Hanna was a typical result of the dehumanizing capitalist spirit.

From a local power in Cleveland, Marcus Hanna soon moved into statewide politics. In 1883 he was appointed to the state party finance committee, where his own generosity and genius for fund raising brought him influence and notice. He became friends with Governor Foraker and an intimate and political advisor of Ohio Congressman William McKinley. Soon, however, the political activities of Foraker and Hanna began to conflict. As early as 1885 disagreements over the distribution of the important state patronage arose between them. Foraker chose his own man as state oil inspector (who disposed of many appointments across the state) in preference to Hanna's candidate. Again in 1887 Foraker disregarded the Hanna-McKinley candidate, this time awarding the prize post to his ally George Cox. Hanna also protested Foraker's choice for railroad inspector.[21] The state could not compatibly sustain two Republican organizers who were competing for the same offices. Both Foraker and Hanna came to see the need to gain supreme control of the state organization.

In 1891 Hanna supported the successful candidacies of McKinley for Governor of Ohio and John Sherman for Senator over Foraker himself. The election of McKinley to the Presidency in 1896 seemed to epitomize to many the victory of both big business and its seamy political allies, in national politics. Hanna, the "Cleveland boss," was credited with winning the election for McKinley and the business interests.

However, Hanna and business Republicanism were not the sole source of corruption in Ohio state government. In 1911, seven years after Hanna's death, nine legislators, from both parties, were indicted, and six were convicted for receiving bribes. In these cases the bribes were really extortions, payments to stop a "milker" bill.[22]

Corruption in the West and South

Many states besides New York and Ohio had "machines" of a greater or lesser degree of perfection during this century. The state government of Missouri was already corrupt by the 1880s. A St. Louis grand jury reported in 1904 that "our investigators have gone back twelve years and during that time the evidence shows that corruption has been the usual and accepted thing in State legislation...."[23]

Claude Wetmer's book *The Battle against Bribery*[24] gives details of the purchase of members of the Missouri legislature in 1899, for enactment of a bill forbidding sale of baking powder with alum—to ensure sale of one company's brand.

Oklahoma came into the Union in 1840 with charges of bribery and unethical behavior as to the location of the state capitol.[25]

Montana entered the Union in 1889 with bitter party rivalry and some charges of bribery. In 1899 there was fairly clear evidence of bribery to elect the wealthy William A. Clark to the U.S. Senate. Clark resigned after a few months because of these charges. Very substantial sums were also spent to secure location of the state capitol at Helena or the alternative city, then known as Anaconda.[26]

In the South, the peculiar circumstances resulting from the Civil War resulted in a brief but intense period of state corruption. The charges against the postbellum governments of Southern cities and states are familiar. They are that the South, as a result of the Reconstruction Act, was burdened with corrupt and irresponsible governments of ignorant and vengeful blacks, led by avaricious and sly carpetbaggers.

The South was now plunged into debauchery, corruption, and private plundering unbelievable—suggesting that government had been transformed into an engine of destruction. It was fortunate for the South that its officials were bent on private aggrandizement and personal gain, rather than on a fundamental class overturning which would have resulted in confiscations and an upset of civilizations. This condition was, therefore, nothing more than the Southern side of the national picture. Corruption permeated government from the statehouse to the city hall....[27]

The corruption charged to these radical governments was enormous. South Carolina, Louisiana, and Arkansas were the most severely affected. But even in Florida, "the cost of printing in 1869 was more than the entire cost of the state government in 1860," and over 1.1 million acres of state-held land was sold for 5 cents per acre by the legislature. Similar examples of corruption and mismanagement were detected in all the Southern states.

Corruption on the Reconstruction scale created large debts and high taxes in most Southern states. In South Carolina the legislature paid $700,000 for land worth $11,000 for resale to blacks and issued $1,590,000 worth of bonds to redeem $500,000 worth of bank notes. In Louisana legislative costs rose from $10,000 to $1 million a year. In Arkansas a black was given $9000 for repairing a bridge which had cost $500.

The charges against Henry Clay Warmoth, a governor of Louisiana, denounced by conservatives as an archcorruptionist, supplies a grim picture of the era, but one differing in magnitude rather than nature from the situation prevailing in the worst-governed Northern states.

According to the conservatives' account, . . . Warmoth had made himself the "idol and hero of the negro race" and, thereby, governor. He then proceeded to set up a dictatorship. With the aid of a compliant legislature, he concentrated all the registration and election machinery in his own hands. His most ingenious creation was the Returning Board, which could sift the election returns from every parish and throw out those that, in its judgment, had been invalidated because of bribery or intimidation at the polls. Governor Warmoth also secured the passage of police-constabulary laws which created, both in New Orleans and in the parishes what amounted to a standing army under his personal command.[28]

Richard Currant, in reviewing these charges, revises the unreserved condemnation of Warmoth. The widespread lawlessness and intimidation exercised by Democratic conservatives across the state, he argues, made the police and voting measures necessary, and since the state legislature soon opposed the governor, a personal "dictatorship" was impossible. However, the charges of corruption which attach to Warmoth and the legislature of the era cannot be so easily dismissed. Warmoth himself was accused of assigning all public printing to a newspaper owned by his friends, netting $1 million for work valued at about $50,000. He sold state-owned stock in a railroad to a friend, receiving $100,000 for himself on the deal. He issued $3 million in levee construction bonds, but only $1 million in construction was completed, with the remaining money returning to Warmoth and his friends. He set up a franchised city slaughterhouse for the city of New Orleans, charging all butchers to use it. And finally, the governor accepted bribes to pass legislation and used his veto to extort money for the passage of bills.[29] While denying that these actions were corrupt, on the basis that each act brought needed improvements, Currant admits that there was "a frightful amount of corruption" in Louisiana—but that the bribers were as much to blame as the bribe takers. And the bribers were prominent conservatives. Currant, acting as Warmoth's defender, concludes that the legislature was itself corrupt, as were prominent Democrats who bribed freely for their own ends. He concludes about Warmoth himself that "though he undoubtedly profited from some dubious deals, he apparently was guiltless of the grosser forms of corruption, such as the taking of bribes."

Even those sympathetic with the radical governments cannot demonstrate that widespread corruption did not characterize the turbulent era of reconstruction in the South, as it did the last quarter-century in the North.

The dramatic end of Reconstruction resulted in the crushing of black political power and the deportation of the carpetbaggers. It also created a need for a strong, centralized, and cohesive Democratic party in the Southern states, as a means for retaining white power and preventing a return to the politics of the Reconstruction era. "In this State for some time to come there is but one issue. All know what it is," a Mississippi newspaper proclaimed.[30]

The hallmark of the post-Reconstruction Southern Democratic party organization was the state "ring" or "courthouse clique." "The extent of their domination and the nature of their machinery of control varied among the state rings, but the ring was always present."[31] The Virginia machine established a typical hierarchy. The state Democratic party chairman issued orders to the county chairman. The county chairman selected an electoral board, which was ratified by the state legislature. Then the electoral board appointed election judges and clerks elected by the county chairman. Using these officials, money, and pressure, the chairman was able to oversee the selection of virtually every elected and appointed official from the county, from revenue commissioner to state legislator. Numerous methods were used to retain the new regime in power and destroy the power of the carpetbaggers. Primarily these devices were intended to disenfranchise blacks and poor whites. Preregistration, election fraud, intimidation, gerrymandering—all were widely employed. But aside from this, the rings and machines of the post-Reconstruction South seemed to be less corrupt than those of their predecessors. In fact, their principle was retrenchment and good business principles. There were differences between states. Louisiana had much more corruption than Virginia.

Van Woodward comments on defalcations of state officials of several Southern states in the Redemption period (following Reconstruction) including Virginia, Tennessee, Alabama, Arkansas, Kentucky, Mississippi, and Louisiana. The sums involved were small, and the corruption probably less than in Northern states. But the South did not escape the low public morals of the period. Fraudulent grants and sales of public lands occurred in Texas and Florida.

When Progressivism came to the South at the turn of the century, it had a peculiar character. It was a reaction against the bosses and machines, largely because of their alliance with Northern business interests. The professional men and small businessmen who filled the ranks and offices of the progressive groups helped eliminate the caucus system and institute the direct primary, thus allowing a free choice by the franchised voters of their representatives. But still, poll taxes and other restrictions retained the white, and not poor white, character of the Southern political system even after the fall of the party-caucus ring system.[32]

Land Corruption

Lying entirely outside the circle of state corruption caused by machine politics was another smaller but still important field of corruption, primarily of individuals and small groups for strictly personal gains. At the state level, this usually resulted from opportunities for illicit profit opened up by westward expansion and by the rapid expansion of state responsibilities.

The opening of new lands to settlement accounted for a prolonged furor of speculation, intrigue, and corruption of both state and federal governments. Before the Revolution, land speculation in America was a large and lucrative business. But since much of the land was awarded and sold by the government, in either London or the colonial legislatures, "grants of land in the southern colonies were a source of continued political intrigues."[33]

Wild land speculation continued after the Revolutionary War, with several instances of fraud and deception and a few examples of improper use of political influence. Alvin Phelps, a member of the General Court of Massachusetts and the Governor's Council, used his political influence to obtain Massachusetts' title to the western portion of New York State, although the concession was eventually voided. During the exploitation of New York's open lands by the New York Genesee Land Company, the promoters of the scheme "employed agents to go about the state, lavishing presents on the politicians . . . to win their favor." Likewise, when the promoters of the Scioto land project sought to purchase 5 of 6 million acres in Ohio from the Continental Congress, they exerted influence on members of Congress through government officials who were involved in the scheme."[34]

These land schemes were rife with speculation, political intrigue and favoritism, and often with fraud or mismanagement; few actually involved political corruption. However, the largest and most notorious of the early land schemes, the Yazoo land frauds in Georgia, was a marvel of corruption. There was a large tract of virgin land to the west of South Carolina, to which the federal government, Georgia, and numerous Indian tribes had claims. Georgia was anxious to sell her doubtful claim at the highest obtainable price. First the legislature sold the "Yazoo" territory to four companies at about 1 cent per acre in 1791, but this deal fell through. Three years later a new deal was arranged with four new companies. The terms of sale were hurried through the state legislature, and the 30 million acres were sold for $500,000, or at 1.5 cents per acre. The haste of the legislature in concluding such an unprofitable sale was apparently the result of the attentions paid them by the companies which had peddled shares at very low prices to nearly all the legislators. However, the outright dishonesty of the companies in reselling their questionable purchase to settlers, and the public anger roused by the unfavorable terms of the contract, led to the election of a new legislature which voided the Yazoo Act.

As the United States expanded westward, land speculation continued, affecting one territory after another and bringing frequent allegations of favoritism or outright corruption. But in general, while the schemes generated fraud and deception, they relied on political mismanagement rather than corruption.

An unusual wrinkle to the land fraud business was discovered a century after Yazoo in the disposal of public school lands in the West (Montana, Oregon, and California) during the 1890s. The system of fraud employed there was complex and profitable. During Lincoln's Presidency, the federal government had allocated sections of public land to be sold for the support of public schools. Later it was decided to recover some of these lands for inclusion in forest reserves. Consequently, the federal government agreed to compensate the states and any private purchasers of reclaimed land with unclaimed land elsewhere. Cliques sprung into being to profit from these laws. A group operating in Oregon and California was typical. "They would settle dummies upon school lands. . . . Then they themselves would map out a forest reserve to cover those claims." This of course required corruption of land office officials. Next, the clique "got from the states wholesale rights to take up magnificent timber and other valuable lands elsewhere . . . [which] they sold in the open market at great profit."[35]

Corruption of officials supposedly protecting the public trust lands was essential to the operation of these schemes. It was readily obtained. In Oregon, the clique included the district superintendent of forests, the U.S. District Attorney and District Marshall, a state legislator, a congressman, and the Commissioner of the Land Office in Washington, Binger Hermann. The schemes also obtained the connivance of the two Oregon senators.[36] The local graft schemes seem to have been devised by private individuals, but since that involved public lands and federal regulations, they immediately demanded the participation of government officials. The scheme, beginning at the local level but working easily to corrupt state and federal officials, demonstrated the interrelationship of corrupt forces between levels of government. It also demonstrated the susceptibility to corruption of officials at all levels of government which characterized the end of this century.

Railroad Corruption

The construction of American railroads, especially the great transcontinental lines, was another source of state corruption. The railroads were the object of "strike" legislation in some states. In others, they anticipated this by actively bribing the legislature. Once the states took on the task of granting railroad franchises and regulating their operation, they became the object of every brand of railroad speculator. The activity of the Central Pacific group in California politics is the most notorious example of railroad corruption of the states.

The Southern Pacific-Central Pacific railroad system maintained a state machine in California from 1870 to 1910. The purposes of the machine were to secure high rates and low taxes for the railroad, to keep a monopoly of transportation in California, to develop a new transcontinental route to the South, and to favor Southern Pacific interests including some questionable land titles. Lawyers, editors, and many politicians were paid annual retainers by the railroads. Alliances were kept with traditional-type city machines in San Francisco and Los Angeles. Republicans and Democrats, governors, legislators, judges, and other officials were often recipients of bribes from Southern Pacific agents.

The Southern Pacific machine, which had links with the Ruef machine of San Francisco and a smaller Los Angeles machine, continued to be all-powerful in California affairs into the first decade of the twentieth century. In addition to harsh treatment of land "squatters" in the San Joaquin Valley, the machine won special fame via the letters from Collis Huntington in New York to General Colton in California. These letters explicitly described bribes and other favors to members of Congress and of state legislatures.[37] The machine was finally defeated in the 1910 elections by a "Lincoln-Roosevelt" league, headed by fewer than 30 active journalists, lawyers, and smaller businessmen. The 1910 election, won by Governor Hiram Johnson, eliminated the railroads' major power and overnight transformed California into one of the best-governed states in the Union, a position which it has held ever since. Initiative, referendum, and recall provisions were put in the constitution; perhaps more important, an effective civil service was begun.

The Southern Pacific may have found its way eased by a history of corruption. In 1851 Vallejo was selected as a state capitol, with charges of bribery being rife. In 1854 the senate investigated complaints of bribery by a member and reached an unsupportable conclusion that the bribe had not been offered but that the decision did not reflect on the honor and dignity of the senator who charged that it had been offered. A California state treasurer and a comptroller were impeached and then indicted in 1857. Election of a U.S. Senator in 1867 was quite possibly a result of corruption.[38]

The California legislature seems to have been badly organized and corrupt through the post-Civil War period.[39]

When the railroad's influence was added to other corruption, California almost went under. Professor Alexander Callow has written about the legislature of 1891 as the "legislature of a Thousand Scandals."[40]

In the last half of the nineteenth century, railroads had generally developed a free-pass system for important public officials; usually the man in charge of legislative relations was in charge of free-pass distribution. To underpaid legislators the opportunity to move freely between state capitol and home was very important. The possibility of losing such passes led legislators to hestitate to vote against railroad-sponsored legislation. In a state like Nebraska, the free-pass system underlay railroad political control of the state, in spite of its contradiction of the oath for public officers.[41]

Bribery of state legislators was a frequent tool of railroads working for lower taxes, more open franchises, or higher rates. Senator Robert M. La Follette's autobiography gives examples of bribes and economic pressure on members of the Wisconsin legislature in the early 1900s.

Influence of Immigration

Except as the presence of immigrants helped the formation of city machines, which had an adverse effect on state politics, it would be difficult to ascribe much of state corruption to immigrants. Leaders in state affairs were generally of "original stock"; immigrant groups rarely dominated states as they did cities. "Old stock" farmers usually offset big city immigrant groups, and so ethnic controls became less possible.

Influence of States on Local Government

Although the state governments created local governments, outlined their responsibilities, set up their frameworks of government, and authorized their financial activities, the states showed little concern about the honesty of local government. There were occasional investigations of cities like New York, and a few states provided for state appointment of police commissions for major cities, but both of these seemed to be viewed as political more than administrative measures.

Conclusions

State corruption prior to World War I was not as universal as was that of the cities. Eighteen states are mentioned in this chapter; there was probably some major corruption in another twenty during the 1880s and 1890s and 1900s. New York led a change of American political life for the worst, in the form of seeking spoils machines which speedily became corrupt, involving both public business like the Erie Canal and private operations like the Erie and Pennsylvania railroads. Pennsylvania had a record of political corruption similar to New York's, although even more persistent. In Ohio the state machine was a collection of city machines. Railroads led the corruption in California and were important in many other states.

Business efforts to control were more general in state governments than in nineteenth-century city governments, but even in the states it was sometimes hard to distinguish between government extortion and business bribes.

After the Civil War, the South had excessive corruption brought on by carpetbagger governments. After the fall of the carpetbaggers, many Southern states became more nearly honest than their Northern counterparts for decades.

Land speculation was a field in which state governments were universally susceptible to corruption. From the Yazoo land frauds of the Georgia legislature in the 1790s to the Oregon land grafts of the early 1900s, this function seems to have been open to corruption. The railroads, seeking charters, routes, lower taxes, and higher rates, were a corrupting force in many states.

5

Federal Corruption in the Nineteenth Century

Briefly, the federal government went through four epochs in its first century and a quarter. The Federalists and Jeffersonians set a "high tone of conduct."[1] Then the new ethos of the Jacksonian democracy resulted in increasing amounts of partisan politics and of corruption which culminated in the Buchanan administration. During and after the Civil War, the federal government had much corruption, especially in the Grant administration, 1869-1877. From the 1870s on, principles and program of reform were actively championed. They were applied earlier and with more success to the federal government than to the cities or the states. From the time of President Theodore Roosevelt (1901-1909) civil service was secure.

The Federalists and the Jeffersonians

President Washington, by his personal demeanor and his scrupulous regard for fitness in the selection of officers of the federal government, established a tradition of honesty and high ethical practice which survived through the first quarter of the nineteenth century. In the main, Washington was adhering to the high-minded principles of good, free, and honest government which had motivated the separation from England. To improve upon the old model seemed to be essential to justify that revolution and to prove viable the great experiment in free government.

Washington made fitness for office the sine qua non for selection; despite the violent party struggle which engulfed the United States in subsequent years, the succeeding Federalist and Republican Presidents in the main adhered to this standard.

Given these standards for appointment and expectations of performance, it is no surprise that the early years of the nation are seen in retrospect as a "golden age" of ethical propriety. There were, however, a few isolated instances of questionable conduct or corruption. Moreover, by the 1820s, the spoils system, patronage, and the other accoutrements of regularized party politics in the new, popular, democratic mold were beginning to question the prerogatives of the "first characters" and to threaten the standards of conduct which they had established.

One of the first suspected cases of the corruption of a high federal official resulted in the resignation of Edmund Randolph, in 1795 Secretary of State

73

in Washington's Cabinet. An intercepted French dispatch indicated that Randolph had approached the French minister, offering favorable treatment of French interests in return for money. Randolph resigned when shown the dispatch by Washington, but later sought to vindicate himself in a book which Jefferson, among others, found convincing.[2] Randolph's guilt or innocence remains uncertain.[3]

The corruption of General James Wilkinson, commanding general of the U.S. Army and sometimes governor of Louisiana Territory under Jefferson, is more certain. Allegations were circulated that Wilkinson was in the pay of Spain during the Washington and Adams administrations and again while he was Governor of Louisiana in 1806. He was, in fact, receiving money to disclose military and diplomatic information to the Spanish in west Florida. Jefferson ignored the charges against Wilkinson, removing him as governor in 1807 only because of his involvement in the Burr conspiracy. However, Jefferson cooperated with House and military inquiries into Wilkinson's dealing with Spain in 1808. When both inquiries failed to convict him, Jefferson surprisingly reassigned the suspected Wilkinson to a new command in New Orleans. The Wilkinson problem was seconded to Madison's administration. Wilkinson was investigated by the House in 1810 and court-martialed, but he was cleared in 1811. Remarkably, at this point Madison restored Wilkinson to active duty. Finally, after mismanaging a command in the War of 1812, the general was dismissed from active duty for good. Wilkinson was guilty of corruption, if not treason, but Jefferson and Madison have been blamed only with credulity and poor judgment in the prolonged affair.[4]

In the lower ranks of the federal administration, there were some charges and a few revelations of official misconduct. Fiscal agents during the War of 1812 were supposed to have used government money for private profit, and some prize agents were thought to have misreported prize money and the property of ships and crews. A congressional investigation in 1818 indicated that some government clerks and agents in the Treasury, Post Office, War Office, and Naval Office had acted as agents for claimants whose cases they would inspect. These individual cases were condemned, but "the committee on the whole cleared the public service of infidelity to its trust."

The most notable defalcation of the "golden era" came near its close. The newly installed Jackson, convinced of the corruption of the John Quincy Adams administration, had his subordinates minutely examine the records of all the federal departments to substantiate their suspicions. They found only one case, but it was notable and politically advantageous. The close friend whom Adams had appointed fourth auditor, Dr. Tobias Watkins, was discovered to have embezzled $7000. He fled upon discovery, but was subsequently arrested, convicted, and imprisoned.[5] These few facts tend to mar the overall impression of the high quality of public service during the era, but they comprise a large part of the instances of corruption in the federal government from 1789 to 1829.

Yet, by the end of this era, the groundwork was being laid for a new manner of politics, a manner inherently biased toward favoritism in the selection of officials, if not toward actual corruption in the conduct of official duties.

The Jackson Era and the New Politics of the Democracy

During the election of 1828, incumbent President John Quincy Adams became convinced that his Postmaster General, John McLean, was using the patronage of his office to secure the election of General Jackson. This suspicion was probably unjustified, but Adams's perpeturbation suggests the potential for political manipulation inherent in the patronage appointments of the federal government, particularly in the post office.

By 1820 the use of patronage to secure partisan control of elections was well established in New York and Pennsylvania.

By the year 1828 . . . in every state throughout the North and West the spoils systems was either established or there existed an element eager to introduce it. . . . It was but a question of time and circumstances when the custom would become national.[6]

The federal government generated more and more patronage jobs as its operations grew; the advantages from turning this patronage (widely distributed across the United States) to partisan or factional advantage advanced apace. In 1820 the Tenure of Office Act was passed, directing that a considerable portion of federal officers responsible for collecting or disbursing money be appointed for terms limited to four years. It is unclear if the purpose of the act was to render the public service more accountable or more partisan; the end result was the latter. A correspondent warned Jefferson of the dangers of the act:

It saps the constitutional and salutary function of the President and introduces a principle of intrigue and corruption. . . . This places, every four years, all appointments under their power, and even obliges them to act on every one nomination. It will keep in constant excitement all the hungry cormorants for office, render them, as well as those in place, sycophants to their Senators, engage these in internal intrigue . . . and make of them what all executive directories become, mere sinks of corruption and faction.[7]

The key warning was that officers, holding their jobs for a fixed term, would become sycophants to those who held the power of appointment. They could be forced to do political work. Senator Benton in 1826 reported this danger to the Senate.

Power over a man's support, has always been held and admitted to be power over his will. The President has "power" over the "support" of all of these officers; and they have "power" over the "support" . . . of an immense number of individuals . . . to whom they *can* and *will* extend, or deny a valuable private as as well as public patronage, according to the part which they shall act in *State,* as well as in *Federal* elections.[8]

These dire predictions of the consequences of the partisan use of patronage, combined with the principle of rotation in office, were rapidly and amply justified.

General Jackson swept into office at the head of the new democracy in 1829, springing more from the new egalitarianism of the West than the old aristocracy of the East. The early days of his Presidency saw an unprecedented, and for those days unseemly, scramble for public office. The supporters of Jackson were boastfully confident that he would interpret reform as they desired. *Reform* meant the elimination from office of those who opposed Jackson and the appointment of his supporters. Within limits, the expectations of "reform" were fulfilled. John McLean, the Postmaster General whom Adams had denounced for his partisanship, was swiftly "kicked upstairs" to the Supreme Court, presumably because he was unwilling to accept the wholesale replacement of postmasters required by the new regime.[9] Jackson himself enunciated his policy and its justification in his first annual message to Congress in 1829. Indefinite terms in office, he said, led men to be unmindful of the public interest, and perhaps prone to corruption. Further, since "the duties of all public offices are, or at least admit of being made, so plain and simple that all men of intelligence may readily qualify themselves for their performance,"[10] then more was to be gained than lost by short, fixed terms. He then called for the extension of the 4-year-term rule to virtually all federal appointments. Although Jackson himself used the spoils system judiciously, and replaced only 10 to 20 percent of federal government employees during his administration, still Pandora's box was open; the system, with its potential for partisan abuse and its inclination to select unfit characters, was adopted and extended by successive administrations. Both Democratic and Whig Presidents followed Jackson's principle, until in 1857 Buchanan showed the full malevolent power of the rotation principle. Rotation did lead to corruption, often if not always.

The picture drawn by Professor White and by others of President Jackson as the unwitting father of corruption, through introduction of rotation of office, needs some sharpening. Jackson was personally honest and did move against speculative (and often corrupt) federal land sales.[11] But Sam Houston's efforts to secure a noncompetitive contract for furnishing Indian rations at a price unfavorable to the government were advanced by Secretary of War Eaton with Jackson's concurrence. On several occasions Jackson failed to disapprove the clearly illegal conduct of Houston who physically attacked Congressman Stanberry because of the latter's unreasonable complaints against the unethical and illegal procedures favored by Houston.[12]

Corruption during the Jacksonian Era

Under the Jacksonian Presidents, the Post Office, with its thousands of local patronage appointees, was developed into a limited national political machine at the personal disposition of the President. The growing reliance of federal officeholders on a machine-style organization was not the only circumstance responsible for the transformation of the federal government during the 1820s and 1830s. The institution of regularized partisan politics and the rise of popular democracy made long-term officeholding by a qualified elite appear to be both bad politics and bad democracy. The development of the political machine in cities and states provided a ready model for the operation of the federal government under party control. The replacement of the upper classes by professional politicians in a large portion of the public service facilitated the adoption of methods which were now deemed necessary, but formerly would have been rejected as corrupt by the more scrupulous. These changes yielded predictable results:

That traditional standards of public service morality were in decline could not be denied at the close of Andrew Jackson's administration. The decline continued, with variations and exceptions, through the years ending with the dreary term of James Buchanan. The standards of official conduct in 1860 were consequently regrettably inferior to those which had been nurtured and protected by the Federalists and Republicans alike.[13]

White has an interesting page on the decline in ethics which underlay the rise of political corruption under the Jacksonians (and which led to even worse corruption in the last half of the nineteenth century). He quotes an editor who found a lack of integrity among business people—in regard to business transactions. The reasons he suggests include a more complex society in which fraud is less easily punished and there are the temptation of "the great prizes in railroad construction, shipping, and manufacturing," the spirit of speculation, the anonymity of urban life, and the varying standards of morality resulting from immigration.[14]

The decline which White notes was characteristic of both Congress and the executive branch. There were few proved cases of corruption in Congress between 1828 and 1861, but corruption was widely suspected and easily believed. Adept managers of party caucuses and machines had generally replaced the notable and respectable characters who dominated Congress earlier years. There were charges in 1837 that travel allowances were being claimed fraudulently. The growth of lobbying provided new temptations to congressmen. Several lobbies were operating by 1850, one of which was formed specifically to guarantee the renewal of the patent on the Colt revolver. The notorious activities of the Colt lobby led to a committee investigation which, although it could not verify the bribing of members, did conclude that the lobby had spent money lavishly on entertainments, gifts, and the like for congressmen. In 1853 the first rules were drawn up to regulate members' relations with lobbyists, also establishing penalties for the bribing of congressmen. Nevertheless, in 1857 four members of the House were recommended for expulsion.[15]

Of the documented cases of corruption during these years, most were in the administration, and particularly in the federal field service. Federal government employees in the field were in intimate contact with the corrupting influences of the state and urban political machines, and often were simply creatures sponsored by it and nominated by friendly Presidents or congressmen. In the territories officials regularly fell prey to speculators or were themselves drawn by the allurements of speculation.

Federal officers colluded with speculators or speculated themselves with government funds. Congressional reports in 1835 and 1839 disclosed serious fraud in 75 land offices.[16]

At the beginning of President Polk's term in 1845, a large sum of government money was advanced from the U.S. Treasury and from a Pennsylvania bank owned by Simon Cameron, newly appointed senator to fill Polk's unexpired term. The money was used to purchase the Washington Democratic newspaper, the *Globe,* for an editor friendly to Polk. It was already accepted practice to allot U.S. government printing contracts to the party newspaper in the capital city, but the loan of government funds to purchase the paper was a clear departure from accepted practice.

The Whig administration of President Zachary Taylor witnessed a tumultuous but indecisive partisan struggle over the alleged conflict of interest of three cabinet members. The Treasury Secretary and Attorney General decided in 1850 that the United States should pay a private claim against the federal government for $235,000. But it was soon shown that the Secretary of War, George Crawford, was the attorney for the claimants and that he was to receive half of any settlement. The Democrats protested noisily, but Crawford argued that his fee was legitimate, while the Attorney General and Treasury Secretary said they had not even known of Crawford's financial interest in the case when they made their ruling. The House accepted these protestations, but Taylor had evidently decided to replace the three Cabinet members at the time of his sudden death.

The Buchanan administration is considered the most corrupt of the antebellum years. While this reputation is probably deserved, it is also true that one reason so much corruption was discovered was because it was assiduously sought out. The Republicans obtained a majority in the House in 1859, and forthwith instituted numerous congressional investigations to expose and embarrass their Democratic rivals. Many of the malefactions discovered had probably been employed in previous administrations as well, but had not been disclosed.

Both the corruption of government functions for party advantage and corruption for personal gain were revealed. The Democrats had used several federal programs as sources of income for the elections of 1856 and 1858. A personal friend of Buchanan's promised several firms naval construction contracts in return for campaign contributions. Fowler, in the New York Post Office, directed large amounts of government money to various Democratic campaigns, before absconding. Wendell of the Washington *Union* testified that he gave more than $100,000 to Democratic campaigns—part of his enormous profits from government printing contracts. Most of this money was used for legitimate campaign activities, although some probably went to finance large-scale naturalization of immigrants, to purchase votes outright, or to transport "repeater" voters to critical states.[17]

Federal government contracts had been used since Jackson's administration to support friendly printers, frequently on the expectation that a percentage of the resulting profits would be plowed back into party coffers. There was, consequently, a disincentive for those contracts to be awarded to low and honest bidders. The printing costs were higher than necessary, and the excess went to finance explicitly partisan activities. A congressional committee (the Covode Committee) in 1858 investigated and exposed this system, in which, it was shown, Buchanan himself had been involved. In 1860 a government printing office was established to terminate this particular source of government corruption.

The Republican Covode Committee investigating the Buchanan administration discovered that the Attorney General had sent an agent to the editor of the Philadelphia press, offering him $80,000 worth of printing contracts if he would stop opposing the LeCompton constitution. The discovery seemed reasonably well corroborated.[18] This kind of flagrant effort to buy a change in newspaper attitudes seems to rank with Jefferson's action in the Burr trial, and the Watergate actions—a kind of corruption which threatens democratic government.

The Lincoln Administration

The system of favoritism and corruption which had attached itself to the granting of federal government contracts did not miraculously disappear when the Civil War broke out. Instead, the rapidly expanding demand for supplies to equip the Northern forces provided larger, lucrative targets for the corrupt operators. Consequently, the familiar charges of inefficiency, favoritism, and corruption were leveled against Lincoln's departments. The War Office was presided over by the Pennsylvanian Simon Cameron. Under this guidance, the War Office was plagued with inefficiency. Competitive bidding was replaced with the granting of contracts to favored middlemen, in order, it was argued, to expedite acquisition rather than to debase it. But because of fraud, duplication, and inefficiency, the War Office entered into numerous contracts which were exorbitantly wasteful. Lincoln removed Cameron, and the audit of contracts by the incoming

Secretary saved the government $17 million.[19] Similarly, the Navy Department's purchasing received criticism, largely because the Secretary's brother-in-law was awarded the department's agency for New York. He subsequently earned a fortune by arranging contracts there. But the Navy Secretary successfully defended himself against charges of graft or favoritism by arguing that all the contracts had been valid and that by relying on a trusted individual, the contracts had been let swiftly and efficiently.

Some features of the federal corruption carried over to the state and local levels. John Niven, in *Connecticut for the Union*,[20] writes that government contracts were peddled in Hartford as well as Washington; this may have been a result of the recruitment of troop units from states. He even writes of a ring of Hartford Baptists which secured a lion's share of state contracts from their fellow Baptists, the adjutant general and the quartermaster general, until both officers were dismissed by the governor for misconduct. Legislators also entered extensively into contract getting and influence peddling.

Finally, Lincoln's Treasury Department was acknowledged to be a source of corruption in its administration of commerce in occupied Southern territory. The opportunity for large profits there from trade in cotton led to suspicion that speculators were bribing both Treasury agents and army officers who were administering occupied areas.

Corruption and Reform in the Postbellum Years

The years between the Civil War and World War I saw both the most widespread and the deepest corruption that the federal government was ever to endure, but this was slowly superseded by a gradual drive to reform government and eradicate corruption. Leonard White provides a brief overview of the period:

The Republican era opened in moral chaos. It remained sunk in moral degradation throughout Grant's two terms, during which members of Congress, high executive officials, and subordinate administrative agents were guilty of one dereliction after another. Improvement began with Hayes and was sustained by Garfield and Arthur. Cleveland did much, and the quality of presidential and Cabinet leadership during and after his administration helped restore the reputation of the government.[21]

The Grant administration has one of the seamiest reputations in American history, much of it deserved. Scandals reverberated throughout his administration. Congress, during these years, seemed equally prone to corruption. The most notorious episode involving Congress, however, the Credit Mobilier and Credit Foncier frauds, although uncovered during the Grant years and frequently associated with the other Grant scandals, actually took place before Grant took office.

The Credit Mobilier was a construction company formed by some of the larger stockholders of the Union Pacific Railroad. They planned to direct to Credit Mobilier the contracts to build the Union Pacific. In other words, as stockholders in the Union Pacific and members of Credit Mobilier, these men contracted with themselves for construction. They paid themselves exorbitant dividends on Credit Mobilier stocks and paid over to the construction company much of the cash earned by Union Pacific stock sales. To prevent congressional investigation of these enormous profits that the directors were reaping, one member of the clique and U.S. Representative from Massachusetts, Oakes Ames, distributed stocks at par among selected members of Congress. In 1872 the history of Credit Mobilier's operations and of Ames's bribes was uncovered. A House investigation into the scandal led to the expulsion of Ames and another congressman, James Brooks. The expulsion of Senator Patterson of New Hampshire was recommended. Former Vice President Wilson and outgoing Vice President Colfax were implicated and disgraced, and several other congressmen, including James A. Garfield, were not charged but were widely throught to have been guilty of accepting bribes.

During the Grant administration proper, a series of scandals touched directly or indirectly on President Grant, several of his close associates and Cabinet members, and numerous lower officers of the federal administration. The revelation of these corrupt schemes discredited Grant's administration and threw doubt on the respectability of the federal government in general. The first, known as the Sanborn contracts scandal, involved the Secretary of the Treasury, William Richardson. Prior to 1872, informers who reported federal tax delinquents had been rewarded with a percentage of the recovered taxes. In 1872 this practice was abolished by Congress, but Senator Benjamin Butler attached to the repealing legislation a provision allowing the Treasury to let three contracts for the collection of specific delinquent taxes. Under this provision Sanborn, one of Butler's political protégés, signed a collection contract with Richardson, then Assistant Secretary of the Treasury. Sanborn was to receive a 50 percent bounty on any taxes he collected. The contract, although unusually lucrative, was not illegal. However, Sanborn proceeded to collect taxes which the Treasury would have recovered in due course anyway and to rake off his bounty. When this contract was investigated in 1874, Sanborn was shown to have received $213,500 of rewards, on $427,000 worth of delinquent taxes, virtually all of which would have been collected by the Treasury without his intervention. The committee reported that Richardson deserved "a severe condemnation," but the Treasury Secretary resigned before a vote of censure would be passed through the House.[22] To the chagrin of reformers, Richardson was then appointed by Grant to the court of claims.

The Whiskey Ring scandal, which broke in 1875, reached much further into the federal administration than did the Sanborn contracts. Federal officials and employees, from clerks to the private secretary of President Grant, were implicated or convicted of corruption. Since Andrew Johnson's administration, rumors had circulated that distillers were defrauding the government of tax revenue. The government displayed a mysterious reluctance to investigate these charges. In 1874 Richardson's successor at the Treasury received information about the distillery rings and decided to investigate. Avoiding the regular Treasury personnel, whom he distrusted, the Secretary sent hand-picked inspectors to the distilleries, where they found that an elaborate apparatus of fraud had been constructed. Distillers falsified reports of the quantity of liquor they produced and then bribed government inspectors at the distilleries to verify the fraudulent reports. In some Internal Revenue districts, higher officials, up to and including the district collector himself, were brought into the ring. Moreover, some members of the Treasury's Bureau of Internal Revenue in Washington were also "in," and they provided the rings with advance notice of inspections or investigations.

The Whiskey Ring included [Grant's friend] General John A. McDonald, collector of internal revenue in St. Louis ..., other collectors, notably in Chicago, Milwaukee, and San Francisco, subordinate personnel in considerable numbers, the chief clerk of the internal revenue division of the Treasury Department in Washington, and an unknown number of informants to the ring in Washington and elsewhere. It also included General Orville E. Babcock, President Grant's private secretary....[23]

In the end, over 350 distillers and government officials were indicted. The numbers involved in the Whiskey Ring, and the availability of corruptible officials at all government levels, indicated a degenerative malaise in the public service of the 1870s. Interestingly, this scandal did not go as high in the Bureau of Internal Revenue, as did the scandal of the Truman administration six decades later.

The infamous record of the federal government under Grant provided a stimulus to the government reform movement, which was then concentrating on proposals for the institution of civil service. President Grant who, despite the willful corruption of his nearest associates and appointees, was apparently personally incorruptible had advocated the creation of civil service in his Presidential campaign. Again, in his second inaugural address, Grant asked Congress to create a law governing the manner of making all federal government appointments. In the form of a rider to an appropriations bill, a limited provision for civil service passed through a reluctant Congress in 1872. The bill, however, left everything to the President's discretion. The new civil service rules were first applied to the Washington departments and to federal offices in New York, but the President himself soon violated the rules by some of his own appointments.[24] The ultimate success of federal government reform was to result only from a long and desperate struggle with the entrenched forces of corruption, as well as the partisan political forces which had come to rely on the existing interplay of interests and power.

Thinking about a corrupt period like that after the Civil War is sometimes marred by overemphasizing the names of Presidents. The fault of Grant and many of his successors did not lie in personal dishonesty but in weak attitudes toward officials who were dishonest. Congress, over which he had no control, was very corrupt. Collis P. Huntington of the Southern Pacific said the Forty-fourth Congress was made up "of the hungriest set of men that ever got together."[25]

Patronage here, as elsewhere, led to further corruption. Reform Senator Carl Schurz was especially critical of the "general order" business of the New York Customs House. Overnight storage of goods, at an exorbitant rate, had to be paid to a Grant employee.[26]

Reform and Relapse from Hayes to Roosevelt

President Hayes was favorable to the civil service, devoting two paragraphs of his inaugural address to the subject. Congress, however, proved unwilling to act upon Hayes's proposals. And even Hayes, for his part, while insisting upon and aiding the elimination of patronage as a basis for appointment in some departments, personally devoted himself to the distribution of key patronage posts in others. A recent observer concludes, "to most historians today, it appears that Hayes' record of inconsistency on reform rests less on any inclination on his part to subvert effective reform than on the practical necessity of working within a system that was not yet prepared to accept reform."[27]

President Hayes also made another notable gesture toward federal reform; this one concerned the time-honored custom of assessing officeholders for party activities. He directed that no federal officeholder be allowed to participate in partisan organizations or activities, nor should any officeholder or his subordinates be allowed to be assessed. However, as with the patronage, Hayes himself was unable to abide this directive. In the 1878 campaign, a Republican politician sent out a letter, apparently with Hayes's knowledge, indicating that all federal employees earning over $1000 should contribute 1 percent of their salaries to the Republican campaign.[28]

The public demand for reform was strengthened during the Presidencies of James Garfield and Chester Arthur by the discovery of the star routes fraud in the U.S. Post Office. The ring which initiated the fraud was actually established during Hayes's term, but was detected and prosecuted under Garfield and Arthur. The star routes were special postal routes designed to provide postal service by men, horses, wagons, or stagecoaches to rapidly developing areas of the West. Congress periodically delineated the new routes that were needed across the country. Then the Second Assistant Postmaster General was authorized to let 4-year contracts for these star routes by competitive bid, and to supervise their operation. However, he also had the authority both to require the upgrading of service on routes after the granting of contracts and to authorize higher payments for the upgraded service. Thomas Brody, who had been appointed Second Assistant by Grant in reward for his service to the Republicans in the 1876 election, saw this last provision as an opportunity for fraud. During Hayes's administration, Brody ordered improved mail service, with maximum increases in compensation, on star routes contracted to a small group of men. But the routes did not need improved service, and the extra compensation did not buy improvement. It only brought cash into the pockets of the ring members, who included Stephen Dorsey, Secretary of the Republican national committee and manager of Garfield's Presidential campaign in 1880. Garfield, until his assassination, and then Arthur pressed forward the investigation and prosecution of the principals in the case, even though they were aware that it might implicate close associates and weaken the Republican party. As a result of jury fixing and faulty prosecution, those indicted were never convicted. But there were certain "happy results" from the case. "The accused men were driven from the government service; the Post Office Department improved in personnel and saved some $500,000 per year. Public opinion was aroused against corruption in office and more impetus given to the movement for civil service reform."[29]

Eaton's 1881 book indicates some results of Arthur's Customs House administration. "There were strong reasons for believing that the numbers on the official payrolls at New York were excessive, that not a few officials were incompetent—that fraud and smuggling were considerable." The spoils system caused as bad or worse problems of administration in the New York Post Office.[30]

The Jay Commission in 1877 heard evidence of the duty-free passage of wire intended for an official, fraud in importation of silks, inefficiency of patronage employees, acceptance of bribes by officials, and political assessment of employees.

Secretary of the Treasury John Sherman, supporting Arthur's removal in a letter to the Senate on January 15, 1879, noted the high costs of collecting the customs, irregularities on the part of the weighers and gaugers, and resistance of Arthur and his colleague to reform.[31]

However, under Hayes, the minority wing of the state party was favored by the President, and a great battle was waged over the control of the Customs House. Hayes, seeking to replace Arthur, was viewed as the champion of civil service principles, and Arthur was the Black Knight champion of patronage, the Conkling machine, and the corruption which traditionally surrounded the Customs House. His selection as Garfield's Vice President, following his removal from the collectorship, had resulted from the Conkling machine's influence. Consequently, there was little in Arthur's past to indicate that he was anything but the most thorough spoilsman. Moreover, during the 1882 congressional campaign, assessments were again levied against federal officeholders with Arthur's approval. Yet the defeat of the Republicans in those congressional elections, which returned a Democratic majority to the House, seemed to persuade Arthur and his party that civil service reform was demanded by the public and could be postponed only with the most dire political consequences. Not only did Arthur support the comprehensive civil service law, but he also promised legislation to prevent any further assessments. In December 1882 the Pendleton Act was passed, and in January 1883 it was signed by President Arthur.

Yet even the passage of the Pendleton Act was insufficient to retain the support of the public for the Republican party. The Democrats successfully ran Grover Cleveland, reform governor of New York, for President against Republican James Blaine, of questionable reputation. The public was in the mood for continued reform.

The election of William McKinley to the Presidency in 1896 dismayed many reformers. McKinley's chief organizer was the Cleveland "boss" Marcus Hanna, so it was feared that the new administration would resort to the old system of spoils and corruption. Yet even McKinley made explicit his intention to uphold and extend the civil service and to "press forward with federal government reform." Despite his statement, however, McKinley slightly contracted the coverage of the civil service. About 10,000 jobs were removed from the civil service rolls, and the restrictions on transfers and reinstatements were eased. But these revisions were minor; the civil service had come to stay.

During McKinley's tenure of office, corruption was discovered in the temporary administration of the Cuban Post Office, and inefficiency or corruption was charged against the War Department in the conduct of the war with Spain. At the end of the Spanish-American War, the Postmaster General appointed Estes Rathbone to administer temporarily the Cuban posts. Rathbone was an intimate and advisor of Hanna, and of the First Assistant Postmaster, Perry Heath. It was soon discovered that Rathbone and the director of the Cuban postal finance office had stolen $130,000. Hanna used his influence to protect his protégé, but McKinley allowed the investigation to go forward and Rathbone was eventually indicted.[32] The result of a War Department investigation was different. The Secretary of War was thought by all to be grossly inefficient, but the commission organized to investigate the conduct of the war concluded that he and the department were guiltless of corruption.[33]

Theodore Roosevelt, who had made a national reputation as a reformer, became President in 1902. His election was yet further proof that reform had been irreversibly sanctioned. However, the discovery of more corruption in the Indian Service, Land Office, and the Post Office Department during his administration, though perpetrated by appointees of his predecessors, reflected badly on Roosevelt's terms of office. Sizable contributions to Roosevelt's 1904 campaign by giant corporations, and the President's questionable explanations of them, also removed some of the luster from his reputation.

Finally, corruption discovered in 1903 in the Post Office Department had begun in 1893 and continued throughout Cleveland's second term and McKinley's administration. A group of high postal officials (fourteen of whom were eventually indicted, including the assistant attorney general, the superintendent of free delivery, and the superintendent of salaries and allowances) "operated principally in the fraudulent purchase of postal supplies, in the illegal appointment of political favorites, and in the sale of promotions."[34]

The extent and duration of these misdeeds under McKinley indicated that lax discipline still prevailed in the federal administration at the beginning.

In 1908, William Randolph Hearst read to an Ohio gathering a series of stolen letters which indicated that Senator Joseph B. Foraker had been receiving retainers from Standard Oil apparently in return for supporting and opposing legislation. Foraker's answer was that he served Standard Oil as a lawyer. Foraker was generally criticized by the press, and he was not nominated to succeed himself.[35] The corruption of so many, and the acquiescence of countless others who must have been aware of the waste and duplication, pointed out that public service ethics, even after decades of improvement, still retained some of the old standards.

The federal administration's difficulties in the nineteenth century should not be left without alluding to the close relationships between corruption on the different levels of government. New York and Pennsylvania presumably brought the spoils system to the federal government. Federal patronage at the post office and in collection of customs helped sustain local and state political machines. But while the corrupters ran nimbly up and down the ladders of government, the slower-moving forces of legal rectitude tended to ignore the levels of government other than the one for which they were legislating. The spirit of reform did seem to stir the federal government before it developed extensively in state and local governments. There were, of course, state and local imitations of federal civil service and perhaps other reforms, but except by example the federal government did little to help improve the quality of state and local government. Bad federal examples like the corruption of the Buchanan and Grant administrations probably encouraged more local dishonesty.

Conclusions

This review of federal government prior to World War I indicates that America is slow in learning how to conduct democracy honestly. The national government, which in most modern democracies is the enforcer of honesty, went through the same cycle as the people. First, there was a "golden age" of revolutionary enthusiasm for new democratic ideals; second, the discovery of the spoils system enabled democratically chosen rules to keep their power longer on a largely nondemocratic base. In this stage, the federal government became the tool of state and local politicians. Third, the spoils system degenerated into the real corruption of the Buchanan administration, the Civil War mistakes, and the stealing which went on in the Grant and later administrations. Fourth, a spirit of reform began to grow, perhaps best symbolized by the Pendleton Act of 1882, a reform which even in the twentieth century leaves America an ethically backward nation.

In this whole process, the federal government shared state and local corruption but kept itself on a higher plane. Professor White's administrative history gives the impression that lack of adequate administrative supervision was the reason for most federal corruption, in contrast to administrators who wanted corruption in some states and many cities. The federal government was clearly the first of the levels to begin consideration of serious reform.

Some of, but by no means all, the federal corruption was initiated by business. The Credit Mobilier scandals and the Southern Pacific and Pennsylvania Railroad efforts to locate congressmen were business-initiated, although even here it must be noted that the government wanted the railroads. Much personal corruption like the Randolph and Wilkinsen matters had no connection with business. The misuse of patronage and exploitation of customers in customs houses and post offices were against rather than for business. However, Colt Revolver did initiate the congressional legislative corruption to secure renewal of its patents. Some of the land office fund corruption was business-initiated; most was not. The misuse of funds from government printing contracts for political purposes probably should not be called business-initiated. Civil War corruption was partly, but not all, due to business. The Sanborn contracts were not. The Whiskey Ring was. The Foraker situation was probably an example of business-initiated corruption.

6

Local Corruption since World War I

Introduction

Prior to World War I, American city government was still very generally corrupt. New York, Philadelphia, Boston, and Chicago all had high degrees of corruption administered by major political machines, either continuously or on an off-and-on basis. There was substantial corruption in cities such as Cincinnati, Cleveland, Detroit, Kansas City, St. Louis, Minneapolis, Seattle, San Francisco, Baltimore, New Orleans, and many smaller cities. Corruption was less widespread than in 1890, but not much so.

Detailed studies of corruption in county government are not generally available, but what evidence exists indicates there was a great deal. Political machines in New York, Chicago, Kansas City, and elsewhere automatically included county government whenever they could. During the La Guardia administration in New York the New York counties were machine-dominated, and worse off than the city.

Corruption is important in many suburban areas, for example, northern New Jersey, but almost nonexistent in others. Rural corruption exists, but we know little about it except that the opportunities are less and the published studies are rare.

Since World War I, there had been a gradual elimination of the major multiethnic machines and some corresponding reforms. By 1977 the only surviving centralized machine in a major city was in Chicago. Nevertheless, law enforcement and some other corruption continued to be widespread, especially in the formerly machine-run cities like New York, Philadelphia, and Boston. Organized crime has been and remains widespread, and is especially strong in the cities formerly dominated by machines although an awakened federal government has begun prosecution of a large proportion of the gangsters.

After describing the death of the old machine and the institution of organized crime, this chapter will review in detail the cities of New York, Philadelphia, Chicago, and Kansas City. All but Chicago have made the transition from the old machine to the partial corruption of today in which law enforcement corruption is predominant and organized crime has a main role. Many examples of the interlocking of organized crime with corrupt politics are given. There follow briefer reviews of various cities, where the available evidence is only fragmentary.

Political Machine to Organized Crime

As Prof. Raymond E. Wolfinger has pointed out in *The Politics of Progress,* the corrupt political machine is not yet dead. He describes the "macing" (compulsory campaign contributions) of employee salaries, the spread of "honest" graft, and the selling of patronage which have been occurring in New Haven, Connecticut, since the 1950s. Newfield and DuBrul, in *The Abuse of Power* (1977), describe similar operations in New York City today. While these corrupt activities are particularly strong in the Middle Atlantic and New England states, they are not infrequent throughout the rest of America.

The new pattern of corrupt machines does not include extensive bribery of officials or direct stealing from the city treasury. Except for Chicago, the boss of an entire city has become extinct. Ward politics, however, which are based on persons seeking patronage appointments or other favors, still exist. Ward politics now depend more fully on "honest" graft which includes noncompetitive bids; high-priced insurance, legal, or architectural services; and purchases of city services through agencies connected with political bosses. Ward politics are often closely interrelated with organized crime.

Why has the central machine largely disappeared? First, the argument is often made that the national government's assumption of welfare services has reduced the necessity for machine-dispensed jobs and Christmas baskets. However, there are obvious difficulties with this theory. Many machines disappeared prior to the New Deal. Some, like those in Chicago and Reading, have become stronger since the New Deal, and many have continued their corrupt activities without visible central leadership. Wolfinger notes that locating jobs or help in the new federally financed agencies offers the machine greater opportunity for service to its supporters.

A second argument suggests that as immigrant groups become more familiar with American language and institutions, they became less dependent on the machine. Again, there is validity to this argument in some cities, but it should be remembered that both disappearing and continuing machines also existed in nonimmigrant areas. For example, the reform of civic institutions in Dallas and Houston, Texas, was not related to the Americanization of ethnic groups. In states such as Massachusetts, Connecticut, New York, New Jersey, and Pennsylvania, ethnic voting is still very important, which may help explain the continued corruptibility of government in those states, but it is not the sole cause.

A third argument is that the corrupt machine declined as a result of the general spread of education and the subsequent opportunities it provided to help individuals succeed without machine assistance. Wolfinger notes, however, that these advantages are not available everywhere in the United States.[1]

The conclusion of this analysis is that no one or two or three reasons can be found for the decline of the corrupt political machine. Rather, a variety of influences have operated in a variety of circumstances. For example, the spirit of the Age of Reform inspired 30 Californians to lead a crusade which eliminated the Southern Pacific machine from California politics in 1910. A small group of socialists reformed Milwaukee during the same period. Beginning in 1937, the leadership of a small citizen council initiated reforms in Dallas with the intention of improving the city; they were sometimes aided by one of the factors previously mentioned.

Corrupt politics, however, did not perish with the Age of Reform. Indeed they provided the important vehicle by which organized crime gained a foothold in many American cities.

Many techniques of American organized crime originally came from western Sicily, but organized crime or the "mob" is independent of Italian control. Hence, the word *Mafia* should be applied only to the Italian organization and not to the American one; indeed, some of the leadership has been Jewish, and persons of other ethnic extractions have been included. There is much talk today of black, Chicano, or Chinese "Mafias." In America, a *capo* (head) is supported by a *consigliere* (counsellor), by *caporegimas* or *capo decinas* (lieutenants), and finally by "soldiers," or triggermen. Organized crime directs and draws its revenues from gambling, bookies, the numbers racket, prostitution, labor racketeering, narcotics, and pornography. Criminal entrepreneurs are forced to pay "protection" to the "family" which controls the specified racket. Failure to pay incurs penalties ranging from vandalism to death. Insubordination, the possibility of testifying in court, and the espousal of unpopular points of view are difficulties which are generally resolved by skillfully executed "hits" or murders. The Sicilian code of *omerta,* or silence, discourages testimony in court, thus crippling law enforcement efforts to prosecute organized crime killers.

Although there were traces of it in the nineteenth century, organized crime's major appearance in America occurred in the early 1900s. Criminal techniques and leadership developed in New York City and spread elsewhere in the 1930s—Al Capone and Johnny Torrio to Chicago; Meyer Lansky to Florida and the Bahamas; Owney Madden to Hot Springs, Arkansas; Bugsy Siegel to Nevada and California; Phil Kastel to New Orleans; Albert Anastasia to New Jersey; Charles "King" Solomon to Boston; Abner "Longy" Zwillman to New Jersey; and the Bernsteins to Detroit.[2]

Prohibition greatly aided the growth of organized crime. Organized crime's control of the industrial rackets, protection payments, prostitution and gambling, however, would probably have developed without Prohibition. Tammany Hall's Mayor Jimmy Walker did encourage gangster involvement in bootlegging simply by not enforcing Prohibition. During this period, Arnold Rothstein, Frank Costello, and other gangsters purchased the tacit cooperation of the New York City Police Department with numerous bribes. Costello functioned through Jimmy Hines, a Tammany district leader who acted as a liaison between organized crime and the city government and who was Franklin Roosevelt's major Tammany supporter before the Chicago Convention of 1932. Costello's payroll helped support Hines, and Costello worked closely with Hines in Democratic politics.[3]

Growth of organized crime's activities depended on political corruption principally at the municipal level, but occasionally at the state or federal levels. Honest, dedicated municipal police and prosecutors could have eliminated most of the rackets with a few exceptions. While organized crime was initially aided by political corruption, it has since become a major source of corruption itself.

Hank Messick, a newspaperman who has written several books on organized crime, concludes that Franklin Roosevelt irreparably damaged the old machine by taking over the welfare programs and by weakening the city bosses, thus permitting gangsters more freedom.[4] While this may have occurred in some cities, organized crime has flourished with the bosses and has not been strengthened by their demise.

Daniel Moynihan, in a 1961 article, suggested that government "at many levels is controlled by massive and sinister commercial interests that the individual dare not defy."[5] He points out that the political reputations of men like Thomas E. Dewey, Averill Harriman, and John F. Kennedy were partly made by attacking organized crime, a practice which none of them continued from higher office. The financial resources of the gangsters and the weak policies of the Federal Bureau of Investigation (FBI) are suggested as reasons for organized crime's growth.

Professor Donald R. Cressey has suggested that in 1969 organized crime's controlled illegal gambling, loansharking, narcotics, certain unions and businesses, the cigarette vending machine industry, the juke box industry, and a variety of retail firms such as restaurants, bars, hotels, trucking companies, food companies, linen supply houses, garbage collection routes, and factories. Since Cressey's book was written, the publication and sale of pornography have become largely a mob business. Until recently, organized crime dominated Las Vegas in addition to controlling state legislators, federal congressmen, and other officials in legislative, executive, and judicial branches of government at municipal, state, and national levels. Some government officials, including judges, have even been considered to be active members of the mob.

While organized crime has made some appearances in relatively uncorrupt areas such as southern California, most families have established themselves securely in cities which have had continuous records of political corruption. New York City, the birthplace of organized crime, has five or six "families" and perhaps the longest history of continuous law enforcement corruption by organized crime. Boston, Kansas City, New Orleans, Providence, and Detroit had in 1969 at least one family each. It was then estimated that nationally there were at least 24 tightly knit families.[6] There have also been small families, or "syndicates," which have conducted organized crime operations in cities like Albany, Rochester, Syracuse, Buffalo, Reading, Newark, and Jersey City, almost always with the aid of some corruption of law enforcement.

Organized crime frequently moves between cities. Gangs in large cities often dominate some of but not all the surrounding suburbs. When New York

City developed an uncomfortable climate for certain organized crime operations in the 1930s, these activities shifted to northern New Jersey. In the 1950s, Philadelphia was reported as having its organized crime activities administered from New Jersey; it now has its own independent families. The Torrio-Capone group developed control of suburbs like Cicero because they feared possible law enforcement in Chicago. There are also "open areas," like Las Vegas and Florida, in which several families may operate. Occasionally, locally established gangsters cooperate with emissaries of any family which has operations in the area.

Some families have widespread criminal operations. The Cleveland syndicate has operated illegal gambling operations in the Kentucky suburbs of Cincinnati, other operations in Miami, and others in Las Vegas.[7] The Carlos Marcello family, operating from New Orleans, has operations in Texas, Nevada, and California, as well as in other states.

In 1967 the National Commission on Law Enforcement issued a report listing nine cities which had failed to report on whether or not they had organized crime. These cities were Buffalo, Flint, Kansas City, Milwaukee, Mobile, Nashville, New Orleans, Oakland, and Youngstown. The commission noted that federal agencies believed that organized crime existed in six of the nine.[8] Organized crime certainly exists in Buffalo, Kansas City, New Orleans, and Youngstown.

All organized crime's activities profit through political corruption. Strict law enforcement would greatly reduce, if not eliminate, most of them. Even organized crime's "legitimate enterprises" have been extended through the forcible elimination of competitors, when corrupt law enforcement authorities have permitted it. The following studies of four cities will indicate how closely organized crime has been tied to corruption in each of them.

A Study of Four Cities

New York City

The dawning of the twentieth century marked the decline of Tammany Hall. For the first 25 years of the century, Charles F. Murphy was Tammany Hall's leader. A quiet but firm figure, he very carefully controlled the district machinery, the police department, and the politicians. Although Murphy tried to actuate Tammany's complete transition into the "honest" graft category, New York City remained immensely corrupt. The impeachment and conviction of Governor Sulzer, who failed to follow Murphy's instructions regarding state appointments, typified Murphy's power. Two mayors of New York City, George McClellan (1903-1905) and William J. Gaynor (1909-1913), tried to function independently of Tammany, but neither was successful.

Corrupt Tammany politics merged with organized crime when Arnold Rothstein, a founder of American organized crime, began his gambling career in New York City under the protection of Tammany leader, "Big Tim" Sullivan, and his successor, Tom Foley. Once, when Rothstein was booked for murder, a Tammany-controlled judge freed him because of "insufficient evidence." In another instance, when Rothstein was charged with felonious assault, he succeeded in having the case dismissed and in turn engineered the indictment of the police inspector who had charged him. The inspector was subsequently sentenced to five years in prison.

Rothstein's Tammany connections led him to partnership with Robert P. Brindell, who controlled the building trade unions in New York City. Rothstein also worked with Theodore Brandle, the northern New Jersey labor boss and businessman, and with "Waxey" Gordon who was heavily involved in narcotics. Bucketeering (the selling of fraudulent securities) provided Rothstein with an important source of revenue during the 1920s. He obtained protection money from "bucketeers" and, in addition, worked through the district attorney, the police, and Tammany legislators to preserve and extend his rackets.

The advent of Prohibition caused Rothstein to develop his unique genius for criminal organization. Aided by his political contacts and the Coast Guard, Rothstein financed and protected the "Legs" Diamond gang which smuggled rum and hijacked other bootleggers' shipments, which were then sold to Rothstein. Rothstein, however, soon left the bootlegging business since he could not dominate it.

While New York State had rigorous laws enforcing Prohibition, there were very few convictions. Rothstein prospered in his bonding business. He also used a loophole in the New York law which enabled a landlord to secure injunctions against future raids if a first raid did not secure a conviction. Rothstein bought leases of properties which had been raided and, on occasion, used his police contacts to schedule raids.[9]

Italian-American gangs followed Rothstein's lead in organizing criminal activities and became politically important in the late 1920s. Expanding into bootlegging, racketeering, gambling, and speakeasies, these gangs found Rothstein's political connections useful since Tammany district leaders relied on them at election time.

George Olvany succeeded Murphy in 1924 and thus emerged as a representative of an altered Tammany. He was removed from the leadership in 1929 after supporting Al Smith's unsuccessful Presidential bid. John F. Carey, a more traditional Tammany politician, replaced him. The underworld connections with Tammany Hall were dramatically illustrated in 1929 when Magistrate Albert H. Vitale, previously charged by La Guardia with borrowing money from gangster Arnold Rothstein, was guest of honor at a dinner of the Tepecano Democratic Club. Some of his fellow guests had police records, including Cerro Terranova, who headed the artichoke racket. The dinner was held up by armed men, but

Magistrate Vitale promptly got the loot back through Democratic Club-underworld connections. With Jimmy Walker as mayor (1925-1933), corrupt Tammany Hall operations accelerated until the Seabury investigations, commencing in 1930, and the election of Mayor Fiorello La Guardia in 1933.

Three investigations conducted by Judge Samuel Seabury played a very important part in Tammany Hall's decline in the 1930s. The first was of the magistrates' courts, the second was of the district attorney of New York County, and the third was of the whole city. All three were ordered by state authorities. These investigations found scores of police officers and magistrates who were banking sums far beyond their annual salaries. Hundreds of innocent women were arrested by police, falsely charged with prostitution, and then forced to pay the policemen in order to avoid prosecution. Seabury disclosed "how inept and unethical attorneys had obtained positions as magistrates," paying for the job and offering cooperation to machine leaders.[10] Much damaging evidence was found in an investigation of District Attorney Thomas C. T. Craig. Sheriff Thomas M. Farley of New York County was removed from office because he failed to explain to Seabury how he had accumulated $400,000 in six years on an annual salary of $8500. In a state investigation of New York City, Judge Seabury showed that unemployment relief funds had been used for Democratic political purposes. Finally, Seabury found that Mayor James J. Walker had received some substantial gifts from persons who wished to influence city street railway policy. The effect of the Seabury investigations was to force Mayor Walker's resignation and to excite a substantial anti-Tammany feeling, which led to the election of La Guardia. Dewey's prosecutions later showed that Tammany gave complete immunity from prosecution to favored gangsters. Tammany had engaged in too much corruption even for New York's tolerant citizenry. The shutting off of immigration, the Roosevelt welfare state, and the increased vote also contributed to Tammany's downfall.[11]

La Guardia's reform administration (1933-1945) deserves special mention. La Guardia was the first reform mayor to be reelected since Tammany came into power in 1869. His ticket was fusionist, consisting of Republicans and reform Democrats. La Guardia gained support from his colorful personality, his half-Italian, partly Jewish background, and his liberal views. Although President Roosevelt was nominally of a different party from that of La Guardia, he still supported him.

La Guardia helped Thomas E. Dewey to be elected district attorney in 1937. Dewey, in his roles as Chief Assistant and then U.S. Attorney (1931-1933), special deputy district attorney (1935-1938), and district attorney (1938-1942), did much to reduce the power of organized crime. The police cooperated fully, both when Dewey was special prosecutor and after he became district attorney.

Depression conditions and the glamour of the work helped Dewey recruit a brilliant staff of investigators, accountants, and lawyers, who succeeded in jailing "Lucky Luciano," "Waxey Gordon," a dozen other gangsters, and Tammany leader-mob liaison Jimmy Hines, and prosecuting Dutch Schultz until his gangland assassination. Never before, and almost never since, was so much accomplished against organized crime.[12] For a time, New York City experienced relatively effective law enforcement. Yet even under La Guardia, who publicly destroyed Costello's slot machines, Joe Adonis was enabled to continue major gambling and organized crime in Brooklyn because he supported La Guardia. Concurrent with La Guardia's reforms, the numbers racket expanded under Dutch Schultz, waterfront pilferage increased, and floating dice games were frequent.[13]

Impetuous La Guardia gave New York City the most honest administration it had every known. Sincere but unsuccessful efforts were made to eliminate organized crime, gambling, and prostitution. Racketeering (extortion of funds for permission to stay in business), which was highly developed in markets like that for artichokes, was successfully attacked, although much continued to exist. Recent evidence suggests that areas within the police department remained corrupt. Frank S. Hogan, one of Dewey's deputies, succeeded Dewey in 1941 and kept an honest prosecutor's office in New York County (Manhattan). With federal funds, La Guardia promoted building, health and welfare services, and education. Graft on school site purchases was eliminated, and a crusade against weight-measure frauds was instituted on behalf of consumers.[14]

By the early 1940s, however, organized crime was controlling Tammany Hall. In the winter of 1941-1942, Costello controlled a majority of votes on the Tammany executive committee, which selected Tammany leaders.[15] In 1943, District Attorney Frank Hogan's office released a tape of a telephone conversation in which a recently nominated New York State Supreme Court Justice, Thomas A. Aurelio, protested "undying gratitude" and loyalty to Frank Costello. Thomas Lucchese, boss of a mob family, had 22 judges as guests at charity dinners.[16]

In 1945 William O'Dwyer was elected mayor with the support of Tammany Hall and organized crime, even though O'Dwyer had started as a rackets buster in his days as prosecutor in Brooklyn. Later, in his service as district attorney, O'Dwyer had shown signs of organized crime connections. After winning a second election as mayor in 1949, O'Dwyer was forced into an ambassadorship in 1950, to save the party, as his organized crime connections became apparent. When O'Dwyer became mayor, Tammany was operated by Frank Costello and other organized crime figures. In 1949 Costello, who had wearied of politics, transferred control of Tammany to Carmine de Sapio, instructing him to keep clear of the rackets.[17] De Sapio, the first non-Irish leader of Tammany, endeavored to rid it of organized crime connections. Although he eventually claimed that he had reduced organized crime infiltration, he maintained some connections himself. The interest of organized crime in New York politics was only partially due to the rise of the Italians in Tammany Hall. Charles Garrett suggested that:

The decline of Tammany, it is important to note, was reflected in a change in the relationship between the Hall and the underworld. While the machine was growing poorer, gangland was wealthy and its leaders not unaware of the importance of political connections. The result was what one could expect; the balance of power in the ancient alliance tended to shift from the politician to the gangster. The outstanding manifestation of the shift was that the underworld, instead of just buying protection as in the old days, came to install its own district leaders.[18]

Carmine de Sapio supported Robert F. Wagner, Jr., as borough president and mayor. Wagner performed reasonably well until 1966, breaking with de Sapio in 1961. Members of organized crime were voted out of Tammany district leaderships in the 1953 mayoral election, turning over control of Tammany Hall to de Sapio. Although Wagner was not another La Guardia and even made many Tammany appointments, he did not cultivate organized crime contacts. De Sapio had formerly defended Tammany Hall against the Kefauver committee's demonstration of organized crime connections in 1951, but was eventually overthrown by a reform Democratic movement that was incensed by Tammany's mob contacts. After his dethronement, de Sapio acted in one instance as a negotiator of a bribe for organized crime, for which he was later convicted.

The election of reform Mayor Lindsey in 1966 did not exempt New York City from further corruption by organized crime. A department head, James Marcus, let himself become involved in a "kickback" arrangement worked out by organized crime.[19] In 1968 District Attorney Thomas J. Mackell reported that organized crime was "siphoning off as much as $50 million a year" from cigarette bootlegging, clearly with some official cooperation.[20] Mackell was himself indicted in 1975 for obstructing a prosecution.[21] In 1972 District Attorney Eugene Gold of Brooklyn handed subpoenas to five hundred mobsters, a score of judges and politicians, and more than 100 policemen. The subpoenas were based on electronic surveillance of a trailer in an automotive junkyard, a summit headquarters for organized crime.[22] In 1973 Ted Gross, former Youth Services commissioner, pleaded guilty to accepting bribes over a 16-month period.

The *Knapp Commission Report on Police Corruption* in 1971 viewed organized crime as one of the primary sources of police corruption. The commission noted that since its founding in 1844, the New York City Police Department had had some continuous corruption.[23] Police corruption was largely based on extortion of funds from persons who were in violation of "morals" legislation. Brothel owners and bars which operated illegally made payments which, under Tammany administrations, went to the political machine and then to the police department. Once the machine collapsed, however, the payments went directly to police officers at various levels. Gambling operations were also extorted on a systematic basis, with planclothesmen receiving monthly bribes of $400 to $1500.

Narcotics control was the greatest problem facing the police department. Police were bribed not to arrest and start prosecution; policemen sold heroin or other illegal drugs themselves. Since the location of narcotics sales varied, police extorted large single payments from narcotic deals rather than smaller monthly payments.

The Knapp Commission found that bribes to police by contractors and subcontractors were "the rule rather than the exception." There were also bribes to inspectors and personnel from other agencies. Bribes were paid to avoid the necessity of securing permits for rearing fences, wooden walkways, even for moving vehicles across the sidewalk or double parking. An elaborate system of intradepartmental payments permitted desk officers to share in the illegal income of officers. Payments were also made for departmental citations, for temporary and permanent assignments on lucrative jobs, for medical discharges, and for selling blackmail information on criminals.

None of the Knapp Commission report indicates that any of the bribe money went from the police to a political machine. The decline of Tammany was a break for corrupt police who no longer had to turn over a percentage of illegal take to the local boss. By the same token, the police lost the political support of the local boss and were more vulnerable to investigatory commissions and reform actions. However, the Knapp Commission did find organized crime behind much police corruption.

The Temporary Commission of Investigation of New York State confirmed and extended some of the conclusions of the Knapp Commission in 1972. Until the end of the 1960s, there had been a general wish among policemen to remain in "honest" graft (defined by New York police as excluding direct bribes). By 1971, however, patrolmen and detectives were receiving direct payments from drug importers and were often becoming partners in the business, helping make New York City the heroin capital of the United States and drug abuse the largest reason for the death of New York City teenagers.

Police were concentrating on arresting retail violators of drug laws, largely ignoring the more important wholesalers on whom federal and state enforcement agencies were concentrating. While there were many New York Police Department arrests on drug charges, almost two-thirds were misdemeanor charges; and two-thirds of them resulted in acquittal or in dismissal of charges. Almost 40 percent of drug felony arrests also resulted in dismissal or acquittal.

The commission concluded that the drug control efforts of the New York police were a failure. In the special narcotics division, a quota of so many arrests a month per officer resulted in many unimportant arrests. Large-scale or long-time investigations were not encouraged. The addicts—the easy targets—were arrested. Inadequate supervision and poor equipment made it easier for corrupt police to avoid detection. In one instance, police officers forced a woman addict into becoming a pusher of drugs. In another, a patrolman, whose locker had been found to contain three guns and over fifty pieces of narcotics contraband and who had criminal associations, was kept on the force surprisingly long. Another "Narco" officer attempted to bribe an assistant district attorney to dismiss a narcotics charge.

In summary, New York City's long tradition of political corruption has made it possible for organized crime to establish itself there and then flow out to the rest of America. Organized crime flourished so strongly that for a time it had control of the city political machine. The New York City electorate, however, rejected the machine once this association was apparent. New York City is still not "reformed"; remnants of the machine and organized crime families continue to enter into its political, economic, and social life. In a recent book, Newfield and Du Brul state their belief that mob control over politics is now decreasing, but they clearly view it as still of major importance. Their book has a chapter on "The Political Economy of Organized Crime."[24]

Chicago

By 1900, a combination of the Republican Lorimer machine, the Democratic Sullivan-Hopkins machine, the Yerkes Traction Companies, two gas companies, and the Walsh banks was dominating city, county, and state politics.[25]

During the progressive era of the 1900s and 1910s, Chicago had an antivice crusade which almost closed down the red-light district by 1914.[26] Unfortunately, William "Big Bill" Thompson, who was elected mayor in 1915, cooperated extensively with the Torrio-Capone organized crime family. Thompson's administrations were as bad as any in the city's history. City employees, ranging all the way from day laborers and doctors in the sanitarium, were assessed for political contributions and required to attend ward meetings. Patronage rolls were extended. Dives which had been closed during the previous administration were reopened. Ward committeemen designated their police commanders. Even doctors in the city sanitarium were ordered to campaign for Thompson's tick. Under Thompson's direction, the criminal activities of Torrio and Capone were subject to a minimum of police harassment. Capone's henchmen supported Thompson's campaign in return. In 1923 Thompson was succeeded by the honest, well-meaning, but ineffective Mayor Dever. Thompson was reelected to a last term in 1927 but served only until 1931, when Cermak defeated him.[27]

Chicago and several of its suburbs were almost literally controlled by organized crime during Prohibition. In 1920-1922, Johnny Torrio, with help from Al Capone, expanded gambling and prostitution in Chicago Heights, Cicero, Posen, Blue Island, and Stickney by corrupting local officials. Capone was arrested several times but not brought to trial, until the federal government sent him to jail for income tax and Prohibition penalties in 1932. Capone's immunity from prosecution partly resulted from *omerta* and from the willingness of police, prosecutors, or judges to release him. Temporary efforts of Mayor Dever to reform Chicago merely led Torrio and Capone to develop Cicero as their center of operations—indicating how the great decentralization of American law enforcement is a boon to organized crime. The low standards of certain Chicago judges also helped organized crime. For example, Judge Howard Hayes restored to Johnny Torrio the incriminating ledgers which a temporarily honest police force had seized. Police who escorted the O'Bannion gang in hijacking bonded liquor were temporarily suspended, but soon restored to full status. Few wished to serve on juries which might have to find gangsters guilty and face reprisal efforts the rest of their lives.

In 1927 Bill Thompson estimated the total payoff to police from all sources at $30 million a year. Capone's payroll listed half of the entire Chicago police force. After the assassination of gangster Jack Zuta, Chicago police found correspondence discussing payments to two judges, two state senators, two police officers, the business manager of the board of education, a newspaper editor, the William Hale Thompson Republican Club, and the chief of police of Evanston.[28]

Anton J. Cermak, elected mayor in 1931, received support from Moe Rosenburg, the Democratic boss of the West Side and junk dealer; Jake Arvey, a lawyer and political leader; Al Capone, the head of organized crime; and Pat Nash, an Irish-American political leader. Nash, Rosenburg, and Arvey subsequently profited from public contracts. After Cermak was assassinated during an attempt on President Roosevelt's life in 1932, the Democratic county chairman, Patrick A. Nash, suggested Edward J. Kelly as mayor. Kelly was elected by successful machine politics, reducing the Republican organization to bankruptcy and making business pay tribute.[29]

Chicago's corruption gained momentum in the 1930s with contracts going to favored contractors and the police department cooperating and sharing its profits with organized crime. "Protection" was afforded gambling establishments, off-hour liquor operators, and brothels. The establishment of the national racing wire in Chicago furnished the "catalyst of syndicate crime" through the nation.[30] Meanwhile, basic city services declined. Garbage collection and street cleaning were haphazard, and public transportation became disorganized.[31]

In the late 1930s, the syndicate decided to require Chicago restaurants to pay "protection" money to the syndicate-controlled Drugstore, Fountain and Luncheonette Employees Association. Property was vandalized, and owners and patrons were injured through beatings and bombings until the restauranteurs agreed to pay the union; yet employees failed to benefit and remained at low wages. This terroristic control was largely dependent on local government's failure to enforce the laws, a failure which rose from its close alliance with organized crime. For example, a syndicate representative, Lawrence Rossano, who burned a restaurant was arrested and promptly turned loose by Judge Alexander J. Napoli. In another type of city-mob cooperation, a syndicate-controlled company had extensive city contracts for paving.

After Cermak's assassination, Frank Nitti became head of the underworld for a decade—a decade of great prosperity and immunity from both federal and local arrest—until his suicide in 1943.

During World War II, gambling and prostitution provided servicemen with continual entertainment. The Loop (central business district) and the North Side were riddled with gambling and assignation joints, many of which were operated by precinct captains and politicians. In 1944 Arthur X. Elrod, Democratic committeeman from the Twenty-fourth Ward on the West Side and protector of the mob in this area, received a telegram from Franklin Roosevelt congratulating him for the tremendous vote in his ward.[32]

Mayor Kelly retired in 1946 after an unenviable record. The National Education Association made a study of the Chicago Board of Education and was appalled by the ineptitude and corruption of Kelly's school system. Taxes were high, the city bankrupt, and police captains wealthy from gangster payoffs. The rector of the Faculty Presbyterian Church complained to Kelly that he was being propositioned by prostitutes when he went out for air on Northern Michigan Avenue during the evening.[33]

From 1932 to 1950, Captain Dan "Tubbo" Gilbert served as chief investigator for District Attorney Thomas J. Courtney and two other district attorneys. Gilbert worked closely with organized crime and was indicted in 1938 for helping a milk-price racket, but the indictment was dropped. Gilbert, in addition to his official duties, helped organized crime establish a score of unions and gambling and handbook joints and was a "wheelhorse in the Democratic Party." He operated his own gambling joint, lived briefly with two syndicate gamblers, and kept a lively interest in crime and vice. Gilbert told the Kefauver committee little about his finances, but his wealth was far beyond the potential of his salary. He, however, was not unique in this respect; Arthur Madden, Treasury agent in Chicago, estimated that 40 police captains were worth more than $1 million each.[34]

When the Kefauver committee came to Chicago in 1950, two witnesses, one a former police captain, William Drury, were killed to keep them from testifying. Drury had been fired from the force because he had insisted on questioning Jack Guzik, Capone's chief financial man. Mayor Martin A. Kennelly, successor to Kelly, who naively announced his belief that there was no syndicate, was excluded from syndicate political activities. Kennelly also failed to control the political machine, which was then presided over by Col. Jacob Arvey. Kennelly's efforts to support civil service reform offended ward leaders who needed patronage as well as bribes.[35]

In 1953 Richard Daley became county chairman, and in 1955 he defeated Kennelly for the Democratic mayoral nomination. Vanquishing Alderman Robert E. Merriam for election as mayor in 1955, Daley's victory came largely from West Side wards, the ones controlled by the former Capone block. A review of the politics of several wards is a tedious recounting of the interrelationships of organized crime and machine politicians. Frank Annuzio operated the 1st ward as a fief of the syndicate. Vito Mazzallo, Democratic committeeman and alderman, had Capone machine backing in the 25th ward. Bernard Neistein, Democratic committeeman of the 29th ward, took his orders from the syndicate controller. Similar connections are pointed out by Demaris in the 24th, 3d, 4th, 6th, 20th, 27th, 28th, 31st, and 42d wards.

One West Side bloc leader, Roland Libonati, was elected to Congress with 89 percent of the vote in 1957, despite connections with Al Capone and other gangsters and a record of serving his own interests in the state legislature. While in Congress, where he served on the House Judiciary Committee, Libonati maintained organized crime contacts. While in Washington, Libonati had worked on behalf of "civil liberties," introducing a bill which "would have made it a crime for federal agents to keep gangsters and criminals under surveillance." He also sponsored a resolution asking the House Judiciary Committee to investigate the "persecution" of the Teamster's Union leader, James R. Hoffa, by the Justice Department. In 1963 Sam Giancana, leader of organized crime in Chicago, ordered Libonati to retire from Congress, which he did. Frank Annuzio was Libonati's successor. It is said that Attorney General Robert F. Kennedy threatened to prosecute Libonati if he returned to Congress.

Needless to say, Chicago elections have often been of a scandalous nature. The election of 1960 has been of national concern, when part of John F. Kennedy's slim victory margin came from corrupt, machine-dominated Cook County. In 1962 the Joint Civil Committee on Elections reported large quantities of "assisted" Democratic voting. In 1964 Sheriff Richard B. Ogilvie, despite lack of cooperation by the Chicago Elections Commission, found several thousand "ghost" voters who were dead or had moved away.[36]

An analysis of the Daley machine presents an image of organized labor and organized crime being integrated with corrupt politics. In Chicago, every mayor for the last four decades, up to Mayor Daley's death, has been an Irish Catholic; Irish Catholics have also controlled the city, county, and state governments. Irishmen were more acceptable to other minority groups in certain mixed wards. This, in addition to Irish ability at political organization, may explain their political strength, which is vastly greater than their proportion of the population, which is estimated to be from 4 to 10 percent.

The 50-man council was well controlled by Mayor Daley and a few powerful aldermen. Aldermen who disagreed with the top group found their wards discriminated against by the reduction or suspension of city services. The party ward committeeman, who usually held a good public service job, was more important than the alderman and usually told him his duties. The major part of the ward committeeman's time was taken up with "services" to his constituents and supervision of his precinct leaders. He, like the alderman, could always be controlled by the central committee through the threat of withdrawing services from his ward.

The Daley machine raised cash by assessing the salaries of people it appointed to public position, by ward-sponsored social affairs, and by contributions from individuals and organizations who wanted to be on good terms with the party. The donors, of course, included gambling houses, taverns, and nightclubs, all wanting special and illegal favors. Some politicians joined with racketeers to form criminal syndicates, operating under the protection of organized crime. Patronage extended beyond jobs to racetracks, public utilities, and the Transit Authority.[37]

The Chicago Sanitary District has traditionally been a major source of political patronage. Syndicate friends have been rewarded with jobs, and sanitation contracts have been inflated. Frank W. Chesrow, president of the district from 1958 to 1966, had a brother who traveled with gangster Tony Accardo and Sam Giancana. Chesrow was himself a product of the First Ward machine. Vincent D. Garrity, the district's vice president, was one of Sam Giancana's political hacks. A series of *Tribune* stories indicated that district employees were falsifying time sheets, padding payrolls, and participating in insurance kickbacks and rigged contracts. Richard B. Ogilvie found a list of 36 district employees with syndicate connections. A new executive manager from the West Coast, Vinton W. Bacon, forced on the district by reformers, attempted to act against overpaid companies, but the courts and the district trustees stopped the lawsuits. When Bacon discovered that a civil service examination had been rigged, efforts were made on his life in true syndicate fashion.

Unions were well represented in the Daley machine; they supported the mayor, and he in turn appointed their leaders to public office.

The Daley machine was not as crude as some of the Tammany operations uncovered in the Seabury investigations or as Chicago's own First Ward politics under "Bathhouse John" Coughlin and "Hinky Dink" Kenna during the first decade of the century. The machine has cooperated with the downtown businessmen's association and has received much business backing. Chicago's "loop" has been relatively well policed, clean, and orderly. Many business and professional people believe that Chicago is an efficiently managed city under the Daley machine. It has not shared New York City's financial troubles, nor does it report as high crime rates to the FBI.

Crime rates rose during the 1950s, however, but since half the crime was in the ghettos, no one worried about it. The state's attorney complained that five defense attorneys and a few judges handled most of the important criminal cases. Judge Joseph A. Pope, "who reputedly served at the pleasure of the crime syndicate's boss of Chicago's First Ward," presided over half the big cases involving organized crime and passed out acquittals freely.

Daley divided graft opportunities with his aldermen who controlled council committees which had power to grant franchises. He also controlled the choice of political captains, deals with departments, and driveway permits.[38]

There have been occasions when the Daley machine bowed to public opinion. A reform police chief, O. W. Wilson, was appointed in 1960 after the

Republican state's attorney had discovered a number of police scandals. Wilson made a vigorous effort to make the police department honest and effective. However, he admitted in a *Harper's* article that little progress had been made against the higher officials of organized crime. Indeed, Demaris contends that organized crime had connections high in the police department four years after Wilson came in. Wilson told the McClellan Committee (a federal committee investigating organized crime in 1957-1960) that the problem of fighting organized crime was too great to be handled by the Chicago Police Department. This was supported by a federal report which clearly indicated many police-syndicate connections.

The Chicago government, however, temporarily stiffened its attitude toward organized crime after the police scandals of 1960. A "federal report" indicates that Alderman John D'Arco, a conduit for syndicate requests, found Mayor Daley more likely to reject them.[39] D'Arco was dropped, ostensibly on grounds of ill health in 1962, and the machine-nominated successor was Anthony J. DeTolve, Giancana's nephew by marriage. Mayor Daley defended him against charges of gangster connections, but DeTolve was quietly removed from the race. The new candidate for alderman, Mike Fio Rito, resigned when his residency was questioned. His successor was Donald Parrillo, who had been vice president of a syndicate-controlled company and partner of a syndicate operator.

Despite seven years of honest leadership by Wilson, Chicago's police force declined rapidly. In 1972 a federal grand jury "had its sights set on more than sixty policemen from the city of Chicago, up to the rank of district commander." Williams grants that some cities remained relatively honest. While Cicero was the headquarters of the Capone syndicate, gangsters avoided nearby Oak Park.[40] In 1972, 24 Chicago police, including a captain, were indicted.[41]

Demaris's own interviews with policemen led to a consensus that Wilson, although himself honest, was too naive to combat the machine. Wilson retired in 1967, whereupon Mayor Daley returned to a more customary chief of police and to police operations more typical of machine politics.

Syndicate connections in the Cook County sheriff's office seem to have been numerous, and a reform-minded sheriff, Richard Ogilvie (later governor), was no more able to eliminate organized crime's influence than was Superintendent Wilson in the city police department.

Important judges at the federal, state, and local levels have been controlled by the Chicago syndicate since political requirements for appointment exist at all three levels. Organized crime's close relationship with the political machine has meant the appointment of many judges who are lenient on syndicate criminals. Efforts of the police or the state attorney's office to enforce the law are easily upset by a syndicate-influenced judge.

How accurate is Demaris's view of the close relationship between organized crime and politics in Chicago? Other books appear to confirm it. John Kobler's *Capone* gives many examples of such interrelationships during the 1920s. A less detailed book, *Chicago Confidential* by Jack Lait and Lee Mortimer has a chapter which confirms this relationship as of 1950. The Kefauver commission report of 1950 has similar evidence. Another book, Ed Reid's *The Grim Reapers,* has a chapter on Chicago which carries the story to the late 1960s. Reid wrote that ". . . for the past generation, it [organized crime] has been building up insulation in this country in the form of judges, courts, and cops who 'bought' and then owe the mob something."[42] Salerno comments: "As late as the middle 1960s, the local chairmen of both parties 'cleared' their lists of candidates with Sam Mono Giancana, a successor of Capone."[43]

Heroin sales to blacks, syndicate betting, and bordellos flourished quietly in Daley's Chicago, with appropriate amounts being paid to the machine. The syndicate was "bombing its way into control of the restaurant industry's supply and union needs, and had murdered its way into a takeover of the black police wheels. . . . One of the worst public health departments in the country, politically corrupt, was no better after four years. City inspectors of all kinds were shaking citizens down, as were the police."[44] In 1974 U.S. authorities indicted 70 Chicago policemen, including 4 district commanders, on charges of extortion. Most were convicted.[45]

In 1975 a special Cook County grand jury accused the Chicago police of "burglary, illegal electronic eavesdropping and incitement to violence" in the department's infiltration of community political groups since 1969.[46]

Other negative aspects of Mayor Daley's administration are portrayed by Chicago reporter Mike Royko in *Boss:*

Out of $113 million in bond revenue, only $20 million was to be used for slum land clearance and community conservation. But since the civic leaders, downtown merchants, and newspaper editors did not live in slums, it was not the sort of inequity that would bother them. Not that the slums, among the worst in the nation, did not interest them. In a one-month period, thirteen black adults and children died in a series of slum fires. Most of the buildings had been illegally converted to cubbyhole units. The newspapers' solution was to rake a few of the slum owners across the coals of public opinion. The fact that the city's building department was taking bribes faster than it could spend them was of less concern to them. The blacks were jammed into the ghettos because the city made no effort to crack the closed real estate market and let them out. During his gala first term, Daley allowed this policy to continue. His urban renewal program amounted to a stack of charts and blueprints. Rats gnawed on black infants' feet, while money was used to build new police stations around the corner.[47]

These activities indicate how corrupt politicians, police, judges, and organized crime have worked together for several decades in Chicago. As in New York City, the success of organized crime would have been substantially less if a corrupt political machine had not protected it. Likewise, the life of the political machine would have been considerably briefer if organized crime had not given it support. Unfortunately, the overthrow of the machine in New York City through the democratic process has not been emulated in Chicago. This can partly be attributed to the shrewdness of the Chicago machine leaders in carefully shaping public opinion.

A different view of the Daley administration is presented by Professor Rakove, who has worked in the machine. He finds that Chicago has made great physical progress and improved the quality of public services; that government is more responsive to the citizenry; "and that Daley has unquestionably been the most effective and efficient mayor in Chicago's history."[48] However, he qualified his comments by doubting the regime's impartiality, sense of justice, and concern for the general citizenry and those most in need.

It is too soon to know whether Mayor Bilandic, Daley's successor, will initiate any major moves toward independence of the city government from its political machine and organized crime allies.

Philadelphia

During the nineteenth century Philadelphia was very corrupt. Nine Republican bosses—William B. Mann, Robert Mackey, James M. McManes, David Martin, Israel Durham, Boies Penrose, Edwin H. Vare, and William S. Vare—ruled Philadelphia from 1849 to 1933. The Republican machine was occasionally defeated and occasionally split, but it survived without genuine opposition until the Roosevelt campaign of 1933.[49]

James McManes, a Scots-Irish Presbyterian, was appointed to the Gas Trust board in 1865 and promptly took a leading position. He probably received his reward in the form of rebates on high-priced coal puchased by the trust.[50] Meanwhile, the Gas Trust was accused of defrauding the people of $1000 a day. The collector of delinquent taxes made $200,000 a year. In 1881 a Republican convention was filled with officeholders and policemen, and federal officeholders were brought in to stuff ballots. The Gas Ring was thrown out by Matthew Stanley Quay in 1888. However, other machines followed, and Philadelphia politics remained corrupt, centering largely on high-priced contracts and rebates.[51]

The three Vare brothers, for example, of old "American" stock, controlled Philadelphia from 1916 to 1933 with sporadic regaining of control later. From 1890 on, their contracting company throve on public and private business. Their chief rival was the Penrose organization, a rival state Republican machine. Professor J. T. Salter wrote a description of several of the ward leaders of the Republican Vare machine, which was defeated in 1933 but not finally eliminated from power until 1951. The Vare machine found its revenue in assessment of job holders and payment on contracts. In the M Ward, all but three committeemen had jobs in the city hall. One of the three had a brick company which sold many bricks to the city, another was an attorney who received all the lucrative master appointments he wanted, and another had a son with a city job. The Vare machine literally controlled certain aspects of Philadelphia life.

Throughout Philadelphia votes were bought and poll taxes of acquiescent voters were paid by the Vare machine. City officials were ordered to make life unpleasant for a black family that had moved into an area, offending the resident voters. Assessments were lowered for friends of the machine. Voters were helped with the election machine, and bootlegging and the numbers racket were protected. Court verdicts were arranged in advance, and manslaughter charges were fixed for a few dollars.[52]

A modification of this analysis of corrupt Philadelphia is offered by James Reichley.[53] He indicates that the Republican political machine described by Lord Bryce in the *American Commonwealth* in 1889—a machine giving the city the title "corrupt and contented" by Lincoln Steffens in 1904—continued in power until 1951 when Dilworth was elected mayor with Republican support. The Republican machine functioned under the "general guidance" of representatives of distinguished institutions like the Pennsylvania Railroad, the University of Pennsylvania, Drexel and Company, and several banking houses. Graft was limited, and the city received a relatively clean administration. A highly respected mayor, Robert Lambertson, was elected in 1939, but he died in 1941. The machine's limits on graft are sometimes disputed, but Professor J. T. Salter's *Boss Rule*[54] seems to confirm Reichley.

Despite the overtones of general guidance, Philadelphia politics remained corrupt. In 1948 the Committee of Fifteen found "well-organized systems of extortion in the Fire Marshall's Office, the Department of Public Works, the Water Bureau, the Department of Supplies and Purchases, and the Receiver of Taxes Office." An Amusement Tax Office employee committed suicide at the same time, leaving a note implicating his fellows in embezzlement.[55] In 1949, reform Democrats Dilworth and Clark were elected treasurer and controller, their election largely being the result of the 1948 disclosures. In 1951 Clark was elected mayor and Dilworth district attorney. The Democratic party organization had given them only partial support. In 1954 the Democrats elected a governor who gave a great amount of patronage to the Philadelphia Democratic organization, which now developed genuine strength as the Republican machine died. Clark's popularity soared, although most people were not aware of the good things his administration had done. His patrician air and his ability to suggest that he was fighting alone against corruption aided him politically. However, Clark did not file for reelection when the organization differed from him.

In 1955 reform-minded Philadelphia Republicans succeeded in nominating a reformer for mayor, Thacher Longstreth, but he quarreled with the Republican machine and was easily defeated by the Democrats whose candidate was Dilworth. Republican river ward organizations kept control of the party if not the electorate.

In 1957 Victor Blanc, a Democrat with organization backing, was elected district attorney against the wishes of Mayor Dilworth. The Democrats, as Reichley's account closes in 1958, were divided between the reformers led by Senator Clark and Mayor Dilworth and the organization which was biding its time awaiting nonreformer control of Philadelphia. An analysis of the Philadelphia Republican and Democratic organizations is revealing. The Democrats obtained funds readily from "$100 dinners" attended by businessmen, wealthy well-wishers, and especially present or would-be officeholders. The Republicans secured less financial support because business had become mistrustful of the local party organization.

In Philadelphia, as elsewhere, bans on "gambling and excessive moneymaking" have not worked. These forbidden practices became available through the cooperation of law enforcement agencies with organized crime. The rackets were tied into "the national syndicate" through a "big-time operator" in New Jersey. Payments for protection did not go to leading officials in the reform administration, but to "professional politicians of both parties" and to members of the police force. Sometimes the money was called a campaign contribution, but the professional politicians tended to regard it as personal spoils. The key was "a cooperative police force and a compliant minor judiciary and district attorney's office." Dilworth, as district attorney, had some success in prosecuting dope pushers, but his assistant and then successor, Sam Dash (of later Watergate fame), did not have time to obtain convictions of anyone in the numbers racket. When Victor Blanc, an organization-supported man, came in as district attorney, such prosecutions stopped.

In the Philadelphia of the 1950s, the party organization, now chiefly Democratic, relied heavily on fraudulent voting practices. Reichley doubted if the organization could shift back from Democratic to Republican and doubted its absolute control of more than a few voters. The committeemen's loyalty was best ensured by government jobs and distribution of funds. However, most have some other means of obtaining a livelihood. They, whether Irish, Jewish, Italian, or black, work hard at politics because politics gives them a sense of prestige which the dominant Protestants would not let them attain in business or philanthropic endeavors. Organized crime was related to political machines, but was not as strong as in Chicago or New York.

There may be truth to the statement of organization leaders that they are rendering a service to citizens which "more coldminded civil servants . . . do not provide." However, the organization operated by the "boys" is resistant to technical improvements in government which would reduce patronage jobs; helps antisocial forces by its favors; discourages popular interest in government; and in the long run produces the kind of disorder which engulfed the Philadelphia Republican organization of the 1940s.

The Clark-Dilworth reform years lasted from 1951 to 1962, when James H. Tate Jr. succeeded Dilworth as mayor. Philadelphia's efforts at reform were concentrated too much on upper-class objectives and were too sporadic to be effective. Dilworth's campaign, for example, tended to be against gangsters, of whom he convicted relatively few. Clark may have been more successful, but he admitted that he never solved the problem of permanent reform. The late Prof. Kirk R. Petshek[56] pointed out that the Clark-Dilworth decade resulted in Philadelphia's making substantial progress for what might be called the social and economic aspects of good city planning. Petshek believed that Reichley underestimated the social goals of the reformers, but neither Reichley nor Petshek comment on "reform" barely penetrating law enforcement agencies.

Rubinstein's *City Police*[57] and the reports of the Pennsylvania Crime Commission indicate that a continuous history of law enforcement corruption was only briefly, if at all, interrupted by mayors Clark and Dilworth. During the 1950s and 1960s, organized crime appears to have grown in Philadelphia. It is probable that the desire for patronage which Petshek views as important in the return of machine politics was also supported by a desire for kickbacks and loansharking, the customary syndicate goals. The Pennsylvania Crime Commission in 1974 found corruption was "ongoing, widespread, systematic and occurring at all levels of the Police Department." More than 400 police officers were identified as frequently receiving bribes to overlook liquor establishments operating at illegal times or using women enticers. Illegal gambling was also conducted at over 200 places as a result of police bribery. Prostitution was prevalent with payment of police both in money and in sexual services. A large number of businesses were paying police for functioning as private guards, for providing confidential criminal records, for extra protection, for "good will," and for overlooking building traffic or other code violations. Police often received cash from stalled motorists and pillaged unprotected property. The corrupt environment of the department forced some young officers into corruption. The internal control mechanisms of the department were vague, fractionalized, and almost totally ineffective." Drug abuse was widespread, and the police department "had a very poor program of drug law enforcement."

Since the Pennsylvania Crime Commission was statewide, its reports give a picture of how corrupt conditions spread out of a metropolis. In a 170-page report on organized crime, the commission noted that state police had arrested "significant Cosa Nostra and independent gambling racketeers in Allegheny, Bucks, Chester, Erie, Lackawanna, Luzerne, Mercer, Northhampton, Schuylkill and Westmoreland Counties in 1969." The commission estimated that over 375 legitimate businesses in Pennsylvania were controlled or linked to organized crime. There were five Cosa Nostra families in the state, three of which were represented at the Appalachian conference of heads of organized crime families in 1957. Robert W. Duggan, elected district attorney of Allegheny County in 1971, compelled employees to contribute to his campaign funds. Gambling and political corruption in Carbondale and in Phoenixville were reported. Corruption was prevalent in the New York Police Department. An extensive gambling ring with major out-of-state connections operated in Johnstown.[58]

What lessons are to be drawn from Philadelphia's unsuccessful attempts at reform? Some of the difficulty is to be ascribed to that problem of New York City, Chicago, and other of America's great cities—the movement of many potential leaders to the suburbs, leaving people who lack the time, background, education, and experience to solve urban problems. Another difficulty is that the state of Pennsylvania has failed to promote honest government in its cities. A third difficulty may be the tradition of corruption that is so deeply embedded in Philadelphia that eleven years of better government could not change it. The experience of that city appears to be closer to that of New York City than to that of Chicago. Organized crime came to Philadelphia later than to New York City, but in recent decades it has gained disproportionate momentum in Philadelphia.

Kansas City

Kansas City has long had a history of corruption. Boss Thomas J. Pendergast acquired full control of Jackson County (including Kansas City) in 1922 and of the city in 1925, until the defeat of his machine in 1940. Kansas City was vulnerable to all forms of vice, with rampant corruption, connections with organized crime, miscounting of electoral ballots, intimidation of voters, and the other customary features of machine politics. Pendergast, however, was not always in control; strong reform groups occasionally won elections. The state of Missouri generally controlled the appointment of the police commission. While this control has at times been purely political, it has sometimes meant better administrative standards.

The Pendergast machine was frequently able to control the Jackson County prosecutor's office, which was as essential as the police for the machine's type of operations. Much of this control continued after the defeat of the Pendergast city machine.

Pendergast's career began when he replaced his ailing brother Jim on the city council in 1910. By 1916 he controlled the county and city Democratic committees and had secured the Democratic governor's choice of Kansas City police and election commissioners. He was also well equipped with corporations in the petroleum, construction, and concrete ready-mix fields, which served as channels for routing city and county money to him.

In 1925 reformers in Kansas City succeeded in passing a council-manager charter. Pendergast, however, won control of the new council and put in his man, Judge Henry McElroy, as manager. Some 6000 Pendergast supporters received city jobs, with large kickbacks to the boss. Some business support was ensured by "selective lowering of tax assessments on the home and company property of influential businessmen."[59]

Pendergast followed the traditional methods of obtaining ward political support by giving gifts to the poor and by establishing social-political clubs for the middle class.

I know all the angles of organizing and every man I meet becomes my friend. I know how to select ward captains and I know how to get to the poor. Every one of my workers has a fund to buy food, coal, shoes and clothing. When a poor man comes to old Tom's boys for help we don't make one of those damn fool investigations like those city charities. No, by God, we fill his belly and warm his back and vote him our way.[60]

The Pendergast organization had its savage side, probably growing in part out of the impossibility of discipline in a corrupt machine. Girls who were enticed to live at the county farm were sold to New Orleans brothels. Gangster methods were used to win elections, frightening opposition voters away. All varieties of vice were welcome, at a price.

All holders of city and county contracts found it wise to use Pendergast's Ready Mixed Concrete Company from which he netted $500,000 in a single year. His insurance business and other concerns also flourished as it became obvious that his customers received important government favors.

In 1932 Pendergast put Judge Guy B. Park in as Governor of Missouri, who, in turn, cooperated with him on appointments. Pendergast also secured considerable help from New Deal patronage and money, especially the state Works Progress Administration (WPA).[61]

In 1928 Johnny Lazia, a one-time protégé of the Pendergast machine, led an Italian revolt against the Irish-controlled machine. Pendergast took Lazia on as a partner, and the machine found a new emphasis. The St. Louis *Post Dispatch* wrote of Kansas City: "The underworld has got the upper hand. Organized lawlessness is the law. An irresponsible political machine concerned solely with spoils is in full terrifying control."[62]

In 1933 Lazia was indicted for income tax evasion, but Pendergast intervened through political channels and the U.S. District Attorney announced that the case was being put aside on "orders from Washington." He reopened it, however, after federal and local police officers in the investigation were shot and killed by gangsters. Even a conviction and a year's imprisonment did not prevent Lazia from employing murder and violence to help Pendergast win a municipal election in 1932. In 1934 one of every ten men on the Kansas City Police Force had a police record.[63] Although public opinion was inflamed by these tactics, Pendergast succeeded in electing county Judge Harry Truman to the U.S. Senate.

The gang assassination of Lazia in 1934 did not eliminate Pendergast's ties with organized crime. He needed money to bet on horses, and he continued to extract it from Kansas City. Charles V. Carrroll took over the organized crime activities from Lazia and became the Pendergast leader on the North Side.

In 1934, for a $750,000 consideration, Pendergast made arrangements to settle a rate case which had been under litigation between the state, the insurance companies, and the policyholders. A historian comments:

In the final analysis, this insurance scandal helps us understand why Pendergast was so successful as a political leader. In this case, we have the perfect example of this technique. He took a cut for himself, but at the same time, he provided something for a diverse community of interests.[64]

However, only 20 percent of the state-ordered refund went to the policyholders.

Like many local bosses, Pendergast also had influence in the federal government. Early in the first administration of President Franklin D. Roosevelt, Pendergast persuaded Jim Farley to secure a pardon for a "Republican" friend who had been sentenced to federal prison for running an illegal lottery.[65]

In the mid 1960s, President Roosevelt stiffened his opposition to Pendergast as did Governor Lloyd Stark, who was elected by Pendergast in 1935, but who subsequently became one of the bosses' staunch opponents. Election frauds in Kansas City were prosecuted in 1937, and in 1939 Pendergast was sent to Leavenworth for evading income taxes on the large insurance deal previously mentioned. His resulting 15 months in jail did not prevent his machine from operating. However, a federal parole provision against political activity kept him from regaining political strength before his death in 1945.

After Pendergast, Kansas City enjoyed relatively honest government under a business-led Citizen's Party. City Manager L. P. Cookingham, appointed in 1940, was among those who greatly improved the administration of the city. In 1950, however, the Kefauver committee found Kansas City to be in poor shape with a "mobster-politician machine." Large vote frauds were engineered in a 1948 congressional race. Illegal gambling grossed more than $34 million a year. The police department had some good officers, but the county sheriff's department was clearly under racketeer influence. Binaggio, the chief gangster, had been leader of the First Ward Democratic Club and later became an overall political leader, until his murder in 1950. Binaggio also sponsored a candidate for governor in order to secure control of the Kansas City Police Commission.[66]

A Kansas City grand jury report of 1951 revealed a deal between the syndicate and some members of the police department for operating gambling joints, after-hour liquor sales, prostitution, and fencing operations. The jury believed that gambling establishments had been running for years with the full knowledge of the police department.[67] From 1969 to 1971, federal lawyers in the organized crime section of the Department of Justice broke up a major gambling ring and two narcotics rings in Kansas City.[68]

The police corruption of the early 1960s has been largely cleaned up. Clarence Kelly, state-appointed chief of police from 1961 to 1973 and head of the FBI until the end of 1977, gave Kansas City police an honest administration, and the department is generally given a very high rating.[69] However, the recent suspension of six detectives for corrupt activities and reports of organized crime operations suggest that Kansas City is still experiencing some difficulties.

The Pendergast machine's loss of control in Kansas City may be attributed to the combined excesses of organized crime and the fact that the political machine drove the business and professional leaders of the city, as well as the federal government, into opposition. Organized crime operations, however, have continued after the demise of the machine. Kansas City has intermittently enjoyed good government; the quality of the police department has been improved by state control. However, the machine persists in Jackson County, and the county prosecutor's office has been of value to corrupt elements.

The Present State of Municipal Corruption

Since World War I, there has been much improvement in the quality and honesty of municipal government. Only one large city—Chicago—still has central machine control, and it is subject to minor controls by public opinion. Many small and medium-size cities are well run, frequently by the council-manager plan. In the South and the West, a number of large cities are honestly and efficiently managed.

The pattern of municipal graft has changed from the open bribes of the nineteenth century to more concealed, legalistic corruption like the "honest" graft which a personally honest individual like Robert Moses dispensed in exchange for power. Sometimes honest graft could become big money, as when a political corporation was set up to handle relocation of tenants ousted for a public works project at a cost of several hundred thousand dollars. Organized crime has made its way into many such deals.[70]

A number of large cities, in addition to the four discussed earlier, have had major corruption in recent decades. Such corruption is not necessarily continuous; it varies greatly in amount between cities. Some of the cities have improved, but according to the reports received by the Center, corruption is important enough to mention. Substantial corruption in the metropolitan county may be a reason for listing here. Many other cities should be on this list, but it is limited to those cities for which we have specific data.

> Albany, New York; Atlantic City, New Jersey; Baltimore, Maryland; Boston, Massachusetts; Buffalo, New York; Chicago, Illinois; Cleveland, Ohio; Denver, Colorado; Detroit, Michigan; Des Moines, Iowa; East St. Louis, Illinois; Gary, Indiana; Hot Springs, Arkansas; Jersey City, New Jersey; Las Vegas, Nevada; Miami, Florida; Newark, New Jersey; New Haven, Connecticut; New Orleans, Louisiana; Paterson, New Jersey; Pittsburgh, Pennsylvania; St. Louis, Missouri; San Francisco, California; Seattle, Washington; Syracuse, New York; Tampa, Florida; Utica, New York; Youngstown, Ohio.

A number of cities have made themselves substantially more honest during this century. The special enthusiasm of the Age of Reform (1890-1910) has been followed by a consistent movement toward better government, especially in the South and the West. In addition to the 2356 council-manager cities (mostly small), the following large municipalities are known to have made real progress. There are doubtless many other cities which belong on this list, but the list is large enough to be significant.

Atlanta, Georgia; Dallas, Texas; Dayton, Ohio; Houston, Texas; Cincinnati, Ohio; Jacksonville, Florida; Los Angeles, California; Milwaukee, Wisconsin; Minneapolis, Minnesota; Oakland, California; Portland, Oregon; Richmond, Virginia; St. Paul, Minnesota; San Antonio, Texas; Salt Lake City, Utah; Rochester, New York; San Diego, California.

Geographical Considerations

In both the nineteenth and twentieth centuries, corruption has been infectious. The highly publicized Tweed Ring graft must have inspired machine politicians in cities throughout the United States. Poorer suburbs in the Boston, New York City, Philadelphia, or Chicago areas are more likely to be afflicted with corrupt government than poorer suburbs in the better-governed Milwaukee, Portland, or Los Angeles areas. Organized crime, a particularly mobile part of corruption, moved out of New York City into cities like Syracuse, Utica, and Buffalo. Pennsylvania Crime Commission reports seem to indicate that corruption has spread from Philadelphia into several other Pennsylvania cities. Organized crime has covered much of northern New Jersey.

State boundary lines have a surprising effect on corruption. Maryland is heavily corrupt; and yet, across the Potomac, Virginia is quite honest. Illinois is quite corrupt, but Wisconsin's government is generally honest. Nevada has much corruption, but California is reasonably honest.

The differences between areas are partly explainable by foreign immigration or by the migration of rural Americans to the cities. Late-nineteenth-century immigration and industrialization in Baltimore created an attitude toward government vastly different from that in Virginia. Likewise, Chicago's long record of migration and immigration had a substantial effect on the quality of government in Illinois. Wisconsin had as high a proportion of immigrants; but there was no large city like Chicago, and accordingly the population had different notions about the purpose of government. As Wolfinger has commented, the manner in which immigrants are received may also be important. His theory is that large California cities with a high percentage of immigrants, but with fewer ethnic lines drawn by a more mobile population, have less corruption than in Eastern states where immigrants were coldly received.

Another factor which may affect the spread of corruption is the attitude of state governments toward corruption in their localities. New York State has had a relatively honest administration for half a century, but it has been reluctant to assume much responsibility for the honesty of its cities and counties. New Jersey is assuming some but only belatedly; Maryland has little; California has a surprising amount of unpublicized influence on local law enforcement. More detailed information on state supervision is given in Chapter 7.

Our evidence indicates that Kirkpatrick Sale, who in *Power Shift*[71] endeavored to show that corruption was greater in the "Southern Rim" than in the rest of America, was incredibly wrong in his assumptions. Sale cited a number of examples of corrupt men from California in the Nixon administration and various problems in Louisiana, Texas, and Florida. While most of his examples were correct, he ignored the blatant corruption in the Northeastern and Midwestern cities.

Many observers have been puzzled by the more frequent presence of reform in the South and in the West than in the East and the continuation of organized crime corruption in the extended Northeast, including Chicago, Kansas City, and St. Louis. A meeting on police corruption had a round-table discussion on East Coast departments versus West Coast departments, with all attendants admitting that there was a profound difference. The difference is puzzling since Seattle, San Francisco, Los Angeles, Dallas, and Houston have all experienced severe corruption at one time. Some of the difference clearly stems from the bad administrative traditions of the old machines in Eastern cities. Another explanation may also lie in a different attitude toward government within the growing, economically developing South and West.

The pattern of organized crime development is obvious and quite alarming. After developing strongly in the Northeastern and Midwestern states, it has spread heavily into parts of the South, notably Louisiana and Florida. Presently, reports indicate that it is intent upon corrupting the relatively virgin lands of the West. Mobster incursions into *Des Moines, Tucson, Phoenix, Seattle, Denver,* and *Las Vegas* have been noted. *Bakersfield, Fresno,* and *Stockton,* California, have likewise felt the breath of organized crime. Recent evidence of land frauds in Arizona and their subsequent spread into Utah testify to organized crime's mobility. *Los Angeles,* California, a city with a history of small syndicate operations, has recently been alerted to the threat of a massive organized crime invasion through the pornography industry which is centered there. Clearly, mobsters are beginning to descend upon the "Sunbelt" states, particularly in the West, after belatedly recognizing their bright economic prospects. Finally, *La Costa,* California, has been a prominent vacationing spot for gangsters who like residing in a Teamster-financed hotel located there.

The Western states must organize themselves to repel this invasion before they suffer the fate of the large Eastern cities. California has taken some preparatory measures in its attorney general's office, but Arizona, New Mexico, and Utah need stronger state law enforcement machinery. Nevada is already in serious trouble. The Los Angeles Police Department has remained quite honest because of the tradition of excellent leadership established by the late Police Chief William Parker. Parker was an extremely tough, resilient individual who demanded much from his men; he would not brook police corruption or police incompetency. This is the kind of police leadership that large cities in the West and elsewhere need in order to defeat organized crime.

Conclusions

The rate of improvement of America's political machinery is discouraging. Of the four cities discussed in detail, three have slowly reached a state of suspended lawlessness, in which the law enforcement machinery can be only partly effective. The fourth city, Kansas City, has attained an efficient police force but apparently suffers from the indifferent prosecution of law. In all four, organized crime has continued to function largely because of the existence of a corrupt machine which has permitted growth of the mob.

It is impossible to estimate the amount of corruption caused by organized crime. In New York City, Chicago, Philadelphia, and Kansas City, detailed evidence indicates that a high percentage of corruption, perhaps 50 percent, comes from the mob. It may have been as high as 80 percent in Atlantic City under Mayor Enoch Johnson or in Newark under Mayor Addonizio; in other cities, it may have been lower.

Is organized crime likely to strengthen its control over political life in the United States? Probably not, since Americans are more likely to fight it, as they did in New York City and in Kansas City, when its excesses become conspicuous. But it has great staying power. Organized crime's role in labor and business enables it to survive several terms of reform government, which the old political machine could not have lived through.

There are other kinds of corruption to which organized crime makes no contribution or in which the contribution results from the mob's weakening of law enforcement. Individual bribes in exchange for specific government action still occur, although on a smaller scale than in 1890. "Honest" graft is presently more common than direct bribes. The number of prosecutions of local officials for bribery or extortion by the federal government is still surprisingly great, although there are many honest cities in which no such prosecutions are made. No longer are "repeaters" voted in several polling places or is money stolen in the wholesale fashion of the Tweed Ring. There is still, however, in at least half of the larger cities, a large amount of "honest" graft, influence peddling, and petty bribery.

Can municipal corruption be cured? Probably not completely, as the experience of better-administered law enforcement systems in Japan and England indicate. There will always be a few corruptible people. But there have been enough reformed cities in America to show that it is possible for American city government to be honest.

What is the social impact of the change from the corruption of the old political machine to the corruption of organized crime and honest grafters? There are many points of similarity between the two. Both are thoroughly dishonest and illegal, and greatly lower the administrative effectiveness of the city government. Both concentrate on paralyzing law enforcement through the selection of compliant judges or prosecutors as well as through the control of police. Both have an especially adverse effect on the life of the poor and result in a cynical citizenry. But there are also significant differences. Organized crime is more sophisticated, more wealthy, and more cruel, using terror and murder as instruments of policy. Since it is lodged in unions and businesses, as well as government, it can survive reform victories and can easily cross political boundary lines, thus making federal action the only practical means of control. Organized crime, however, does keep itself in more closely defined functional fields than the old-time machine politics.

Municipal corruption of the twentieth century is generally not business-instigated. Individual businesses start some of the corruption; more are forced into it. Much of local corruption is simply a relationship between government officials and individuals or organized crime from which bribes and kickbacks are extorted.

7 State Corruption since World War I

Role of the States

The states, which as colonies were the beginning of the American union, have remained strong in American emotions. In the 1860s loyalty to the states was almost strong enough to disrupt the United States. Even today many people identify themselves by their home states and sing songs of those states with extra emotional force.

But the governmental role of the states has changed tremendously since the birth of the Republic. The state militia, which made up most of Washington's colonial army, is now trained in a "national guard" and has become a reserve for the U.S. Armed Forces and a backup for local police forces. Three of the major functions of most states are the care of the insane, prisoners, and university students. The states are fiscal equalizers and important regulators of monopolies. The states also function heavily in road construction and in public welfare.

Some of these functions can lead to corruption, but a few important ones are protected from corruption. Universities have been accustomed to autonomous administration for so long that state government corruption has not often appeared in academic form. The states' fiscal equalization function is closely scrutinized by hundreds of hungry local governments. Regulatory and tax and institutional management functions are all subject to potentially corrupt activity, but even these are impersonal and aloof when compared to similar functions at the local level. Thus, it is no accident to discover that the states, even more than their local governments, have been improving in level of governmental honesty during this century. However, the improvement has been slower than it should have been.

Unlike the Canadian province, the Australian state, and the German land, the American states are intermediate federal units which operate under the divisive effect of separation of powers. Separation of powers, in spite of its many advantages, can facilitate corruption in government. If the mob cannot hire a judge, it hires an assistant attorney general or a deputy chief of state police or a well-placed legislator. But separation of powers at the state level makes it harder for the mob or other corrupting force to maintain continued control. In a number of cases including California and Montana, the corrupting corporation has given up in part because corruption of the three different parts of a state government was too expensive.

Various levels of politics are usually more closely integrated than are levels of administration. Local political figures often want to become state political figures, and then national political figures. National and state figures wish to keep their state and local bases of power, and local machines may control state and federal political appointments. Administrative efforts to keep the levels of government legally separated may have given political corrupting forces an extra leeway. Yet as individuals move up through the levels of government, their chance for continuous control and hence for corruption is lessened, although Mayor Curley in Massachusetts and Governor Agnew in Maryland have showed us that it is possible to be corrupt at three different levels.

The shift of governmental functions affects corruption. As the states early in this century took over the function of utility regulation from local governments, they decreased the opportunities for local corruption but increased the field for state corruption. As the federal government has made financial contributions to welfare, unemployment, and other fields, it has often taken steps to reduce dishonest state and local administration in those fields. But the major steps it has taken to reduce dishonesty in overall state government or in the law enforcement field have been confined to the prosecution of a relatively small number of state and local officers for bribery or extortion.

The states do have the advantage of being more remote from the would-be briber than the local government. But they also have the disadvantage of receiving much less publicity than the federal government or the government of larger cities. In securing material for this book, the Center staff found state materials were less accessible than federal or local materials.

In some ways, the most disappointing aspect of the twentieth-century state government has been its failure to set standards of honesty for its local governments. In American constitutional legal theory, local government is the creature of the state government. State constitutional and legal provisions establish the machinery of local government or authorize local government to establish its own machinery. State governments determine the main outline of local finance. However, few states have displayed a concern to see that the local governments established under its auspices are honestly run. Legal machinery for grand juries and prosecution of offenders is usually established. But few states require annual audits, make thorough audits themselves, or use their grant-in-aid relationship or their prosecuting power to improve the honesty of their local governments.

Although the states have constitutional authority over their localities, Albany, Harrisburg, Springfield, and Jefferson City have not done much to ensure good government in New York City, Philadelphia and Reading, Chicago, and Kansas City. Some efforts have been made: for instance, Governor Roosevelt removed a few New York City officials; Pennsylvania inspected Reading after four decades of corrupt government; Missouri appointed police and election commissions for Kansas City and St. Louis; New York State's investigation division reported on local crime; and Pennsylvania's Crime Commission did the same. Many state attorneys general have the power to intervene in prosecutions, sometimes with the assistance of state police or highway patrols. But such efforts have been sporadic and often political. Nowhere is there a forceful state program designed to ensure honesty in local governments.

Corruption occurs less frequently in state governments than in municipal governments, certainly in proportion to dollars spent and probably in proportion to number of employees, in part because of the nature of state functions as remarked above.

Corrupt States

Early in this century, corporate or individual corrupters and corruptees flourished. The Southern Pacific railroad machine dominated California from 1870 until 1910. Montana Power and Light combined with Anaconda Copper to keep a good grip on the Montana legislature in the first quarter of the century. In Louisiana from 1928 until 1933 Huey Long was noted chiefly as a demagogue but was also a high-level grafter, until the assassin's bullet ended his career. Artie Samish, the artful lobbyist, exerted great control over the California legislature in the 1930s and 1940s, although he never had a real grip on the entire state government.

Another substantial quantity of corruption was brought into state government by outreaching city bosses, as in the nineteenth century. Tom Pendergast of Kansas City controlled several Missouri governors.[1] Tammany Hall elected Governors William Sulzer, whom it later impeached, and Al Smith of New York State, although neither man remained bossed. The Chicago Democratic machine, predominate since 1930, has often wielded some influence on Illinois state government although it has controlled few governors entirely. Prior to Huey Long, Mayor Behrman of New Orleans ran Louisiana politics corruptly, but not nearly as thoroughly as Long.

The number of state officials found guilty of corruption in recent decades is high. As Reichley noted in a 1973 *Fortune* article:

The last two years alone have seen: the conviction of Federal Judge Otto Kerner for taking a bribe in the form of race track stock while he was Governor of Illinois; the conviction of Attorney General of Louisiana Jack Gremillion for perjury; the conviction of Gus Mutscher, former Speaker of the Texas House of Representatives, for participation in a stock swindle; the conviction of former U.S. Senator Daniel Brewster for taking a bribe; the indictment of close associates of Governor William Cahill of New Jersey for promoting a scheme to evade income tax laws covering campaign contributions. None of these deeds approached Watergate in seriousness, but all are evidence of the low level to which ethical standards have fallen in many areas of government.[2]

State corruption is even more widespread than Reichley's comment would indicate. When Governor Marvin Mandel of Maryland and five associates were indicted in December 1975, the *Christian Science Monitor* (December 16, 1975) discussed the incrimination of two others:

... Governor David Hall of Oklahoma was indicted early this year with Dallas financier Warren W. Taylor for conspiracy to bribe the Oklahoma Secretary of State to invest retirement funds in one of Mr. Taylor's companies. Both men were convicted and sentenced to prison terms.

Neal R. Peirce in 1977 listed Maryland, Illinois, New Jersey, New York, Pennsylvania, Florida, and West Virginia as chronically corrupt.[3] For this book, working papers have been assembled on corruption in 35 states. In this group there is evidence of major corruption in the last score of years in at least a dozen states: Alaska, Florida, Illinois, Louisiana, Maryland, Massachusetts, Nevada, New York, New Jersey, Oklahoma, Rhode Island, Texas, and West Virginia. This list includes the states on the Reichley and Peirce lists.

Types of corruption vary. In Alaska, Florida, Louisiana, Nevada, and New Jersey, organized crime has had a major role in corruption within a state. In Maryland, Massachusetts, Oklahoma, Texas, and West Virginia, corruption seems to be individual and endemic. In all states where corruption exists, it is more sporadic than in the cities. There is today no continuous machine control of any state like the Kelly-Kennelly-Daley machine in Chicago or Tammany Hall in New York. Some of the older examples of continuous corporate control of states like Anaconda Copper in Montana, Southern Pacific in California, and the Cameron-Quay-Penrose machine in Pennsylvania have long since disappeared.

Almost all states have made progress against corruption in some departments where federal grants are extensive and where there is federal supervision of methods of personnel selection and federal audit of accounts; for example, large scandals are less likely to occur in unemployment compensation or welfare. They may, however, occur in another field—highways—where federal grants are important but where supervision of personnel is less detailed. Similarly Law Enforcement Assistance Agency (LEAA) grants are now quite substantial but are not accompanied by regular checkups on administrative honesty.

A 1973 book garishly entitled *The Finest Judges Money Can Buy*[4] lists 74 judges from 22 states as well as the federal system who have been removed from office in the last two decades for various offenses but usually including bribery of other misuse of judicial power for personal gain. A surprisingly large number of cases come from the federal courts, from New York State, and from New Jersey state courts. That there are so many of these cases is the result of our poor system of selecting judges, and at times of a generally corrupt tradition of government.

Individual States

Literature on state corruption is much less abundant than on municipal corruption, so it is not possible to prepare detailed studies like those of New York, Chicago, Philadelphia, and Kansas City which appeared in Chapter 6. Also our working papers on states are much smaller than those on cities. Nevertheless, this section will give examples of a few states which have had severe corruption in recent decades, as well as a few which have reformed themselves. The corruption may have been entirely in the state governments or partly in counties which are state subdivisions. Listing here does not necessarily mean that the state is presently corrupt.

Alaska is an unhappy example of a state which has recently been affected by an economic force which brought corruption with it. The building of the Alaskan pipeline represented a multibillion-dollar effort, requiring speedy action. The Teamster's Union, with markedly closer ties to organized crime than other unions, appears to have secured major authority for certain aspects of this construction, with resultant stealings estimated at $1 billion or more. The initial resistance of state authorities to investigation would seem to indicate that there has been some degree of state complacency about illegal operations.[5] It is still too early to know how much ongoing corruption will be left in Alaska government as a result of the pipeline scandals. Since organized crime was involved, and it has a characteristic of taking firm root, the prospect of Alaska's becoming a reformed state in the near future is not large.

Florida has been heavily invaded by organized crime, especially in the South, which has of course brought corruption with it. Law enforcement has at times been largely taken over in Dade (Miami) and Broward counties.[6] Fighting organized crime has been a feature of state elections, but the success of such efforts is not yet clear.

In sharp contrast to its Midwestern neighbors like Wisconsin and Minnesota, *Illinois* has had fairly continuous trouble with corruption. Since Governor Frank Lowden (1917-1920) tried to reform the state, there have been consistent corruptive trends which have been subjected to sporadic resistance, but no real resumption of reform has been noted. Republican Governor Dwight Green (1941-1949) had a good deal of scandal. The death of Democratic Secretary of State Paul Powell in 1970 led to an incriminating investigation of the source of his $3 million estate. Former Democratic Governor James R. Kerner went to federal prison for bribery, income tax evasion, mail fraud, and conspiracy while governor. However, the election to the governorship of James R. Thompson in 1976 may presage a better future. Thompson, as U.S. Attorney for northern Illinois, directed numerous prosecutions of many corrupt officials of both parties.

On the surface, the major reasons for Illinois's ongoing corruption appears to be the corruption of its very large city, Chicago. The fact that the machine is Democratic and some of the corrupt state officials have been Republican should not mislead us. Corruption has been known to jump from one party to the other in several states and cities.

Louisiana has perhaps been the most corrupt state in the Union since the Civil War. Carpetbagger Governor Henry Clay Warmoth set a model of complete control over local as well as state government, which in the 1920s was repeated by Governor Huey Long. In the earlier 1900s, Mayor Martin Behrman of New Orleans dominated most of the state, again employing corrupt activities as a major vehicle.[7] Huey Long's regime was quite corrupt, and several of his successors have not raised the state's reputation for honesty. Governor Sam Jones, sincere reformer of the early 1960s, was unable to leave much permanent reform behind him.

Louisiana's ongoing corruption has several causes. New Orlean's corruption, to be expected in a port city with a lax attitude toward corruption, has intermittently influenced the state. Organized crime has been consistently present and pervasive since Carlos Marcello began operating in New Orleans in the 1930s.

Maryland, next door to honest Virginia, has virtually embraced corruption as a way of life. During the period 1958 to 1962, nearly a third of the 152 legislators "customarily received salaries or other emoluments from state executive agencies, courts, or local government bodies."[8] In the early 1970s both Republican and Democratic congressmen had scandals; one went to jail, the other committed suicide. Two state legislators were indicted in 1973 alone. The story of Vice President Agnew's acceptance of bribes and the indictment of his successors in the governor's office as well as in the Baltimore County executive are well known.[9]

Why has Maryland had so much corruption? One reason is that Baltimore in the nineteenth century became a multiethnic city, with a multiethnic machine (one of the few which was led by Germans). Since the city represents a large part of Maryland, much of its corruption spread. Another reason is the inadequacies of the state law enforcement machinery.[10] Much of the current trouble has been, as in New Jersey, kickbacks from engineers, architects, contractors, and suppliers, a form of graft multiplied by state construction of schools. The basic reason is perhaps the bad ethical habits which Maryland legislators have acquired.

Massachusetts at one time was perhaps one of the half-dozen best-run states, but since 1930 it has tumbled into being at times one of the worst-run states. In 1940 the Republican floor leader of the House was convicted of accepting bribes for passage of a dog racing bill.[11] In the mid-1940s there was bribery of pardons from the governor's council, including one for Raymond Patriarca, the head of New England organized crime.[12] In the late 1940s and early 1950s, extensive bribes of state officials were discovered.[13] In the mid-1950s, the state crime commission charged that $2 billion of illegal gambling flourished in the state and that prostitution, theft, and narcotics were tied to it.[14] In the early 1960s a dozen high state officials were indicted and convicted for conspiracy, bribes, and larceny.[15] In the 1970s, Massachusetts' political history included both genuine reform efforts and some clearly corrupt activities.

How could the quality of Massachusetts government have gone down so far so rapidly? Part of the trouble may be attributed to the weakening position of the Yankees (along with their moralistic ethics) as other groups took over.[16] One writer, Murray Levin,[17] believes it was the loss of public-spirited citizen leadership. Another author suggests that the corruption of the Boston area led to a general cynicism throughout the state.[18]

In *Montana*, in the first quarter of the century, Anaconda Copper Company, at times working with Montana Power, controlled Montana state government a large part of the time. Somewhere around 1930 the corporations suspended corrupt activities perhaps because it became too expensive to pay off against "strike" bills.[19]

Nevada has tried, with varying degrees of success, to keep organized crime from infiltrating its legally sanctioned vice. In the early 1950s organized crime circles controlled much of Las Vegas, the surrounding area, and some high officials of local and state governments. A combative newspaper, the *Las Vegas Sun,* exposed much of this and prompted the state to impose an increased scrutiny of legalized vice.[20] In the 1960s, however, the state government tended to defend Las Vegas casino owners against charges of skimming and gangster ownership.[21] Some organized crime control has continued into the 1970s.[22]

Northern *New Jersey* has become famous as a center of organized crime and corruption of local governments. As in Massachusetts, Maryland, and Missouri, corruption seems to have spread to New Jersey from its local governments. Mayor Frank Hague, boss of Jersey City, secured control of state tax and highway machinery in 1919 and subsequently selected some not-very-honest governors. New Jersey has selected honest governors (from both parties) from time to time but has never succeeded in securing honesty in northern New Jersey's multiethnic areas. Organized crime's movement out from New York City in the 1930s also added to New Jersey's predicament.

As in other instances of state corruption, corruption in New Jersey has been bipartisan. In 1975 Neal R. Peirce wrote of recent events. "The New Jersey scorecard [convictions] includes two secretaries of state, former mayors of Newark, Jersey City, and Atlantic City, the President of the Newark City Councils, the Democratic boss of long corrupt Hudson County, and the Republican state chairman."[23]

New Jersey has, of course, had corruption for a long time. Governor Woodrow Wilson, in the first decade of this century, battled with political bosses there. But the particularly bad record of the mid-century seems to have been a result of undigested ethnics, of organized crime, and of a state government which did little to ensure honesty within its local governments.

New York is a puzzle. It was quite corrupt, especially in the legislature, until Charles Evan Hughes's insurance investigation threw light on corrupt spots of government, and his subsequent governorship (1906-1910) did much to clean up the state government. Governor William Sulzer was elected by Tammany but impeached by the Hall and its allies in 1913. Since 1920, however, New York has had substantial party rivalry for the governorship, which has seemed to produce reasonably honest candidates from both parties. As a result, the state administration appears to have been relatively free of scandals. Exceptions include a few state troopers engaged in heroin trafficking, some liquor distribution, license bribing, and some excessive pardoning.

In the meantime, however, New York City, Syracuse, Utica, Buffalo, and other cities have had real plagues of organized crime and associated corruption, and Albany has continued to house an old-fashioned machine. Aside from a few thorough investigations, New York State has done little to keep its localities honest. Some of this may have been the result of a legislature which has been much more corrupt than the administration.[24] Election reform legislation of the 1970s did not succeed in cleaning up elections.

Ohio, up to his death in 1904 from his Cleveland base, Mark Hanna commanded a statewide machine. Ohio's level of politics showed up in Washington in the unsavory "Ohio gang" of President Harding's time. In the late 1930s, there were a number of scandals in Governor Martin L. Davey's administration.[25] In the 1960s, there was some evidence of liberal treatment of gangsters by the state government. In the 1970s there were a significant number of prosecutions of public officials. Election reform legislation did not mean a general reform in Ohio state government.

Oklahoma has had an uncertain political record for many years. In the late 1950s the troubles of Selected Investment Corporation brought out the fact that a Supreme Court Justice, Nelson S. Corm, had accepted bribes systematically for 23 of the 24 years he had served on the bench. Another justice was convicted, and a third impeached by the state Senate for the same offense.[26] A fourth former justice resigned from the bar under charges of bribery.[27] Early in 1975 defeated Governor David Hall and a Dallas financier were indicted for conspiring to invest state retirement funds in the financier's company. Both men were convicted and sentenced to prison.[28] In 1968 county judge Glenn L. Sharpe was impeached and convicted for receiving gifts for waiver orders in connection with marriages.[29] Federal Judge Stephen S. Chandler was stripped of his caseload in 1965 because of bias against litigants, abuse of litigants, and other problems.[30]

Pennsylvania in 1876, Senator James Donald Cameron (whose father Simon Cameron had been dropped as Secretary of War in the Civil War because he allowed so much corruption):

... took his father's place in the councils of the party and at the head of the state machine, where he was seconded by Simon's best lieutenant, Matthew Quay. Their clever combination of the coarser methods of Tammany and the arrogant autocracy of the Southern Pacific made Pennsylvania a Republican bulwark.

The Camerons did not soil their hands with dirty money for the protection of saloons, bawdy houses and criminals. They shared no fraudulent bills paid by city or state. They did not bribe party politicians of local influence. They simply permitted all these things in exchange for a regularly delivered, overwhelming Republican majority.[31]

Matthew Quay's state machine collected fees from state employees and speculated with state funds in the 1890s.[32] Quay, as state treasurer for 30 years, demanded political contributions from banks and in return deposited state money at no interest.[33] Boies Penrose, a Philadelphia aristocrat and Harvard graduate, joined Quay and later took over his machine.[34]

The Roosevelt victories brought the Democratic party into power in Pennsylvania government. The administration of Governor George H. Earle (1935-1938) was indicted for fraud on highway contracts and other kinds of graft.[35] According to Herman A. Lowe, a former Philadelphia reporter writing in 1949,[36] Pennsylvania had largely boss-ridden politics, with sporadic corruption in administrations of either party. After publication of the Kefauver report in 1950, federal Judge Albert W. Johnson, a product of Pennsylvania politics, resigned. Kefauver reported that Johnson's "decisions, decrees, orders, and rulings commonly were sold for all the traffic would bear."[37]

Governor George Leader in 1955-1959 led a Democratic "reform" administration. Judging from Reed M. Smith's account of this administration, Pennsylvania state politics were still afflicted with excessive patronage, a term which included some contracts as well as personnel.[38]

In 1974-1975 William R. Caspar, treasurer of the Democratic state committee, was indicted and convicted of criminal conspiracy and solicitation, exacting funds from state employees. The state secretary of property and supplies, Frank C. Hilton, was indicted for receiving a kickback on a state insurance contract.[39]

The Keystone State could hardly have been expected to resist organized crime infiltration, in view of the amount of mob activity in Philadelphia and other cities. Indeed, Governors John Fine, George Earle, James Duff, and George Leader granted pardons to a number of mob members. A surprising number of state and local public officials have appeared as character witnesses for mobsters.[40] In the 1970s Pennsylvania continued to have sporadic corruption and showed no great enthusiasm for election reforms.

Texas in the early 1900s the company that became Gulf Oil easily secured leases from the Texas legislature. Colonel Guffey, then head of the company, said he won over members of the legislature by giving leases to them; "it was again impossible to tell whether the statesmen were blackmailing the industrialists or being bribed by them."[41]

In the post-World War I era the conviction of Governor James E. Ferguson for misuse of public funds attested to Texas' unhappiness. Ferguson was banned from holding office in the state of Texas but succeeded in electing his wife, "Ma Ferguson," in 1924 and 1932, and proceeded to run the administration through her, with continued misuse of funds. Dan Moody, attorney general under Ma, recovered several hundred thousand dollars from overpayments to contractors, and was eventually elected governor.[42]

Jack Halfen in the 1930s established a strong syndicate operation in Houston. According to one source, the payoffs from this syndicate included state as well as local officials.[43] Halfen claimed that he was a major contributor to Lyndon Johnson's campaigns. However, the material available to us does not name any Texas state official. Beaumont, Texas, was filled with casinos and "raped" by organized crime. In the early 1960s a citizens' revolt with federal cooperation led to a reform.[44] In the 1950s a state land commissioner diverted millions from a veterans' homestead program, but wound up in jail. Two former state insurance commissioners were indicted for their role in a fraudulent insurance empire. In the 1960s Billie Sol Estes made away with funds in cotton allotments and nonexistent fertilizer.[45]

In 1970 the banking and insurance empire of Frank W. Sharp of Houston collapsed, leading to the "Sharpstown scandals" of 1971-1972. Securities and Exchange Commission investigations showed that Lt. Governor Ben Barnes had been involved with Sharp, who had pushed special banking bills through the legislature. The Speaker of the House, Gus F. Mutscher, Jr., was indicted and later convicted of accepting a bribe to help secure the passage of a bill for state insurance of bank deposits. Governor Preston Smith had made over $60,000 in Sharp stock, probably arranged to influence him, but had vetoed Sharp's bill and thus removed himself from the bribery suspect list. A state representative and an aid to Speaker Mutscher were also convicted. Although few were convicted and the court sentences were low, several state officials were defeated in the next election as a result of the Sharpstown scandals. Legislation regarding financing of elections and official ethical conduct was also passed.[46]

For several decades, Texas has housed the dictatorial rule of George B. Parr over a largely Latin American group in Duval County and the adjoining Jim Wells and Naeces counties. Just how Parr controls the area is not clear, but shifts in ballot votes indicate a very close control. He has served as county judge and as state senator and has become wealthy through oil and farming. He served one jail term.[47] In 1955 Judge C. Woodrow Laughlin, in spite of Parr's backing, was removed by the Texas Supreme Court for misconduct.[48]

There are recent reports that Southwestern Bell Telephone Company, in addition to its own private scandals, has been charged with using illegal means of influencing Texas regulatory bodies.[49]

West Virginia Democratic Governor William Wallace Barron was inaugurated in 1961. One of his primary opponents had charged an earlier attempted bribery; Barron did not look strong prior to the election. In 1952 he was appointed alcoholic beverage commissioner, was soon fired from that job, but was elected state attorney general in 1956. Early in 1961 Barron's close associate, Bonn Brown, and a friend, Al Schroath, established four dummy corporations—one in Ohio and three in Florida. These corporations received kickbacks from contractors who received state jobs on noncompetitive bases. Barron did not run for reelection. In February 1968 federal indictments were brought against him, three top members of his former administration, and two of his associates. The indictments were based on the use of interstate commerce facilities, the mail, and telephones to establish dummy corporations to facilitate bribery. All but Barron were found guilty, although he later paid the Internal Revenue Service a substantial tax on the proceeds of the dummy corporation. In November 1968 a Republican, Arch A. Moore, Jr., was elected governor largely because of his pledge to restore honesty and integrity to the government of West Virginia. A Purchasing Practices and Procedures Commission established by the 1968 legislature uncovered information which brought in 107 indictments against 11 corporations and 32 individuals, including 13 state officials (among whom were Barron and the state's new Republican purchasing director). All these indictments were invalidated by the Supreme Court on technical grounds. However, Barron was then convicted of bribing the jury foreman during his 1968 trial.[50]

Corruption in West Virginia has not been confined to the Democrats. Governor Arch A. Moore, the Republican who campaigned for honesty, was indicted by a U.S. Attorney in a Republican administration in 1976 but was acquitted

State Police

A special note about state police is needed since police corruption has been such a tremendous factor in local government. In *The Tarnished Badge,* Ralph Lee Smith notes that state police in general have had a higher morale than local police. They have less close relationships with people from whom temptation can come. Much of their work in highway patrolling is more impersonal than that of local police. They are usually more smartly equipped and uniformed, and frequently are better educated than local police. There is clearly less corruption.

However, corruption has reached state police forces. In 1962 it was discovered that in northern Illinois a general program of paying off state police for permission to overload trucks had been in effect since "around 1945."[51] Payoffs were made to all ranks up to captain. One careful state policeman left in his car a notebook showing payoffs from 90 firms. In one district alone, 40 of the 60 assigned police admitted receiving payoffs. All were suspended.

Another scandal was discovered in 1963. Tow truck operators were kicking back to state troopers a third to a half of the $15 charge for hauling damaged cars off the highway. Further, troopers were using state credit cards to pay for fuel or accessories for their private cars.

These scandals must be appraised in the light of Illinois's unfortunate reputation. As previously noted, Illinois has not attained the higher ethical level reached by state governments in the nearby states of Michigan, Wisconsin, Minnesota, or Iowa. Apparently the state police force was used for political patronage jobs until about 1950, and, as noted in the case of municipal corruption, the evil tradition carries on. It was also noted that these troubles came in well-defined areas, probably as a result of incompetent leadership in those areas. Salaries were also low—$5000 to $6000 a year.

A few New York state troopers have been involved in heroin scandals. One police lieutenant and three troopers were charged with organized crime connections in the late 1960s.

Michael Dorman's *Payoff* gives an account of a rather lethargic attitude of the Pennsylvania state police toward corrupt law enforcement in Reading, Pennsylvania. It was even reported that some state police were themselves accepting payoffs in about 1960.[52]

At least until recent times New Jersey state police seems to have been ineffective in resisting the intrusion of organized crime into that state.

There is a constructive side to state police forces. While a few troopers were involved in narcotics, the New York state police has consistently maintained a much better record on corruption than has New York City, Buffalo, Albany, or Syracuse. There are frequently cases in New York where no arrests are made by local forces because of racketeer pressure, but the state police have functioned in a competent manner.[53]

Approximately half of the states have state police forces. The others (except Hawaii) have state highway patrols. Collectively they have over 40,000 sworn officers—about twice the number of federal police personnel and one-sixth that of local personnel. Over half of the state forces are empowered to give some help to local police forces.[54] If the state police forces, with their relatively higher standards of honesty, could be so used, they could help raise the level of honesty of local law enforcement agencies.

Reformed States

In this century a number of states have made real progress and established traditions of administrative and, less frequently, legislative honesty. California's reform of 1911 under the progressive Republicans was permanent except for sporadic outbreaks of corruption in its legislature and an irresponsible attorney general elected in 1946. Wisconsin's reform under the leadership of Robert M.

La Follette was successful. New York's reform after the insurance investigations seems to have endured fairly well although a few departments have had troubles and the legislature has often had corruption. Virginia has had little dishonesty since Reconstruction, Vermont has been fairly continuously honest, and Michigan has done reasonably well since reforms in the 1930s. There has been little outright corruption in Utah state government since 1948 when Governor Maw had troubles in several departments. Nebraska, which had railroad control in the 1890s, now has had several decades of no machines and little corruption.

Neal R. Peirce, in an April 1975 article on state corruption, corroborates the rectitude of some of the states listed above.

It has been years since a major scandal rocked Wisconsin state government. Official corruption is virtually unknown in Vermont. Michigan, Minnesota, Virginia and South Carolina are exceedingly clean by national standards. Utah hasn't had a major corruption case since a mayor of Salt Lake City was jailed for misconduct several decades ago.

Even in California, the most heavily populated state, the amount of official corruption is amazingly small. By one count, the level of recent indictments in California is only one-tenth of that in New Jersey, a fifth of that in New York and Texas and a tiny fraction of the Illinois level.[55]

Peirce should have added that Utah had corruption in several state departments in 1948 and 1949. In most of these cases, the reform of state government has been led by individuals in business or the professions. Lawyers and newspapermen have certainly had an impact. These reforms have rarely, however, been the work of predominant business interests.

Reasons for Reform and Corruption

Why do states like Louisiana, Maryland, Massachusetts, and West Virginia have frequent outbursts of corruption which affect leaders of both parties, while states like California, Michigan, New York, Oregon, Utah, and Wisconsin remain relatively free of corruption at the state level?

The author agrees with Neal Peirce that healthy, balanced party competition provides one of the answers. There are real interparty battles in the better states. New York State, for example, has kept its government at a level above that of its cities, largely through party rivalry. Party rivalry has been said to be the reason for Nebraska's good record.

There have been strong reform movements in the better states. Perhaps the superior foresight of the leaders of these reforms is the key point. Progressives— headed by Hiram Johnson in California, Charles Evans Hughes in New York, Robert M. La Follette in Wisconsin, Harold Stassen in Minnesota, and a New Deal reformer like Frank Murphy in Michigan—have helped establish better standards, even though their respective parties did not remain in power. But why did Lowden in Illinois or Sam Jones in Louisiana fail to establish better standards in their states? Personal leadership is surely an important factor in bringing a state up or down.

Peirce also suggests that:

The honesty level is highest in states with a high level of personal morality— Yankee probity in Maine and Vermont, Mormon principles in Utah, the standards of an old aristocracy in Virginia and South Carolina.[56]

J. E. Lawrence of the *Lincoln Star* in 1949 attempted to attribute Nebraska's honesty to its agrarian economy.

... these forces have molded a smug, stubborn, conservative political philosophy which accepts established order when things go well but which breaks out in angry rebellion in times of desperation. They pay little for public service, demand and get a great deal in the form of honest handling of public affairs, especially in the expenditures of taxes.[57]

The author agrees with these comments but acknowledges the need for further exploration. How does a state attain a "high level of personality morality"? Chapters 11 and 14 will address this subject.

"The standards of an old aristocracy" in Virginia and South Carolina break down into largely ethnic factors. These states had much less European immigration in the nineteenth century than did the Northeast. Some of the leading families went into politics because it was the thing to do. They may not have been progressive, but they were honest. The Byrd machine, for example, ruled Virginia for several decades with almost no charges of corruption. Many of their poor people, i.e. the blacks, were taken out of politics by Jim Crow legislation.

An effort to systematize knowledge about political ethics in the American states is relevant here. Daniel Elazar in the early 1960s made a classification of states as "moralistic," i.e. (among other things), viewing public service as demanding higher moral obligations than other activities; "individualistic," i.e., government viewed as a part of the marketplace, a specialized business but with no special obligations; and "traditionalistic," i.e., a paternalistic and elitist conception of the Commonwealth with a positive but limited role in the community. Elazar traces these three cultures from New England, the Middle Atlantic states, and the Southern seaboard states; notes that immigration sometimes reenforces or changes the culture; and maps out the United States into his three cultures, including some hybrids.[58] Elazar's material has been adapted to table 7-1. Kevin Mulcahy and Richard Katz have noted several correlations in the states as classified by Elazar. The moralistic states had a higher percentage of voting in 1970; the traditionalistic states were lower. Persons were more likely to split tickets in the moralistic states. Politics in individualistic states is competitive and partisan. The greatest political activity is in the moralistic states.

Table 7-1
American States and Their Political Cultures

Moralistic	Individualistic	Traditionalistic
California	Alaska	Alabama
Colorado	Connecticut	Arizona
Idaho	Delaware	Arkansas
Iowa	Hawaii	Florida
Kansas	Illinois	Georgia
Maine	Indiana	Kentucky
Michigan	Maryland	Louisiana
Minnesota	Massachusetts	Mississippi
Montana	Nebraska	Missouri
New Hampshire	Nevada	New Mexico
North Dakota	New Jersey	North Carolina
Oregon	New York	Oklahoma
South Dakota	Ohio	South Carolina
Utah	Pennsylvania	Tennessee
Vermont	Rhode Island	Texas
Washington	Wyoming	Virginia
Wisconsin		West Virginia
Total = 17	Total = 16	Total = 17

Elazar and Mulcahy would almost certainly agree that the character of these political cultures may vary rapidly, as people move to other areas. One phase of economic development has had profound effect on a state like Alaska. So we can hardly expect to extrapolate an understanding of the reasons for corruption from this culture analysis alone.

Nevertheless, there are one or two interesting relationships. None of the states which Peirce or the author classify as chronically corrupt are listed in Elazar's early 1960 list of moralistic states. However, several of the moralistic states have had chronic corruption in the past (perhaps at a time when "moralism" was less firmly rooted). California and Montana had continued corruption up to 1910 and 1925, respectively. Colorado, New Hampshire, Washington, and Wisconsin have had at least sporadic instances of corrupt behavior.

The author would classify 13 states as being sporadically but substantially corrupt (with large agreement from Peirce): Alaska, Florida, Illinois, Louisiana, Maryland, Massachusetts, Nevada, New Jersey, Oklahoma, Rhode Island, Texas, and West Virginia. Elazar's individualistic group includes 6 of these: Alaska, Maryland, Massachusetts, Nevada, New Jersey, and Rhode Island. His traditionalistic category includes the other 7. No moralistic states are on the list. A conclusion which may be drawn from this comparison of our studies with Elazar's is that the "moralistic" political cultures provide an infertile climate for the development of corrruption. The "traditionalistic" and "individualistic" cultures seem to be equally vulnerable to corruption. It is perhaps reasonable that the states in which the population is trying to accomplish some objective through government, are more likely to find leadership against perversion of government.

However, the proof of this point is rather theoretical. Further observation can be enlightening.

The author views a healthy administrative tradition as one of the surest means of escape from corruption. California's civil service tradition, which goes back to the progressive reforms of 1911, has more than once been helpful in overcoming would-be corruptive forces in Sacramento. New York State's administration has helped keep that government above the level of its principal cities and of surrounding states. The excellent administrative tradition of Wisconsin has certainly helped that state.

Programs for Reform

It is hard to predict what will bring our states, or the rest of American government, up to a reasonable level of honesty. Later chapters of this book will suggest specific methods of reducing corruption. This section will supplement the discussion by listing the Common Cause packet of campaign cost controls, the development of better administration, the sharpening of law enforcement methods, and the cultivation of popular pressures for honesty.

Many states have passed conflict-of-interest and financial disclosure legislation, mostly as a result of Common Cause and Watergate (although conflict of interest was only remotely connected with Watergate). Twenty-six states had established laws governing some possibilities of conflict of interest; at least 33 states adopted new legislation or amended old statutes from 1972 to 1975.[59] As of 1975, 42 states had adopted major ethics legislation, and 37 of them applied the laws to legislators. Such laws forbid officials' taking public action involving conflict of personal interest, and require publication or filing of statements of the officials' own assets and income.

The effectiveness of these laws is still far from certain. A score of the states have created commissions or boards to enforce these laws; however, some of these commissions cannot be expected to function actively. Disclosure statutes or codes of ethics may not have much impact on the type of financially serious corruption which accompanies organized crime. It is also possible that disclosure statutes will keep some wealthy people from entering politics so that they may protect the confidentiality of their personal finances, thus strengthening one-party control of state legislatures and decreasing the possibility of investigation of corrupt groups. Clearly, further studies of the new legislation are required.

Seventeen states have extended this legislation to cover local government. Again, it is not possible to judge the effectiveness of such statutes. If properly enforced, they might help reduce local corruption significantly.

There undoubtedly has been progress in a number of the better-run states where good administrative capacity is developing. California, Wisconsin, Michigan,

Oregon, and Washington are probably examples. The federal government has aided this progress to a certain extent with audits of grants made to state or local governments, but has displayed no concern for the administrative capacity of state governments as a whole or of the vitally important law enforcement (except in individual prosecutions).

Control of corruption requires effective law enforcement, and state governments generally have been weak in law enforcement both for themselves and for their local units. Unlike other modern democratic federal systems (West Germany, Australia, Canada), state governments have no officer responsible for law enforcement. States have largely ignored repeated recommendations by outside commissions that they strengthen themselves in law enforcement. Only half have state police forces; the others are limited to highway patrols. Attorneys general often do not have power to investigate local law enforcement inequalities. In addition, help to local prosecutors is sporadic.

The courts, which are usually state-established, are often inadequate. Their procedures are painfully slow, far slower than in any other modern democracy.

States give some help to training local police, chiefly with federal LEAA funds. But training programs are almost everywhere too brief and inadequate. State governments often give technical services such as crime laboratories and fingerprint or automobile license identification, but again largely with LEAA funds. Almost no states have a major program to keep local police forces honest.

State help to local prosecutors is quite spotty and sporadic. Almost all county prosecutors are elected; frequently they are attorneys with no law enforcement background. In many small counties there is only one prosecuting attorney; sometimes he or she is not full-time. State attorneys generally may intervene in local prosecutions under various conditions, but little of this is done in most states. Rural areas of many states are wide open to the organized crime type of corruption; no local official has the ability or staff to investigate and prosecute such corrupters.

The federal government's individual prosecutions of corrupt state and local officials is to be commended, but Washington needs to do more to ensure honesty at the lower levels of government. Chapter 12 suggests some formalization of existing grants for law enforcement agents. If the federal government makes such a requirement, it can be anticipated that most of the states would establish machinery for auditing the honesty of local units of government.

Conclusions

In this century, state corruption became more sporadic than local corruption. No state machine has gripped its state as the Southern Pacific machine did California or the Cameron-Quay-Penrose group did Pennsylvania in the nineteenth century. But the fact that over a quarter of the states have had ongoing spasms of corruption and a much larger number have had some corruption tells us that the Age of Reform (1900-1914) missed many capitals. Florida, Illinois, Louisiana, Maryland, Massachusetts, Montana, Nevada, New Jersey, Ohio, Oklahoma, Texas, and West Virginia may have been among the worst. Review in connection with federal grants has enforced more honesty in some states. Since state functions are limited, more of state corruption has come from business. Some state police forces (far less than municipal) have gone astray. The existence of several really honest states, like California, New York, Wisconsin, Vermont, Utah, Virginia, and South Carolina, seem to show that honest government is possible at this level. But it is not clear why there are great moral differences between state governments. The passage of Common Cause-type legislation against conflict of interest in many states has been a good sign, but there is not yet much evidence of the effectiveness of these laws.

The greatest sin of the states is the failure of most of them to try to ensure honesty and efficiency in the local governments which they control legally and financially.

8

Federal Corruption from World War I to 1969

This chapter on problems of corruption in the federal government in the last half-century is divided into four sections, each of which discusses varying areas of government with vastly different problems. One is the Congress, in which reasonable representation of economic interests sometimes overlaps or appears to overlap situations of undue pressure by such interests; this results in a confused Congress which has moved very slowly in setting ethical standards for itself but has been useful in investigating ethical delinquences in the administrative branch. A second section deals with the federal administration in which a difficulty appears to have been misguided Presidential support of corrupt subordinates. A special section on organized crime is appended since it has had so much influence on corruption in state and local government. A third group of problems arises in the administrative tribunals which sometimes appear to take on the viewpoint of the industry they are regulating. A fourth section deals with the judiciary. The reader is reminded that the complex of charges called "Watergate" is omitted. While these events are of special importance, they are an aberration from the mainstream of American corruption and have been discussed in an avalanche of publications.

The federal government has had corruption, but much less than some state and local governments. However, contrary to what many of its critics suggest, it should be noted that the federal government since World War I has *not* proved to be an example of major corruption. Its actions are simply much more publicized than those of state and local governments. It is true that the federal government has very great administrative problems, and is probably trying to do more things than any one government can do.

Congress

During the period under discussion, Congress has had no major widespread scandal like that of Credit Mobilier in the 1870s. It has, however, been plagued with a series of ongoing incidents of actual dishonesty, with serious ethical problems regarding campaign support and with a lack of concern about the unethical conduct of individual members. Although Congress has shown a deep and healthy concern over the honesty of federal administrators in both investigations and legislation, its concern over the standards of conduct of its own members had been low. The net result is that congressional standards of ethics are probably below those of the federal administration.

The biggest ethical problem of Congress is to sort out the difference between legitimate representation of the economic or political interests of the legislator's area or the nation and the selfish representation of a congressman's or senator's own interest. For many years Senator "Cotton Ed" Smith of Mississippi voted and worked hard for cotton price support, which a majority of Mississippians undoubtedly wanted but which also was of very real financial value to Senator Smith personally. The vote and the work were probably not unethical but could easily have become so. Had a majority of his constituents and his own view of public policy shifted to support lower price subvention for cotton, then the Senator's work and vote would have become unethical. It would clearly be impossible to ban all votes on matters in which a legislator has a personal economic interest. How could any legislator vote on banking or retail sales problems if there were a ban on all interested votes? How could former labor union officials in Congress, whose only career possibility in the event of defeat is a return to union work, not vote on labor legislation as their union constituents want them to vote? Edmund Beard and Stephen Horn quote the late Senator Robert Kerr: "If everyone abstained from voting on grounds of personal interest, I doubt if you could get a quorum in the United States Senate on any subject."[1]

A position as delicate as Senator Smith's was presented by Senator George Smathers of Florida. As a member of the Senate Commerce Committee, he played an important role in rewriting the Transportation Act of 1958, which had provisions desirable to the Seaboard Coast Line Railroad, which in turn was paying very substantial fees to Smather's Miami law firm. He also put an amendment in the 1961 tax bill eliminating an excise tax on railroad, airline, and bus tickets, again benefiting Seaboard and another client, Pan American Airways. Smathers may have had sincere convictions on these votes, but he was certainly guilty of conflict of interest. Similarly, Senator John W. Bricker of Ohio drew his salary from a law firm which received substantial fees from the Pennsylvania Railroad, while stalling off the St. Lawrence Waterway which the railroad did not want.[2]

Congressmen themselves have a variety of reactions to the conflict-of-interest problem, according to a study by Beard and Horn. This study suggests that it is customary to vote for personal interests which coincide with constituent interests. It acknowledges the reasons why outside interests are necessary for a legislator—chiefly as a means of support in the event of defeat. It recognizes the uniquely delicate position of maintaining outside law practice, which at least a quarter of congressmen did at that time. Often the conflict of time is more important than that of interest. The 1977 pay raise and new ethics legislation may eliminate all such law practice.

Bribery is, of course, a form of conflict of interest which most congressmen disapprove. However, congressmen are much more divided about the ethics of receiving honoraria for lectures or speeches from a group which has legislative interests. They disapprove of diversion of campaign funds to personal purposes, but up to 1977 they have not been greatly concerned about lobbyists paying entertainment costs, leasing or selling automobiles at a discount, or furnishing free transport on private planes or free trips around the work "junketing." In general, they believed national standards of legislators to be higher than state standards.

It will be seen in a later section of this chapter that it has been possible to legislate with at least partial effectiveness against many varieties of conflict of interest (bribery, postgovernment employment, benefiting one's own company) in the administrative service of the government. For the reasons mentioned above, statutes against conflict of interest by members of Congress are weak. Members of Congress are forbidden to accept bribes, to receive compensation for services to the government, and to present cases before the court of claims.[3] But until 1977 there was no more general provision against conflict of interest.

A major suggestion has been that of disclosure of interest. If members of Congress in voting (or perhaps speaking) for or against a measure were required to publish how the vote or speech affects their personal economic interest, more careful and statesmanlike votes would result. So goes the theory, but Congress has accepted only a small part of it.

Although requiring disclosure of assets (usually to the Secretary of the department) by higher-paid government administrators, Congress has been very slow to require disclosure of its own members. Public listing of all assets, which would enable the voter to judge a legislator's vote, would also enable attack by anyone who disliked a business in which a legislator had a share. Complete publicity might even keep able candidates out of politics. It will take time to find out how valid this argument is.

In 1977, under heavy pressure induced by Common Cause and even more by concern about public reactions to a large salary raise, each house passed stricter codes of ethics. The House code required all members and principal staff to prepare for publication lists of income, financial holdings over $1000, liabilities in excess of $2500 and security and real estate transactions over $1000. Gifts of over $100 from any lobby or lobbyist or foreign national or agent are prohibited. Unofficial office accounts are prohibited. Franked mass mailings are prohibited in a period 60 days before an election in which the member is a candidate. Outside earned income may not exceed 15 percent of a member's salary, and an honorarium may not exceed $750. The Senate code is similar; but in addition it prohibits ex-senators from lobbying until one year after retirement from the Senate, forbids race or religion or sex or handicap discrimination in employment of staff, prohibits employees from personal services for senators and from substantial campaign activities.

Representative J. Parnell Thomas of New Jersey was convicted in 1949 of forcing employees to endorse government paychecks over to his secretary (for his own pocketing). He resigned in 1950 and hence had no postconviction disciplinary action. Representative Walter Brehm of Ohio was convicted of receiving salary kickbacks in 1951, with no disciplinary action by the House.

Representative John M. Coffee (Washington) was alleged to have received a campaign contribution of $2500 for exerting pressure to secure a contract for constituents. The committee which exposed this did not recommend condemnation. Representative Eugene Cox (Georgia) accepted a $2500 retainer fee from a broadcasting corporation in apparent violation of a conflict-of-interest law as a result of a Federal Communications Commission revelation. He secured appointment of himself as chairman of a select committee to investigate the FCC, and he was not prosecuted.

A few congressmen are incorrigibly wrong. Representative Andrew Jackson May of Kentucky, as chairman of the House Committee on Military Affairs, did all sorts of wrong things during and just after World War II. He intervened with the War Department to get a man released after six weeks of service, to bring a friend's son back from the Pacific, to influence a court martial, to get war contracts for his friends, and to influence the renegotiation of contracts. He was convicted of bribery and conspiracy and sentenced to prison, but was not disciplined by the House. He was defeated for reelection in spite of pleas of major leaders of his party.

In a few cases, a part of Congress displayed some concern about one of its members. Senator Theodore G. Bilbo of Mississippi was found guilty of accepting expensive gifts from war contractors, and he was not seated at the opening of Congress. He died in 1947. Representative Adam Clayton Powell was ousted for misspending public funds.[4]

Senator Joseph R. McCarthy of Wisconsin was censured by a partly partisan vote of the Senate in 1954 because of his noncooperation and abuse of persons appearing before Senate committees and subcommittees. The fact that he had received $10,000 from a corporation under the jurisdiction of a committee on which he served was largely ignored.

Another example, discussed more fully in Chapter 14, is that of Senator Thomas J. Dodd, who was censured by the Senate, and subsequently defeated for reelection, because he took loans from absentee members of his staff, used "political contributions" for personal purposes, and accepted gifts and travel funds from economic interests which he had a possible responsibility for investigating.[5] A senator lost his seat at the 1968 election, at least in part because of conflict of interest. Senator Edward D. Long of Missouri received large "referral fees" from a Teamster's Union lawyer, while his subcommttee was conducting wiretap investigations which could have been beneficial to James R. Hoffa.[6] Shortly after a May 9, 1967, hearing, *Life* published an article which revealed that Senator Edward Long had used his committee (investigating electronic eavesdropping) in behalf of Hoffa. The article claimed that Long received thousands of dollars from Hoffa's chief counsel, Morris Shenker. It later developed that the amount was over $100,000 and that Edward Long had not practiced law during the time of payments.[7]

This lack of concern by Congress for the moral standard of its own members is quite contradictory to practice elsewhere. It is true that in some of the American cases the constituency has refused to reelect a guilty person. In other cases the constituency has reelected such people after congressional action, which leads to a natural doubt as to whether the American people want strictly legal and moral persons in public office. The whole shoddy business seems to reflect a low national standard of public morality. There can be little doubt that all the transgressors cited above would have been asked to resign from the British Parliament.

Another bad practice of a few congressmen has been the working with "fixers" for a price. Robert N. Winter-Berger's *The Washington Payoff* (Dell Books, 1972) tells of a "fixer," Nathaniel Voloshen, who worked for a number of years out of the office of Speaker John W. McCormack. According to the book, Voloshen paid McCormack $2500 a month for the privilege of using the Speaker's office. If a business received an unfavorable ruling from a federal agency and lured Voloshen as its "fixer," he would clear the matter quickly with the Speaker and then contact the federal agency as if he were representing the Speaker. Federal bureaus and commissions pay great attention to influential members of Congress who may have profound effect on their legislative status; so it was often easy for Voloshen and the company's attorney to secure a more favorable ruling. The company paid a substantial fee, sometimes $25,000 or $50,000, to Voloshen, who split the fee with the Speaker and perhaps one or two others. Again, according to the book, the Speaker would route some of the contribution to his campaign fund, and some to more personal uses.

An equally bad example of influence peddling was that of Bobby Baker, secretary to the majority leader of the Senate when Lyndon Johnson was majority floor leader. The story of Baker's activities is clearly outlined by Clark Moellenhoff in *Despoilers of Democracy* (Doubleday and Company, Garden City, 1965). Baker accumulated over $2 million largely trading on the influence of leading senators or his influence on them. With collaborators he entered into a series of business enterprises, most of which prospered because of governmental favors or the promise of governmental favors. His vending company secured contracts to operate at North American Aviation. Some Baker dealings involved Las Vegas gambling figures. Baker probably secured a $35,000 overpayment on a performance bond on the District of Columbia stadium, an overpayment made by a Democratic contractor. Baker used constitutional immunity to refuse to answer questions about these and similar activities. Senator Johnson's office entered into some of these transactions. Some Republicans still believe that certain senators showed a heavy partisan bias, failing to push the investigation of President Johnson's affairs but pushing the investigation of President Nixon's affairs. It should be noted that different types and orders of criminality were involved.

Not all such influence peddling is connected with Congress. The "Ohio gang" in Harding's administration sold their presumed status with President Harding or Attorney General Daugherty. The "five percenters" in the Truman administration used both congressional and administrative contacts; some companies found them essential to securing Reconstruction Finance Corporation loans.

Such influence peddling is probably not available to a majority of congressmen. It may start as a legal transaction, but it easily slips over into illegality. The Voloshen and Bobby Baker stories are striking examples of misuse of congressional power.

Congressional Investigations

Before a review is undertaken of the record of congressional investigations in control of corruption, a few general remarks should be made about the process of inquiry by congressional committees.

Such inquiry is, of course, essential to the effective operation of our system of separation of powers. Congress must have power to find out what is necessary for legislative action. If it had to rely on the administrative departments for all information, the opportunities for deceiving Congress and the public would be greatly increased. Several of the problems of corruption discussed here simply would not have been known if congressional committees had not conducted inquiries. The revealings of the Harding oil scandals, the operations of organized crime in labor and management, and the problems of Internal Revenue in the Truman administration, are all examples of congressional initiative. Even if the main result is only publicizing a problem which some people had known about but most had been ignoring, the job is worthwhile. Every effort should be made to improve and strengthen the congressional investigation process.

However, there are important drawbacks to the process. Congressmen are busy people, and hearings are often conducted by a very few members of a committee or subcommittee—a fact of which Senator Joseph McCarthy took advantage when conducting individual subcommittee hearings where he often abused the witnesses. If a chairman is not effective or has not secured competent staff assistance, the committee's hearings may soon become fruitless, as was the case with Senator Wheeler's hearings on the Attorney General's office in 1924 or the Senate's investigation of the Bureau of Internal Revenue in 1926. Congressional committees are made up of members who belong to political parties, and sometimes a majority does not commence or continue a hearing because it may be politically embarrassing. The Senate Rules Committee's abrupt halt of hearings on the Bobby Baker case in 1964 is a frequently cited example.

As far as the administrative departments are concerned, a major problem of congressional inquiry is the number and overlapping of congressional committees. Committee chairmen, prodded by a union or a disgruntled employee, may demand volumes of materials and conduct lengthy hearings on matters which are far removed from their normal legislative jurisdiction. Cabinet members or bureau chiefs may find a large proportion of their time spent in preparing evidence and giving testimony at hearings before a half-dozen or more separate committees. There are, of course, cases where Congress should investigate and does nothing.

In spite of these difficulties, the student of political corruption is grateful for the many congressional hearings in the period since World War II. In 1923 the Senate Public Lands Committee, with Senator Thomas J. Walsh of Montana acting as chief inquirer, ploughed through mazes of technicalities on oil leases without much result. But information came to Walsh that former Secretary of the Interior Albert Fall's ranch in New Mexico had been improved and extended at considerable cost in late 1921. Then other witnesses came in, and the Teapot Dome and Elk Hills scandals were blown wide open. The Senate committee had discovered things which an administrative investigation might well have hushed up. However, investigations leading to court prosecution and some convictions were conducted by special prosecutors appointed by the President and confirmed by the Senate.

In contrast to Senator Walsh's success, Senator Burton K. Wheeler (also of Montana) was not very successful as chief prosecutor on a Senate special committee investigating Attorney General Harry M. Daugherty's affairs in 1924. The committee's hearings did force Daugherty's resignation but only because Daugherty illegally (and vainly) used Justice Department facilities to harass and block the investigation. Reaction against these foolish and illegal efforts led President Coolidge to request Daugherty's resignation.[8] Daugherty was later prosecuted, but charges were dropped after two hung juries.

The Senate Select Committee on Investigation of the Veterans' Bureau initiated an investigation of the Veterans' Bureau in 1923. President Harding, knowing that there was corruption, had previously secured the resignation of Director Charles R. Forbes but had taken no other action. Shortly after the Senate inquiry began, Charles F. Cramer (the general counsel of the bureau and a close friend and collaborator of Forbes) committed suicide. The Senate committee developed clear evidence that Forbes had made arrangements to secure one-third of the profit from construction of veterans' hospitals for himself. He also arranged to receive large sums on grossly overvalued land bought by the government for hospitals. In addition, he sold government supplies at a low percentage of costs for which he received kickbacks. Forbes was tried in 1924; he received a 2-year jail sentence and a $10,000 fine.

Congressional investigations of corruption in the Hoover and Roosevelt administrations tended to sputter out rapidly—generally for lack of real evidence of lawbreaking. One exception was the Senate campaign expenditures committee, chaired by Senator Morris Sheppard of Texas, which did find evidence in three states of pressure on WPA workers for political purposes. The Congress, without executive leadership, did pass legislation to attempt to prevent this practice.

In 1941 Congress established a special committee to oversee the defense program. This committee was chaired by Senator Harry Truman until he resigned to run for Vice President in 1944. It uncovered evidence of fraud in defense businesses but little government corruption. Two exceptions were evidence regarding Representative Andrew J. May's connection with a munitions manufacturer and Brigadier General Bennett E. Myers, who drew simultaneous salaries as an Army-Air Force officer and as administrator of a defense subcontractor. May was defeated for reelection, and Myers was sent to prison.

As we have already noted, congressional investigation played an important role in the Truman administration. Senator Clyde R. Hoey's committee produced a perjury conviction of John Maragon and severe criticism of General Harry H. Vaughan of the White House staff and other influence peddlers. The President did not respond constructively.

Another Senate subcommittee, headed by Senator J. William Fulbright of Arkansas, investigated political favoritism in awarding Reconstruction Finance Corporation loans and found many important problems. These investigations were resisted by the President, but they forced reorganization of the RFC and ultimately its abolition.

Also in the Truman administration widespread corruption in the Bureau of Internal Revenue was discovered, first by the efforts of an individual senator, John J. Williams (Republican of Delaware), and later by a subcommittee of the House Ways and Means, chaired by Representative Cecil R. King, Democrat of California. The investigations resulted in the removal of 9 of the 64 district collectors of Internal Revenue, the firing or forced resignations of 166 Internal Revenue officials, several convictions, and finally a reorganization of the bureau. Much of the investigation was conducted without great administrative cooperation.

A subcommittee of the House Committee on the Judiciary, chaired first by Representative Frank L. Chelf (Democrat of Kentucky), reported highly unsatisfactory conditions in the Department of Justice. One example stated: "... the Government has actually recovered much more in voluntary refunds from contractors who were merely overpaid, than the Department of Justice has succeeded in collecting in a vastly larger number of cases where the Government had absolute rights to recovery against contractors who had defrauded it."[9]

A special three-man panel of the Anti-Trust and Monopoly Subcommittee on the Senate Judiciary Committee helped develop public knowledge of the conflict of interest of Adolphe Wenzell, vice president and director of First Boston Corporation and unpaid consultant to the Bureau of the Budget in the Eisenhower administration. President Eisenhower did not follow the conflict question aggressively. The House Special Subcommittee on Legislative Oversight in 1958 developed the facts about Sherman Adams's acceptance of gifts from Bernard

Goldfine, whom he had introduced to the Federal Trade Commission chairman. The President defended Adams, but did accept his resignation.

In the Kennedy administration, two congressional subcommittee hearings found serious defects in the Department of Agriculture in its inquiry into the Billie Sol Estes scandals. The Permanent Subcommittee on Investigations arrived at no effective conclusions on the selection of the company to build the TFX, or the possible conflict of interest of Deputy Secretary of Defense Roswell Gilpatric, but it did uncover evidence of conflict leading to the resignation of Secretary of the Navy Fred Korth.

Much investigation in the Johnson administration centered on the White House staff and the President's career in Congress prior to the Presidency. Fortunately for Johnson, his party's large majorities in Congress and acquaintanceship built up by his own congressional career resulted in Congress's "taking it easy." The unhappy affairs of Bobby Baker, appointed Secretary of the Senate under the majority leadership of Lyndon Johnson, were uncovered largely by senatorial investigation. This was one of the cases in which party bias probably kept a committee investigation from going as deeply as it could have gone. In later years, Republicans were especially unhappy about Senator Sam Erwin of North Carolina, who voted against pressing the investigation of Bobby Baker in a way which might damage President Johnson but voted for investigating Watergate in a way which might damage President Nixon.[10]

In a later section of this chapter dealing with federal administrative tribunals is an account of a House commerce subcommittee investigation of tribunals which was sabotaged by the subcommittee members.

Congressional investigations frequently have political overtones. Insofar as the purpose of the party system is for the "outs" to watch the "ins," this partisan bias is valuable. In all fairness, Republican-majority Congresses did investigate the Harding scandals, and Democratic-majority Congresses did investigate some of the Truman scandals. But a greater degree of zeal for good government in spite of party loyalties would be helpful.

The general record of Congress's investigating corruption since World War II has been fairly good. Senate and House committees have explored matters which the White House or the executive department probably would not have explored. One can regret the omissions but be glad for the achievements.

Corruption in the Administration

During the period under discussion there have been two major outbreaks of corruption—one under President Harding (1921-1923) and the other under President Truman (1945-1953)—about which there has been so much discussion that each will be given separate treatment. Then there will be a section on certain types of ongoing breaking of laws, regulation, or ethical standards, which seem to appear in every administration.

World War I

Woodrow Wilson did not succeed in getting through World War I without some corruption. One of the worst examples resulted in the nation's failure to build airplanes, while the executive in charge of producing them was making money from government purchase of lands and letting contracts to firms in which his partners and his wife were concerned.[11]

Harding Administration Scandals. Corruption in the Harding administration was the most widely publicized since the Grant administration, and for various reasons the Harding scandals were perhaps the best publicized in American history, until Watergate. However, it was probably no larger than (if as great as) that in the Truman administration; but unlike the other, it involved one Cabinet member directly and two indirectly. It also was a major point of debate in two presidential campaigns (1924 and 1928).

Most publicized of all the Harding scandals was that in which Secretary of the Interior Albert Fall (in office March 4, 1921, to March 17, 1923) leased on favorable terms Naval Reserve oil fields, located in Elk Hills, California, and Teapot Dome, in Wyoming, to companies largely owned by oil millionaires Edward Doheny and Harry Sinclair. After Fall's resignation, senatorial investigation disclosed that he had received gifts or loans totaling over $400,000 from Doheny and Sinclair. Fall was convicted of bribery in 1928 and served 9 months in jail. Doheny and Sinclair were both acquitted in spite of overwhelming evidence of guilt. President Coolidge appointed as special prosecutors two distinguished attorneys, one Republican and one Democrat, who succeeded in having the leases canceled, though they were less successful in securing convictions.

Less publicized than the oil leases, but costing the government more money, was the large-scale corruption in the Veterans' Bureau under Col. Charles R. Forbes, who lacked both the character and the administrative capacity for handling this large, new agency. Forbes had been at one time an army deserter, but served well in World War I where he won a Congressional Medal of Honor. Forbes sold millions of dollars of government property to selected contractors on highly unfavorable terms for the government. He apparently also bought property on terms unfavorable for the government. The extent of the kickbacks he received is not known, but some evidence was substantial enough to send Forbes to Leavenworth.[12]

Another particularly bad spot of the Harding administration was the Prohibition Enforcement Bureau. Harding, publicly dry, continued to drink himself.[13] His "Ohio gang" friends made whoopee with confiscated liquor at the "Little Green House on K Street." The Prohibition Bureau was located in the Treasury Department, exempted from civil service, and placed under Commissioner Roy A. Haynes, former mayor of a small Ohio city, who was selected by Wayne Wheeler of the Anti-Saloon League. Close control of the bureau by "drys" did not result in high-quality enforcement.[14]

Corruption in Prohibition enforcement cannot properly be assigned only to the Harding administration. It began in the Wilson administration, developed in the Harding administration, continued in the Coolidge administration, was brought under some control under Hoover when it was shifted from Treasury to Justice, and of course went out with Prohibition in the first year of the Roosevelt administration. It is relatively unusual for a federal bureau to remain so corrupt so long. The responsibility for this unhappy state of affairs lies partly in the unenforceable nature of Prohibition, partly in the administrative weaknesses of a sick Wilson and a weak Harding, and partly in the corruptness of state and local law enforcement agencies which, especially in the Northeastern cities, did little to help enforce Prohibition in spite of numerous state enforcement acts and were themselves easily corrupted. Congress also must receive some blame for its action in requiring senatorial confirmation of all appointments above $5000, which meant that almost all Prohibition administrators were political appointees.

Witnesses for the Wickersham commission testified that at least half the personnel of the Prohibition Bureau were incompetents and crooks. In Chicago, within three days of the Volstead Act's effectiveness, three federal agents were arraigned—two for taking a bootlegger's bribe and one for selling confiscated liquor.[15] In December 1921 the New York office fired 100 agents. In the decade, 1587 of the 17,816 persons who worked for the Bureau were dismissed for cause. Most of the causes involved corrupt activity. There were, of course, many other agents whose acceptance of bribes or indulgence in other corrupt activities was not discovered.

Because of the support of Wayne B. Wheeler of the Anti-Saloon League, Harding appointed Roy Asa Haynes—a Republican politician, Methodist, and "dry," but a weak administrator—to the directorship of the bureau. Haynes, until his dismissal in 1927, issued reassuring reports while Prohibition enforcement grew weaker. Agents accused of venality included the Chicago director in 1923, the Ohio director in 1925, the former administrator of Buffalo in 1927, the deputy administrator of Fayetteville, North Carolina, and the former chief of the New York druggist permits. The type of men employed in the bureau was generally scorned. Lack of civil service and low salaries contributed to the poor morale.

Nor was the corruption all with the agents. Bootleggers arrested in New York and Chicago were quite likely to be released by the courts (including federal courts) and often not to be prosecuted very hard by the attorneys. The courts themselves were swamped by the number of bootlegging cases.

A major bootlegger was George Remus of Cincinnati. He operated largely on the basis of withdrawal permits (a legal means of withdrawing liquor from bonded warehouses) bought from Jess Smith, famous unofficial "fixer" of the Harding administration. He bought the Jack Daniel's distillery in St. Louis, piping the whiskey directly to waiting trucks. He was well on his way to control of a third of the nation's bonded whiskey when he was arrested, convicted, and sent to Atlanta, in spite of further bribes to Jess Smith.

The Treasury intelligence division was never corrupted as was the Prohibition Bureau and was responsible for some notable law enforcement triumphs.

Another group of scandals centered on the Department of Justice. Jess Smith—a nonofficial friend of Attorney General Daugherty from Washington Court House, Ohio—along with Howard Mannington of Urbana, Ohio, and Fred A. Casley of Marietta, Ohio, ran the "Little Green House on K Street" where shady politicians were welcome guests, and accepted substantial sums of money for promises to see that persons were not effectively prosecuted. The example cited most often is that of George L. Remus, mentioned above, who claimed that he furnished Smith $250,000 to avoid prosecution, but was sent to Atlanta anyway. Gaston Means, an FBI agent until Attorney General Daugherty discharged and prosecuted him for conspiracy and bootlegging, also took substantial bribes. In spite of a Senate committee investigation, which led to President Coolidge's requirement of Daugherty's resignation in March 1924, clear evidence of Daugherty's participation in bribery or fraud was not secured. However, he was far more deserving of sharp criticism for using the Department of Justice staff in an effort to obstruct and discredit the Senate investigating committee.

Thomas W. Miller—a lawyer of good standing, Yale graduate, Episcopalian, a member of leading Philadelphia clubs—was Harding's Alien Property Custodian, responsible for handling German property taken over in World War I. He paid off a German claim for several million dollars and received $49,000 worth of bonds for his action.[16]

It is only fair to add that other parts of the Harding administration were quite honestly run. No major corruption charges were brought against Secretary of Commerce Herbert Hoover, Secretary of State Charles Evan Hughes, Secretary of War Weeks, Secretary of the Treasury Andrew Mellon (except the Prohibition division, which was actually run by the Anti-Saloon League and the White House). Secretary of the Navy Edwin Denby was forced to resign because he had cosigned Fall's oil leases, but no one seriously accused him of corrupt practices. On the plus side, it was during the Harding administration that the Budget Bureau and General Accounting Officer were established.

The scandals were large enough and reached high enough in the government to become a major source of political controversy. The Democratic party used the issues substantially in both the 1924 and the 1928 Presidential campaigns, without overwhelming success, but perhaps with more success in congressional campaigns. The political usefulness of the Harding scandals to the Democrats was limited by two facts. The law firm of one of their principal 1924 candidates, former Secretary of the Treasury William G. McAdoo, had received substantial fees from Edward L. Doheny, and McAdoo himself had represented clients before the Treasury Department while the Wilson administration was still in power. The 1928 Democratic candidate, Governor Aldred E. Smith, was handicapped by his Tammany Hall connections when he attempted to use the corruption issue.

In spite of these handicaps, however, Democrats and insurgent Republicans talked enough about the Harding scandals to make future Presidents more careful about corruption.

In examining corruption in the Harding administration, the motivations of some of the principal participants, including the responsible President, become apparent. There is no real evidence that Harding went out to seek money for himself or, indeed, that he was fully aware of the corruption which transpired under him, except for that which had been discovered in the Veterans' Bureau, prior to his death. There are two major criticisms to be leveled at Harding. One is his inability to come to grips with his own mental distress, especially after the suicides of Charles Cramer and Jess Smith.[17] But the greater criticism is that he had no real understanding of the responsibilities of high federal offices or of the caliber of men needed to meet those responsibilities. He appointed Forbes head of the important new Veterans' Bureau, with no real knowledge of Forbes's background, and kept Forbes after a number of people had told him that the bureau was being badly handled. He made Daugherty his Attorney General, although nothing in Daugherty's background indicated capacity for that important post. He made his brother-in-law, Herbert H. Votaw (an ex-missionary), Superintendent of Prisons, which Votaw knew little about. He let the Anti-Saloon League and the Republican party mechanism fill the new Prohibition Bureau with incompetents. His ineptitude effectively paved the way for the corruption in his administration, even if he was not corrupt himself. His other weakness was, of course, the hypocrisy of his positon as a political supporter of Prohibition while privately remaining a heavy drinker.

Judgment of Harding is handicapped by the fact that his death in 1923 eliminated the possibility that he may have initiated reform measures. He did learn something of Colonel Forbes's corruption in the Veterans' Bureau and promptly fired the Colonel, but he took no steps for prosecution or investigation. Harding had apparently heard of Jess Smith's money making as an "in-betweener," and told Daugherty that Smith should be dropped from the Presidential party to Alaska and should leave Washington—this latter, plus Daugherty's own criticisms, resulting in Smith's suicide. But the other scandals probably had not come to President Harding's attention before his death. He did know that some of the most respected leaders of his party thought the appointment and continuation in office of Attorney General Daugherty were a mistake, but he ignored their advice.

Moving from the President down to the guilty officials, there are differing remarks about motives. Daugherty seems to have been moved more by political ambition than by desire for money. For three years he managed to keep himself in a position well above his abilities. His major faults were the abuse of the power of his office and a tendency, natural enough for a former participant in Ohio politics of his time, to surround himself with men of ability well below that needed for the job. One of the unhappy consequences of appointing a man like Daugherty to a job well above his capacity is that he in turn will probably make similar poor appointments.

Jess Smith was a person of low ethical standards who never should have been brought to Washington, as Harding finally recognized. His friendships with the President and the Attorney General seem to have gone to his head.[18]

Albert Fall was a bright man, whose chief handicap was that he accepted the job of running a government department in whose purpose he did not believe. He was a Westerner who believed in the development of the resources of the West. He said that his "borrowing" from Doheny and Sinclair may have been unethical, but he did not realize it at the time. This may have been true; if so, our government's officials needed far stricter training in administrative morals.

Daugherty was never convicted of anything, though he did refuse to testify about some funds which may have come into an account held jointly by Jess Smith and himself. He was acquitted by the jury and may have been innocent of bribing. He was certainly guilty of misusing the staff of the department more than once, but expressed no contrition for it. Any analysis of his motives would have to include his background in Ohio politics.

Charles Forbes was a curious man. His excellent military record in World War I, leading to the Congressional Medal of Honor, must be set against the complete irresponsibility of his earlier days. He apparently was completely dishonest.

Alien Property Custodian Thomas Miller's case seems to have been one of those inexplicable lapses into temporary criminality of a man otherwise and afterward honest.

Gaston B. Means of the Federal Bureau of Investigation seems to have been a career man in crime.

In addition to Daugherty and Jess Smith, the other members of the group vaguely called the "Ohio gang" were perhaps accustomed to corrupt politics and viewed Washington as the best place for the biggest operation. One of them, Howard Mannington, showed his attitude to a friend seeing him off from Ohio. The friend observed, "You ought to be in a position to get pretty much anything through down there, if it's right." Mannington winked. "Hell, if it's right, they won't need me."[19]

Shifting from personal to more impersonal factors, other reasons can be cited for the miserable record of the Harding administration. Bureaucracies take time to develop first-class traditions. Although civil service was almost a half-century old, it had not developed traditions of leadership in many departments. The administration's troubles were located mostly in new agencies, like Prohibition and the Veterans' Bureau, or ones like Interior, which had not developed solid administrative traditions or adequate internal controls. In defense of civil service, it should be noted that the corrupt, ineffective Prohibition Bureau was exempt from civil service.

The suggestion that the Harding scandals grew out of the times presents an intellectual challenge. Certainly America's moral climate was not at its best in the 1920s. The postwar relaxation, renewed interest in commercial concern, a literature of cynicism, a further decline in religious ethics, and the problem of enforcing Prohibition were all unpropitious for the maintenance of governmental morality.

Neither President Calvin Coolidge nor President Herbert Hoover had major difficulties with corruption in their administrations. President Coolidge did fairly well in cleaning up the Harding scandals, but did not try very hard to put Prohibition enforcement on a higher plane. Hoover did attempt that, without great success.

FDR and Political Administration. During his 12 years of office, Roosevelt was quite successful in avoiding high-level scandals. He did, however, encounter a good deal of political activity by subordinates which constituted misfeasance if not malfeasance. For example, he agreed to a suggestion of Postmaster General Farley that prosecutions of Democratic gangsters in Louisiana and Missouri be stopped. More is said about this in a later section on organized crime and the federal government.

One of his greatest controversies was with Senator Huey Long. Roosevelt fairly clearly used federal income tax indictments as a means of trying to control the politically ambitious Senator. In a few months after Long's assassination, the indictments of Long and his associates were dropped.

Work relief, the WPA, was sufficiently forced into politics by an act requiring senatorial confirmation of all officials making less than $5000. There were widespread charges that administration candidates had enlisted the WPA to bolster their finances and their support at the polls. The Sheppard committee reported a half-dozen states where WPA workers were solicited for political purposes.

Corruption in the Truman Administration, 1945-1953

Corruption was probably greater in the Truman administration than in any previous administration. Whether or not it was greater in proportion to the size of the administration is difficult to determine. An offhand judgment is that it was probably greater in proportion to the size of the administration than that which transpired under Harding, but not than the corruption with which the Grant administration is charged.

The book's account of the Truman administration's misdeeds will be shorter than that of the Harding administration because much less literature is available.

No Cabinet member was directly involved, but one appointments secretary went to jail for crimes in the White House, two White House aids were censured, an assistant attorney general was fired (and later tried and jailed), a commissioner of Internal Revenue was tried and jailed, and many lower-level tax officials were removed and later tried and convicted. The party's national chairman and Attorney General Howard McGrath were forced to resign for reasons connected with the scandals. President Truman moved to oppose corruption but did it slowly and with undue regard for the feelings of some of the men involved.

Most extensive of the Truman scandals were those in the Internal Revenue Service. In 1951 alone, 166 Internal Revenue officials (a number of officials larger than were involved in all the Harding scandals) were fired or forced to resign in one year, 1951.[20] Former Commissioner of Internal Revenue Joseph D. Nunan was tried and convicted in 1954. Herman Oliphant, general counsel of Internal Revenue, resigned apparently because he had involved himself in a tax case at the suggestion of a tax fixer.[21] Theron Lamar Caudle, Assistant Attorney General in charge of tax litigation, was removed from office in 1951 and later tried and convicted on conspiracy charges. Collector of Revenue James P. Finnegan (St. Louis), a friend of the President, was removed from office and later tried and convicted.

The Nunan case was almost unbelievable. Joseph D. Nunan served as Commissioner of Internal Revenue from March 1944 to June 30, 1947. He was convicted and sentenced to 5 years for evading $91,000 for income taxes from 1946 to 1950. Although a lawyer, a former legislator, and one time collector of Internal Revenue for New York, he kept no books or personal records. When a House of Representatives investigation was initiated in 1951, he filed amended returns for 1949 and 1950, affably explaining that he was a lawyer, not a tax man. Many of his transactions were cash (often an indication of questionable transactions). His statements to the Internal Revenue agents were contradictory and untrue.

The chief action for which a large number of tax collectors were tried was acceptance (or extortion) of bribes in return for administrative action lowering or eliminating tax liability. For example, Patullo Modes, a New York dress manufacturing company, paid $100,000 through Henry Grunewald, a fixer, to Daniel A. Bolich, an assistant commissioner. Bolich thereupon found legal reasons for not prosecuting the company which had a $.25 million liability. In 1955 Grunewald and Bolich both received 5-year sentences.

Collector Denis W. Delaney, of the Boston area, was convicted of accepting bribes and other forms of corruption. He was found to have secured a new Cadillac on very easy terms, for introducing a friend who wanted a radio station license to important persons in Washington. In addition, he helped a cafe avoid a tax liability when the owner provided him with a rent-free cottage. Delaney's chief field deputy testified that he had lifted many liens. He was sentenced to jail for a year.

The Reconstruction Finance Corporation's granting of loans was, perhaps, second only to tax collection in its degree of corruption. The RFC was more or less honestly administered in the 1930s by Jesse Jones, but when he was dropped in 1945, the agency was encouraged to make more liberal loans. A loan of $1.5 million was made to the Saxony, a "swank hotel" in Miami Beach, after the RFC examiner and his wife and daughter had spent a free 10 days there. An arms company received a $300,000 loan shortly after its principal owner was appointed an RFC director. Merle Young, a former RFC employee and husband of a White House secretary, was made a vice president of Lustron, builder of prefabricated homes. While in this position, he sought a large fee for securing a loan to another corporation, Texmass, and to Kaiser-Fraser Auto Corporation. Lustron finally was foreclosed on by RFC, but only after Young and others had tried to secure control of it. American Lithofold Company hired Collector of Internal Revenue James P. Finnegan (St. Louis) and William Boyle, then vice chairman of the Democratic National Committee, to help secure an RFC loan.

Politically potent friends of President Truman in Missouri formed the Midwest Storage and Realty Company of Kansas City, which leased government-owned storage space from the War Assets Administration and then leased the space back at a large profit to the Commodity Credit Corporation. Large sums were also made out of insuring Federal Housing Agency projects. If the company could inflate the costs which FHA insured, it would reap substantial profits. Substantial gifts were made to FHA employees who approved these inflated costs. There were other cases of mismanagement in the Post Office, the G.I. educational program, and the Alien Property Custodian offices.[22] Defense Department and Maritime Commission contracts or other transactions were negotiated "five percenters" (the size of the kickback), or sales were made at low prices to those with Democratic party support.

The reasons for the outbreak of corruption in the Truman administration are not easily ascertained. Less is known of the personal motivations than in the case of the more elaborately documented Harding scandals. Again, as in the Harding and Grant scandals, there is no evidence that Truman was personally involved but much evidence of his being slow to move against old friends. James Boylan concludes:

President Truman has not been found directly to have ordered or otherwise to have caused any of these transgressions. Yet many of them clearly took place in circumstances in which the transgressor gave the impression that the power of the President was behind him. The loyalty he gave so unstintingly to his associates was not always returned in the same measure.[23]

President Harding's early death keeps us from knowing what he would have done to clear up the corruption in his administration. But President Truman was in office longer and obviously did take some clean-up opportunities. In 1952 he announced a reorganization of the Internal Revenue Service, which eliminated the 64 collectors' offices and established an independent inspection service; Congress accepted the plan. Further "reform" of a sort was imposed by Congress when it abolished the Reconstruction Finance Corporation program.

It may be appropriate to point out that both Harding and Truman had their original political training in below-average state and local political mechanisms. Both had only minor administrative responsibilities prior to their ascension to the Presidency. The responsibilities of the great office made each personally honest; in fact, there is little evidence of personal dishonesty on the part of either in earlier dealings. But each had learned to associate with dishonest characters and to overlook dishonesty. It is interesting to observe that each of these Presidents made appointments of responsible men to the highest positions in foreign affairs, a field in which neither man was well versed. Oddly, both made their worst appointments in the fields with which they were familiar, often of men they knew well. Both these outbursts of corruption came in an immediate postwar period, as did the Grant administration scandals. This time coincidence leads one to think that ethical standards may bear some relation to the national sense of patriotic duty or, conversely, to a general cultural relaxation.

The Scotch verdict, not proved, seems to be an appropriate judgment on this guess. There were not similar lapses after the Revolutionary War, the War of 1812, or the Mexican or Spanish-American wars. The similar thread in Grant, Harding, and Truman administrations seems to have reflected the attitude of the appointing President. Perhaps the nature of each represented a national reaction to the wartime leadership. Yet the initial steps taken to select Truman were taken during the war, when the need for effective leadership should still have seemed important.

Conflict of Interest in the Eisenhower, Kennedy, and Johnson Administration

Little of the outright bribery and extortion which discredited certain bureaus in the Harding and Truman administrations appeared, at least in high levels, in other administrations, which confirms this book's earlier generalization that corruption has not been a frequent feature of American federal administration in this century.

There has, however, been a continuous outcropping of a lower order of corruption which is usually described as "conflict of interest." This is a political malaise with which Americans are particularly likely to identify, since our bar associations generally recognize it as a major legal evil and many of our active politicians, at least at the federal level, are lawyers. Conflict of interest in a broader sense is defined by David A. Frier as "any situation in which an official's public responsibility and private interests conflict and does not suggest that the clash has been resolved to the interest of the private rather than the governmental interest."[24] Conflict of interest is a real problem in government service because many people are brought into political office from business, where conflict of interest is a lesser problem.

Professor Frier's scholarly study is written in an effort to indicate that Eisenhower had attacked the Truman administration and then permitted equal evils in his own administration. This book is not particularly interested in rating Truman versus Eisenhower, but is glad to use Frier's compendium, supplemented by *Responses of the Presidents to Charges of Misconduct,* as examples of a conflict-of-interest problem which must annoy every President and which brings discredit upon the American federal administration.

President Eisenhower's most publicized problem centered on Sherman Adams—an automobile dealer, then governor of New Hampshire and an early Eisenhower supporter—who for six years wielded great power as chief of staff for Eisenhower. Adams accepted some moderately valuable gifts, such as an oriental rug, a vicuna coat, and a number of payments of expensive hotel bills from his old friend Bernard Goldfine. On at least two occasions, Adams got in touch with the chairman of the Federal Trade Commission to make an appointment for Goldfine or himself to discuss problems which one of Goldfine's mills had with violation of FTC regulations. When these connections were brought out by the House Special Subcommittee on Legislative Oversight, Adams eventually resigned. Eisenhower accepted the resignation with expressions of deep regret and appreciation of Adams's services. Adams insisted he had done nothing wrong, and Frier is probably right in concluding that Adams had simply failed to understand the impropriety of his actions. Frier is sharply critical of Eisenhower for moving slowly in securing Adams's resignation. The criticism is justified, and unfortunately reminiscent of Presidents Harding and Truman.

Another major incident of corruption in the Eisenhower administration was the Dixon-Yates affair. To avoid expansion of the Tennessee Valley Authority (TVA), officials in the Budget Bureau worked out a scheme by which the new Mississippi Valley Generating Company was to build a steam-operating power plant in West Memphis, Arkansas, largely financed by federal funds. Utility executives Dixon and Yates organized the company. The plan aroused a good deal of opposition from the TVA, Boss Crump of Memphis, and other organizations. The conflict of interest was committed by Adolphe H. Wenzell, former vice president and director of the First Boston Corporation (which had arranged the financing), who had also acted as consultant to the director of the Bureau of the Budget while the arrangements were being made. Wenzell was unpaid. Wenzell himself recognized the embarrassment in his position and consulted First Boston's lawyer, who advised him to resign promptly. The firm decided against asking a fee because of the circumstances. Frier believes that Eisenhower was inadequately informed about the affair throughout and that he should be viewed "as something of a contemporary U.S. Grant, i.e., a man who was disposed to do the right thing but was so totally uninformed about the affairs in his own Administration that he was unable to carry out his altruistic goals."[25] To this can only be added that Wenzell and Rowland Hughes, the director of the Budget Bureau, were unbelievably inept to have permitted such a conflict of interest to rise in this very controversial field.

Secretary of the Air Force Harold Talbott sent out letters on Air Force stationery to a number of firms, including defense contractors, asking them to use the management services of Talbott and Mulligan, a management firm of which he was half-owner. He later argued that he had never used his official position to bring pressure on the firms. He knew that RCA had asked for an Attorney General's opinion on the propriety of a contract with the Mulligan firm, but Attorney General Herbert Brownell had refused to give such an opinion. After severe public criticisms, Talbott's resignation was promptly accepted. He was seen out of the Pentagon with a military review and the Medal of Freedom—inappropriate rewards for a man who could not distinguish public from private interests. Apparently he had been guilty of some improprieties during World War I.

Drew Pearson in 1955 drew attention to the fact that Peter Strobel, Commissioner of Public Buildings, maintained his connection with Stroebel and Salzman, a consulting engineering firm. Strobel had formulated rules that the firm should accept no contract from the General Services Administration (of which Public Buildings was a part), take on no new clients who were interested in Public Buildings service, and was to have no financial interest in any architectural or construction firm. However, Strobel delayed in signing the standard of conduct form, and attached reservations when he did. He also delayed in furnishing a list of his firm's clients to the Office of Compliance of General Services. After being sworn in, Strobel did press a claim for $7500 on the Corps of Engineers on a contract entered into earlier. He also negotiated a new contract with the Corps on March 31, 1954—the day before he was sworn in as a consultant to Public Buildings. (He became commissioner on July 1.) Had the Corps of Engineers known that he was becoming a federal employee, they probably would not have signed the contract. Strobel also recommended to the New York regional director of Public Buildings use of the Serge Petroff firm, one of his firm's clients, without telling the regional director of the close relationship. During his term a contract was granted by Public Buildings to another Strobel client in Atlanta. Of fourteen names of architectural firms submitted for the Central Intelligence Agency building, eight had or had at one time had some relationship with Strobel and Salzman.

After pressure was applied by the House antitrust committee of the Judiciary Committee, Strobel resigned. Eisenhower was ill in a Denver hospital and could not have asked for the resignation. Strobel insisted that he never used his official position to advance his private interests. "In politics I was out of my element." Frier comments that Strobel, like Talbott, had an "unbelievable naivete." No one seems to have viewed him as a scoundrel.

The case of Robert Tripp Ross, Assistant Secretary of Defense for Legislative and Public Affairs in the Eisenhower administration, raised another issue. His wife, Clair Wynn Ross, headed a company, Wynn Enterprises, in which he had no financial interest and held no position. Wynn Enterprises had an $800,000 contract to furnish trousers to the Army. Another company, headed by Ross's brother-in-law, the Southern Athletic Company, had received substantial government contracts in the past, some of which were not on a competitive basis. After querying by Senator McClelland's Committee on Government Operations, Ross offered his resignation, which was accepted with thanks for his services. The Senate investigation was then dropped.

May an official have conflict of interest because of his wife's business? The official here was also far removed (in the Defense Department) from the procurement processes of the Army. He had arranged by telephone one appointment with a marine general for his brother-in-law, but otherwise had not participated in the procurement process. The Senate committee was pushing conflict of interest near its ultimate limits when it pushed Ross to resignation.

Frier, noting in a chapter appropriately entitled "It Didn't End with Ike," tells us Fred Korth, Secretary of the Navy under Kennedy, used a Navy yacht to entertain "some extra-good customers" of the Fort Worth bank with which Korth had been connected. Perhaps more serious, he participated in discussions regarding the award of the TFX contract to a General Dynamics plant located in Fort Worth and a customer of the Continental Bank with which Korth had been connected. President Kennedy apparently asked for his resignation with speed but with no public statement of the reasons.[26]

In the Kennedy administration it became public knowledge that an agricultural entrepreneur, Billy Sol Estes, had built up an enterprise in West Texas on the basis of chattel mortgages on nonexistent fertilizer, fraudulent cotton allotments, and lucrative federal warehouse allotments. Estes had bought clothing for the deputy administrator of the Stabilization and Conservation Service, who resigned when this information came out. An aide to a former Assistant Secretary of Agriculture was fired because he refused to appear at a Texas inquiry. The former Assistant Secretary was himself fired when it was reported that he had charged long-distance phone calls on Estes' charge card. An Assistant Secretary of Labor resigned when his receipt of a $1000 gift from Estes became public.[27]

When the Defense Department decided to award the TFX contract to General Dynamics, several political as well as conflict-of-interest questions were raised. The Vice President came from Texas, as did the Secretary of the Navy. Texas had far more electoral votes than Washington and Kansas, homes of rival facilities. Area competition for the work made the Senate committee of investigation unusually sharp in its queries. Deputy Secretary of Defense Roswell L. Gilpatric had performed legal services for General Dynamics and had attended its corporate board meetings. His old firm was counsel to General Dynamics. The conflict of interest was blatant. His defense was that his law firm had represented many firms in defense industry and that he could not disqualify himself from participation in all contracts involving the firm's clients.

In President Johnson's administration, Assistant Secretary of Commerce Herbert W. Klotz received a stock tip from a *Newsweek* reporter, a former employee of the Commerce Department. He acted on it and cleared a generous profit. After a court suit was filed against insiders (not including Klotz) of the company, Klotz's participation was made public, and President Johnson soon secured his resignation with no statement of the reasons.

Another conflict-of-interest arrangement which affected President Johnson greatly was the Bobby Baker affair, discussed in the analysis of Congress and corruption.

The problem of conflict of interest is still present in the federal government. A Los Angeles *Times* story of December 4, 1975, cites General Accounting Office studies of the Interior Department and several other federal agencies in which a number of workers owned stocks which "could create at least the appearance of conflict of interest." The department's chief of audit and investigation responded that no "actual" conflict of interest was discovered but that tighter rules were being drafted.

On December 11, 1975, another *Times* news story indicated that Robert D. Timm resigned as a member of the Civil Aeronautics Board after the White House had exerted pressure for his resignation. At least one of the major charges against him was that he spent a weekend in Bermuda as the guest of an airline regulated by the CAB.

Why have conflict-of-interest cases bobbed up so frequently under every President, in view of the embarrassment they bring to the President as well as to the person whose interests conflict? One part of the answer is that the question of what constitutes conflict of interest is not easily ascertainable. Some of the cases discussed in this section are disputable. Did an Assistant Secretary of Defense really have a conflict of interest over the sale of trousers to the Army by a company of which his wife was president? At some not easily determinable point of indirectness, Congress should shut off condemnations of conflict of interest.

But there is a deeper factor which is harder to appraise. In many business operations, conflict of interest need not be so closely regarded because of the assumption that no responsible executive will damage his company's net income statement by accepting offers against the interest of the company. In a highly competitive world, someone will soon succeed him if he fails to make money. At governmental levels, however, the executive must recognize that he is in a monopolistic position. If he accepts even a small gift or a hotel room for a few nights, he is leaning unconscionably in the direction of the donor. The maintenance of high governmental standards requires his avoidance of such situations as far as is humanly possible. American businessmen serving in government have too often failed to learn this lesson.

Conclusions on Administrative Ethics

In summary, the amount of loss to the nation from corruption in the national administration has not been high. Three bureaus were widely corrupted, and two departments had spasmodic corruption in the Harding administration. The toll under Truman was similar. In addition, the appearance of occasional instances of corruption and the fairly frequent difficulties with conflict of interest in practically every administration must not be ignored.

How important is all this? The total dollar amount lost by the federal government, or by persons from whom bribes were extorted, is not very great; it would hardly total a fraction of a percent of the present federal budget. Mistakes in congressional policy, like Prohibition, farm price support, and some veteran bonuses, have cost the national government much more. The psychological loss to the citizen is, however, far greater than the dollar loss of federal administrative corruption. The white light of publicity shines very clearly on mistakes in federal administration. The Harding scandals were amplified by newspapers and later by historians into a legend that Washington in the 1920s was entirely run by sinister men who, as they played poker and smoked cigars, bargained away the public interest. Hard-working public servants under Secretaries Hoover and Hughes must have found this picture uncalled for.

But the corruption that did take place in the Harding, Truman, and other administrations, plus the attendant publicity, has had some real impact on American thought. To what extent is the ongoing large-scale corruption in many of our cities the result of an assumption that all government, from the Capitol down, is corrupt? "If the feds are getting it, why don't we?" may be a natural reaction. The indifference of voters to corruption may be a result of a similar feeling. "Everybody is getting some graft. Let's vote for the person we like best, regardless of honesty."

If the national examples of corruption have this unhappy imitative effect, the costs of national corruption may be very great indeed. If local corruption is imitative, the costs of poor law enforcement resulting largely from corruption are very substantial. Estimates of the costs of crime to America range from $50 billion to $100 billion—enough extra burden to affect the cost of living and our international trade balance. So national administrative corruption may be a very serious factor in our lives. What can be done about it?

Most accounts tend to blame the Presidents, who with one exception are themselves guiltless; their fault may be attributed chiefly to their inaction in removing the offending officials or the Cabinet members who were responsible for corrupt officials. Dr. George A. Graham, a distinguished scholar with extensive administrative experience, who admired President Truman in many respects, wrote in 1952:

> No matter what his private position may be, he has publicly defended and continued the associates who have embarrassed him, and they have lacked the good grace to get out from under his feet. The President has been more considerate of them than they of him. The effect upon the morale, the attitudes, and the standards of the administration is inevitably depressing.[28]

Why did Truman and other honest Presidents move slowly to rid themselves of dishonest associates? Several excuses come quickly to mind. In politics, an outstanding virtue is loyalty to one's friends, for the obvious reason that they will support you only if you support them. Unfortunately for Truman, some of these friends had established their ethical standards earlier in Missouri politics.

Another reason for slowness in removing offenders is the legalistic habit of waiting for the court to make a decision on individual cases: "Judge not until the judge has decided." This position obviously can become absurd. One does not keep a deputy attorney general in office until he is indicted or convicted; but this position, nevertheless, influenced the decisions of many Presidents.

A third consideration is perhaps the President's greatest difficulty. Most major appointees have the blessing of senators, congressmen, or political leaders from their home area. If the Democratic senator from Missouri believes that the St. Louis collector of Internal Revenue was too summarily removed from office, the President may have difficulty securing the cooperation of the senator from Missouri.

There have been substantial efforts to work out codes of official conduct which ban all corruption and most conflict. Unfortunately, these codes are frequently not read or understood by political appointees from business or local political fields where easier standards prevail. Presidents and department heads could help themselves greatly by talks to staff groups, perhaps as often as annually, in which they emphasize the importance of avoiding any impropriety or appearance of impropriety. Such talks are seldom held, perhaps because the executive shares the customary American aversion to discussing uncomfortable things like ethics.

The consistent reappearance of ethical infractions in national administration leads some to search for mechanical checks. George Graham raises the question of a higher-level civil servant group who would be especially trained to maintain professional standards. Such a group would correspond to the top class of the British civil service or to those regular officers of the armed forces who are destined for high command. It is true that such groups have been effective in maintaining high ethical standards. A problem with developing such a group is the fundamental American antipathy toward setting aside positions which cannot be attained by anyone coming up from the bottom.

Another possibility is that of developing a high-level inspection group, similar to those adopted in large city police forces. It had been hoped that the General Accounting Office management audit would serve this purpose, but its management audits have not gone into questions of individual honesty nor do its personnel appear to be of the type who could undertake such surveys. Some individual departments have had success with inspection services, but they are not likely to be a highly favored introduction to American national government. It is not probable that a strictly administrative change can vastly alter the situation.

The Federal Government and Organized Crime

In Chapters 6 and 7 this book has indicated how large a role organized crime has played in the corruption of local governments and in corrupt attacks on state governments since World War I. How has the federal government, which is the only level that can control organized crime with its mobility and financial capabilities, fared against organized crime?

There has never been a danger of organized crime's taking over the federal government. Most of the corrupt federal actions discussed in this book are not related to organized crime. However, the federal government has had many problems of law enforcement which are related to organized crime. Income tax evasion, importation of drugs, and interstate conspiracies are many areas in which the mob commits federal offenses. By and large, the federal prosecution of organized crime has been effective—certainly more so than state or local prosecution. But the federal government, large and impersonal though it may appear to be, has not been unsusceptible to politico-criminal approaches. Back in 1921, Ignazio Saietta, a major figure who had transferred his Mafia activities from Sicily to New York, was pardoned by President Harding. Prohibition brought out a surprising amount of federal (as well as local) corruption in Coast Guard and alcoholic control units.

"Lucky" Luciano claims that F.D.R. in preconvention 1932 agreed to call off Judge Seabury in return for organized crime's securing support of the Tammany delegation.[29] It is certain that Jimmy Hines, Tammany's chief contact with organized crime, was a leader for F.D.R. President Franklin D. Roosevelt removed Thomas E. Dewey, appropriately according to political tradition, from the U.S. attorneyship but substituted a man, Francis W. H. Adams, who later became Lucky Luciano's attorney. During World War II the United States government is said to have informally approved a "deal" by which chief gangster Luciano agreed to protect the New York waterfront and was released from prison at the end of the war. Governor Dewey commuted his sentence because of presumed help to our armed forces.[30]

Even though several federal statutes were often violated, Al Capone's reign in Chicago was for years not seriously interrupted by the federal government, until President Hoover put pressure on Secretary of the Treasury Andrew Mellon to do something about him. The omnipotent gangster's indictment on charges of income tax evasion and Prohibition violations finally came in 1931. The federal government did succeed in putting Capone in jail, but did not end the organized crime regime he had established.

Kansas City presented a problem of mixed political loyalties to F.D.R. John Lazia, Boss Pendergast's organized crime lieutenant, was under indictment, but prosecution was stopped by Postmaster General Farley, who possibly acted after consultation with F.D.R. However, after some local gangland killings, the income tax case against Lazia was reopened largely because Secretary Morgenthau persuaded Roosevelt to approve this action.[31] In the 1940s it was a federal income tax prosecution which finally ended Pendergast's career.

In the Truman administration, Robert Gould, a black-market whiskey dealer who at times worked with the Cleveland syndicate, secured a quick federal parole after making a "campaign contribution" to the Democratic party.[32]

In April 1964 Lyndon Johnson commuted the sentence of a labor union official who had been convicted of shaking down a contractor and who in turn made a contribution to the Democratic party.[33]

More recently, James Hoffa, leader of the Teamster's Union (which has maintained very close ties to organized crime), was pardoned by President Richard Nixon, whose campaign had received Teamster support.

There are, of course, countless individual cases in which Mafia members have had contacts with the federal government. Messick gives a more amusing one in which the Undersecretary of the Treasury in 1947 urged the special agent in New York to pursue Frank Costello, which later resulted in that special agent's being indicted himself for bribery to fix tax cases. More tragic, in 1932 presumed agents of John Lazia (Tom Pendergast's organized crime man) "kicked out the brains" of the Internal Revenue agent who had asked about his income.[34]

Another interesting problem in intergovernmental relations occurred when Treasury agents investigating tax liabilities in Enoch Johnson's Atlantic City political machine—crime organizations—found themselves followed by Atlantic City cops. However, they persevered and in 1941 sent Johnson to prison in addition to collecting $1 million in taxes and penalties.

During the Truman administration when Joe Nunan was Commissioner of Internal Revenue, organized crime came, perhaps, closest to running a large federal bureau. Fortunately, Nunan was himself convicted of tax evasion, sent to jail for 5 years, and fined $15,000.

Louis B. Nichols, former assistant to J. Edgar Hoover, resigned to become executive vice president of Schenley Industries in 1957. Lewis S. Rosenstiel, board chairman of Schenley, had numerous organized crime connections. These did not keep Nichols from lobbying hard and successfully for the Forand bill (passed in late 1958), which altered the length of time whiskey could remain in a bonded warehouse, greatly to Schenley's advantage. There is no proof of corruption here but indeed certain evidences of the political influence of organized crime.

Congress has similarly not escaped from the political influence of organized crime. At any given time, there may be a score of congressmen who are directly obligated, and many more who would not wish to offend organized crime, in their districts or states. In 1953 Congressman Ronald Libonati announced his intention not to run again, probably because Sam Giancana, then head of organized crime in Chicago, ordered him not to run. In 1970 an aide and an associate of House Speaker John W. McCormack were indicted, and later convicted of perjury and of misusing the Speaker's office. Both had close mob ties.

The slowness of the FBI, or rather of J. Edgar Hoover, to acknowledge the danger of organized crime is almost unbelievable. In 1950 it had only five men probing racketeering in the New York office—a figure which was raised to 85 after Robert Kennedy became Attorney General and forced more attention to organized crime.[35]

Dorman cites an interview with an unnamed former Assistant Attorney General who said that a federal investigation of rackets in Chicago hasd been called off by the White House, after the Chicago political machine had impeded the investigation at every level, by Chicago officials, by members of the local U.S. Attorney's office, and even by federal judges. Dorman's account is probably trustworthy, but of course would be helped by more details.[36]

Even after the Apalachin conference of 1957 and the McClelland Committee hearings, the National Commission on Law Enforcement and Administration of Justice (appointed by President Johnson in 1965) would have omitted organized crime had it not been for the arguments of Henry S. Ruth, the deputy staff director. Ruth cited "his own experiences in the investigation of a Pennsylvania city where criminal corruption has pervaded the entire structure of the government, and in the prosecution of a New York State Supreme Court judge for conspiracy to fix a trial." Ruth won, and a report was prepared.[37]

The chief reason for federal unwillingness to move against organized crime, of course, has been the result of political resistance which the mob can bring against federal investigation. A secondary reason has been that many mob actions do not violate federal laws. There is also a possibility that J. Edgar Hoover's friends may have misled him on the magnitude of organized crime activity. But the fact still remains that the federal government is the only body which has the staff, funds, and territorial coverage to control organized crime adequately.

Organized crime connections occur in the hectic life of many leading political figures. With varying degrees of remoteness, mob connections appear in the acquaintance of Presidents Roosevelt, Truman, Eisenhower, Kennedy, Johnson, and Nixon, as well as many other political leaders. Usually the mob connections have propelled themselves into the President's acquaintances.

Administrative Tribunals

The administrative tribunals of the federal government are in a never-never land halfway between the administrative departments and the courts. This in-between status raises special problems of corruption. The Sherman Adams case indicates that it is wrong for a White House staff man to contact an FTC commissioner about a case before the FTC. However, Adams probably would not have been condemned for a similar contact with a bureau chief in an administrative department while he probably would not even have thought of contacting a federal judge on a similar plea. But contact with the commission for a friend who had given him expensive favors cost him his job. Clearly, the standards of conduct in the Federal Trade Commission are different from those in the ordinary administrative agency.

The independent agencies' varying ethical standards so not seem to have prevented some conflict-of-interest charges. Hugh Cross, chairman of the Interstate Commerce Commission (ICC), was questioned in 1955 about his getting in touch with several railroad presidents on behalf of Railroad Transfer, a company owned by John Keeshin (a long-time friend of Cross), who was considering asking Cross to head the company if it were enabled to secure contracts with the railroads for transfer of passengers and luggage. Since the ICC had the authority to schedule rates charged by the railroads, these inquiries by the chairman in behalf of a company for which he might work were highly inappropriate. Cross's resignation was requested and received, and an investigative congressional subcommittee subsequently dropped the matter.

Chairman John Doerfer of the Federal Communications Commission in 1958 accepted expenses and an honorarium for attendance at a meeting of the National Association of Radio and Television Broadcasters, for which he also received government reimbursement. On other occasions Doerfer and his wife were known to have been entertained in Florida by members of the industry. After these facts were made known, Doerfer's resignation was requested and received. National Airlines hired an attorney, Thurmond Whiteside, to press an application for a broadcasting license in Miami. Whiteside happened to be a long-time friend and occasional financial helper of Richard Mack, a member of the Federal Communications Commission, which granted the license. Mack resigned, probably by request.[38]

A more general charge against the commission has been made often in recent years. Commissions are too prone to be "industry-minded," i.e., to adopt the point of view of the industry which they are supposed to regulate. After expiration of their terms, commissioners may be appointed to good jobs in the regulated industry. Or an ex-commissioner may join a law firm which is helped by fees from a firm which the commissioner has regulated.[39]

Questions have often been raised as to how the Lyndon Johnson family built up a major fortune during a lifetime of public service. Mrs. Johnson bought a small radio station in 1942 for $17,500 plus an agreement to pay off its existing debts of $40,000 to $50,000. The station expanded, bought other stations, and became a multimillion-dollar business. The unanswered question is whether the Johnson television station became prosperous in part because of receiving favorable rulings from the Federal Communications Commission.[40]

One congressman commented:

It should be apparent that the President, Vice President, and others of high rank in Government should not obtain interests in a Government-controlled industry. There is either direct control of appointments to the Federal Communications Commission, as in the case of the President, or the troublesome situation where high officials have great influence that might be misued in associating with the F.C.C.

It should also be apparent that members of the House and Senate have a position of some control over the F.C.C. through legislation, proposals of legislation, through appropriations, through investigation, and otherwise through political links.[41]

Professor Bernard Schwartz has published a book on his role as chief counsel of a House subcommittee investigating whether or not the regulation agencies were doing what Congress had intended. Schwartz discovered that a majority of his subcommittee did not wish a genuine investigation, partly because of the economic interests of committee members in regulated industries, partly because of their own philosophies which called for limited regulation. Schwartz was fired from his position; nevertheless, he unearthed evidence of impropriety which led to the resignation of one FCC member. The greatest concern raised by the deposed counsel is that of the congressional committee's lack of concern about regulatory commission members who receive expensive favors from regulated bodies.[42]

Corruption continues to be a problem in some of the commissions. The *Washington Post* (June 9, 1977) recently carried a story that two top staff members of the Interstate Commerce Commission were put on "administrative leave" as a result of possible organized crime influence on ICC trucking decisions.

The Judiciary

In this book, corruption of judges has been treated as an integral part of state and local corruption. Tammany Hall as well as other machines have controlled local judges rather freely. The federal judiciary, however, has been a different story. Lifetime appointments and generally higher salaries have usually made federal judgeships more independent of political control than is the case with their state and local counterparts.

A recent study of the federal judiciary reveals many weak appointments and many purely political appointments. However, it cites only one instance where appointments were initiated through corrupt processes—the Chicago federal judges appointed by the Daley machine in the 1950s and 1960s. The best-known example is, of course, the unhappy case of Circuit Court Judge Otto Kerner—two-time Governor of Illinois, United States Attorney, Major General in the National Guard, and former trustee of his alma mater, Brown University—who was convicted of conspiracy, accepting a bribe, income tax evasion, mail fraud, and perjury, for transactions in racetrack stock while he was governor. Other Chicago federal judges have not been convicted, but have frequently conducted themselves in most unjudicial manners.[43]

Tom Dewey's staff in 1949 had assembled data which led to the resignation and later conviction of federal appeals judge Marvin Manton, who had accepted several bribes.

The general standing of the federal judiciary is approved by statistics. More than 2000 persons have served as federal judges; only 8 have been impeached, and of these only 4 have been convicted. "By contrast, that many members of Congress have been convicted as felons in a single session."[44] However, 55 judges have been investigated with the threat of impeachment, and 17 have resigned during the process.

In 1963 the *Wall Street Journal* published information on bank and corporate directorships held by federal judges. There were also two scandals regarding former Supreme Court Justice Abe Fortas, who received high fees for lectures at American University and consultant fees from the family foundation of adventurous businessman Louis Wolfson, when Wolfson had legal problems. After several efforts by the Judicial Conference to agree on a code and by some members of Congress to secure legislation, the Judicial Conference finally settled on requiring a semiannual report of gifts to federal judges of more than $100 and any income from outside work. A federal judge is also required to disqualify himself if he has any financial interest in a case and is prohibited from serving as an executor or trustee except for the estate of a family member.

Conclusions

The federal government has had less corruption than state or local governments in this century, but it nevertheless occurs, including even some influence from organized crime. Congress has the worst record, perhaps in part because of the difficulty of distinguishing between proper and improper recognition of economic interests in disputes which must be settled through legislation. Only very recently has Congress required its own members to disclose conflict of interest. Congress has made a few efforts to discipline its own members but essentially seems to be waiting for the courts to determine penalties for misconduct. Congressional investigations have played an important role in scrutinizing honesty of conduct, although some of them have been terminated too quickly.

Administrations have varied since World War I. Wilson had troubles with wartime contracting and with Prohibition. Harding had severe problems with oil reserves, veterans' affairs, Prohibition and alien property. There is little evidence of corruption during Coolidge's and Hoover's terms of office. F.D.R. kept his administration fairly clean, in spite of a heavy retrogression to political appointments. Truman had the largest amount of corruption in the twentieth century, having difficulty with the Reconstruction Finance Corporation, the Federal Housing Administration, and other agencies; although he eventually made a laudable effort to clean up his administration, he still deserves criticism for poor appointments and too slow removals. There was not much bribery or extortion in the Eisenhower, Kennedy, and Johnson administrations, but there were a good many publicized cases of conflict of interest which generally prompted quick resignations.

9

Corruption in American Elections

The fundamental test of elections in democracies is whether they can bring into being governments that rule with the consent of a free people. American elections have managed this very well. Yet there are also problems, many of which involve various kinds of political corruption. In this chapter, we canvass three problem areas: the administration of elections, the conduct of campaigns, and money in elections.

The Administration of Elections

Writing in 1929, Joseph Harris observed that "little progress has been made in the technique of elections in this country. Probably no other phase of public administration is so badly managed. Our elections have been marked by irregularities, slipshod work, antiquated procedures, obsolete records, inaccuracies, and many varieties of downright fraud."[1] A generation later, V. O. Key, the successor to Harris as the leading authority on American elections, confirmed this judgment and declared that a "hair-raising volume descriptive of electoral frauds" could still be compiled.[2] Today, although some of the older forms of electoral abuse have declined, an unenviable reputation for fraud continues to attach itself to the administration of American elections.

Charged by the U.S. Constitution with responsibility for conducting elections, the states publish detailed administrative regulations in election codes. Often bewildering in their complexity, these state codes are frequently revised, usually to suit the convenience of the party in power in the state legislature. Generally, the actual administration of elections is given little or no central supervision by state agencies, being left to local governments whose officials are often closely identified with one party or the other. It is this weakness of central administration in the states combined with the powerful role of partisan interests that together explain many of the principal abuses of American election administration.

Most election frauds occur in areas of one-party dominance, especially in the very poorest wards and precincts, the grossest forms flourishing in the remaining strongholds of "bossism." Party primaries, much more than general elections, are the principal stage on which the tricks and dodges of election fraud continue to be worked.

169

Disorder, Violence, and Intimidation

History records a number of occasions on which American elections were disrupted by unruly crowds, perhaps the best known being the mayoral election of Fernando Wood in 1856 in New York. The Wood supporters, supplied with brickbats, clubs, axes, and pistols, made war on their foes; the anti-Wood men destroyed ballot boxes in addition to assaulting, stabbing, and shooting at their opponents. The twentieth century has seen few incidents of disorder on such a scale, an improvement we may ascribe partly to some general betterment in the standards of civic conduct, partly to the absence from recent American politics of issues as explosive as those of the Civil War period—and, perhaps, partly to the enforcement of state legislation forbidding the sale of alcohol on election day.

Organized violence and open physical harassment of individual voters at the polling place also have almost disappeared in the second half of this century. The era of greatest abuse seems to have been the decades after 1840 when the electoral system experienced the rapid expansion of the suffrage and then, after the Civil War, the influx into the cities of large numbers of immigrants. Some of the groups that had benefited from the earlier restricted suffrage now attempted violence against the new voters. Violence was also employed by the big city machine as one tactic among many for the control of the expanded urban electorate. Examples of violence at the polls in the twentieth century have occurred in a number of Northern cities and in rural areas of Southern states. One of the worst examples of machine-organized violence at the polls occurred in 1934 in Kansas City. Four murders, eleven cases of critical injury, and more than two hundred cases of assault were reported.

The decline in organized violence at the polls must be attributed partly to the secret, or Australian, ballot which was adopted in a majority of the states by 1850.[3] In the colonial period and throughout much of the early history of the United States, voting was *viva voce*; that is, the voter would announce orally his voting preference to election officials. Later, many states took up the use of private ballots, printed by the parties or the candidates and employing their own distinctive colors or symbols, which were then furnished to the voter for presentation at the polls. Both the *viva voce* system and the private system, allowing bystanders to know how votes were cast, provided occasions for organized violence against voters. The Australian ballot, however, practically ensuring the secrecy of the voting act, deprived observers of much of the incentive to interfere. In most states, further limits were placed on the violence of bystanders by enforcement of code provisions specifying the number and duties of "poll-watchers" and controlling electioneering activity near the polling place.

Although overt violence at the polls has almost disappeared, there is still some intimidation of voters, or the use of threats and harassment short of violence. There is probably somewhat more intimidation to be found at the registration stage of the electoral process. In the last decade, for example, blacks were still frequently deterred from registering to vote in some Southern states. Until the early 1960s, black registration in Alabama, Georgia, Mississippi, and South Carolina was consistently less than 20 percent of those eligible to vote[4] – a fact that must be ascribed partly to black fears that attempted participation in elections would elicit reprisals. Of course, black registration rates were also depressed by a range of official devices, the most important of which were the literacy test and the poll tax. Such registration hurdles were the basic means of limiting voter participation—of poor whites as well as blacks—throughout the South.[5]

Some reduction in the incidence of intimidation of registrants has been achieved by new methods of registering voters, particularly systems of permanent registration. Originally, voters in all the states would present themselves to election officials on the day of the election, establishing on the spot their qualifications to vote—a procedure during which unscrupulous officials might easily exert pressure on or threaten the voter. By the beginning of the twentieth century, however, most states had established their qualifications to vote, thus securing a position on an official registration list prior to election day. This type of periodic registration has today been widely displaced by systems of permanent registration in which the voter makes an initial appearance before a registration official and, thereafter, until he or she changes residence or dies, his or her name remains on the registration list. In such ways, registration has been made much less of a hurdle to voters in all parts of the country—and also less of an occasion for voter intimidation. In those areas of the South where registration of blacks continued to suggest special problems, a variety of legal actions has been undertaken to prevent intimidation and harassment by registrars.

Illegal Voting, False Registration, Bribery, and Illegal Assistance

Of the many varieties of election fraud involving illegal voting techniques, perhaps the most notorious are "repeating" and "personation." In the heyday of machine politics, the use of repeaters and personators—to "vote early and often"—was widespread, from the North Side in Kansas City to the South Side in Chicago, from the Strip in Pittsburgh to South of the Slot in San Francisco. No less important, and generally used in conjunction with these, was the practice of wholesale manipulation of registration lists. The names of aliens (sometimes as the result of illegal naturalization), minors, and nonresidents were added to the registration list, along with fictitious names and the names of reliable nonvoters. In combination, such illegal techniques could yield large numbers of fraudulent votes. In the 1869 election in New York, for example, between 25,000 and 30,000 votes were attributed to repeating, false registration, and illegal naturalization.

Partly because of the decline of city machines and partly as a result of the use of permanent registration methods, these types of illegal voting are much less common. It would be a serious mistake, however, to think that they have disappeared. In Pennsylvania (especially in Philadelphia), in Illinois (especially in Cook County), in Texas (especially in central and south Texas), and in several other states (in both urban and rural areas) their use has continued well into the second half of the twentieth century.

The "endless chain" or the "Tasmanian dodge" is another form of illegal voting. Impracticable in jurisdictions where voting machines are in use, it is a device frequently associated with petty bribery of voters for the use of their ballots. First, an official ballot is obtained and marked as desired by the politician; it is then given to a reliable voter who substitutes the marked ballot for a fresh one and deposits the marked ballot in the ballot box; the voter then returns with the fresh ballot to the politicians, and the cycle begins again with the politician marking up the new ballot for another reliable voter. In many states, prior to the use of voting machines, some check was achieved on this practice by numbering the ballots.

Outright bribery and the purchase of votes, once common in many American jurisdictions, are now almost certainly quite rare. Money still changes hands in questionable ways in the poor wards of cities such as Philadelphia and Chicago or Detroit (for example, in the guise of payments to "party workers"). And even in states such as California, "street money" is still quite widely used by Democratic politicians in dealing with black voters, the typical contact being the black "reverend" who is presumed to have a measure of control over the votes of his parishioners. Thus, the Los Angeles *Times* reported the use of $5000 of "street money" channeled through four black ministers by the Carter campaign in the California primary of 1976.[6] But these practices have faded with the growth in affluence of the electorate. Much more frequent is the use of illegal assistance in voting. Sometimes the voter will expect some future services for allowing the politician to accompany him into the voting booth; sometimes he will allow it in recognition of past services; and sometimes he may simply prefer not to antagonize the politician, his neighbor. Whatever the reason, large numbers of voters undoubtedly continue to yield control of voting machine levers to local politicians. Thus, *The Philadelphia Inquirer* reported the estimate of a federal grand jury that approximately 100,000 people in Philadelphia were losing their franchise each year to election frauds, the majority as the result of manipulation by district politicians rendering illegal assistance in the voting booths.[7]

Alteration of Ballots, Ballot-box Stuffing, False Counting, and Certification of Results

The various techniques of illegal and deceptive voting that have been described rely on the existence of rather large numbers of pliant voters, effective ward or district organization, and the disbursement of substantial funds. Cheaper devices, often capable of delivering much larger numbers of votes, yet involving only a few party workers and therefore carrying less risk of detection, are forgery and false accounting by election officials.

The alternation of ballots, often during the ballot count, may accomplish many objectives, including completion of a ballot on which the voter has failed to make a preference for all the offices or issues; spoiling ballots cast for the opposition, for example, by marking more than one preference for an office; and correction of ballots cast for one's party or candidate. Sometimes premarked ballots are substituted for those cast by the voters; sometimes genuine ballots are removed and destroyed; and sometimes additional premarked ballots are simply added to the total. The last of these ploys brings us to the practice of "ballot-box stuffing"—the wholesale voting of names (whether on the registration list or not) by election officials. If there is any fear of a later investigation, the practice will generally be to vote only the names of registered voters; a little riskier is the voting of fictitious names previously added to the registration list (or, as in the case of "cemetery voting," the use of names that have not been removed from registration lists after the voters' demise); and riskiest of all is the voting of names that make no appearance on the registration lists.

The simplest way to change vote totals, of course, is to miscount. This is done where the political organization feels itself strong enough to deter or control later investigations. Sometimes the count in certain wards or precincts will be postponed until the results from all the other areas are available; then, when it is known how many votes are required for victory, the "count" provides them. Sometimes, the "count" is predetermined to achieve a quota established by the organization. And sometimes, even when the ballots have been correctly counted and honest totals recorded on the tally sheets, it will be found possible to falsify the certificate of results.

A Final Note on Abuses in Election Administration

Although we have cataloged a variety of illegal practices, it is hard to know how much fraud really occurs in the administration of American elections. Unlike most other things of value, elections can be stolen without the theft being discovered; it may be, therefore, that many frauds have gone undetected. On the other hand, since there is nothing to prevent losers from crying "thief" when no theft has occurred, it is perhaps more likely that there is exaggeration in the claims of abuse.

It is still harder to know how to judge the significance of election frauds. Compared with the massive official chicanery in the elections of communist states and other totalitarian regimes, American election frauds are on a trivial scale. Compared with the scrupulously administered elections of a few Western European democracies, they appear more serious—although it may also be remarked that there are obviously many more opportunities for electoral abuse in the United States, since the number of offices and issues subject to election is vastly greater than in other democracies.

The Conduct of Campaigns

The American voter is often charged with being too tolerant of the misconduct of candidates. Certainly, the struggle for election leads candidates (or their campaign managers) into many kinds of unscrupulous competition, and many American campaigns do see more rough-and-tumble tactics than campaigns in some Western European countries. Yet it must also be said that in all democracies close-fought elections may involve reprehensible and illegal behavior. Ruthless campaign tactics have brought men to power in the best-ordered and most law-abiding modern democracies. In democracies everywhere, the statements of politicians seeking election have always required a pinch or more of salt. And always, too, the powerful have been able to manipulate the system to their advantage in elections.

Campaign Tactics: "Dirty Tricks"

Election campaigns, not unlike campaigns in war, often seek information through espionage. Sometimes the spy is a "plant," a paid worker from one campaign intruded onto the staff of another; sometimes bribery reveals the secrets of the opposition; sometimes electronic eavesdropping is the means. Espionage, of course, was the motive of the Watergate break-in of 1972.

Sabotage is also not uncommon; some of its milder forms have even attracted specialist practitioners to campaign staffs. Thus, the political saboteur who defaces the billboards or tears down the lawn signs of the opposition, sometimes replacing them with his own candidate's posters, is commonly known as a "snipe." The agitator who leads a demonstration against a campaign headquarters, perhaps with the purpose of harassing campaign staffers or rattling the candidate, is generally referred to as a "crowd worker." Similarly, advance men, when not accompanying their candidates, and other junior campaign staff are often used for organized heckling of the opponent, disrupting his speeches, or asking "planted questions."

There are also much more serious forms of sabotage. Theft or diversion of campaign mail, for example, has led many campaigns to employ professional guards at their direct-mail houses (and even to use special precautions to ensure timely delivery by the U.S. Post Office). Sabotage of precinct operations is also frequently attempted. Generally, this is done by violence against the opposition's precinct workers, but there are also more imaginative means. It has not been unknown, for example, for a campaign to hire blacks to pose as workers for the opposition campaign and then to send them from house to house in blue-collar, white precincts to urge a vote for "their" candidate in terms of an allegedly radical stand on civil rights. Campaign headquarters and candidates' residences are frequent targets of sabotage and have been set on fire or even raked with machine gun bullets. Such violence, of course, may produce a sympathy vote for the victim, and desperate candidates, understanding this, have sometimes stage-managed attacks on their own headquarters, even experiencing "near escapes" from flames or gunfire.

Candidates and their managers use many other dodges and ploys to discommode opponents. Among the most effective is the harassing suit. Although the grounds may be slight or nonexistent, a suit may focus "negative press" on the opposing campaign and absorb the energies of its senior staff. Similarly, injunctions are often sought to halt mail deliveries or the use of television commercials. It may be noted that legal actions of this kind often focus on the detail of recent election reform laws, the plaintiff thereby seeking to identify himself with the cause of reform and his opponent with its breach.

It should be said, of course, that cutthroat competition and such ruthless tactics born of malice prepense are often relieved by more playful politics. The prankster, no less than the spy or the saboteur, may find a home in a campaign, and many a lighthearted practical joke has been played out in good humor between opposing campaigns.

"Voter Misinformation"

Walter Quigley was among the first of the twentieth century's technical specialists in "voter misinformation."[8] A self-styled expert in "political dynamiting," Quigley sold his services to campaigns throughout the Midwestern United States in the 1920s. His special skill was the design of pamphlets and brochures to blacken the reputation of opponents with "believable lies." Quigley's innumerable modern successors have been much assisted by the development of the computer printer and the rotary press. Computerized letters (with "variable messages") and glossy color brochures the now mailed out by the millions every election year. The advantage of the computer letter is that it can be used to address different "personalized" messages to voters in dissimilar areas of a district. This is achieved by using vote history data to determine the issue stands most likely to appeal to voters in different precincts; and the "personal touch" is achieved by use of the voter's name at some point in the text, by reference to some local problem, or by the use of the signature of a local notable. Many lies are told in such communications to voters, but the worst are always reserved for the last. The "Election Day Gutter Ball Special" is a well-known tactic of unscrupulous campaign managers. A mail piece filled with charges against the opposing candidate is delivered at the last possible moment prior to the election, too late for response or effective challenge. Late mail deliveries may also include pieces attributed to one campaign, but actually authored by the other, the purpose of which is to undermine established voter support.

Electronic media techniques have led to the development of new forms of "political dynamiting." Television or radio commercials, designed by "image experts," have been widely used for this purpose. Again, last-minute denunciations of opponents—the "negative media blitz"—are a favorite technique of unscrupulous management.

Although there is little hard evidence on the point, it seems clear that another technique of voter misinformation involves manipulation of survey research results. Polls paid for by a candidate notoriously favor the client. Independent surveys should be more reliable, but discrepancies among the results produced by different polling companies have sometimes been so great as to lead to charges of deception. Of course, the influence of poll results on the average voter is probably quite slight; but they are often closely read by financial contributors.

"Working the System"

The well-placed and well-connected candidate who knows how to "work the system"—and get away with it—may do much to aid his campaign. There is nothing illegal, of course, nor even much that is reprehensible to some of this. Everyone understands that the candidate with friends in high places may have special access to official information and may use it in planning his campaign. Similarly, there are special advantages to incumbency that no one is expected to forego. But there are limits beyond which candidates may be involved in real abuse. Thus, the congressional frank and some of the official mail privileges extended to state legislators have been used by some incumbents for blatant electioneering. Sometimes, too, members of an incumbent's staff have been taken off their official duties and involved full-time for long periods on campaigns.

Manipulation of official powers goes well beyond such misuse of incumbent privileges. Threats of legislative or regulatory action against financial interests have been used to swell campaign coffers; powers over government contracts may be translated into covert campaign services; official contracts with business interests may be used to manipulate newspaper editorial and endorsement policies (via pressure on advertising revenues); legislative votes or executive decisions may be bartered for endorsements; executive and judicial appointments may be promised in return for support; and in many other ways the system may be squeezed for electoral advantage.

Money in Elections

The loser's cry that an election was "bought" is as familiar as the cry that it was "stolen." Innumerable controversies have arisen over the role of money in American election campaigns, many of them developing into major political scandals and leading to the enactment of new election laws.

Until the closing decades of the nineteenth century, controversy focused on forced campaign contributions from government employees. Thus, one of the earliest provisions of federal law on campaign financing, incorporated into the Naval Appropriations Act of 1867, provided that: "No officer or employee of the government shall require or request any workingman in any navy yard to contribute or pay any money for political purposes, not shall any workingman be removed or discharged for political opinions." The restriction did not prevent the Democratic claim against the GOP congressional committee in 1858 that 75 percent of its funds came from federal officeholders and government workers.

Major scandals arose over the use of federal employee funds in the political campaigns of 1876 and 1800. Among other allegations, it was said that James Garfield had pressed his national chairman for information on campaign contributions of top bureaucrats, by implication threatening their dismissal if they had not paid. Reform agitation led Congress to the passage of the Civil Service Reform Act (the Pendleton Act) in 1883. This legislation declared, "No person in the public service is for that reason under any obligation to contribute to any political fund . . . and he will not be removed or otherwise prejudiced for refusing to do so."

The practice of forced employee contributions to campaigns remained undisturbed for much longer in state and municipal governments. Some states were laggardly in the disestablishment of patronage and spoils systems, continuing to permit forced political contributions by state employees well into the present century. In other states the old ways continued despite prohibiting legislation. Thus, in New York, where a law prohibiting solicitation of campaign contributions from state employees was enacted in 1883 and another requiring candidates to file sworn financial statements was enacted in 1890, Tammany long continued to "mace" city salaries. Tweed's successor, "Honest John" Kelly, instituted a system of fixed contributions to a general campaign committee by all candidates, and officeholders owing their positions to Kelly were assessed contributions from their salaries according to a sliding scale. In Louisiana for many years, the "macing" rate was a flat 10 percent of salary. In Pennsylvania the rate was a mere 2 percent in 1882; but by 1900 the schedule ranged from 3 percent for salaries of $600 to $1200 to 12 percent for salaries above $10,000. Although fourteen states had enacted some kind of campaign legislation by 1905, they achieved little regulatory effect. As Justice Felix Frankfurter observed in *U.S. v. D.A.W.* in 1957, most of these laws quickly "became dead letters or were found to be futile."

The spotlight next shifted to corporate contributions. The Blaine campaign of 1884, widely denounced for its reliance on corporate funds, furnished one of the first examples of the risks, rather than the advantages, of fund-raising success. In the course of his campaign, Blaine attended a dinner at Delmonico's given by some wealthy friends, including John Jacob Astor II, Cyrus W. Field, Jay Gould, Levi Parsons Morton, and Russell Sage. Reporters being excluded from the affair, it became a cause célèbre, and Blaine was pilloried as "Balshazzar" dining on "Monopoly Soup," "Lobby Pudding," and "Gould Pie." Four years later the antiprotection issue drew large amounts of corporate money into the presidential campaign, and from then on there were few major elections in which the role of business funds failed to attract the attention of the press. In 1904 the National Publicity Law Association, headed by Perry Belmont, took the lead in urging federal legislation to limit corporate contributions, and the issue was seized by Theodore Roosevelt in his State of the Union messages in 1905 and 1906. Finally, in 1907 Congress passed the Tillman Act, prohibiting any corporation or national bank from making "a money contribution in connection with any election" of candidates for federal office.

The use by very rich candidates of their personal fortunes, particularly the purchase of votes in state legislatures for election to the U.S. Senate, now became a major controversy. Scandals in several states led to federal legislation (the acts of June 25, 1910, and August 19, 1911) imposing new restrictions on campaign expenditures.

In 1925 the Federal Corrupt Practices Act was passed, a law reflecting a climax of public concern over the Ford-Newberry election scandal in Michigan, the findings of the Kenyon committee, the Teapot Dome disclosures, and revelations of corruption in the Harding campaign of 1920. For nearly half a century, this legislation remained the basic federal law on campaign finance. Except when major scandals arose, its regulations were poorly enforced or ignored. Much the same must be said of the additions that were made to the law by the Clean Politics Act of 1939 (the Hatch Act) and the Taft-Hartley Act of 1947.[9] In particular, the prohibitions of the Hatch Act on the use of relief funds for political purposes and on campaign contributions by federal contractors seem to have been widely evaded, as also were the Taft-Hartley provisions forbidding labor union contributions to political campaigns.

The next major federal regulation of campaign financing occurred in the form of the Federal Election Campaign Act of 1971. Shortly afterward, the Watergate affair began another major national scandal, important phases of which centered on the misuses of money in presidential politics. The aftermath saw a flood of reform legislation—26 states enacting campaign finance legislation in 1974 alone. The most far-reaching of this legislation was California's Proposition 9. Finally the controversy over the fund-raising tactics of the Committee to Re-elect the President led Congress to provide for public financing of the 1976 Presidential campaign—a step that many of the reformers now hope to follow with public financing of other federal and state elections.

Extortion of Contributions by Candidates

The extortion of contributions by politicians is an abuse as old as politics. In this century, the practice of "macing," or the levying of assessments on public salaries for contributions to campaigns, has dwindled as patronage itself has contracted. It persists where patronage and machine organization also persist.

Pennsylvania, New Jersey, Indiana, and Illinois are the states where practice seems to have lasted with most vigor. In 1944 the U.S. Civil Service Commission ordered the dismissal of the secretary of health in Pennsylvania's state government, along with two other top officials, on grounds of violation of the Hatch Act and forced contributions of state employees to campaigns. Pennsylvania's governor ignored the order. In 1950 the Jersey City auditor reported that the Hague machine had collected $361,649 from 3000 city employees during the previous year—a rate reflecting 3 percent of each employee's salary. There have been numerous reported incidents of the same kind in Cook County politics. Elsewhere, kickbacks from the salaries of staff members—whether for personal or campaign use—constitute a contemporary substitute for the practice.

The sale of government jobs, another traditional resort of politicians seeking campaign funds, has not followed macing into decline. The exchange of postmasterships and other minor federal positions for campaign contributions, although it persisted until very recently, is now certainly much reduced. But other, very much more prestigious or more lucrative positions are apparently still available to major campaign donors. Thus, it is clear that the sale of embassies flourished extensively under Richard Nixon, his 1972 campaign reaping $1,324,442 merely from the eight individuals who headed embassies in Western Europe at the time. After this reelection, Nixon made ambassadors of a further eight individuals, each of whom had given no less than $25,000 to the campaign, and in aggregate $706,000. In February 1974, Herbert Kalmbach, Richard Nixon's personal attorney, pleaded guilty to a charge of promising J. Fife Symington, the ambassador to Trinidad and Tobago during 1969-1971, a more prestigious European ambassadorship in return for a $100,000 contribution to be divided between Republican senatorial campaigns and the Committee to Re-elect the President. Although Symington did not in fact receive a European appointment, there were thirteen appointments of noncareer ambassadors soon after the close of the campaign. It is also noteworthy that a condition of Kalmbach's guilty plea was that he be granted immunity from further prosecution in connection with "contributions from persons seeking ambassadorial posts."

Pressure on government contractors for campaign contributions is another age-old abuse still vigorously pursued at many levels of government. In 1972 executives of 28 corporations holding federal contracts gave $2,691,775 to the Committee to Re-elect the President, nearly half in the form of pre-April 7 "secret gifts." Of these contributions, all purportedly from individuals, some were proved to be corporate funds. As Governor of Maryland and as Vice President, Spiro Agnew received "political contributions" from government contractors amounting to between 3 and 5 percent of the value of the contracts. It is a practice that remains common in many states, having led to 46 convictions in one recent 3-year period in New Jersey. The convicted included two secretaries of state (one Democrat, one Republican), a former Democratic mayor of Newark, and a Democratic congressman. Reports from Philadelphia indicate that 5 percent of the value of public works contracts there is diverted to party committees, and in New Orleans the rate is said to be a flat 10 percent. In Illinois a stockbrokerage firm contributed $20,000 to a fund-raising dinner to pay off gubernatorial campaign debts, and one of its partners bought $6000 of additional tickets; shortly afterward, his firm was retained as advisor to the state on a $100 million bond issue, with a fee estimated at $75,000 to $100,000.[10]

"Milker," "squeeze," "pinch," and "cinch" bills—known as "margarine bills" in Oklahoma, where dairy interests are powerful and oleo manufacturers easy prey—are devices for the extortion of funds from lobbyists. The bills are designed to threaten established interests; but, for a fee or a campaign contribution, they will be withdrawn or voted down. Jess Unruh, former Democratic speaker of the California Assembly, made masterful use of this tactic of milking legislative lobbies. A variant of the practice is the speech in which a legislator publicly signals a possible shift in his issue stance, thus requiring emergency action, perhaps in the form of an additional campaign contribution, by the concerned lobbyists.

Deals with campaign vendors and manipulation of campaign accounts are another means by which candidates fund their election efforts. Polls surreptitiously provided to a campaign may be billed by the polling firm to a commercial client; the management firm may perform at a fraction of its usual fee if some of its personnel are found berths on commercial payrolls; and, of course, all types of campaign services may be provided at low costs if a commercial client is being charged for a "business expense."

Finally, American politicians have developed fund-raising and extortion techniques that hinge on manipulation of the system of justice. Both the "protection" extended in certain areas of the country to the activities of organized crime and the "fixing" of traffic tickets, which occurs nearly everywhere, yield contributions to campaigns. At one extreme, millions of dollars are involved (according to the 1973 estimate of the National Advisory Commission on Criminal Justice Standards and Goals, $20 million, or 15 percent of all the funds contributed to municipal and state election campaigns); at the other extreme, the *quid pro quo* may be no more than the expectation of the purchase of a ticket to a fund-raising dinner. Between these poles lies a wide range of illegal activity, from promises of intervention in the regulatory process to the sale of pardons.

Abuses of Contributors

Contributors employ a variety of means to achieve the effect of a personal campaign contribution without actually parting with their own funds. The principal abuse is probably the simple diversion of corporate funds to personal political use. Another device relies on the expensive distinction the tax laws make between campaign contributions and business expenses. The concept of transforming a campaign contribution into a tax-deductible business expenditure—a practice usually referred to in campaign parlance as "double billing"—is one that underlies many manipulations of campaign accounts. The 1964 Pierre Salinger campaign in California, for example, engaged in several maneuvers of this kind, receiving more than $20,000 in campaign contributions from firms which were then provided with bills "for services rendered" on tax-deductible items such as public relations programs. In 1969 several firms owned or controlled by Howard Ahmanson, including the Home Saving and Loan Association, were fined for disguising campaign contributions to Democrats as advertising expenses.

Concealment of campaign contributions is the motive of another series of abuses. The purposes range from hiding the true magnitude of the contribution, through evasion of adverse publicity, to hiding the fact that contributions have been made to more than one candidate in the same race. Much used techniques for ensuring the anonymity of donors include under-the-table cash contributions; surreptitious gifts of valuables (credit cards, telephone lease lines, postage and bulk mailing costs, automobile loans and use of airplanes, and polling and other forms of research); hidden salary subsidies to the candidate and his staff; diversion into the campaign of questionable funds as the result of complex, third-party transactions ("hot money" and "laundering"); and postponement of contributions until after the reporting deadlines, undeclared loans, and private assurances to cover campaign deficits (the last of which is known in campaign parlance as a "downstream marker").

Routine Circumvention of the Law

Perhaps the greatest abuse involving campaign financing is the use of loopholes in the law by both candidates and donors. Testifying in 1966 before the House

Administration Subcommittee on Elections, Representative James C. Wright (D.-Tex.) declared that legislation on campaign financing was "intentionally evaded by almost every candidate." He added, "I dare say there is not a member of Congress, myself included, who has not knowingly evaded its purpose in one way or another."

The limitations of the 1925 Federal Corrupt Practices Act on the amount of money candidates may receive were typically evaded by reliance on the phrase in the law referring to the candidate's "knowledge or consent." The candidate simply made certain that he knew nothing about campaign contributions or expenditures. Thus, in 1968, when Senator George McGovern (D.-S.D.) was questioned on his failure to report receipt of funds by his reelection campaign, his assistant noted, "We are very careful to make sure that Senator McGovern never sees the campaign receipts."[11]

Another widely exploited loophole was the restriction of the provisions of the 1925 act to political committees operating in "two or more states." If a committee operated in only one state and was not a subdivision of a national committee, the law did not apply. Nor was a committee covered by the law if it operated only in the District of Columbia and then mailed out checks to candidates in a particular state. Thus, the former chairman of the House Special Committee to Investigate Campaign Expenditures, Representative Thomas P. O'Neill (D.-Mass), used a District of Columbia committee for receipt of contributions to his 1970 reelection campaign.

Loopholes exploited by donors are of many kinds. To evade the application of reporting of publicity requirements, the practice has been to give a trifle less than the amount that the law provides must be reported (for example $99.99 in the case of $100 reporting requirements) and to give such sums to a large number of committees, each of which supports the same candidate. To evade the limitation on total contributions (for example, the $5000 individual limitation under federal law), the donor contributes funds to other groups (state or county or private associations) which pass along the money in their own names; or he privately subsidizes his relations, so that not only his wife, but many members of his family give $5000. Corporations and banks have evaded restrictions on their involvement in campaigns by contributions to trade associations (which then pass on the money to candidates); by giving bonuses or salary increases to executives (who are then expected to make personal contributions to candidates); or by loaning or renting to campaigns their billboards and equipment and offices and airplanes (and then writing off the loans at less than the market rate or declaring the rental fees uncollectable). Similarly, unions collect political funds which they claim not to be membership dues; or they conduct "nonpartisan" registration and voting drives in only those areas where their own candidates benefit; or they make use of union publications to promote pro-union candidates. All these practices, exploiting loopholes in the law, are common at every level of politics and seem not to be effectively checked by repeated efforts at reform.

Thus, one of the toughest state laws on campaign financing was enacted by Massachusetts in 1962. As reported by *Congressional Quarterly*, the law limited the number of committees supporting a candidate to three; required each committee to have a bank account and the bank to report money deposited or paid out; and required public reports on the names and addresses of donors of more than $25 and the addresses of persons whose bills were paid. It was noted that "despite the supposed stringency of the law," when Edward M. Kennedy in 1964 reported expenses of $100,292.45 for his successful campaign for the Democratic nomination for the U.S. Senate, realistic estimates of his actual expenditures amount to "ten times that sum."

Conclusions

It is clear that there has been a real improvement in American standards of election administration in the past half-century. The massive ballot frauds and election-day violence of the nineteenth century have almost disappeared. The credit appears partly due to refinements in the techniques of election administration (chiefly, the secret ballot and permanent registration) and to new election technology (the voting machine and computerization). But the principal causes are the improvement in the civility of the American electorate itself and the spread of two-party competition to most areas of the country.

The underhanded tactics of the 1972 Committee to Re-elect the President attracted much attention and inspired reform efforts at all levels of government. Whether the new laws, regulations, and bodies such as California's Fair Political Practices Commission will succeed in improving the overall conduct of campaigns remains to be seen. One may be permitted to doubt, however, that the excesses of candidates and their managers will be so easily checked. Legislative and regulatory provisions, federal and state commissions, even improvements in the vigilance of the press and media—none of these is sufficient to limit the reach for power that inspires the use of "dirty tricks" in political campaigns. Moreover, the more worrying forms of campaign misconduct—the new types of "voter misinformation" and the use of official powers for campaign advantage—have attracted relatively little notice. Again, the hope for improvement must lie principally in the standards that the electorate requires of candidates and in the self-interest of competing politicians.

The century-long effort to control the use of money in elections remains far short of its goals. Partly, the repeated evasions of the reform laws may be the result of the unrealism of their provisions. One may argue that the attempt to purify completely a process, politics, which involves the clash of the major interests in the society, is itself unrealistic. Or one may attribute the unrealism to the origin of much of the legislation in the heat of scandal, a time when the tides of popular reaction sweep all before them. Partly, too, evasion and abuse may result from those elements of self-serving partisanship that are to be found in the law, some provisions being enacted with the sole purpose of perpetuating the dominance of the majority party.

It is also true that the aims of much of the reform legislation on campaign finance have been frustrated by the success of yet other reforms. There is a fundamental inconsistency in the ambitions that have guided the campaign reform legislation of the last century. On the one hand, there is the effort to control the costs of the election process, while on the other there is the effort to greatly expand popular participation in that process (particularly at the stage of nominations). Thus, the Tillman Act limitations on expenditures were quickly ruined by other successes of the Progressive movement: both the Seventeenth Amendment to the U.S. Constitution, requiring the popular election of U.S. Senators, and the widespread adoption of direct primary laws greatly increased the costs of campaigning in populous states.

At bottom, however, the failure of much of the reform legislation on campaign finance is explained by the attempt to block the intervention in the political process of immensely powerful groups—often at the very times when they perceived their interests as most threatened. Thus, coincidentally with the early reform legislation, government was thrusting itself ever more deeply into the economy (the Underwood Tariff Act); the impact of politics on business, sharpening the inducement to businessmen to involve themselves in campaigns, increased. In the same way, with the enactment of national and state labor legislation, unions' financial ties to politics grew apace. Legislative regulation could not be more than a trivial check to the efforts of these groups to protect their interests in politics.

Today, much reformist enthusiasm focuses on public financing of elections. The belief seems to be that private contributions to politics are inherently corrupt. Thus, according to the authors of a recent study, "the interface between economic resources and political power that occurs primarily in election campaigns and . . . the inequities it produces" are a "major source of systemic corruption in America." They explain that:

The need to finance election campaigns by private contributions has helped to nurture a close relationship between candidates and officeholders and the individuals or organized interest groups with the resources available for investment in politics. At its best, this relationship tarnishes the credibility of all government officials in the eyes of the public; at its worst, it is a "mutual benefit society" whose politics serve the public only fortuitously. Unfortunately, politics, at its worst, has too often been characterisitc of the American system of private campaign financing.[12]

The proposal for public financing of elections rests on a radically overdrawn indictment of the corrupting influence of campaign funds. Indeed, in the effort to make their case, some of its advocates would cast suspicion on all forms of interest group politics, even on representative democracy itself. Thus, in some versions, public financing is merely the preface to the instutition of "periodic plebiscites," experiments in participatory democracy, or a fundamental restructuring of the electoral process to "increase the accountability of public officeholders."[13]

The problems of funding are only one source of corruption in American elections. Public financing will not remedy corruption in the administration of elections or in the conduct of campaigns. Indeed, it hardly touches the problems of the abuse of official power. New forms of corruption would undoubtedly be generated by public financing, and loopholes would soon be discovered. The risk is especially great that it would afford dangerous opportunities for official manipulation. One must be even more suspicious of reform proposals that view public financing as a first step toward new kinds of "direct democracy." Watergate, like other major scandals before it, gave impetus to radical critiques of American institutions. Neglecting the extraordinary achievements of democracy in this country, they seek to use the evidence of corruption in elections as the basis for changing the whole system of representative government.

True reform should have as its goals the effort to maintain and increase effective competition in elections and to attract candidates of the highest abilities and personal qualities to public office. The best protection against corruption in elections is found in the open controversy of campaigns and in the conscience of candidates.

10

Costs of Corruption

In the last few decades a substantial social science literature in support of corrupt machine politics has developed. This chapter will give a few examples of such literature. It will then indicate the destructive side of corrupt machine politics, its creation of cynicism in politics, its destructive effect on city finances, its deleterious effect on government departments, its effect as a gateway for organized crime and help to other crime, its support to police brutality, and its impact on people.

Intellectual Arguments for Corrupt Machines

The human mind moves readily to rationalizations of the status quo, however undesirable it may be. Before the current academic arguments for corruption are cited, it is interesting to note that somewhat similar arguments were raised by informed persons in the first decade of this century. These arguments and convincing reasons against them appear in Robert R. Brooks's *Corruption in American Politics and Life*.[1] One was the argument that corruption made for more active business partly because people spend more for the vice, which corruption permits, and partly because they can do more business with the favors granted by politicians. The second argument is that corruption may be more than paid for by the greater efficiency of those who engage in corruption. A third apology is that "it saves us from mob rule." The machine protects society against the attacks of internal barbarians. The fourth apology is that corruption is part of an evolutionary process, the ends of which are beneficial.

Brooks disposes of all four arguments readily. There is no need to repeat his arguments. Few people today would take any of them seriously. But they are cited to give the reader perspective. Some Americans of the first decade of this century used what they knew about evolution and societal order and business development to rationalize corruption rather than undertake the hard work of elimination; some American writers today have found new rationalizations but are repeating the process.

Current academic apologies for corruption are numerous. John F. Davenport, a graduate student in American history, asks: "In the last analysis is there really that much difference between George Washington Plunkitt and William Ronan?"[2] Plunkitt was a Tammany politician who described his cheating the city on land deals in humorous terms which have apparently misled Davenport.

Ronan was a member of the New York Port Authority and later chairman of the New York Transport Authority—a hard-working, well-educated, capable public servant, who unwisely took a personal gift from Governor Rockefeller, but a gift which was not intended for any antipublic purpose and was not illegal.

Another apologist for the corrupt machine is Prof. Robert K. Merton of Columbia University. He writes: ". . . the functional deficiencies of the official structure generate an alternative (unofficial) structure to fulfill existing needs somewhat more effectively. Whatever its specific historical origins, the political machine persists as an apparatus for satisfying otherwise unfulfilled needs of diverse groups in the populations."[3]

Another apology for corruption comes from Prof. Samuel P. Huntington of Harvard. This comment was written for developing countries.

Just as the corruption produced by the expansion of political participation helps to integrate new groups into the political system, so also the corruption produced by the expansion of governmental regulation may help stimulate economic development. Corruption may be one way of surmounting traditional laws or bureaucratic regulations which hamper economic expansion.[4]

A historian, Sam Bass Warner, Jr., criticizes nineteenth-century reformers for their failure to undertake economic reforms and praises Martin Lomasney of Boston (ward leader in the first three decades of the century) and Charles F. Murphy of New York (Tammany leader from 1902 to 1924) "who used their success to represent their constituents."[5]

Professor Smelser has written an article about corruption which seems to share the belief in its usefulness:

The functionalist treatments of corruption did not manifest the naive moralism of the preceding page, but a new kind of moral stance . . .; a sense of moral superiority that arises when one assumes a new and more enlightened moral posture toward a phenomenon based on some new knowledge about it.[6]

Smelser, however, smells more of a rat than do the other writers quoted above. He notes that corruption "leaves the regime in a position of reduced flexibility and maneuverability," which "may lead to a vicious circle of declining legitimacy in the long run."

Another historian, Prof. Joel Arthur Tarr, has a chapter on "The Political Machine as Public Servant."[7] This chapter is as much an attack on reformers as it is an outline of public services from the machine. Corrupt activities of the Lorimer machine are duly cited, but there is little recognition of their disadvantageous consequences to Chicago or its citizens.

A historian who is more conscious of the disadvantages of the corrupt machine is Prof. Alexander B. Callow, Jr. He notes the drift of his colleagues:

Present day urban historians tend to minimize corruption, in the belief that excessive emphasis on it in the past has obscured the facts on how the machines worked, and the point that the bosses contribution to the social mobility of the poor may have outweighed his social misdeeds.

But he goes on to say:

Graft is still graft. Perhaps the heart of the issue is not the kind of graft or who perpetrates it or even its magnitude but rather its impact upon the democratic process. Graft of any kind breeds distrust. Distrust breeds cynicism. Cynicism is the most powerful enemy of the democratic representative process.[8]

All these scholars are undoubtedly reporting aspects of the truth about corrupt machines as they see the truth. Chapter 11 tries to appraise some of their theories. But few of these apologists go on to comment about the disastrous consequences of corruption. This chapter will outline some of those consequences, so that the reader may have a more nearly complete picture, and then suggest some noncorrupt methods of bringing government closer to people.

In the following lists of costs of corruption to government and to the public, the reader should keep in mind that many difficulties arise in appraising the consequences of corruption. It is often impossible to determine the exact proportion of the extra costs or poorer service which is due to corruption and what proportion is due to normal bureaucratic ineptness. The author has tried to limit this chapter to unusually poor results which seem to come from dishonest administration. In some cases like "honest" graft, the extra costs of dishonesty are clear. In cases where intergovernmental comparison is possible, the costs of corruption are reasonably clear. The tendency of corrupt police departments to be cruel in dealing with the poor seems to have been amply established and is confirmed by other writers and police executives. But how much corruption had to do with tragedies like the Iroquois Theater or Triangle Shirtwaist fires mentioned later in this chapter is less certain. In both these cases, the corrupt city regulatory bodies were delinquent. But would honest city governments have done much better with the deficient techniques of the times?

Development of Cynicism

The first section of this chapter quoted Professor Callow who properly viewed the development of cynicism as a major disadvantage of corruption. Throughout the United States, able people stay out of politics, refuse to run for office, or support less able candidates because they have come to believe that "politics is all corrupt." However, this book has noted that politics is not all corrupt; that most of the federal service is free of corruption; that almost no states have had continuous corruption; and that much of local government is now honestly run. But there is still enough corruption to keep cynicism alive.

The reader must also consider the impact of police corruption on youth and on the population generally. As Professor Bahn has observed, the public tends to place great confidence in police officers as defenders of law and order, perhaps a greater confidence than the police can hope to fulfill. The boy who at a certain age wants to be a policeman is expressing this confidence. When the police become corrupt, the result is a shattering of the confidence of much of the public, but especially of youth.

The *Knapp Commission on Police Corruption* in New York declared in 1972:

But perhaps the most important effect of corruption in the so-called gambling control units is the incredible damage their performance wreaks on public confidence in the law and the police. Youngsters raised in New York ghettos, where gambling abounds, regard the law as a joke when all their lives they have seen police officers coming and going from gambling establishments and taking payments from gamblers. . . . While it is certainly not true that all police officers, or even a majority, get rich on gambling and narcotics graft, the fact that a large number of citizens believe they do has a tremendously damaging effect on police authority.

Elsewhere the report added (page 113): "The complicity of some policemen in narcotics dealing—a crime considered utterly heinous by a large segment of society—inevitably has a devastating effect on the public's attitude toward the department."[9]

The New Jersey Commission on the Newark riots of 1967 reported that the constant air of corruption in Newark had much to do with inciting the riot. John Gardiner, discussing the consequences of corruption in Wincanton, comments that the most damaging result has been the weakening of public support for local government, a weakening attested by both a survey and individual interviews. Many businessmen also felt that community growth suffered because of the city's reputation for corruption and gambling.[10]

The Costs of "Honest" Graft

It has been noted earlier that smarter corrupt politicians have been moving toward "honest" graft. How much do the politer forms of "honest" graft handicap a government's operations? An analysis in Moscow's sympathetic but usually objective book on Tammany boss Carmine de Sapio claims that in recent years in New York there has not even been the kickback on contracts by which Hague in Jersey City and Pendergast in Kansas City made large sums. Profits on contracts are now usually made by rings of contractors who buy up small city officials without the cooperation of the top political leaders.[11]

The chief polite form of moneymaking cited by Moscow is done by the political figure who goes into a business which by its nature offers a front for selling political influence. Law and insurance are frequent examples, but architecture and public relations have become quite frequent. In one era, says Moscow (himself at one time a Democratic officeholder, but a relatively objective ex-newspaperman as far as the authors know), various New York Republicans made fortunes practicing as attorneys for liquor license seekers before a Republican-controlled state liquor licensing board. One Tammany Hall leader in the 1920s made more than $3 million in five years of practice before the city Board of Standards and Appeals, which would relax zoning laws at his request. Another Tammany leader controlled the man who ran the Department of Buildings. Persons who bought insurance from his agency received no notice of violations; others found every technicality used against them. Other leaders sold performance bonds to contractors who wanted the city jobs. Boss Ed Flynn of the Bronx, who claimed complete honesty, was a partner in a "political law firm," which insisted that the staff other than Flynn do the legal work. Carmine de Sapio, the Tammany leader from 1949 to 1961, was in the insurance business.

In de Sapio's regime, as under the leadership of other Tammany leaders, men selected for judgeships were asked to make contributions to Tammany political funds (some of which probably went to Tammany leaders). The amount was at one time as high as $100,000 but was later cut down to a year's salary. Some judgeships were given as rewards for political endeavor.

How damaging to the city are these methods of "honest" graft, many of which are legal, at least on the surface? Most of them, of course, mean higher costs and poorer services to the city since competition is limited to those corporations which have bought their insurance or secured their legal services at the "right" place. Some, like the control of building restrictions, are a means of extortion which is both expensive and aggravating to the businesses concerned. The large contribution required of judicial candidates probably results in poorer judges.

Effect of Corruption on Governmental Finance

Gosnell's account of machine politics in Chicago makes it clear that machine-granted favoritism and corruption in the assessment office had much to do with Chicago's financial difficulties in the Depression.[12] Undoubtedly the background of Tammany mismanagement is related to the current (1977) financial difficulties of New York City. Wincanton, Pennsylvania, after its decades of corrupt leadership, ranked "*last* in the state in the average ratio of observed to estimated performance on taxation and expenditure policies."[13] Many of Boston's financial difficulties have been ascribed to its generations of misrule.

Similar problems can occur in state government. To quote Tyler Draa's study of Louisiana politics:

However, the fact remains that Huey Long was responsible for the design and success of Louisiana's most corrupt political regime, and the cost to Louisiana's citizenry was tremendous. For instance, competitive bidding for public contracts was all but abandoned. The cost per mile of Huey's highways were almost twice that of a neighboring state, which had constructed wider highways with higher quality concrete on terrain which was not as flat as Louisiana's. These excessive costs resulted from corporate kickbacks and payments to Long machine intermediaries. By 1932, the Highway Commission was bankrupt, and necessitated Long's extensive bond legislation. . . . Yet these bonds only represented one-half of the costs of building Long's doubly expensive highways, the other half came from existing gas taxes. It has been estimated that for every dollar spent on the public, two more went into the Long machine's treasury or individual members' pockets.[14]

To take a more recent example in Wincanton, Pennsylvania, city land was sold at a very cheap price, with a similar amount distributed to officials. The buyer subsequently sold the land for 4 times the city price. On almost all major city contracts, the price was higher because of fees paid to politically selected architects, engineers, or contractors. Gardiner concludes:

. . . in the long run, the corrupters and corruptees—have retarded progress more than they have assisted it. The wide open gambling and the free lance corruption of the Donnellys and Walaseks have made it harder, not easier, to recruit new industries and investors to replace the declining or departing corporations which built the city at the turn of the century.[15]

Much financial burden comes from the appointment of incompetent officials by corrupt machines. The La Guardia administration found many incompetent Tammany appointees in the holdover county governments. The Commissioner of Records in Kings County, Hyman Schorenstein, could not read or write, or spell his own name. The 102 employees of New York District Attorney Dodge received $433,845 a year for paying no attention to the rackets which Dewey discovered in a few months and for slow or no prosecution in other cases. There were also 85 unnecessary positions in the county registers' offices, costing $178,000 a year, and unnecessary positions costing $45,000 a year in the offices of the Commissioner of Records. A Deputy Tax Commissioner in the Bronx drew his salary while working full-time for the Lackawanna Railroad. He was removed, but a Tammany majority of the Board of Estimate voted him his pension.

Tammany used municipal court clerkships as a means of paying the politically faithful but administratively absent.[16]

All the above costs of corruption of course add to the cost of government to the taxpayer, or reduce the value of government services, or both.

Quality of Administration

Nineteenth-century political machines often had a disastrous effect on administrative quality. The Philadelphia Gas Ring, under boss James McManes, produced real administrative chaos. A citizens' committee asking the legislature for a new charter in 1883 noted:

Philadelphia is now recognized as the worst paved and worst cleaned city in the civilized world. The water supply is so bad that during many weeks of the last winter it was not only distasteful and unwholesome for drinking but offensive for bathing purposes. The effort to clean the streets was abandoned for months. . . . The physical condition of the sewers is dangerous to the health and most offensive to the comfort of our people.[17]

John Powers, boss of Chicago's Nineteenth Ward (1896-1921), was reported to be generous to his constituents, but in 1896

—Hull House investigators found public schools badly overcrowded, with 3,000 more school children in the ward than seats available. Dirt, garbage, and other refuse filled streets and alleys and constituted a serious health hazard for inhabitants. The area badly needed parks and bathhouses. Well aware of the community's desperate plight, Hull House women determined to improve the situation, but they quickly found themselves outmaneuvered by the boss, who benefitted from maintaining the status quo. Reformers soon discovered that similar situations existed in other areas of the city.[18]

On December 30, 1903, a fire in the Iroquois Theater of Chicago killed 572 persons. Carter Harrison, then mayor, reports that the city council (a largely corrupt group) had two months earlier ordered that "further action against theater violations be stayed until the committee on judiciary reports an amendatory ordinance."[19] The problem was the burning of crowded inflammable scenery, ignited by a gas jet.

When reform Mayor Hazen S. Pingree took over in Detroit on January 1, 1890, he found that the preceding corrupt administration had left Detroit with expensive rolled wooden pavements, difficult to clean and poorly drained. Poor contractors, with good Democratic party connections, had done all they could to take advantage of the city. Recently constructed sewer lines were also rotting and crumbling. School board members had been bribed into agreeing on contracts.[20]

In Baltimore in 1892, "Pigtown," the worst black slum where people lived under abominable conditions, received no city inspection whatever from the Rasin-machine-run Baltimore government. Sweatshops were also inadequately inspected, as was milk.

At a Baltimore citywide congress on municipal government in 1911, Dr. Herman M. Briggs of New York spoke of health. Briggs and William H. Welch were reported by Crooks to have argued: "In Baltimore, as across the nation, there was a shortage of trained personnel. This shortage, argued both men, was largely due to the spoils system in city government which prevented careers in public health work."[21]

Some of the worst effects of corrupt governmental regimes are felt by the reform administrations which succeed the bosses. Reform mayors like Lindsay in New York and Clark and Dilworth in Philadelphia were largely unsuccessful in reforming police departments. Perhaps too large a personnel turnover would be required; perhaps the men in uniform have too much political power; perhaps police is a mysterious field into which mayors dare not look. Whatever the reasons, New York and Philadelphia have shown us that reform mayors may have little impact in reforming police departments.

Reform mayors also often run into the problem of too many headaches coming at once. An interesting book by Diana Gordon, *City Limits,* cites several problems encountered by the Lindsay administration, all of which were made worse by the neglectful and corrupt administrations of preceding mayors. The drug problem was clearly a consequence of corruption; the others may or may not have been so. The Lindsay administration had great difficulty trying to work out appropriate programs for drug addicts. Addiction was a major cause of death among teenagers and also a major source of crime. New York was probably the worst city of the country in amount and proportion of drug addiction. Gordon grants that, "Finally the shadow of police corruption and involvement in the narcotics traffic hung over police attempts to round up pushers and users." A New York State Joint Legislative Committee on Crime estimated in 1969 that organized crime revenue on heroin alone was pulling out of three ghetto areas (Harlem, South Bronx, and Bedford Stuyvesant) a sum of money (ranging between $122 million and $238 million a year) equal to at least half of welfare monies expended in the same area.[22]

Lindsay's substantial difficulties with New York City's prisons certainly grew in large part out of staff inadequacies, in both numbers and training, which as surely went back to political machine policies, or the lack thereof, in the past. Previous warnings about prison inadequacies had been disregarded by earlier administrations.

Royko, in his penetrating study of Mayor Daley's administration of Chicago, noted that while Mayor Daley was putting an old family physician in charge of public health, Chicago's tuberculosis rate was twice the national average and the infant mortality rate was climbing (against a national trend) to a point higher than in all but two nations of the developed world. Daley's unqualified public health head ignored a flu epidemic and let his neighborhood health clinics be "filthy and understaffed."

A ring of Chicago police under Daley was stealing and carrying loot home in squad cars. The corrupt police department was, not surprisingly, inefficient. Crimes would be reported several times on the police radio, as there was no immediate investigation. While Daley was applauded by business leaders for downtown development, "The syndicate was still putting bodies in sewers and in car trunks, bombing its way into control of the restaurant industry's supply and union needs, and had murdered its way into a takeover of the black policy wheels."[23]

New York City's record shows similar unhappy experiences. Crippled and disabled men had to pay $1000 to $7000 to the machine for licenses to run newstands in the pre-La Guardia years.[24] The superintendent of the city home on Welfare Island for aged, friendless, and destitute people not only permitted horrible living conditions but extorted their small savings from these poor people.

Additional evidence comes from a careful study of Philadelphia. "Still, the fact that corruption, generally accepted by Philadelphia's population, had led to the neglect not only of the city's public improvements but also of its social and economic problems made the effects of the Depression particularly shocking."[25]

Time magazine, September 27, 1972, gives a picture of what municipal corruption can do to local and national elections. A *Tribune* reporter became an election clerk in Chicago. He and his coworkers found more than 1000 election law violations, mostly forgery. A federal inquiry resulted in 40 indictments of "political small fry" but little sign that Mayor Daley would move toward more honest elections.

Effect of Corruption on Crime

It is certain that the great extension of racketeering in New York City in the 1920s and 1930s was largely a result of police "protection" furnished by the Tammany machine. Tammany district leaders were the main go-betweens.[26] Obviously the efficiency of the police was lowered and crime increased by this type of transaction.

Organized crime, or any other sort of corruption, is likely to have very negative effect on the morale of public officials, especially, of course, on police. Gardiner notes that in Wincanton, departmental morale and esprit de corps of the police have been low because of political meddling and because of the general public belief in the existence of police misconduct.[27]

Police corruption damages the effectiveness of the police force in its important crime control and public order maintenance activities.

Curiously, some of the police chiefs with whom the authors have talked have not recognized the effect of corruption on crime rates. The relationship is important enough to deserve analysis. So many factors other than law enforcement affect crime; amount of corruption is so difficult to measure; and crime statistics are still so unreliable that mathematical correlations have not been adequately investigated. But one must not ignore the national correlation that American rates of crimes of violence and American corruption rates appear to be higher than those of most other modern democracies.[28]

The simple problem of time is also hard to deny. How could a police force like that of New York City in 1969, with a substantial fraction of its staff spending much police time collecting bribes or stealing, be effective in running down criminals?[29] The same query must be raised about most other cities where substantial corruption is to be found.

Several studies[30] indicate that punishment does discourage crime. If this is the case, the failure of a police force to start the punishment process because of corruption must lead to more crime. The discouraging effect of corruption on individual police incentives to action must also be considered. If an arrested criminal can buy himself out, at higher police levels or at the prosecution level or at the courts, the patrolman or detective who made the arrests must be discouraged.

There can be little doubt that certain kinds of undisciplined police action can lead to riots. Paul Chevigny gives an example of how Puerto Rican youth in the lower East Side were ready to riot because a youth arrested for burglary was dead by hanging in the jail and because police, for no apparent reason, had summarily ordered Puerto Rican youth out of a park. Similar cases appear elsewhere.[31] It is probably fair to guess that undue police provocation of this type is more likely to occur in more corruptly run departments.

Since the Civil War, there have been examples of police brutality which was closely associated with machine politics. The Lexow committee in 1894 and the Mazet committee in 1900 found it in New York. In the 1900 riots in New York City, blacks were beaten up mercilessly. The police board refused to take any serious action.[32] The Seabury investigations in the 1930s in New York City uncovered cruel treatment of many citizens by New York police.

Rubinstein, studying Philadelphia police, comments that "The real cost [of police graft] is the degradation of the job, the destruction of morals, the exposure of discipline and supervision, and the breakdown of clear standards of what constitutes 'good work' which allows some policemen to become criminals in every sense of the word."[33]

Corruption Spreads

Police are necessarily a major enforcing agency against derelictions by personnel of other departments of the city or county government. The construction inspector who extorts from the contractor, the food inspector who is bribed by the dairy, must be reported by someone to the police and arrested by the police. Corruption in other departments is bound to increase if corrupt police accomplices are easy to find. Corruption in other departments is also likely to foster corruption in the police department, if only by force of example.

One of the methods of judging a district attorney's office is the percentage of convictions. A well-run district attorney's office prosecutes only people whose guilt is reasonably certain. The following figures compare reform attorneys Jerome, Whitman, and Dewey with Tammany district attorneys.

In 1902-1909, William Travers Jerome had made a sensation with 44 percent of convictions from all his trials. In 1910-1914, Charles S. Whitman, the last Republican district attorney, had raised this to 60 percent. The next year Tammany came back and the percentage fell to 50 percent, to 49, to 44, to 45. William C. Dodge brought it back to 51 percent. Dewey shot it up to 63 percent.[34]

The impact of the ineffective district attorneys' office on police and other officials hardly needs elaboration.

The Seabury investigation in New York discovered an assistant prosecuting attorney who testified that he had received $20,000 in bribes in 600 cases to "go light" in prosecution of 900 defendants in the Woman's Court. The discouraging effect on this kind of prosecuting weakness on law enforcement again is easy to imagine.[35]

The Knapp Commission reported[36] that the temptation of police was increased by the knowledge or suspicion of corruption in the prosecution or judicial functions. "Evidence uncovered by the United States Attorney's office in Manhattan in a current investigation of bribery by heroin dealers confirms the fact that corruption in narcotics law enforcement goes beyond the Police Department and involves prosecutors, attorneys, bondsmen, and allegedly even certain judges."

Corruption Aids Organized Crime

As Chapter 6 has shown, organized crime benefits tremendously from police corruption. Former Chief Justice Warren has been quoted as saying that organized crime cannot get started in any community without corruption of some law enforcement agency.[37] It may be that the Los Angeles area is an exception, in which organized crime has continued to operate, although on a reduced basis, in spite of a minimum of law enforcement corruption. But generally, police corruption and organized crime do seem to go hand in hand. Introduction of organized crime is a brutalizing force in any community.

An Italian-American writer, campaigning against the broad application of the term *Mafia* to his fellows, notes:

Incidentally, the American media have totally ignored the fact that in other countries with large populations derived from the Mezzogiorno there is no Italian organized crime. For example, Argentina and Brazil have old Italian communities, and Australia and Germany more recent ones. The absence of Italian criminal organizations in these countries gives the lie to the suspicion that Mafia-type activities are inherent in and inextricable from the culture of ordinary South Italians.[38]

Professor Gambino could also have added that Canada has a large population of Italian extraction with only fallout of organized crime from America and that the Italians sprinkled through England and various continental European countries have not brought organized crime families with them. So we are left with the question: Why did organized crime flourish among Italian immigrants in America, but not among Italian immigrants elsewhere? The corruptibility of American government is one factor. Corruption is probably greater in Argentina and Brazil than in the United States, but it is probably less in the other countries cited.

Most studies of organized crime in America indicate that political corruption is essential to its operation. In *Theft of the Nation* Cressey has a chapter on the political corruption activities which are essential to organized crime. Michael Dorman's *Payoff* is devoted entirely to the role of organized crime in corrupting American politics. Virgil Petersen in the last chapter of his *Barbarians in Our Midst* notes that "Almost everywhere the underworld has become an integral part of the political machine."[39] Chapter 6 of this book demonstrates that organized crime is a major factor in continuing corruption.

Salerno has assembled a number of examples of how organized crime, through its corrupt political influence, can penalize a law enforcement officer who tells the truth about it. The Chief of Police of Tampa and Sergeant Jack de la Llana of Tampa presented evidence to the McClelland committee about organized crime leader Santo Trafficante only to be criticized by the business community in Tampa. ("You're going to ruin the tourist trade if you keep talking about gangsters down here.") In Detroit, Chief of Detectives Vincent Piersante was forced to retire because his investigation showed Detroit policemen who were paid off for protection to gambling. In New York the police sergeant, Edgar Crosswell, who discovered the Apalachin meeting was demoted to a job in New York City's Sanitation Department, the demotion coming as a result of criticism from an official influenced by the Teamster's Union and organized crime. In Chicago hard-nosed Joseph Morris found that the mob made trouble for him at each promotion, and forced him through an expensive trial. After the departure of Superintendent Orlando W. Wilson, Captain William J. Duffy was demoted because he conducted a raid which found lists of Chicago police paid off by gamblers. In New Jersey organized crime influences pressed Jersey City police to drive federal and state law enforcement officials away from the wake of a waterfront mob associate. William J. Brennan, Jr. (son of the Supreme

Court Justice), was sidetracked by the Attorney General of New Jersey, on whose staff he served, because he indicated, truthfully, that certain legislators were "too comfortable" with organized crime.[40]

Organized crime fares well in some courts. In 1971 the New York State Legislative Commission on Crime studied 1762 cases in state courts in the 1960s and found that "the rate of dismissals and acquittals for racketeers was five times that of other defendents."[41]

Effects of Corruption on People, Especially the Poor

In *The Children of Sanchez,* Jesus Sanchez ruminates on the problems of life. One of the most discouraging to him is the quality of his government and its effect on the poor. "The Mexican people are going under, because there's no leadership and no faith, and there's so much lousy corruption, as you can see."[42]

Corruption has a broad effect on people. Feelings like those of Jesus Sanchez are carried over to some of his children who live in the United States. Italian-Americans still show the mistrust of government which their ancestors acquired living under the corrupt Bourbon rule over "El Regno de Due Sicilii" in nineteenth-century Italy.[43]

A striking example of the cost of a corrupt police department to people is found in the East St. Louis race riot of 1917. In this riot perhaps 100 innocent blacks and whites were killed. Presumably the mayor tried to maintain order, and he did ask for National Guard units (who were not very helpful). But some of the blame must go to a corrupt and inefficient police force. The department was reorganized upon insistence of a businessman's committee after the riot, but the reform was only temporary.[44] The Chicago police force was sharply criticized by a grand jury for spying on people, failing to prevent the October 1969 riots, with resultant damage to citizens.

The Libbey commission, investigating the 1967 riots in Newark, concluded that the general atmosphere of corruption in Newark city government was a major reason for those unfortunate riots.[45] Ralph Salerno joined in this judgment:

Negroes criticizing the operation of the Police Department cite, among other things, the 1966 indictment of five members of the auto squad on charges of extorting $9,000 from car thieves. Indictments against one of the five men have since been dropped, but the others are still awaiting trial.

Testimony before the Commission, interviews with responsible people in different strata of the city's life, as well as nationally publicized articles (*Life, The New York Times*) leave no doubt that the belief that Newark is a corrupt city is pervasive. This has implications for the attitudes of citizens toward law and order which this Commission cannot ignore.

One of the most consistent complaints of Negroes about the city involves politics in the Police Department. A priest who is familiar with Negro problems says: The Police are the real breakdown in community relations.[46]

There is also some evidence that corruption was one of the causes of black riots in Detroit in 1967, most destructive of the black riots.

Rubenstein quotes an interview with a former New York police commissioner who resigned under fire:

In the ghetto, the one who is most hurt by police corruption is the ghetto resident; for the most part he is getting little or nothing. In fact he's being hurt tremendously by the corruption. The consideration, even the courtesy extended him is less. Now, when you move from the ghetto and you consider corruption in the middle class and the business community, they are only paying for some service or product and they're getting some worth, so its's really with the poor that corruption makes the greatest impact and hurts the most.[47]

Judge Ben Lindsey, founder of the juvenile court movement in the first decade of this century, described some of the effect on poor children of the jail run by the corrupt machine of Denver at that time.

I found boys in the city jail, in cells reeking with filth and crawling with vermin, waiting trial for some such infantile offences as these I have described. I found boys in the county jail locked up with men of the vilest immorality, listening to obscene stories, subject to the most degrading personal indignities, and taking lessons in a high school of vice with all the receptive eagerness of innocence. I found that the older boys, now almost confirmed in viciousness, had begun their careers as Tony Costello had, or these burglars of the pigeon roost. And I found that many of the hardened criminals were merely the perfect graduates of the system of which I had been a sort of proud superintendent.[48]

Some of the costs of organized crime also are a burden on the more well-to-do. Another cost of political corruption which is overlooked by its academic defenders is the cost of racketeering to the consumer. For example, in the mid-twenties Chicago West Side kosher butcher shops were terrorized into a Master Jewish Butcher's Association, raising corned beef prices to the customer from $.95 to $1.25 a pound. In a Chicago where Al Capone represented authority much more than "Big Bill" Thompson, the public prosecutors made no real effort to fight gangster extortions.[49]

A substantial reason for the tragedy of American blacks today is the poor level of government afforded urban blacks by corrupt municipal machines. Osofsky's account of the making of the slums of Harlem in the 1920s is almost a list of items which an honest and effective New York City government should have prevented. As the blacks moved in, rentals and real estate values rose—something which no government could have long prevented. But these quarters were allowed to become congested and unsanitary (probably through bribing the City Building Department).[50] Apartments were transformed into one-room flats, into which entire families moved. Landlords left halls dirty and dark, permitted broken pipes to rust, cut off heat as the apparatus wore out, and allowed homes to become vermin-invested. Good enforcement procedures of effective city governments would have kept all these things from happening.

With these living quarters and the inhabitants' lack of preparation for urban living, health conditions were appalling. Infant mortality in Harlem in the 1920s was 111 per thousand. Deaths from tuberculosis, heart disease, and cancer were all high. Some of these illnesses could have been controlled by the public health department of a city like New York, if it had been honestly and effectively run.

A Hearst reporter, Nat Ferber, has given us several examples of what Tammany Hall misrule cost the citizens of New York. In the 1920s when these episodes took place, New York was a relatively wealthy city. Sometimes the crusades against these malpractices were motivated partly by Hearst's personal animosities, but Ferber and his reporter colleagues managed to give most of them a reform twist.

The newspaper's reporters took freshly delivered bottles of milk to a laboratory for testing. While some were found to be very good, other brands were loaded with filth and bacilli. Sufficient complaining finally forced Mayor Jimmy Walker to secure more inspectors for a universal guarantee of quality milk.

Another Hearst investigation in the early 1920s was that of bucket shops. These were offices (frequent and large in the early 1920s) for selling securities fraudulently. Frequently the buyer recovered nothing on his investment. The Hearst reporters discovered a number of such organizations. Nothing had been done about prosecuting them until the Tammany authorities were forced into it by the newspaper reporters. Meantime, thousands of small investors had their life savings literally stolen by these conscienceless bucketeers.[51]

Restaurants in Chicago have been forced to take on juke boxes from the syndicate, which received half the gross income, by fear of exposing some technical legal violation to the license department.

Organized crime, which lives by corruption, hits the poor hardest. In 1969 "the Chairman of New York State's Joint Legislative Committee on Crime stated that $223,000,000 was siphoned out of the Central Harlem, South Bronx, and Bedford-Stuyvesant ghettos by numbers bankers and narcotics pushers during 1968, while Federal, state and city welfare funds pumped into the same communities totalled $272,000,000."[52]

Union members, too, may suffer from organized crime's penetration of their unions. On the New York waterfront for decades some "union leaders" have been little more than syndicate bosses.[53] The ability of such "unions" to murder dissident members without penalty was a result of their political connections. Astor adds: "Ghetto residents are firmly convinced that members of the narcotics division have profited from the sale of drugs. One periodic shake-up in 1968 indicted three top detectives for allegedly going into business on their own."[54]

Corrupt police tend to be less disciplined police for the obvious reason that administrators do not dare discipline, for fear of exposure. One of the worst effects of widespread police corruption is the freedom it gives the police to use rough methods on the poor. Williams quotes the Pennsylvania Crime Commission interim report of 1972: "The first victims of police corruption are the urban poor." Certainly, the published hearings of the New Orleans special citizens' committee of 1953 indicated a kind of police brutality toward prostitutes that would sicken most of us. Fifteen officers having intercourse with one woman in rapid succession is as bad as any gang brutality.[55]

Judge Seabury's investigations in New York City in the 1930s indicated that the vice squad, crooked bondsmen, and lawyers had succeeded in extorting substantial sums from large numbers of innocent, respectable women by trumping up charges of prostitution. Forty-eight girls, illegally placed in Bedford Reformatory, were released by the final order of the Court of Appeals.[56]

Beyond the cruelty to poor individuals, corruption damages the public in important ways. The Knapp Commission found that police, in addition to taking bribes, were themselves selling confiscated heroin.[57] It is not unreasonable to deduce that New York City's sad position as the leading heroin center of the country, with "pushers" at every high school, was in part a result of such corrupt police practices. The estimated 15,000 narcotics addicts in Washington are said by Williams to be in part a result of a corruptible police force.[58] When police go in for stealing, as has been the case in recent years in New York City, Chicago, Denver, and elsewhere, the public suffers directly and painfully.

The New York State Joint Legislative Committee on Crime in 1969 reported on the extent of the narcotics traffic in New York. Narcotics at that time received more help than hindrance from some of the New York police and was widespread in the ghetto communities. Many addicts resorted to crime to support their habits. The committee describes the consequences of this aspect of police corruption on the public.

What effect do these criminal activities have on living conditions in the ghetto? Testimony before the Committee revealed that the ghetto resident has become a prisoner in his own home, where he must remain in order to protect whatever worldly possessions he has from theft by the addict burglar. Similarly, the welfare recipient, whose property usually consists solely of his clothing and home furnishings, fears to leave his residence to undertake job training or rehabilitation programs because he knows that any prolonged absence from his home inevitably means it will be burglarized and looted.

As things now stand, much of Harlem considers the police with distrust, as manifest in the fact that several witnesses at the Committee's hearings looked to the State Police or to the National Guard, rather than to the City's police, for the answer to the narcotics problem.[59]

Applicants for naturalization were charged $10 for coming up early in the county clerk's office in the Bronx. Destitute relief clients were given clothing vouchers but shortchanged by agreement between relief and investigators, who received kickbacks, and clothing stores. Clients needing food were also shortchanged. The Building Commissioner of Queens permitted continuing violation of building codes by housing contractors. Scores of applicants for motion picture operator's licenses (the job was very important for public safety) were required to pay bribes to Tammany officials.

One unhappy result of government corruption is that it permits nonpublic agencies to commit cruel acts. Senator McClellan notes 173 separate acts of labor violence (mostly by organized crime) reported to his committee, only 8 of which had resulted in court action of any kind. The acts were numerous and brutal, ranging from severe beatings to murder. Tires were slashed, dynamiting continuous, extortions constant. There is not even the excuse that these actions were in the interest of labor, since the "union" was frequently a device for gangster extortion.[60]

The personal damages caused by organized crime are inestimable. Moynihan has some thoughts:

Organized crime obviously has something to sell that many people want to buy. Yet always behind the pleasures of vice lie the ugliness of degradation and the terror of violence. It is pleasant to think of winning a lot of money, not so pleasant for an Irish tenement kid to stare at what is left of his father's face after the smiling bookies' psychotic "enforcers" have collected the hard way.[61]

When Thomas E. Dewey was functioning as special deputy district attorney of New York in 1935, he secured indictments and convictions of a number of loansharks. A few paragraphs will describe how these sharks, functioning under the relaxed rule of generous and humanitarian Tammany, treated ordinary people. First, two paragraphs from a speech by Dewey in his campaign for district attorney two years later:

The loan sharks had one of the most vicious rackets that ever plundered our city. They got fat on the profits they took from people who were hard up, who needed money to pay for doctors, for groceries, for rent. Usually the loan shark would lend five dollars and demand six dollars back the next week. If the borrowers were not able to pay at the end of the week, they soon learned that they had let themselves in for a much bigger debt, which kept getting bigger and bigger.

The loan sharks organized their racket into a big business. The Russell Sage Foundation found the business was a million dollars a week. The gangsters broke heads and cut men with knives and made their victims lose their jobs. Thousands of people were caught in their net.[62]

Shifting from Dewey's speech to Rupert Hughes's book:

The testimony was harrowing. The sums extorted were appalling. A beauty parlor operator had borrowed $100 in 1934 and agreed to pay $5 a week interest—a small matter of 260 percent a year. She had to borrow another $100 and gave a note for that amount, receiving only $75 in cash. After she had paid

$550 and could still not square the deal, her persecutors threatened to cut her hands off, to cut her ears off, to slice her throat to ribbons, and at last they dispossessed her of her little shop after all.

There is sardonic farce in the political aid given to one loan shark who actually used policemen as collectors. He had no less than twenty-five hundred clients in Radio City. He told the police that his life was threatened and a bodyguard was assigned to him. By the use of this ruse he was able to approach his victims and tell them, "See, the police are working for me."[63]

In 1952 police captain Joseph C. Workman in Brooklyn was sentenced to 2½ to 5 years in prison. Mockridge and Pratt tell us:

Workman, a miserable specimen of humanity, who had thrown in his retirement papers shortly after Gross was picked up, was so involved in corrupt affairs in the police department that he tripped himself up every time he opened his mouth. The forty-eight-year-old captain was so greedy for money that he took not only big cash payments from bookies and policy slip operators, but he shook down respectable merchants in his precinct, and even collected from sick and crippled shopkeepers in the poorest sections of his command.[64]

The horrible example of the Triangle Shirtwaist fire in Manhattan in March 1911, as given by Raymond Fosdick, is an example of the results of corrupt building practices. Some 147 employees, mostly women between the ages of 17 and 25, lost their lives as the fire cut them off from stairways and fire escapes. "Nothing that I saw at the front in the First World War seven years later surpassed in horror that dreadful scene."[65] The tragic results were caused by blocked fire escapes, locked doors, and faulty construction, traceable back to a corrupt and highly inefficient Bureau of Building of Manhattan. Other writers ascribe this fire to "industrialism."[66] Both business and the government trying to regulate it were at fault.

New York State laws provided penalties for failure to put iron stairways and fire-retarding materials in "old law tenements" (built prior to 1902). From 60 to 80 people were burned to death annually in such tenements, but no prosecutions of landlords were undertaken until 1938, when Thomas E. Dewey became district attorney.[67]

How much of this inefficiency and brutality to the poor is a result of corrupt city regimes? An exact answer is not possible. As noted elsewhere, honest governments can be inept. But there seems to be a high correlation between police and some other public official brutality and broad-scale corruption. Corrupt police are not easily disciplined police. It is the cities like New York, Chicago, Boston, and Philadelphia where the officials have been corrupt which also produce the worst stories of governmental brutality.

Is Corruption Needed to Secure Citizen Participation?

Social Excuses for the Machine

In the considerable quantity of social science literature supporting corrupt machines, one of the most frequent occasions for attack on honest government is the charge that it is not human or does not give citizens a sense of belonging. The machine, on the other hand, is pictured as jolly and friendly and considerate. Walter Lippmann has written that the reformers needed to be as friendly as Tammany Hall.

Bosses liked to help build up this picture. Tom Pendergast was quoted by *The New York Times:*

I'm the boss—I knew all the angles of organizing and every man I meet becomes my friend.... Every one of my workers has a fund to buy food, coal, shoes, and clothing. When a poor man comes to old Tom's boys for help we don't make one of those damn fool investigations like these city charities. No, by God, we fill his belly and warm his back and vote him our way.[68]

Earlier in this chapter, several of the social science rationalizations for corrupt machines were listed. One of them was Professor Merton's claim that machines "relieved social tension."

There is validity to the theory that the large modern city government can be impersonal and unfriendly. All large bureaucracies can become impersonal, and a governmental bureaucracy is particularly likely to be so. Nineteenth-century cities were just beginning to learn the methods of large-scale management; probably none of them had given any "public relations" training to their staffs. If the staff of the corrupt machine tried to be friendly, it may well have passed the city employees in friendliness, manners, and helpfulness. The social worker was, and indeed still is, required to ask certain questions of prospective municipal welfare clients. The policeman was certainly critical and authoritarian at times. The tax collector and the building inspector appeared to be dipping into other people's private business. In short, the municipal bureaucracy was bureaucratic, and the introduction of civil service legal provisions against removal probably did not make civil servants any friendlier to outsiders.

Sometimes the social science apologists for corruption attack the "reformers" rather than the city government. The reformers are aristocratic, condescending, rigid, and cold in contrast to the warm, friendly machine. They also tended to be "Wasps" and hence unfriendly to anyone of more recent immigrant stock.

This position deserves careful analysis, but it does not completely conform to the facts. The author has known a number of municipal reformers (going back into the 1900s) who were friendly men, quite the opposite of aristocratic or condescending. A substantial number of them also were not "Wasps." There are also numerous instances where the corrupt machine government has not been jolly and friendly. The reader is reminded of the section on the effect of corruption on ordinary people in this chapter. Surely the immigrant women who were falsely accused of prostitution in New York City in the 1930s or the Appalachian whites who were pushed around in the Chicago of the 1960s or the blacks in Newark could hardly have felt that the corrupt machine was reducing their social tension.

Must Honest Government Be Unfriendly?

There is no reason why government must be dishonest to be friendly with its population. In fact, an honest government should be able to get along better with people it is *not* trying to cheat than a corrupt machine with people it *is* trying to cheat.

There are, however, some things which the honest government can and should do to secure a higher degree of citizen cooperation with, and citizen participation in, government. Had some of the following examples been followed in the last century, it is possible that the corrupt machine might have been less ubiquitous. With the great growth of "participative management" in industry, local governments in the last two decades have thought up a number of ways of securing citizen participation in the governmental process. These will be reviewed in the next few pages, not with the thought that any one of them is the final answer but to indicate some of the ways in which honest government can become closer to its citizens.

The presence of many blacks, Chicanos, and other ethnic groups in central cities adds to the problem of governmental relationships with citizens. Many of these people have never experienced living with a government by language or by ethnic customs. Recognizing these problems, some governments have made substantial efforts to build closer relationsips between themselves and their citizens.

Voting is, of course, a method of citizen participation, but it is far from adequate as our low percentage of voter participation in America indicates. Mayoral elections often interest less than half the registered voters. American states and cities have handicapped the voters by asking them to make more judgments than any "outsider" can make. Those of our cities which maintain partisan elections usually have no real contest in the final election because of the Democratic party predominance.

Community Action Programs

Two federal programs, Community Action in the Office of Economic Opportunity and Model Cities in the Department of Housing and Urban Development

(HUD), have called for establishment of local governing boards by election of poor people and have appropriated funds for social services which could be designated by these local boards. As of January 1972, there were 900 such community action agencies in existence.

There was much opposition to the Community Action program. The programs often tended to be run by factions of the Democratic party opposed to the mayor's faction. The Community Action programs largely disappeared with the Office of Economic Opportunity in 1973. The Model City programs were folded into block grants for community development. HUD continues to have a deep interest in citizen participation. A January 1977 report by the Brookings Institution to HUD indicated a fair degree of success in continuing efforts to secure citizen participation. The citizen participation format that most often was associated with significant influence was public hearings plus neighborhood meetings. Citizen influence was also strongest where local officials were most in favor of it.

Decentralization of City Governments

In the last twenty years, a number of major cities have established local offices to serve the needs of citizens. The primary idea is to have a place where citizens may discover what branch of government can help them meet their particular needs. In some cases there are citizens advisory groups attached to such centers. In some cases an effort has been made to local branches of departments such as welfare, which serve the population directly. An investigation gave particular praise to such centers in Boston, Houston, Los Angeles, and San Antonio. Others exist in Atlanta, Kansas City, Columbia, and New York City.

Neighborhood Development Corporations

A report of the Advisory Commission on Intergovernmental Relations in 1971 found that 16 percent of reporting cities had corporations designed to conduct such activities as low-income housing planning, rehabilitation, and social services. They have often had some governmental powers delegated to them.

If adequately supported, the neighborhood development corporation operating through decentralized offices should serve some of the purpose supposedly performed by the corrupt machine, and more usefully.

Community Control of Schools

As a result of the increase of black self-consciousness, there was a strong movement in the late 1960s for a system of "community control" of schools. The movement was perhaps strongest in New York City where blacks were especially anxious that local school boards have power to pass on tenure appointments in their area, a desire growing out of black fears that certain teachers did not believe that blacks can learn. Less is heard of the movement today as blacks gain political power, but a number of major cities are still experimenting with local boards which consider problems of one or a few schools. Teacher unions which have gained great power in recent years tend to oppose this decentralization. Massive bussing would also weaken the force of it.

Administrative Participation

Probably the most useful method of bringing government closer to people is to organize administrative departments so that citizens may be invited into contact with their governments. This may not be a strictly democratic process, but if administrators listen to advice of their citizens, it may be a very useful relationship. It was the way much local government started in America—the citizen night watch for policing, the volunteer fire department, and volunteer sanitation work. Thoughtful police departments, notably in Los Angeles, Oakland, Indianapolis, Rochester, Dayton, and Dallas, have made a number of reasonably successful efforts to consult with citizens about law enforcement efforts in their area. Health departments are consulting much more. Many departments, however, still have a great deal to learn. Housing and urban renewal projects almost automatically are preceded by extensive consultation with citizens, as a result of the HUD policies noted above.

Conclusions

Had most of the above approaches been in existence in 1890, American cities and states might still have had the corrupt machine. The general low ethical level of the America of that time, the presence of large unassimilated immigrant groups, the naivete of state and local legislation may have made it impossible to secure honest governments. But if the defenders of the machine take seriously its social function, some of them must admit that a good many cities are now trying to secure citizen-government relationships on a more honest basis.

Summary and Analysis

It has been noted that corruption can cost a government, and its taxpayers, large sums through both "honest" graft and the overburdening of the government exchequer. The administrative headaches which come from corruption greatly weaken the efficiency of governmental operations. Crime, and especially organized crime, is far larger in America because of the opportunities for political corruption here. Police brutality is greater in corrupt cities where police discipline is laxer. Finally, corruption has a frightful impact directly on poorer citizens. Numerous examples are to be found in the history of American corruption.

One could wish that the distinguished sociologists and political scientists who have found social or psychological usefulness in corrupt political machines would add an appendix about some of the horrible administrative results. The reader might then have a fairer picture of the tradition of corruption in American life. Professor Wolfinger has made a similar comment.

Several of these writers have tried to put themselves on a plane above "naive moralism." This attitude against "moralism" may grow out of one or more of several intellectual positions. Max Weber's distinction between the "is" and the "ought" has been exaggerated by many social scientists. Freud's most widely read books seemed to deprecate morals as a cause of psychoses. Social anthropologists, when they first discovered that ethical values varied somewhat from nation to nation, jumped to the conclusion that such values were only "conventional" or "relative" and hence not a fit subject for academic study.

Such analyses overlook several facts. Max Weber's own writing was loaded with moral judgments. Freud himself, in his later years, indicated his belief that every society must have a moral code for decent living together. Even Skinner provided some ethical instruction in *Walden II.* Whether or not we grant their universal qualities, most of us must admit that moral codes do exist and that societies and organizations with poorer codes have more difficulty with internal unrest and strife. The social science professors who scorn "naive morality" are usually quite "moral" themselves. So perhaps the early reformers striving for moral improvement of their corrupt cities were not as irrational as Davenport, Merton, Huntington, Warner, Smelser, and Tarr have found them to be.

It is possible that the failure of these social scientists to point out the bad consequences of corruption was simply a result of ignorance. Several of them were theorists, unlikely to be aware of all the practical consequences of corruption. Most professor-written literature tends to ignore administrative or social or economic consequences of corruption; the author has found books and articles by newspaper or magazine writers to be much more descriptive of actual administrative results of corrupt machines than are the academic books and articles. Perhaps as knowledge of these administrative results grows, the theorists will add to their praise of the corrupt machine some indication of its bad consequences. In the interim, however, whole generations of college students graduate with an unduly optimistic view of the corrupt machine. Unfortunately, many of these students continue to view corruption as benign after they become adults. Thus, the social scientists themselves add to the cynicism so well described by Professor Callow.

11 Theories of Corruption

This chapter reviews a list of some of the various reasons for corruption which have been suggested by a number of writers. Their validity is discussed at the end of each section, while a final section attempts to summarize the relationship among them.

As these theories of the causes of corruption are listed, the reader will naturally be thinking of the "cure" for each cause. However, some of the causes are simply not changeable; our heterogeneous population is one such cause. The reader is also cautioned that there may be different kinds of corruption which require different packages of remedies. There is little similarity, aside from moral disapprobation, between the act of the New York police detective who demands protection money from a brothel and the actions of the giant milk cooperatives which finance campaigns of both national political parties in order to secure support for a milk price increase. Both types of corruption would be lessened by ethical education, but other remedial measures would vary greatly.

Benevolence of the Machine

Several writers have commented upon worthwhile products of the machine. Monte Calvert has developed a thesis that urban bosses recognized professional needs of the cities better than reformers in the last half of the nineteenth century. His proof includes Boss Tweed's reorganization of New York City's administration. Alexander Shepherd, "boss" of Washington public works in the 1870s, left more buildings and a better paved city. Calvert also cites administrative mistakes of reformers. Joel Tarr has a chapter on "The Political Machine as Public Servant" in his *A Study in Boss Politics.*

Callow gives several examples from current literature praising bosses as reformers. Pendergast in Kansas City and Robert W. Speer of Denver supported civic improvements. Al Smith and Charles Murphy supported social reform laws. Martin Bohrman of New Orleans was praised for civic improvement. Anton J. Cermak in Chicago and Frank Hague in Jersey City claimed to be upholders of law and order.[1] Callow goes on to point out that the extent of the reform, the intensity of the bosses' efforts, and the political and economic gains to the boss must also be considered.

Appraisal of Theory

The theory of the benevolence of the machine is perhaps best answered by Prof. Charles E. Merriam who knew far more about machines than most political scientists, as a result of his years in Chicago politics.

The Boss gives $100 to charity but accepts $1,000 for voting against an ordinance for better housing. He pays the funeral expense of the man who dies because the boss killed the law to safeguard the machinery on which he worked. He helps the widow whose suit for damages was blocked under a system he was paid to perpetuate.[2]

An equally effective answer is to be found in Quentin Reynolds's description of the cold treatment of a welfare applicant in Hoboken by the "Poormaster" of the local machine in 1938. Since this applicant had supported an opposition candidate, he and his family were treated on an almost starvation basis.

The material in Chapter 10 is another answer. Wolfinger is skeptical of the benevolence argument, and the author shares his skepticism.

The Modernization and Economic Development Theory of Corruption

Political scientists have written much in recent years about a "functional" theory of corruption. Since some writers have used the term *functional* for other purposes, we will call this the "economic development" theory of corruption. One of the principal elaborations of this theory is in Prof. Samuel Huntington's book *Political Order in Changing Societies*. Huntington argues that corruption comes with "rapid social and economic organization." New sources of wealth and power make new demands on government and resort to bribery or other forms of corruption if their demands are not met legitimately. Modernization (use of modern technology) has also changed the values of society toward "universalistic and achievement based norms." It increases the laws and regulations operating over society, sometimes establishing "unreasonable puritanical standards." Reducing corruption may involve scaling down norms for officials as well as leading the behavior of those officials toward the norms. A greater recognition of the difference between public and private interest is required.

Corruption, says Huntington, also appears to be less likely to function in a highly stratified society, which already has a highly developed system of norms. Since corruption involves exchange of political power for economic wealth, the form of corruption depends on whether wealth or political power is easier to gain. "In the United States, wealth has more commonly been a road to political influence than political office has been a road to wealth." In societies which have fairly strong national political institutions, the incidence of corruption is likely to be greater on the lower levels of government.

Huntington's economic development theory of corruption is best summarized by the following quotation:

> Just as the corruption produced by the expansion of political participation helps to integrate new groups into the political system, so also the corruption produced by the expansion of governmental regulation may help stimulate economic development. Corruption may be one way of surmounting traditional laws or bureaucratic regulations which hamper economic expansion. In the United States during the 1870s and 1880s corruption of state legislatures and city councils by railroad, utility, and industrial corporations undoubtedly speeded the growth of the American economy.[3]

Huntington grants that corruption weakens a governmental bureaucracy. However, he believes that corruption may help party organization, which in the long run helps to overcome corruption.

Huntington's thesis has been followed by several other writers. Even Prof. C. J. Friedrich, a strong supporter of morality, has paid a fair amount of deference to this theory of corruption in his *Pathology of Politics*. Professor J. S. Nye carries Huntington's theory further and suggests that "the national integration of millions of immigrants in the nineteenth century" was based partly on corruption.[4] Nye analyzes the costs and benefits of corruption in developing countries and concludes that costs may exceed benefits "except for top level corruption involving modern inducements and marginal deviations and except for situations where corruption provides the only solution to an important obstacle to development." Except for the generalization about the nineteenth century, the article does not relate to the United States.

Professor James C. Scott develops a phase of the Huntington thesis for both America and developing countries. He concludes that the political machine in developing countries and in machine-run parts of America must have inducements to secure support, other than traditional patterns of loyalty to party.

> Frequently a three-cornered relationship developed in which the machine politician could be viewed as a broker who, in return for financial assistance from wealthy elites, promoted their policy interests when in office, while passing along a portion of the gain to a particularistic electorate, from whom he "rented" his authority.[5]

Appraisal of Theory

The economic development theory has been advanced chiefly by students of developing societies, in which it may be largely correct. The author does not know enough about such societies to support or contradict the theory. Some aspects of Huntington's theory are clearly applicable to the United States; two are specifically discussed later in this chapter in the sections on class structure and political parties.

The thesis that corruption comes with rapid social and economic organization may be valid for some of nineteenth-century America, where an economy was expanding, cities were developing, and new immigrant groups were entering communities, as Professors Scott and Nye have suggested. During most of the nineteenth century, many American cities, many states, and at times the national government became very corrupt. "Modernization" may or may not have created new norms, as Huntington suggests (perhaps he was discussing only developing countries), but there were new forms of wealth and power. Huntington's third effect of modernization—creating new laws and regulations—did exist in the United States but was related to only a part of our corruption.

In spite of the brilliance of the theory, a majority of the evidence seems to be against its application in America. In the nineteenth century when our corruption was worse, American government wanted development of business rather than opposing it. America's first great example of corruption, the Tweed Ring of Tammany Hall, did little that could be called development of business. Graft money was made by paying salaries to nonworking people, by collecting kickbacks on city contracts, by paying "salaries" to Tweed, by exacting funds from public employees, and from brothel keepers, saloon proprietors, gambling joints, and other places profiting by illegal action. None of the above were examples of the economic development theory. Tweed did get a gas franchise through the New York legislature, and was paid for his part in the rivalry between the Erie group and the Vanderbilt group, but it is difficult to know if this should be classified as bribery at the instance of business or extortion by the politician. Corruption almost certainly hindered rather than helped the development of many public utilities, as Lincoln Steffens, in *Shame of the Cities,* demonstrates with lists of bribes and counterbribes. The "black horse cavalry" in the New York legislature was extorting from business, not aiding its development.

Another test of the functionalism theory came in Chicago's street car controversies around 1800. No one opposed franchises for street cars. But Charles Yerkes wanted 50-year franchises; Mayor Carter Harrison wanted them limited to 20 years. Yerkes used corrupt methods on both the Chicago city and Illinois state government to achieve his ends, but he was seeking extra privileges, not new development.[6] Perhaps further evidence against the pure form of the economic development theory was found in Mayor Pingree's work in Detroit where the *city government* forced the street car companies to modernize themselves.

Another case in which the functional theory did not apply came up in the trial of Harry Gross, organized crime boss of bookies in Brooklyn in 1961. Assistant District Attorney Helfand pointed out:

This was not a series of isolated conspiracies with individuals or groups of policemen. This is an over-all conspiracy, one entire picture of corruption.

Gross, you know, never sought police protection. Rather it was the police who sought him out and forced on him a verbal contract that assured them regular payments made on the first and fifteenth of each month.[7]

Gross, the gangster gambling chief, defended himself by saying, "I didn't corrupt them. They [the police] corrupted me."[8]

Judge Ben Lindsey describes a corporate control of politics in Denver (Democratic at the local; Republican at the state level) in the first decade of this century which appears to have been primarily business control of politics. There is, however, not much evidence that it was control for reasons connected with the development of the businesses concerned. Large corporations, primarily public utilities, supported corrupt politicians, who also encouraged other illicit activities like gambling, in order to help protect the corporations from effective rate regulation, employee liability suits, normal taxation, and child labor laws.[9] If Lindsey's analysis is correct, it proves that some businesses in the Denver area did share in corrupting government, but more for their greater profit than for the economic development described in the functional theory. The economic development theory further suffers from the fact that the Denver utilities linked their economic demands so closely to political machines which depended on noneconomic functions such as illegal gambling and white slave trade.

Most of the American nineteenth-century machines included funds from both political extortion and business bribery in their income. Many times it becomes a chicken-egg controversy, as to whether business or government made the first suggestion of corruption. In the twentieth century, as utility regulation has been moved to the state level of government, the largest part of ongoing municipal corruption is not economic development, unless the perpetuation of brothels, drug dens, gambling establishments, and pornography is an economic necessity. Very little of America's economic future is dependent upon the police corruption of the big Northeastern cities or the corrupt activities of organized crime in much of the country; on the contrary, the extra costs of corruption and crime are a handicap to economic development. Some elements of corruption for what may be economic development continue at the federal and state levels where regulations regarding prices, rates, types of service, amount of imports, and other controls do affect economic groups, which in turn try to influence government action, sometimes corruptly. As Prof. Paul Douglas suggested in 1962, there should be careful consideration of such regulations to see if the amount of regulation could not be reduced or the process of regulation made more impersonal and automatic to reduce the possibility of corruption.[10] But elimination of all such "functional" corruption would leave intact the great mass of ongoing local government corruption, which consists largely of personal exploitation rather than economic functionalism.

Another example of what might be called corruption for economic development is what the Knapp Commission on police corruption in New York called "the maze of City ordinances and regulations" which cause construction contractors, liquor licensees, and firms which require illegal parking to bribe the police as "easier and cheaper than obeying the laws." This practice undoubtedly occurs in other cities but is rarely encouraged by deliberately unworkable ordinances as in New York. As in the case of so many bribes, this source of corruption should be classified as extortion.

Sociological Theory of Unfulfilled Needs

There has been some theorizing, chiefly by sociologists, on the sociological needs fulfilled by the political machine. This argument does not always include corruption but often does.

Robert K. Merton in his *Social Theory and Social Structure*[11] outlines some functions of the corrupt political machine as an alternative to an ineffective political structure:

1. The political boss becomes a necessary means of centralizing power.
2. The machine becomes a means of securing assistance for individuals or subgroups. These subgroups include poor immigrants who need jobs and business which wants political privileges.
3. The machine offers an alternate route for personal "advancement." This includes the advancement of persons in "vice, crime, and rackets."

An elaboration of Merton's theory has been written by Neil J. Smelser.[12] Corruption, according to Smelser, is "a contrivance that flourishes particularly under conditions of unevenness and inequity in structuring social rewards." He cites, with apparent approval, the modernization and economic development theory. He assumes that a moralistic response to corruption is inattentive to facts.

Corruption, writes Smelser, requires a minimum level of structural differentiation of politics and some normative framework. It also involves a "crossing over" of political and economic sanctions. There must be a specific act—bribery or misappropriation or conflict of interest. Corruption may be regarded "as an accommodation to the ambiguities that arise in the new, generalized relations between bureaucrat and clientele." Corruption flows toward the more valued reward, which may vary with the state of development of the society.

An example of the social fulfillment theory of corruption is to be found in what Dorothy Heid Bracey calls "a functional approach to police corruption." Professor Bracey follows Merton's theory that corruption performs functions not performed by other processes of society. She suggests that the corruption of several policemen furnishes a common activity to help develop police solidarity. Corruption may be a training device or "a rite of passage." Corruption reaffirms the status of superior officers, while confirming their solidarity with their subordinates. Corruption is a stabilizing force between those who wish to see a law changed and those who do not. Corruption is a facilitator of business, which cannot function under many laws and regulations.

Corruption also helps law enforcement in three possible ways:

1. The officer accepts a bribe, letting the lawbreaker off at lower cost.
2. The innocent person finds a bribe less costly than the cost of defending himself.
3. The officer accepts a bribe from a person who is guilty but would not be punished by the system.

Corruption also helps to control crime since it gives a means of forcing persons to give information to the police about more serious crime. It also is a means of securing special services, such as a police escort for funds or scaring criminals away from coffee shops. It enables the police to give special services to a wealthy class.[13]

Appraisal of the Theory

The argument that the corrupt machine fulfills the needs of individual and subgroups for power, for privileges, for advancement, and for awards is probably true for some societies at some times. It is true that persons with political talent in many ethnic groups, however, found recognition in the corrupt multiethnic machines developed in the last century. But did the machine have to be corrupt in order to give this recognition? In Canada many immigrant surnames appear in provincial legislatures, without dishonest conduct to secure election. In California today, there are many ethnic candidates but no signs of corruption. And we must note, with Lincoln Steffens, that much of nineteenth-century political corruption was through Yankee-dominated machines, such as the Gas Ring in Philadelphia and the Southern Pacific in California.

Honestly run cities can absorb ethnic groups more readily than machine-run cities, through better education, better health and welfare services, and more just treatment by the police and other organs of government. But it would be difficult to assemble statistics on the relative assimilative capacity of corrupt and honest cities.

If the sociological argument is taken on a nonethnic basis, it is more significant. Large cities and states have lost some of the sense of citizen participation which Tocqueville thought he saw in the America of the 1830s. There is much current interest in securing citizen participation in the governmental process, as described in Chapter 10. It is perhaps true that rural America, where citizen participation in elections may seem more meaningful, is less corrupt than urban America. However, enough of our large cities and states have become noncorrupt that we may safely assert that corruption is not a necessary means of fulfilling individual needs.

Smelser is perhaps wiser than Merton when he points out the temporary nature of the corrupt machine's help toward release of tensions. Chapter 10 of this book develops the costs of corruption which Merton ignores. They seem to more than offset the sociological values of corruption.

Class against Corruption

Several discerning observers have noted that the lack of rigid class structures in America has facilitated the development of political corruption in this country. Ernest Griffith has stated this theory in terms of respect for officials rather than class:

A respect for office-holding that surrounds the official with a kind of political halo has a profound effect on the official himself. It postulates *noblesse oblige*. In America this respect passed with the entry of the new democracy. Rotation in office and the spoils system destroyed well nigh completely any feeling that office-holding involved obligations. Office-holding had come to be looked upon not as a privilege but as a reward or even as a right. *Noblesse oblige* is impossible in such an attitude. *This was and is the root of American corruption; its converse is the reason for the high British standard.*[14]

Other observers have put the same point differently, that other modern democracies have a ruling class or an upper class which has assumed more responsibility for governing honestly than do the constantly changing groups which find themselves in charge of government in a less class-minded America. Huntington, in developing the theories referred to above, comments:

The degree of corruption which modernization produces in a society is, of course, a function of the nature of the traditional society as well as the nature of the modernizing process. The presence of several competing value systems or cultures in a traditional society will, in itself, encourage corruption in that society. Given a relatively homogeneous culture, however, the amount of corruption likely to develop during modernization would appear to be inversely related to the degree of social stratification in the traditional society. A highly articulated class or caste structure means a highly developed system of norms regulating behavior between individuals of different status.[15]

Today Britain is so little concerned with political corruption that it has not been possible to discover contemporary studies of the relationship of the class structure (now becoming a "meritocracy," of intellectual rather than hereditary choice) to the lack of corruption. But there are two comparative studies of practice regarding corruption in the House of Commons and in Congress which indicate that the British desire to treat MPs as "gentlemen" has resulted in higher ethical requirements for membership in the legislative body than exist in the American congress.[16]

A sociological variation of the class theory has come from the fertile pen of Seymour Martin Lipset. Comparing the United States with Canada, he concludes that Canadians set less store by equality and individual achievement than Americans but value an educated "elite" more. Canadians stress moral values more in education, whereas Americans emphasize "citizenship, patriotism, social skills, and family living." Not surprisingly, there is substantial evidence that Canadians have more respect for law. There is "greater lawlessness and corruption in the United States." Canada is more "collectively oriented" and less business-oriented.[17]

For our purposes, Lipset's comments may be viewed as an illustration and extension of the theory that class stratification helps resist corruption. Lipset extends the theory to indicate that the citizen frame of mind which accepts an elite also accepts government, authority, and honest procedures.

Validity of the Theory

The argument that a class structure operates against corruption has substantial merit. In American history, it is apparently true that the federal appointments made by Presidents from Washington to Jackson tended to be members of "leading families," usually with an above-average education. During that time our federal government was relatively uncorrupt. Since that time there have been fewer class-conscious appointments and more corruption.

The theory of rotation in office—including the perverse idea that any American can fill most governmental positions—was adopted by President Andrew Jackson. It resulted in less attention to family background of appointees, many weak appointments, and much corruption in all levels of government, consequences which Jackson did not foresee. European democracies, which have maintained social classes, now through education rather than inheritance, have had less corruption, at least since 1850.

A possible argument for the class against corruption theory is to be found in the South. There, in many areas, some of the leading families have gone into politics and conducted honest, if uninspired, governments for many decades. Virginia and South Carolina are often cited as states run by honest "machines" of well-to-do people. Until recent decades, the South (except Louisiana) was relatively free of the worst of the urban machines, perhaps because middle- and upper-class whites felt an obligation to participate in politics.

Perhaps another argument for the class theory is that the people who fought the corrupt machine tended to be well-established professional or business people. The argument could be made that, had these people been in more powerful political positions, they might have succeeded in establishing more honest governments. In looking over the list of corrupt machines in American history, it is certainly true that such machines were frequently based in the poorer wards and were often led by uneducated men of poorer background. Some of the early reform movements were probably attempting to keep the poor uneducated out of political power.

There are, however, contrary arguments. A surprising number of educated persons were leaders of corrupt machines, as the list of corrupt educated men in Chapter 14 shows.

Whether or not the class argument is valid, America is simply not going to establish a rigid social class system. America does not have a feudal or a guild background. It has long prided itself on being a place for the young man (and now young person) "on the way up." This tradition of vertical mobility could not be overturned, and very few Americans wish it to be overturned. Means of controlling corruption other than by a class system must be found.

Rigid social classes are not always free of corruption. Die-hard defenders of the class against corruption theory must admit that many social class systems have been useless or worse. For example, the pre-World War I Russian social classes allowed a great deal of corruption to go on.

The real lesson to be drawn from the class against corruption theory is that America should try to eliminate corruption without taking on the disadvantages of rigid class stratification. One way is by the process of indoctrinating most members of the society with the sense of public responsibility which class-stratified societies have given only to the elite. How this may be done is explained more fully in Chapter 14.

The other possibility is that we educate those citizens who are going to have special responsibilities in the public obligations of their future jobs. The American armed forces have certainly been able to produce disciplined, patriotic, courageous, and honest leaders through a long process of education, both in ROTC and the military academies and on the jobs. The civil service and foreign service have not always been successful in inculcating ideas on the job, but their final product has generally been able, conscientious, and honest. Individual state and local governments have also produced incorruptible public servants.

But this piecemeal way of reproducing *noblesse oblige* can be only partly successful. It is nearly impossible to prescribe it for elected officials whether federal, state, or local. There are many governmental tasks for which it is not possible to educate a meritocracy. The freedom of upward mobility in American life which we prize makes it difficult to plan out education in ethical responsibilities for small groups.

Overemphasis on Business Values

Another reason which is often cited for continuing corruption in American life is our emphasis on business values. The theory, as advanced by Lincoln Steffens, was that most of the bribes came from business; the problem was to get business under control. It was on this theory that prosecutors of the Ruef-Schmitz machine in San Francisco turned loose most of the bribe receivers. Their goal was to convict the bribers.[18] An elaboration of this view is that American emphasis on success in business encourages efforts to "get mine" regardless of ethical scruples.

Since the theory is discussed more fully in Chapter 13, no appraisal will be attempted here.

The Party Dominance Theory

Another theory of corruption, heard often in the last quarter of the nineteenth century and the first quarter of the twentieth century, was the dominance of political parties. Direct primary elections, the right of voting referenda on legislation, and recall of public officials were mechanisms intended to reduce the dominance of party leaders. White cites Charles Francis Adams, who put the blame for corruption on party organization "bred in the gutter of New York politics."[19] Ostrogorski, in his classic *Democracy and the Organization of Political Parties,* first published in 1902, agrees with the indictment of parties.[20]

Validity of the Theory

The fact that almost all corrupt political machines discussed in this book were part of a party mechanism, and gained support of honest citizens through that connection, must be cited in support of this theory. Even today, idealistic, reform-minded persons vote with Tammany Hall, the Chicago machine, and similar groups elsewhere, simply because the machines are Democratic. In heavily Republican areas, especially prior to 1932, there had also developed a "machine" which led sincere, well-meaning Republicans to vote for unscrupulous leaders. However, our trouble with reformist Democrats and Republicans may not be with the party system as much as with the naivete of the reformers.

Perhaps because Americans are not ideologically inclined, party groupings in America are based more on considerations of practicality than of principle. Thus, the party that is fortunate enough to put together a winning coalition, as F.D.R. did in 1932 and the Republicans did in 1860, may have too much control. No faction wants to leave the winning coalition. Sometimes America has a one-and-a-half, not a two-party system. This sort of system is helpful for corrupt machine politicians in the big cities, who use the party label to gain some middle-class support and then rely on machine activities for additional help.

On the other hand, there are situations in which party rivalry does help prevent corruption. Since 1920, New York State has had a minimum of administrative corruption (much less than its cities), largely because the party rivalry is so intense that each party consistently nominates honest and able candidates for governor. There are many states which have clean politics because the parties are competitive. On the other hand, New York City, with one party dominant, has had a correspondingly unhappy record of corruption. Chicago's one-party control for 40 years has produced equally bad results. Baltimore, Boston, St. Louis, and many other cities have suffered from one-party control.

An obvious difficulty with the party dominance theory is that other modern democracies have leared to operate noncorrupt politics through party machinery. Professor Huntington even assumes that party organization will end corruption. If other countries can operate their politics honestly with political parties, surely America can learn to do so.

Since no one has devised a way to keep party strengths more or less equal, it looks as if the one-sided nature of the party system will continue to add corruption to America. It may be that the introduction of nonpartisan elections into local government has helped secure more honesty, because it weakens the dominance of the one-party machine. Nonpartisan elections seem to have gone with more honest city government in California and elsewhere. The argument against them—that party responsibility is lost—is offset by the fact that the real contrast in most cities is between nonpartisan elections and one-party elections.

A Note on Patronage

Martin and Susan Tolchin have put together an interesting combination (*To the Victor,* Random House, New York, 1971) of theory and practice on patronage. They define *patronage* to include political appointments not only to full-time jobs but also to "prestigious" boards; contracting of government for architectural or legal services, or, if more competitive bids are possible, for regular contractual services; executive action in easing regulations on taxes; and other practices of aid to political supporters. They recognize the danger that such patronage might bite back politically, but they appear to assume that a certain amount of this type of operation is essential for politically responsible government.

There are, of course, a number of democratic governments which operate successfully with little or no patronage. Many city manager cities, including some fairly large cities, have almost no patronage. People run for the city council for the prestige or the experience or the sense of public service.

In countries like Great Britain, the political turnover of patronage is very small—Americans would think it less than is necessary to see that the new party in power can control the management. In Switzerland it is negligible.

The Tolchins might reasonably argue that in the large American cities, states, and federal government which they are discussing, the operation of separation of powers requires that the chief executive have some leverage in order to strengthen his leverage with the legislative body. The authors have observed enough occasions when Presidents, governors, and mayors have used their patronage for constructive purposes to agree with this point.

Whether or not patronage is necessary in American governments, it is fairly certain to be used as widely as statutes and court decisions will permit. What effect does its existence have on corruption?

Most forms of patronage tend to increase the opportunity for corruption. The Tolchins themselves concede that Mayor Daley's vast control of appointments in Chicago helped to make him unbeatable; and the Daley machine has allowed a great deal of corruption. The typical patronage city government of the nineteenth century was almost invariably corrupt. Unqualified political patronage employees seem to lack a sense of duty and turn to extortion of bribes rather than professional public service.

Some of the financial patronage discussed by the Tolchins is next door to outright corruption. If the law should be altered to forbid granting of contracts except by competitive bid, many of the actions mentioned above would automatically become corrupt. Conflict-of-interest statutes may well be violated when a city government appoints political supporters. The pragmatism which helps keep Americans away from the several ideological splits of Europeans probably helps this patronage become more important than principles in some American political contests.

Weakness in Forms of Governments

In the tradition of the Founding Fathers, Americans have long sought changes in statutes, ordinances, charters, or state constitutions which would presumably eliminate corrupt practices. These changes, of course, assume that present mistakes in the organization of government are the chief cause of corruption.

Civil Service

From the Civil War to the middle of this century, it has been assumed that civil service, protecting government workers from spoils politics, was a reform which would help eliminate political corruption. In some ways this has been an echo of the theory of class against corruption—the differences being that members of the class are chosen by competitive examination instead of aristocratic birth.

In the second half of the last century, civil service reform groups existed in most large cities. Many of their members undoubtedly believed that civil service was a major cure for corruption, perhaps because it was a part of Britain's major reform.[21]

Stronger Chief Executives

Another legal reform which has frequently been advanced is the concentration of political responsibility in a strong chief executive, be he governor or mayor or manager. In the middle of the last century, many city charters and state constitutions, perhaps following the Jacksonian rotation-in-office theory, provided for election of many department heads, judges, and boards of control. In the words of Ernest Griffith:

> . . . in the hodge podge of elected officials in America, in the indefinite relationship between the council and the executive, and between both and the state, and in lack of any sort of statutory budgetary procedure, some coordinating force was needed. In fact some such force was inevitable if the government was to function at all. The boss was a necessary evil.[22]

Observers of more recent political phenomena have also assumed that political power brings coordination at the expense of popular understanding of government. Banfield and Wilson comment: "La Guardia's reforms in New York, Clark and Dilworth's in Philadelphia, and Daley's in Chicago, although strengthening administrative authority, nevertheless weakened the influence of city government as a whole."[23]

Separation of Powers

American observers have not missed the fact that American federal and state government is unique in its doctrine of separation of powers as well as its corruption. Henry Jones Ford has written an article indicating that the separation of the executive and legislative functions encourages efforts of special interests to capture individual legislators. Walter Bagehot had a similar thought.[24] The reform "council manager plan" is itself closer to British responsible government than to our separation of powers. Recent Watergate difficulties have led many people to wonder if we do not need some system by which the executive branch of the national government is more responsive to the legislative branch.

Appraisal of the Thesis

Americans tend to think in terms of constitutional and statutory devices which will keep good government going automatically. Reform campaigns since the revolt against the Tweed Ring have been accompanied by proposals to change governmental mechanisms in order to obviate the necessity of future campaigns.

The proposed changes in forms of government have included civil service, strong chief executives, independent inspection agencies, city managers, city commissions, planning commissions, and many others. Some of these have improved the performance of governments in certain respects. But most of them have not had great effect on corruption. The problem is much more one of failure to elect honest, able people to office than a failure of mechanism. Just how well the political bosses recognized this fact is illustrated by Boss Tweed's action in *supporting* a new charter for New York City which gave the mayor more power. The Pendergast machine rapidly took over the new council manager government of Kansas City.

The system of separation of powers which has been used in our federal and state governments since their beginning, and which is used by a majority of our larger cities, is not an easy system of government to operate. It may be one of the reasons for the constant array of changing state constitutions and local charters. Yet, we have no certainty that eliminating separation of powers would improve our position. As a panel of public administrators pointed out in commenting on Watergate, a series of episodes like Watergate could easily have occurred under a responsible system of government. Separation of powers has served America well for almost two centuries and is likely to continue, at least at state and national levels of government.

Civil service has not been a universally successful reform. It doubtless held spoilsmen in check and resulted in more qualified appointments in many cases. It certainly helped pull the federal administration out of some third-class political traditions and helped produce the relatively honest federal administration of today.[25] States like California, New York, and Wisconsin and cities like Los Angeles and Milwaukee do creditable administrative jobs with civil service. But civil service frequently resulted in "covering in" political appointees.[26] It also frequently became a block to the firing of corrupt or incompetent employees. It has not kept cities like Boston, Chicago, New York, and Philadelphia from a great deal of ongoing corruption. Civil service may help the administration of a city or state through one 4-year term of a bad mayor or governor. But it will not help much if a number of poor top executives are elected.

A trenchant criticism of the strong-mayor thesis has been written by Professor Wolfinger. He notes that Banfield found Mayor Daley of Chicago coordinating only in the last resort, that Sayre and Kaufman found machine-controlled New York to be uncoordinated, and that in other cities machine politics were not accompanied by effective coordination.[27] In the experience of the authors, corrupt machines have rarely run coordinated governments.

In a few cases the reform of governmental mechanisms has brought results. California's change of mechanisms in 1911 heralded a state government which (with the exception of some legislatures) has been as continuously honest as it was continuously dishonest before. The council manager plan has frequently been accompanied by real reform of city government, especially in smaller and medium-size cities. But even in these cases, change of governmental mechanism has not been the sole cause of continued reform.

A Note on Laws by Acton and Friedrich

Lord Acton's famous statement about power calls for a comment here. Lord Acton, famous nineteenth-century British historian, stated a theory of corruption which is related to forms of government: "Power tends to corrupt and absolute power corrupts absolutely." Acton was writing of Pope and King and perhaps would not have applied his remark to democratic institutions like those of the United States. However, the statement often has been quoted on American problems. Professors Harold Lasswell and Arnold Rogow published a book in 1963 which controverts the Acton statement and concludes that in America the more powerful officials of government are not more likely to be corrupt than other officials. The evidence adduced by Lasswell and Rogow is now partly obsolete and not always convincing. The author, nevertheless, is inclined to agree with some of their conclusions. Experiences recorded in this book do not indicate that separation of powers, decentralization of government, and other forms of checks and balances have invariably helped America avoid corruption; in fact, a case could be made that the reduction of responsibility in government resulting from excessive checks has often permitted more corruption. Excessive reliance on democracy, such as the election of judges and prosecutors, and the establishment of inadequately trained local police have not helped secure honest government. Other types of checks and balances such as publicity requirements, inspection from a higher level of government, annual outside audit, or grand jury probes might be more helpful.

Professor C. J. Friedrich tries out an important variation of Acton's generalization:

It is possible to state a 'law' or general regularity by saying that the degree of corruption varies inversely to the degree that power is consensual.[28]

Friedrich's law is supported by evidence which he gives of corruption in totalitarian countries. The law is probably also valid in the United States where corruption almost invariably appears under the boss whose political authority is secured from a machine based on coercive measures, while governments based on honest elections are less likely to be corrupt. However, constructive use of Friedrich's law in American state and local governments is handicapped by the unwillingness of many people to take part in the processes which may lead to consensus.

Money in Elections

Discussion of Watergate has led many people to the opinion that financial contributions to elections are the major cause of corruption. Common Cause legislative proposals for control of elections have frequently been supported on the ground that they would end corruption. Professors Berg, Hahn, and Schmidhauser of the University of Southern California have written a book which maintains that campaign contributions are the main source of corruption.[29] These authors believe that corruption by bribing has fairly well disappeared, and has been succeeded by corruption through contributing campaign expenses to influence policies of legislators and executives.

Appraisal of the Theory

The theory that campaign contributions are the principal cause of corruption is an oversimplification. Most of the political machine income of both the nineteenth and twentieth centuries came from direct bribes or from so-called honest graft. Forced contributions were often exacted from public employees, but this has generally been outlawed and is not the kind of money in elections which Common Cause or the three cited authors view as the source of corruption. Some national and state but little municipal corruption has come from campaign contributions. Corrupt city machines have often secured campaign contributions, but they have other ways of extracting money.

There are important points to be made in favor of public financing of elections. It is quite hard to draw the line between legal campaign contributions and illegal bribes. The same money, passed from and to the same persons, may be legal or illegal depending upon the time of gift, a statement of the intent of the gift, or promises of performance. But it must be pointed out that abolition of monetary contributions will not eliminate pressure of economic interests. Union, corporations, and consumer groups will still find means of exerting influence in elections. And there is nothing in the record to support the supposition that the elimination of monetary contributions would eliminate other forms of grafting. The entire campaign process is discussed in Chapter 9.

Unnecessary Legislation

Many observers have wondered if Americans do not burden our law enforcement people with too many laws to enforce. There are particular objections to laws creating "victimless crimes," examples of which include homosexual (and certain heterosexual) activities between consenting adults, use of marijuana and other drugs, and gambling and abortion. Robert Williams blames police corruption on these unnecessary laws.

. . . the hypocrisy of American society, which wants to indulge itself yet keep its morality intact, at least insofar as the bulging statute books are concerned, must bear the ultimate responsibility for the corruption of police departments throughout the country. And that corruption, without exception, originates in the squads and divisions directly concerned with the enforcement of laws intended to eliminate immoral behavior—laws against gambling, against the sale and use of narcotics or other dangerous drugs, laws against seeking to control and regulate the use of alcohol.[30]

Williams is also convinced that organized crime moves into areas because of laws against "pinball machines, brothels, bingo nights, saloons, and strip joints." More recently, the new industry of pornographic publication, much of it illegal, has been heavily invaded by organized crime.

Appraisal of the Theory

There is much truth in this argument. Prohibition was a badly mistaken way to stop the evils of excessive use of alcohol. Our discussion of organized crime indicates that it is not solely a result of Prohibition, but Prohibition certainly gave organized crime a big boost. A major illegal activity on which most of organized crime operates, and on which a large amount of twentieth-century police corruption rests, is the so-called numbers game, the most frequent form of popular gambling. The effort to enforce laws against Sunday drinking on an immigrant population which viewed a trip to the *Bierstube* as a portion of its Sunday ritual certainly was a help in the corruption of many police forces. Indeed, Sunday "blue laws" were so helpful to corruption that the city machines voted to keep the laws on the books and, hence, the bribes in the pockets. Unfortunately, this kind of legislation continues. Serpico's brother, Pasquale Serpico, was "shaken down" by police officers because he ran his grocery store on Sunday in violation of a "Sunday blue law," which seems quite unnecessary.[31]

Organized crime which operates chiefly in the so-called victimless crime field is closely related to police corruption. Williams notes that *Parade* magazine in December 1970 quoted Chief Justice Earl Warren as saying that organized crime could not exist without corruption of law enforcement.[32] The argument is at least partly persuasive. Organized crime for decades seemed to come into areas first with the numbers racket and with bookies, both illegal because of laws against gambling. Prostitution, which seems to be impossible to eliminate, is another area which promotes police corruption and organized crime.

However, Williams' thesis is probably overplayed. He indicates that organized crime always begins with these victimless crime laws. But the mob has established labor racketeering in areas where victimless crime laws are nonexistent, for example, garbage collection and the restaurant supply business. The recent mob movement into Utah seems to have been in land speculation. One wonders if the legitimatizing of brothels, gambling, pornography, saloons, and strip joints would keep organized crime from operating in the legitimate businesses which it has already penetrated.

The reported conversation of Williams with Rocky Pomerance, chief of police of Miami Beach, also casts some doubt on his thesis. Pomerance quoted a hotel owner who told him that he did not want prostitutes at his bar because the prostitute takes away a customer and unsettles other customers. Backed by this attitude and the opposition of its older inhabitants, Miami Beach has limited its control of brothels and gambling, and maintains reasonably effective law enforcement.

A real trouble with banning victimless crime is the political one of securing passage of legislation eliminating the restrictions. How readily will suburban legislators vote for laws which would force their communities to permit the establishment of brothels? Laws against gambling cannot be repealed without some legislation, which police must enforce, to prevent fraudulent practices by legalized gamblers. Prostitution has been for much of human history a means of enslaving young girls. Does America wish to perpetuate "white slave traffic" or to have its governmental agencies enforce the necessary health regulations and other needed laws for the protection of the prostitute? Similar questions can be asked about repeal of laws against gambling. The government would still have to operate or regulate the gambling in order to ensure honesty and to collect taxes; most efforts in this direction have invited organized crime. Legalizing marijuana may be a reasonable goal, but passing out heroin, British style, involves major problems as Professor Wilson and his collaborators have indicated.[33]

Perhaps the best proof that allowing victimless crime will not remove our corruption problems is the example of Nevada which allows victimless crimes. This state has always been on the alert to avoid organized crime takeover of its governmental agencies, but has continually felt its presence.

Some repeal of unnecessary legislation like Sunday closing laws or penalties for use of marijuana is surely to be encouraged. But very watchful experimentation is needed before a general change of the other laws against victimless crime is initiated. We may then expect compromise laws. Prostitution may be allowed, but, as in Japan, brothels should be forbidden or solicitation controlled as in England. Government sanctioned gambling may finally compete with illegal gambling. Marijuana may be legalized, but certainly not heroin.

Demographic Factors

Most frequently met of popular explanations of America's ongoing corruption is the ascription of it to our heterogeneous population. America has been, more than almost any other country, a nation of immigrants. Many new peoples, unaccustomed to American conventions, either are likely to try corruption as a quick means of getting ahead or are not familiar enough with our domestic evils to advise their children against corruption. A variant of the explanation is that the ethnic political machine more readily misleads the immigrant. Another alternative of the heterogeneity rationale is the argument that the core city is populated by groups which lack the time or education to govern themselves. Robert di Grazia, former police commissioner of Boston, has pointed out that many central cities include many poor people, and a few wealthy people, but only a small proportion of middle-class people. The flight to the suburbs has taken away many of the natural allies of the police.

Analysis of the Theory

Much of our immigrant population as well as the native minority populations has indeed provided a focus for many problems, some of which have led to political corruption, as Professor Maaranen points out in Chapter 2. The venal political machines which developed in the nineteenth century were often dependent upon immigrant groups to whom they gave small favors and upon whose votes they counted. A leading role in many of these machines was taken by Irish-Americans, who did not value "good government" because of their unfortunate experiences under British misrule in Ireland. Since the bad administrative traditions of these machines have lasted into this century, as shown in Chapter 10, the heterogeneity of our population has indirectly contributed to corruption. Immigration has also resulted in the existence of too many varied denominations which have been unable to form any kind of religious front against corruption. Too many varieties of priests, pastors, and rabbis have defended corrupt members of their own religious groups.

But it is easy to make too much of these points. A substantial majority of our immigrants have come from countries which were more honestly operated than our own. They have learned their corruption here, not in the old country. The scores of million Americans of German extraction and 10 to 12 million of Scandinavian extraction have not required corrupt political machines to become assimilated in society. Ethnic groups like the Irish-Americans and the Italian-Americans have contributed to corruption, but members of such groups have also distinguished themselves on the side of reform.

Would America have had the corruption without the heterogeneity of population? This is an "iffy" question which is hard to answer. Canada has brought in millions of immigrants with much less corruption. Some American machines were Yankee-controlled. Perhaps it is fair to say that the number and variety of our immigrants made the situation worse, especially in the last century. Yet one of the strongest arguments against the immigrant theory of corruption was written by Lincoln Steffens in 1904:

When I set out on my travels, an honest New Yorker told me honestly that I would find the Irish, the Catholic Irish, were at the bottom of it all everywhere. The first city I went to was St. Louis, a German city. The next was Minneapolis, a Scandinavian city, with a leadership of New Englanders. Then came Pittsburgh, Scotch Presbyterian, and that was what my New York friend was. "Ah, but they are all foreign populations," I heard. The next city was Philadelphia, the purest American community of all, and the most hopeless. And after that came Chicago and New York, both mongrel bred, but the one a triumph of reform, the other the best example of good government that I had seen. The "foreign element" excuse is one of the hypocritical lies that save us from the clear sight of ourselves.[34]

Steffens was not a good prophet in his appraisal of the status of reform in New York and Chicago, but other "American" cities like Los Angeles, San Francisco, and Cincinnati could be added to this list of places where "native Americans" operated corrupt governments. The authors doubt if they learned it all from the foreigners.

Professor Wolfinger has sharply contested the theory that immigrants and machines go together.[35] He singles out the efforts of Edward Banfield and James Q. Wilson, *City Politics,* to distinguish between "public regarding" and "private regarding" ethos, finding the former in "older stock" residents (supplemented by upper-middle-class Jews). Wolfinger cites earlier corruption in Rhode Island among rural Yankees as a disproof of this thesis. He also cites Indiana as a largely old-stock state where public and private issues were mixed up as late as the 1960s. The authors are familiar with many other examples of corruption in states or cities of predominantly American Protestant origin, including Los Angeles in the first decade of this century, San Diego around 1900, Nebraska in the 1890s, Montana up to 1925, and others. We agree with Wolfinger that too much blame has been placed on the ethnic.

Wolfinger also comments that West Coast cities, where corruption is less, have percentages of foreign-born which closely parallel those of Northeastern cities.

Poorly Paid Public Employees

The National Advisory Commission on Criminal Justice Standards and Goals, in discussing corruption on zoning problems, suggested that public employees dealing with these problems are paid much lower salaries than private workers, and hence are more easily corrupted.[36] Similar suggestions have often been made about the problem of corruption in developing countries.

Appraisal of the Theory

The argument that inadequately paid public employees are easily corruptible certainly had some weight in nineteenth-century America. Even today it is still true in some smaller cities and some of the less well-financed states. But the increase of public employees' compensation in the last two decades (before 1977) has removed much of the force of this argument, without removing the corruption. Congressmen with salaries over $50,000 and a wealth of perquisites still manage to become corrupt. New York City, with some extremely high public salaries and fringe benefits, still suffers from corruption. Few of the organized crime or police corruption rackets noted in recent decades have occurred in the poorly paid forces.

Considerations of equity make it desirable to pay public employees better where they are underpaid. But this reform will have little effect on America's ongoing corruption problem.

Overdecentralization

America has a more decentralized law enforcement system than any other modern democracy. This decentralization permits corruption to continue in local governments, whereas more centralized governments would promptly eliminate it.

Appraisal of the Theory

In Chapter 12 the problem of corruption in levels of government is fully discussed. Here it is only necessary to say that a strong case can be made that excessive political decentralization has helped to produce corruption. America has more political corruption than any other industrialized democracy, and the most decentralized law enforcement system. It is doubtful if any of the other modern democracies would have permitted a city like Reading, Pennsylvania, to have remained a "sin city" for 40 years, or a metropolis like New York to have continued large-scale police corruption for so many decades. The central or provincial government of every other modern democracy has taken steps to ensure the honesty of its local law enforcement.

Chapter 12 discusses corruption at levels of government and develops the problem of law enforcement and corruption, much of which grows out of the American emphasis on decentralization.

Ethical Standards

Several acute observers have commented on the possibility that the weakness in American ethical standards lies behind the ongoing problem of corruption. Ostrogorski believed that the "caucus" (by which he meant corrupt party organization) was diminishing America's moral reserve.[37] Senator Paul Douglas wrote in 1952:

> ... More important than the institutional improvements which I have suggested is our need for a deeper set of moral values. ... The faults which we see in government are all too often the reflection of our own moral failures. All this may dawn upon us, so that we will not only help to reform government but also to reform ourselves.[38]

Professor and former Civil Service Commissioner Leonard D. White, writing in 1957 about the period 1869 to 1901, was concerned about general moral standards but believed that improvement was coming. He commented that "vigilance was still necessary," a remark which is still true twenty years later. Professor C. J. Friedrich comments that corruption may strike a country in its "ideatic core."[39]

Professor Samuel Huntington, in his brilliant observations on corruption in developing countries, clearly indicates the importance of moral norms. The senior author of this book and a colleague have elsewhere indicated their evaluation of ethical instruction in American political affairs. Most social science writers, however, ignore morality as much as they can.

Appraisal of the Theory

There is evidence that the above-quoted writers are correct. Wealthy, well-educated men have participated in corrupt activities enough so that the poverty and family reasons discussed in literature on the causes of crime seem less important here. Victimless crime legislation or immigrant ancestry do not explain the ethical conduct of Aaron Burr, Collis P. Huntington or Charles Yerkes, or James G. Blaine or Albert Fall, or the Watergate group. There is also evidence that ethical instruction was becoming less effective in the America of the last half of the nineteenth century, when our political corruption became severe.[40] It is even clearer that the ethical instruction given in nineteenth-century America did not prepare a person to meet the problems of corruption in the growing new corporate-government society.

In this century, congressional delegates have several times returned men to Congress who had been voted out for ethical delinquencies. Recently a poll of Maryland citizens indicated that they believe Governor Mandel to be a good governor, although they acknowledged his corruption.

These and many other examples seem to indicate that Ostrogorski and White and Douglas and Friedrich were right in being concerned about national moral standards, which will be discussed more fully in Chapter 14.

Faulty Administrative Tradition, Especially in Police

There can be little doubt that some of the worst outbreaks of corruption were fostered by political machines. Whether Tammany Hall taught the New York police to be corrupt or vice versa may be a "chicken-egg" controversy, but the growth of bad police under Tammany and its counterparts in other cities is indisputable.

Today's problem is clearly different. While unsavory ward politics survive in many American cities, the former Daley machine is the only fully centralized, large city machine to survive. Yet police corruption continues to surface in scores of American cities. Former Police Commissioner Murphy quite accurately observes that the New York mayor's office has not appointed corrupt commissioners at least back to Mayor Wagner's time (1952); but police corruption has continued. Such situations have also appeared, albeit on a smaller scale in cities like Indianapolis and Cincinnati, where overhead city administration has been above average.

It is possible that these contemporary examples of police corruption are results of faulty administrative tradition. A young officer entering a police career is likely to be greatly influenced by the older officers to whom he is assigned or attached, following their corrupt practices very quickly. The administrative introversion of police departments, their psychological solidarity, and their unwillingness to accept personnel from other departments help continue this tradition of corruption.

David Burnham has pointed out that in a city like New York, police can become completely cynical. When they see district attorneys letting dangerous robbers off with a light bargained sentence, when judges grant clemency to gamblers with whom they have organized crime connections, when detectives are assigned as bodyguards to a man known to be a Mafia fence, the police naturally become corrupt.[41]

An important cause of police corruption may be the unwillingness of mayors and managers (even reform mayors) to disturb tradition and to hold police accountable for their actions, even though the police department has far more arbitrary authority over citizens and far more chance for corruption than any other department of the city.

Professor Bahn has noted that policemen become "resocialized" when they go through police academy training and join a police force. Police work demands that men assume a "total role," demanding "qualities of judgment, forbearance, patience, courage, stamina, and integrity that are beyond the capacity of most individual police officers to show at all times." Police manuals often require standards of conduct which present an ideal standard but are simply unattainable, thus casting doubt on the value of all rules. The total role also tends to separate police officers from other elements of the community, and, as has often been noted, police tend to develop social contacts among fellow policemen. If veteran policemen are corrupt, the young patrolmen may become corrupt quickly.[42]

Appraisal of the Theory

This argument is that the damage done to good administrative management by several decades of corrupt machine control lives on. In all four major cities discussed in Chapter 6 where corruption by organized crime is still very important, there have been many decades of poor administration. If citizens become adjusted to corruption, it is harder to move them to reform action. If officials are used to corruption, it is harder to persuade them to give up their illegal financial opportunities.

For special reasons the faulty administrative tradition continues in police forces. This is partly because reform mayors often pay least attention to police. Examples of mayoral inattention to police are numerous. Mayor Lindsay of New York was forced to appoint the Knapp Commission in his second term, after *The New York Times* published Serpico's previously ignored complaints. Eleven years of reform mayors in Philadelphia did not forestall the unhappy situation described in Rubinstein's *City Police* or the 1974 Pennsylvania Crime Commission *Report on Corruption in the Philadelphia Police Department.* In the much smaller city of Paterson, New Jersey, Christopher Norwood tells us how reform Mayor Kramer practically ignored his police department.[43]

Administrative nirvanas do not come quickly to police departments. Professor James Q. Wilson's review of the status of the Chicago police force after substantial reforms had been introduced by Chief Wilson clearly shows that some reform of the police will not necessarily increase morale. The sergeants queried by Wilson's questionnaire recognized that the department was better run after four years of reform administration. But the general level of police morale did not rise. Wilson suggests external factors which keep police morale down. The rising spirit of black revolt, the amount of black crime in Chicago, the fact that the courts still made political decisions which nullified police arrests were all more important in keeping police morale low.[44]

Another factor may have been the belief of many police that the Wilson administration would last only as long as Chief Wilson had years of active service. The Daley regime was semipermanent, and Chicago police were likely to revert to type.

The evidence available to the authors indicates that faulty administrative tradition is a very important factor in continuing corruption.

Organized Crime

One of the most important successors of the political machine as a reason for political corruption is organized crime. Clearly, organized crime has a special interest in law enforcement and in the police function. Professor William J. Chambliss suggests that, like his *Rainfall West,* "virtually every city in the United States" has a joint control of politicians and syndicate leaders.[45]

Organized crime's first interest in government is, of course, to secure its own illegal undertakings. If the judge can be bought, a light sentence or dismissal can be secured for the "soldier" who has committed a crime; if the prosecutor or an appropriate attorney in his office can be bought, the prosecution of the "soldier" can be stopped or so weakly conducted that conviction is impossible. If the detectives or patrolmen concerned are bought, there will be no arrest or prosecution.

Organized crime secures further control of the law enforcement process when circumstances permit. The Knapp Commission report showed that policemen had been used as heroin dealers. In other cases, the use of police as fences or guards or full accomplices has been accomplished.

Appraisal of the Theory

Organized crime during and since the 1920s has become a major component in American political life, dominating some corporations, many cities, and many unions. It developed first in the cities like New York and Chicago where old-type political corruption offered a welcome, as shown in Chapter 4. Wherever it can do so, it purchases the cooperation of local governments. Sometimes it corrupts state officials, and it has been known to exert strong enough political pressure to call off more than one federal investigation. Although it may not cause a majority of present-day corruption, it is surely the largest single corrupting force, and it is evidently persistent. New York drove much of it out with Dewey and La Guardia; largely eliminated it from Tammany Hall with Mayor Wagner's leadership; yet found it from the mayor's cabinet to police force in the John Lindsay administration. Reform Chief Wilson tried to drive it out of Chicago but admitted that he had failed on this score. Kansas City's honest administration has failed to eliminate it, largely because of its survival in the county. William J. Chambliss has given an example of how it dominates a Western city of 1 million. It is driving heavily into the Southwest.

As pointed out in Chapter 13, election of reform governments often does not drive out organized crime, which continues to operate in unions or corporations which it controls.

The next chapter discusses some of the measures which may help to control organized crime.

Why Is America So Corrupt?

Although American government is much more honest than that of most countries in Asia, Africa, and Latin America, it is probably more corrupt than other modern democracies—here defined as Britain, Ireland, the Low Countries, Scandinavia, West Germany, France, Switzerland, Australia, Canada, New Zealand, and Japan. American corruption seems to grow out of a variety of historical and contemporary factors.

Some corruption has always existed, but massive corruption began in the first half of the nineteenth century with the organization of political machines, composed of both immigrant and native groups. The situation was made worse by mistaken theories of rotation in office, by city charters which divided power and responsibility among many officials, and by lack of any state or federal attention to honesty of local governments. America was suffering from an excess of dependence on democracy as a cure for all ills which enabled anti-Democrats to obtain and hold excessive power. Nineteenth-century theories attesting to the overriding importance of business values and in some cases the desire to accomplish worthwhile business objectives may have added to public acceptance of these corrupt machines. Equally important may have been the support given by rural native groups to Sabbatarian and other personally restrictive legislation, which was literally unenforceable on immigrant groups in large cities and which led to corrupt action by law enforcement agencies.

Corruption spreads, and the malady in city governments often appeared in state capitols and sporadically in the federal government. There was public concern about this spread; but the overriding sense of business values, a drop in American ethical standards after the Civil War, the absence of Judaic-Christian rules about the ethical problems of large-scale industry and government all weakened the opposition to corruption. By 1890 most large cities of the country were corrupt, as were at least half the states and some part of the federal government.

When the reform movements came, they too often overemphasized mechanical changes in form of government, only to discover after a term or so of power that corrupt machines could also operate the streamlined governments. However, some of the reforms were of lasting value; a large fraction of these were connected with a change in form of government—more important was the council manager plan, which has enjoyed considerable success especially in smaller cities because of its simplicity and its emphasis on professional ethics standards.

A few of the reformers tried to use higher levels of government as a means of controlling corruption. State appointment of big city police commissions was tried in several states but generally abandoned as too political. The European thought of using federal or state administrative inspection to improve the overall honesty of local government or of local law enforcement did not appear in the United States, although many functional controls were legislated.

The poor administrative traditions of the nineteenth century have lasted in many local governments and some states, including jurisdictions which had been "reformed." This poor administrative tradition was reflected in a willingness of the people of cities and states like Boston, New York City, Chicago, Philadelphia, Illinois, Maryland, Louisiana, and West Virginia to accept corruption. Law enforcement agencies were often impervious to reform, giving organized crime (a new source of ongoing corruption) a chance to establish itself very firmly in a number of big and little jurisdictions.

The combination of this bad administrative tradition with the institutionalized corruption of organized crime, even less effective ethical education, lack of continuous central government efforts for honesty, and continued outbursts of ethnic or economic bloc voting regardless of ethics helps explain America's continued corruption.

Can corruption be controlled? America cannot change its heterogeneous population or remove overnight a continuing tradition of corruption. It can, however, use its whole government to control corruption and improve its ethical education. The problems of business and unions, of levels of government, and of ethical education are discussed in the following chapters; it is not possible here to assess their relative importance. Solutions to all are probably necessary if America is to operate on a reasonably high level of corruption control.

12 Levels of Government and Corruption Control

Change and Suggestions of Change

The reader will have noticed that organized corruption has consistently had its major focus in local government. It began in local governments, spread from them to state and federal governments, but has been hardest to eradicate at the local level (as the experience of some of our largest cities clearly indicates). All other modern democracies place more responsibility for honesty of their law enforcement at higher levels. It is not surprising that many persons have suggested changes toward more centralized control of law enforcement, which is essential to corruption control, in America.

Largely in an effort to combat organized crime, which moves quickly across political boundaries to avoid prosecution, Congress has already passed laws to encourage federal prosecution of local corruption, and some administrations have taken steps to enforce these laws. Several distinguished government and quasi-public associations have urged state governments to take a more leading role in law enforcement including corruption control. Some legislatures and state administrations have already taken action, although much less aggressively than the federal government.

Before we discuss these changes in detail, it seems wise to review the major arguments for and against greater federal and state action in corruption control and law enforcement.

Arguments for Greater Federal and State Responsibility in Corruption Control

Americans are a pragmatic people, and the chief argument for bringing state and federal governments into corruption control is that too many local governments, including a majority of the very largest, have been unable to eradicate their corruption during 125 years of effort. There is no doubt that America has suffered far more corruption at local than at state or federal levels. Neither the federal government nor any state government has experienced the degree of semicontinuous corruption of New York City police for more than a century, the more than half-century "city of sin" record of Wincanton, or the continuous corrupt machine control of Chicago for over four decades. There are much less data about rural corruption, but it is probable that many county and township governments have had continuous corruption. Generally, the federal government has been able to resist corruption more than state government, and state government more than local government.

There is less local corruption now than in the last half of the nineteenth century, but it continues to depress the quality of life in America. The end of the centralized political machine has not been accompanied by the disappearance of local corruption. There are few statistics on corruption. But it is a fair guess that between 25 and 50 million Americans live in areas where one or more of the institutions of local government harbor fairly continuous corruption. Certainly the 8 million New Yorkers, 2 million Philadelphians, over 3 million Chicagoans, 750,000 Detroiters, and 500,000 Bostonians must be included in this unhappy list.

Those who are opposed to centralization ask: Why not let the local population improve its governmental experience by reforming itself? The centralizer responds that if such reform has not been effected in the 125 years, it is not likely to be done now. In addition, he points out that corruption in a large city is not stationary; it emigrates elsewhere. Gangsters whose methods were learned and financial support secured in New York and Chicago are now causing major problems for the governments of Los Angeles and Phoenix.

In fact, says the centralizer, states need to be concerned about local corruption for their own safety. Corrupt local machines have frequently attempted to control the state governments. Frank Hague, boss of Jersey City, was frequently a dominant figure in New Jersey state politics.[1] In the mid-nineteenth century, Boss Tweed of New York City put a utility franchise through the New York State legislature, of which he was a member. The Daley machine frequently controlled a substantial number of Illinois state and Cook County jobs.[2] Tom Pendergast, a boss of Kansas City in the 1920s and 1930s, and his gangster successor, Charles Binaggio, elected several governors of Missouri; on one occasion Binaggio succeeding in influencing gubernatorial appointments to the Kansas City police commission.[3]

Centralizers agree that state and federal governments frequently share partial responsibility for local corruption. When federal and state financial systems impoverish cities and counties, or when Congress and state legislatures enact laws which cannot be enforced, federal and state governments are indeed contributing to local corruption.

Sometimes state governments have even corrupted their local counterparts. Huey Long, as governor and as U.S. Senator, did not hesitate to control New Orleans, and other parishes, a lesson which he learned from Louisiana's carpetbag governor Henry Warmoth.[4] In the last century, many state legislatures passed "ripper" legislation to eliminate undesired local officials or agencies. An example of how far ripper legislation can go occurred in Pennsylvania in 1900. Mathew Stanley Quay's state machine joined forces with Thomas S. Bigelow to overthrow the Flinn Magee machine in Pittsburgh. Quay put through the state legislature a bill to abolish mayors in cities of the second class (Pittsburgh, Allegheny, Scranton) and replace them with "Recorders" (a new title for mayor) appointed by the governor. The first recorder of Pittsburgh, Mayor A. M. Brown, resigned shortly after appointment. Governor William A. Stone appointed J. O. Brown, an adherent of the old machine, whereupon Senator Quay persuaded the legislature to abolish the office of recorder and then elect an adherent of the Quay-Bigelow machine as mayor. However, this abuse of the democratic process aroused considerable public resentment.

Although often opposed to local machines, state governments have not always stood strongly *pro bono publico*. Mayor Hazen Pingree in 1892 found the Michigan state legislature firmly opposed to utility reform, which Detroit supported.[5] Fortunately, "ripper" legislation is much less frequent today, and state governments seem to be assuming more responsible attitudes toward localities in the twentieth century.

Centralizers also argue that states have been more successful than local units in resisting organized crime. Ralph Salerno cites three instances in which voters have rejected organized crime encroachments in their states. Claude Kirk was elected governor of Florida in 1966 on opposition to organized crime, after the mayor of Miami had vacillated on the issue.[6] Paul Laxalt was elected governor of Nevada, also in 1966, after an FBI discovery of much "skimming" of casinos in Las Vegas by organized crime and other illegal operations of the mob. In 1967 party control of the New Jersey state legislature was changed on the same issue.[7] In all three cases, the state government and citizenry seemed able and willing to take a firmer position against organized crime than the localities.

A major argument for state help to localities is the fact that successful action against organized crime requires a number of high-quality law enforcement officers which few cities can assemble on their own. The Dewey assault on organized crime in New York in the 1930s or the federal attack on the mob in the Nixon-Ford administration gained results but only by continuous efforts of specially recruited, talented investigators and prosecutors.[8] Organized crime can afford very able lawyers, who will take advantage of every possible Supreme Court decision. Government must have able lawyers if it is to win cases against the mob.

The work of the Kefauver and McClelland committees in waking the nation to the dangers of organized crime could not have been accomplished by state or local governments.

The theoretical argument used by the centralist is that state and federal governments are more remote and impersonal and hence less easily controllable by corrupt political forces. Although the FBI and other federal police forces have their faults, the percentage of their staff who accept bribes is minute compared to many local police forces. The state police have had a few scandals, but all observers report that they are less easily bribed. Many gangsters are well aware of these facts and cheerfully pay federal income taxes on illegally acquired gains to avoid confrontation with federal agents. They remember Lucky Luciano's comment when the Federal Narcotics Bureau put him in jail in 1923: "I tried everything; I offered them three bastards anything they could name, but they wouldn't even look at me."[9] Al Capone learned the same lesson of federal toughness a few years later, when he went to federal jail for income tax evasion and Prohibition law violation, while the brutal murders and scores of other offenses he committed were not even prosecuted by local governments.

The relative impersonality of the federal government needs further comment. During the Watergate investigation, it was said that once an FBI investigation was well started, it could not be stopped. Someone would leak the information, as "Deep Throat" leaked it to the *Washington Post* staff. Perhaps the size of the federal law enforcement unit, perhaps the education and high salaries of the staff, perhaps the Washington publicity make it more difficult to *nolle prosequi* (drop prosecution) in federal cases. President Nixon was driven out of office by the media for assenting to the coverup of two third-rate burglaries, while local administrators in Chicago and elsewhere were illegally securing many millions of dollars of "protection" money. Pleading *nolo contendere* to bribery charges, Vice President Agnew was driven out of office by a federal investigation.

Arguments of Anticentralists

Those opposed to greater federal-state participation in corruption control begin with this argument: Has America not been successful with its old method of law enforcement? If government institutions have worked reasonably well for two centuries, there should be hesitation about recommending change. Theoretically, Americans have feared and distrusted centralized police forces. While this attitude is still prevalent, we today have over 20,000 federal "police" and 40,000 state police.

Over America's twenty decades, a continued faith in decentralized government has probably helped give us a greater sense of popular participation in government.[10] It has given us some guarantee against the application of arbitrary nationwide policies to the varying needs of local press. State and local governments have also proved an important training ground for federal political leadership.[11]

Another argument of the anticentralist is that moving responsibility for corruption control to federal spheres will merely increase the pressure of organized crime and other corruptive forces on the state and federal governments. Then Professor, now Senator, Moynihan noted this argument in an article in the early 1950s. Moynihan's warning had merit; anticentralizers can note a substantial number of cases in which corruptive forces, especially organized crime, have had an impact on state or federal government. In 1935 federal prosecution of Huey Long's followers was abruptly ended. According to an account of Secretary Harold L. Ickes, Postmaster Farley said it ceased because, after Long's assassination, both factions in Louisiana were friendly to the Roosevelt administration.[12] Treasury intelligence personnel opposed dropping the prosecutions and pointed out that most of the accused admitted guilt and reimbursed the Treasury.[13] F.D.R.'s early administration also stopped prosecution of Pendergast supporters; however, later, as Secretary of the Treasury, Henry Morgenthau secured further prosecution of both Missouri and Louisiana gangsters.

Organized crime has frequently demonstrated its effectiveness at multiple levels of government. An Illinois "nonmember associate" of organized crime, who has been arrested thirteen times on murder charges, obtained references to the Swiss government from Senator Dirksen and Congressman Hawkins. A number of bills banning deportation of gangsters have quietly passed through Congress.[14] Those who follow organized crime are aware of its success or near success in establishing some contact with every Presidency in recent decades. Some anticentralists have argued that the Eastern states with their large corruption and organized crime may need some state centralization of law enforcement, but that Southern and Western rural states do not need state centralization. The centralist answer is that the Southern or Western rural states with inadequate state law enforcement machinery and unspecialized local law enforcement personnel are very inviting to organized crime—witness recent organized crime incursions into Arizona, New Mexico, and even Utah.

However, after the arguments of both centralists and decentralists are balanced against one another, it becomes probable that some further pressure from central law enforcement agencies is needed to raise the standards of local agencies. The impact of organized crime and other corruptive forces on the federal government is less damaging than their paralyzing effect on some state and local governments. Apparently both state and federal governments are recognizing the need for greater action on their parts, as the result of this chapter will indicate; the real problem is that of determining which techniques of state and federal action will do the least harm to local self-government while raising the effectiveness of crime and corruption control.

State Efforts against Corruption

America has the most decentralized, most ponderous law enforcement machinery of any modern democracy. Little can be done about the complexity of our legal processes until enough responsible judges recognize that speedier justice is essential. But the state governments can do much to improve police work, prosecution, and judicial selection and thus reduce corruption. The best-known leader of thought in police work, Patrick Murphy, now president of the Police

Foundation and former reform police commissioner of New York City, has stated that we need state agencies which can, among other things,

... Establish statewide standards for the operation of criminal justice agencies in each state, for the personnel of all criminal justice agencies, and for their training;
 ... Influence, either administratively, or legislatively where necessary, changes anywhere within the criminal justice system.[15]

Murphy also states that if the states fail to tighten up and improve their criminal justice systems, the federal government will enter into the field. He is undoubtedly correct. If states will not take action, a national police operation is inevitable. Most of the other modern democracies have already developed such operations.

Recognizing greater resiliency against corruption at the state rather than at the local level, several other states tried state control of big city police forces in the last century. It was adopted for Baltimore in 1860; St. Louis, Kansas City, and Chicago in 1861; Detroit in 1865; and Cleveland in 1866. Of the 23 cities whose population exceeded 250,000 in 1815, state control had been tried in 12. Since then, however, it has been largely abandoned. By 1920 it had survived only in Baltimore, Boston, Kansas City, and St. Louis. In 1963, it was ended in Boston but later revived.[16]

In 1865 the New York State legislature created a metropolitan police force under state control. Local police responded violently.[17] The system of state control of New York City lasted for 13 years. During the Detroit Railway Strike of 1891, Mayor Pingree blamed the violence on the state-appointed metropolitan police commission, and thus quickly secured legislation restoring home rule to the Detroit police department.[18]

In Missouri, state control of local police seems to have alternated between sheer politics and a mild desire to reform. In 1916 a governor, grateful for a political favor, gave Pendergast informal control over police commission appointments. In the 1920s there followed a "wide-open" Kansas City with a state-appointed police board, but with the honest police force subject to budgetary harassment by McElroy, city manager for the Pendergast machine. In 1932 the Missouri Supreme Court ruled that Kansas City could name its own police director. In 1939 evidence of bribing of the police director to protect vice operations resulted in approval of a bill to return control of Kansas City police to the state.[19] In 1948 gangster boss Charles Binaggio was extremely anxious to elect a governor, so he could control the police and elections commissions of Kansas City.

State control of local police continued in only a few cases—notably Boston and Baltimore. One of the major reasons why it failed was because of the criticism that particular jurisdictions were singled out for control.

At present, state appointment exists in the case of St. Louis, Kansas City, and Baltimore, and in them only sporadically. State appointment has failed for two reasons. First, it runs contrary to deeply embedded American theories about the importance of local self-government reinforced by a tradition against central police power. Second, the states have too often used it for reasons of political importance, rather than in the interest of good police administration.[20] Much more sensible than state appointment of police heads would be the development of state training programs and state audit or inspection programs for local police forces.

State governments may control local law enforcement in ways other than appointment of local police commissions. They can designate the methods of selection or training of police officers, prosecutors, or judges. Generally, states have not had an active record in these fields, because of cost and because of fear of invading local autonomy. Law Enforcement Asssistance Agency grants have helped states give greater training opportunities to local police. Some states, notably Missouri and California, have tried to improve the process of selection of judges. Many states give limited training opportunities to local prosecutors. Nevertheless, it is fair to say that few states have recognized any statewide responsibility for establishing a local law enforcement system which would resist corruption.

A real problem is that some states do not have much strength to add to local law enforcement agencies. An attempt by Nevada to keep Las Vegas honest or by West Virginia to keep Charlestown honest would probably fail. Neither state has the experienced law enforcement officials nor the tradition of honest public service necessary for success. However, New York State, Wisconsin, California, or Virginia could easily undertake the task of making their localities more honest.

Most states should organize themselves to help their local governments remain free of corruption and organized crime. Methods of organization would vary in each state, but all should include the following:

(1) Careful review by attorney general and legislature to be sure statutes include modern electronic surveillance and use-immunity laws.

(2) Existence at the state level, usually in the attorney general's office, of a group of professional investigators and specialized lawyers, who can help inadequately staffed local units of government expose and prosecute organized crime and corruption. The large number of states who today are not thus equipped to help fight organized crime and corruption are derelict in their duty to the local governments which they have created.

(3) Authority in the attorney general or other appropriate state offices, to supervise the work of the county prosecuting attorney and sheriff, if necessary. Some states, of which California is an example, have granted such authority. This power is rarely used but is essential to handle those situations where forces of organized crime and other corruption have literally taken over the government

of a local area. The authority of the state official should also include law enforcement in cities if the county does not already have that authority.

(4) Mechanisms of training to build up the professional esprit de corps of the staffs of city and county prosecutors and police officers.

The Knapp Commission in New York recognized that it was hard for a local prosecutor to bring charges against policemen or other officials with whom he had been working; so a deputy attorney general should supersede the district attorneys of New York City for corruption cases.[21] This suggestion has been followed and should now be evaluated. It is in accordance with the procedures of most other modern democracies, where the prosecutor for a corruption case would usually come from a state or national office.

A major problem of law enforcement in America is the uncertain quality and easy accessibility of much local law enforcement personnel. Locally elected prosecutors will often not bring charges, and locally elected judges often fail to give adequate sentences. If these men could be appointed rather than elected and serve for longer periods of time, justice would be obtained more frequently. The decision of whether to prosecute individual cases should, as in England and Canada, be left to semipermanent professional prosecutors, not exercised by an elected county prosecutor or attorney general.

(5) Machinery to secure able judges and to remove from office judges who have demonstrated incompetence. In connection with appointment of judges, it has been interesting to observe in this study that, where corrupt officials have been tried, the judges seem to have set reasonably strict standards in at least half the cases. More care in selection and a greater degree of independence might make the large proportion of American judges capable of handling corruption cases.

More Party Opposition to Keep Law Enforcement Alert

The worst corruption occurs in cities where one political party is usually dominant. If the citizen cannot express dissatisfaction by casting a negative vote, he or she is unlikely to express dissatisfaction at all. The lesson from New York City experience appears to be that the growth of reform influences in the Democratic party has made it easier to fight some kinds of corruption than in Tammany Hall days. But citizens of New York City are deceiving themselves if they expect to secure honest, efficient government without more genuine party opposition.

The striking contrast of bad government in New York City with one party predominant and good government in New York State with two-party rivalry is one which all those examining evidence of corruption should bear in mind. New York State has had relatively little corruption since World War I; New York City has probably never cleansed itself completely.

This comparison supports nonpartisan local elections. Most cities have predominantly Democratic voters; almost all political machines are Democratic (for practical rather than ideological reasons). There is no real possibility of effective two-party rivalry in the large cities. Reforms pointing toward honest law enforcement need the support of concerned people, both Democratic and Republican. But "fusion" tickets are hard to put together. Nonpartisan elections would give reformers of both parties a better chance. Issues of conflict between the parties in national and state affairs are rarely important in municipal affairs.

It is interesting that the British, who use party ties in local elections, have had real difficulties. In some cases one party dominates the local council and makes decisions in private caucuses where conflict-of-interest rules cannot be enforced.[22]

How Administrators May Combat Corruption

The reader is reminded of the suggestions in Chapter 1 for combating certain techniques of graft and the suggestions in Chapter 7 for the states to undertake more positive roles to control corruption in local units of government.

A general suggestion which is applicable at all levels of government is that administrators make clear to their subordinates their desire for honest and legal administration. The point should be made at least twice a year in writing or orally or both; an example is shortly given of reform Commissioner Murphy's ethical directive to the New York police. Similar directives from Presidents, governors, mayors, departments, divisions, and bureau heads would eliminate much corruption and permit executives to leave office with untarnished reputations.

Police Reform

Since much of corruption is in police departments, a few suggestions are added here. There is no easy road to reform of a corrupt police department. However, it is possible to list some of the measures attempted by administrators who have had real cleanup jobs.

The La Guardia administration (1934-1941) eliminated Tammany controls on the police force, but made no effort to go after wholesale police corruption. La Guardia's police executives pursued individuals who were accused of bribery, but thought only in terms of prosecuting individuals.

After the Serpico disclosures, in October 1970, Mayor Lindsay appointed Commissioner Patrick V. Murphy and asked him to eliminate police corruption. Murphy's first step, according to Professor Brown, was to make clear a strong position against corruption. He made this clear in remarks to superior officers in October:

Except for your paycheck there is no such thing as a clean buck. It is just as corrupt to tolerate the bookmaker as it is to ignore the drug pusher. It is just as dishonest to accept the favor of the traffic violator as it is to exact a gratuity from the liquor licensee. Department wide posture must reflect scrupulous honesty. Indications of corruption must be exposed and expunged.[23]

This line had some immediate effect, says Brown. Arrests by policemen for bribery increased fivefold over 1968. Cooperation developed with other agencies fighting corruption.

A second major step was to decentralize the responsibility of corruption control. Field commands were required to set up anticorruption machinery.

Third, machinery for controlling corruption in corruption-prone units, such as narcotics and public morals, was combined into one unit of the Organized Crime Control Bureau.

Fourth, since much of corruption came from inept administrators, new efficiency criteria "with a strong overtone of corruption control" were developed.[24]

Fifth, the department announced its intention to cooperate fully with other investigatory agencies, including the Knapp Commission, the state investigation commission, and several federal strike forces.

Sixth, the department placed emphasis on systematic corruption control rather than a case-by-case basis.

Seventh, a policy of openness on police problems was adopted.

At the same time, certain internal administrative steps were taken:

(1) The office of the first deputy commissioner had incorporated an analysis unit and the Organized Crime Control Bureau mentioned above. A tough professional police executive was put in charge of the Organized Crime Control Bureau.

(2) NARCO (the narcotics division) was reorganized and strengthened, and its top personnel were changed. The department announced policies intended to shift NARCO's emphasis from street narcotics sellers to major traders. Some important new practices were instituted. Officers caught in criminal action were allowed to cooperate. Top staffs created field associates, who received a detective's gold shield for promising to report internal crimes.

(3) A criminal justice bureau was established to analyze criminal cases and keep better touch with courts and prosecutors.

(4) A field-based corruption investigation system was established.

(5) Administrative review units were established to evaluate performance and increase efficiency.

(6) Experimental neighborhood police teams were created.

In August 1971 Commissioner Murphy told the executive force that he was dissatisfied with their progress in reducing corruption. A number of demotions of high-ranking officers were made as a result. Many other changes in personnel practice were made, and the academy program was strengthened to reinforce integrity. The training program for sergeants was augmented to include the corruption problem.

A less formal list of Murphy's anticorruption practices can be picked out of a book, *Target Blue* by Robert Daley, a reporter and writer who served as Murphy's deputy police commissioner for a year, 1971 to 1972. Chief emphasis is placed on Murphy's decision to hold area commanders responsible for keeping corruption out of their areas when the corrupt acts were "so serious, repeated, or widespread that he either knew or by reasonable diligence should have known of them, or that the conditions would not have developed or persisted if he had demonstrated a level of leadership and supervision commensurate with his assignment." Many police executives were demoted or asked to retire on grounds of failure to control corruption in their jurisdictions.

Murphy also decided that men should serve in the narcotics division of plainclothes—a jurisdiction filled with opportunities for corruption—for only two years. He ordered 500 top police executives to disclose all their assets, and he received questionnaires from all of them. His Deputy Commissioner for Inspectional Services, Sydney Cooper, led nocturnal raids on station houses and other places where men on the graveyard shift were sleeping. Six precinct captains lost their jobs because many of the officers in their charge were found "cooping" (New York police jargon for sleeping on the job). Murphy retired a chief in a borough where the FBI had filed an affadavit in court that a gambler was distributing payoffs to policemen, with no action by the chief. He told the chamber of commerce that bribers would be arrested as well as bribees, and later reported to the public the arrests which had been made for bribing. "Christmas lists" of gifts to police were suspended. Perhaps most significant of the actions was an order that patrol forces should limit actions employed against gambling, which had proved unenforceable in the courts, and also against intelligence gathering, response to complaints, and response to nuisance situations.[25]

Reports from persons who are familiar with the New York Police Department in 1976 indicate that organized corruption has been largely eliminated by methods like those described above. Much individual corruption remains, but it is hoped that the amount is decreasing.

Present Federal Efforts against Corruption

Recognizing the arguments for federal action, particularly against organized crime, Congress has passed legislation greatly extending federal power to prosecute certain activities of organized crime and other aspects of local corruption. The Organized Crime Act of 1970 makes it unlawful to use income obtained from criminal activities to establish an interstate business. Long prison sentences may be imposed on racketeers. Gambling operators may be prosecuted, without proof of crossing state lines, if they involved five or more persons working over 30 days who have handled daily bets totaling $2000. It is also a federal crime for local or state law enforcement officers to protect gambling operations. Federal grand juries are empowered to issue reports, as distinguished from indictments, on acts of official misconduct involving organized crime. Since the Johnson administration the federal government has had "strike forces" which combine various federal police agencies to fight organized crime, each one under the chairmanship of a Department of Justice attorney. These statutes are combined with earlier ones which enable federal officials to prosecute state and local officials who accept bribes, and which enable the federal government to enforce laws about drugs, alcohol, income tax, and other fields in which organized crime is concerned.

The FBI's witness protection program, started in 1967, has been one of its greatest assets in fighting organized crime. Every prosecuting agency has been weakened by the fear of witnesses that mobsters would kill them before testimony to prevent talking or after testimony as punishment of a "stoolie." Thus, great care was taken to protect Valachi, Teresa, and Barboza.

Given some degree of involvement in interstate commerce, federal officials can now prosecute state and local officials. Neal R. Peirce quotes James R. Thompson, then (1975) U.S. Attorney in Chicago, now governor of Illinois:

The current wave of prosecution of official corruption can be traced—irony of ironies—to the Nixon-Mitchell Justice Department. No administration ever did more to upgrade, professionalize and staff the U.S. Attorneys' offices in the field, and then leave them unfettered on their choices of prosecution.

Peirce then goes on to comment about the new federal powers to get at state-local corruption through new laws and expanded powers of old laws. However, federal prosecution of state-local misdeeds may not continue. Peirce again cites Thompson:

Ten years ago the U.S. Attorneys weren't into local corruption, and ten years from now they may not be there. They may become politicized or turn their attention to drug traffic.[26]

Federal police forces (about 20,000) are less than state (over 40,000) and local (about 300,000). Similarly, federal prosecuting lawyers are few compared to the staffs of state attorneys general and local prosecutors. The result is that the federal government cannot uncover a substantial fraction of local corruption;

yet federal prosecutors now make perhaps half the prosecutions of corrupt state and local officials—but a great many remain unprosecuted. The general distaste of Americans for expansion of federal law enforcement makes it unlikely that the national government staff will be expanded so that federal prosecution will adequately reduce political corruption.

In July 1977 federal attorneys who had done distinguished jobs of prosecuting corrupt state and local officeholders of both parties were being removed, to be replaced by Democratic appointees of less obvious experience and ability.[27] It remains to be seen if President Carter's administration is going to lower the vigor of federal prosecution of organized crime and corruption. There will be heavy congressional pressure to do so, since most well-entrenched organized crime or other corruptive forces are capable of political pressure on representatives or even senators from its area.

An Alternative Approach for Federal Action

A better approach than more federal prosecution, and the attendant federal policing, would seem to be the strengthening of state and local law enforcement by a federal conditional grant. This method has already been employed with some success by many other federal agencies which depend upon a system of grants, preferably "block grants," for state and local activities in a wide variety of fields such as welfare, road construction, education, vocational rehabilitation, employment, and unemployment compensation. Often the federal grant provides for some standards of selection and educating public employees.

If a grant system is to be used in the law enforcement field, it need not be a large percentage of existing costs, since such costs are already in state and local budgets. Some 10 or 20 percent of costs, or less, might be adequate. The existing LEAA grants would be better used for this than for their present purposes.

One condition which should be attached is that each state or local prosecutor's office which receives the grant must have an annual or biennial audit of honesty. The audit should be made by an outside agency, sponsored by a state government or an appropriate association of local governments or a professional association or some other official group. The U.S. Department of Justice should certify the adequacy of the staff of each agency conducting audits. The requirement of honest operations for receipt of grants is implied if not expressly set forth in most federal grants, but it is especially important here.

Some will suggest that such a provision would result in federal political control over state and local law enforcement officers. This difficulty could be avoided. Federal police and law enforcement agencies which would certify the credentials of the audit agency serve under political department heads, but are themselves staffed by professional men of fairly continuous service. It is hard to believe that these professionals would try to dictate political conditions to the auditing agency. Auditing agencies would, of course, vary in usefulness. States like California, New York, and Wisconsin would set up excellent agencies, because of their excellent personnel traditions. Smaller states like Nevada might have difficulties, making alternative auditing agencies like the International Association of Chiefs of Police or the International City Managers Association perhaps more desirable. Some of the strong leagues of municipalities could set up a law enforcement audit agency.

Would this effort to eliminate corruption at state and local levels bring corruption to the federal government? It is certainly true that organized crime would be unhappy with an effort to ensure honesty of local law enforcement agencies, and might lobby in Congress to weaken the audit provision. But it does not seem probable that such a program would bring the corrupting force of organized crime more strongly into the federal government. Organized crime would certainly be drawn into more efforts to control the Department of Justice if federal prosecution of corruption should become ubiquitous. But it would be harder to apply mob political pressure to an annual audit by professional men.

In fact, the audit of local law enforcement agencies could help bring about a generally desirable closer cooperation of federal, state, and local law enforcement machinery. J. Edgar Hoover used local corruption as a reason for the FBI's policy of "stand off" from local enforcement units. If the honesty of local units could be ensured, much closer cooperation between governmental levels would be possible.

Those who are concerned about loss of citizen participation in local government as a result of overcentralization should reflect that a mild centralization like the one proposed here might produce more local cooperation of the citizenry because citizens would work more closely with better local enforcement agencies. Japanese law enforcement operates under central control, but with more citizen participation (in associations helping police and helping rehabilitate prisoners) than in the United States.

The experience of law enforcement intelligence units (LEIUs) gives a somewhat encouraging basis for interstate inspection of law enforcement units. This association admits only those units of government whose work has been professionally evaluated. Salerno tells us:

Local police corruption usually is obvious to L.E.I.U. men in other cities long before it comes to the attention of local citizens. More than a year before a Dade County grand jury shocked Miami, Florida with revelations of police corruption, law enforcement intelligence men in cities thousands of miles away were aware of the situation. In 1965, the Miami Police Department withdrew its membership from L.E.I.U. It faced suspension there.[28]

The recommended changes could be accomplished with no real loss to America's system of political decentralization. Indeed, the opportunity of citizens to work in their government, to learn to be good citizens, would be increased by steps which would tend to reduce corruption.

13 Business, Labor, and Political Corruption

Introduction

This chapter will attempt to prove that not business nor labor nor government can be cited as the sole source of political corruption in the United States. It is argued that an interrelationship exists between these three institutions and that this interrelationship strengthens and perpetuates corruption. Political reform is viewed as being successful only when the ethical standards of government, business, and labor are raised.

The theory that extensive nineteenth-century business corruption of government was a consequence of rapid urbanization and industrialization which made existing ethical standards obsolete is examined. It is shown that political corruption results from the government's extorting money from business and business's offering bribes to government, rather than business's simply corrupting government. The shift of regulatory functions from municipal government to state and national government and the corresponding shift of various types of corruption from the municipal level are also examined. Finally, it is argued that while businessmen have played an important role in government reform since 1865, they have still not committed themselves to it as fully as possible.

Certain elements of American organized labor are shown to be highly corrupt, and political corruption, particularly at the municipal level, is regarded as the source, more than the result, of union corruption. Politically controlled law enforcement agencies are cited as a frequent reason for extensive union corruption, and instances are mentioned where unions have been both the willing and the unwilling partners of organized crime. The chapter concludes with a discussion of various labor leaders who have tried to rid their unions of corrupt and subversive elements and of the obstacles that hinder internal union reform. These obstacles include the defensiveness of union members regarding external criticism, their frequent lack of an adequate educational perspective, their socioeconomic ties with corrupt local politicians, and an attitude of hostility toward government investigations.

Is Business to Blame for Corruption?

Many writers and groups have assumed that "business" was the source of nineteenth-century corruption. Lincoln Steffens held this theory in most of his writings, although his 1931 autobiography has an easier judgment that some business had to corrupt government to exist. An esteemed political science colleague, Prof. Phillips Bradley, simply assumed that "a politician who promotes a private interest in a political 'deal' is merely following current business practices and ethics."[1] In 1974 the California chapter of Common Cause assumed that limitations on lobbying expenses and business contributions to political campaigns would end corruption in California. In 1910 Professor Brooks had argued that business practices and political corruption were inextricably linked and that competition was the main reason for most forms of corruption. Brooks, however, failed to explain why *monopolistic* industries, such as the railroads and the public utilities, were trying hardest to corrupt government.[2]

Preview of the evidence does not support the theory that business was the sole cause of corruption. But before reviewing the factual evidence, the reader should be reminded that few people in business or politics or elsewhere in the nineteenth century had adequate ethical codes for the problems of a growing industrial America in the last half of that century. The rapid urbanization and industrialization that the United States underwent from 1865 to 1900 required newer and more comprehensive ethical standards than the religions and philosophies of early America had developed. Ideas of "conflict of interest" or careful definitions of the "public interest" were not known. Unfortunately, the need for these standards was not fully recognized until the beginning of the twentieth century, and even then no single body was responsible for framing them. Even business, which was ultimately responsible for regulating its own affairs, possessed few individuals capable of establishing such standards.

The confusion that businessmen and politicians experienced regarding ethical standards can also be attributed to the emergence of new currents of thought in nineteenth-century America. Darwin's *Origin of the Species* and various trends of modern intellectualism undoubtedly weakened the influence of religious institutions which, for many Americans, were essential to the preservation of an ethical code. The effects of this upheaval were quite visible: emphasis on individual ethics in school readers declined, crime increased, and the climate of ideas for ethical democracy was less friendly than in 1780.

Dimly aware of their ethical dilemma, Americans initially sought to use the free market as their new ethical guide. In theory, the free market enabled decisions regarding the allocation of resources to be made on the basis of supply and demand, hence in a manner that minimized corruption. If the market failed to operate in an equitable fashion, frustrated competitors could complain to the government. In practice, however, the unregulated market often appeared to encourage lower ethical standards for business and government.

Business Corruption of Government in the Nineteenth Century

With the exception of a few instances, such as Georgia's Yazoo land scandals, there is little evidence of business extensively corrupting government prior to 1860. Indeed, canal and railroad construction, which was financed primarily with government subscriptions, clearly united politics and business in an effort to answer important questions about routes, financing, and use charges, all of which were critical to the economic development of the United States. Most political corruption during the pre-Civil War period related to the sale of public offices, to extortion of funds from businesses shipping goods through customs houses, and to bribes or kickbacks on government contracts.

From 1865 to the early 1900s, however, America experienced one of the most corrupt periods of her history, an era of rapid economic expansion and frontier settlement in which small and large businessmen were guilty of involvement in corrupt government activities. Many smaller businessmen also conducted their financial operations on fraudulent or near-fraudulent bases, often selling worthless securities to small investors. These activities were not classified as political corruption until governments began devising regulations to end them, and corruption was used to avoid such regulations. Many honest businessmen assumed a leading role in eliminating these bad practices as well as pressing for other business reforms, supporting new federal and state laws in addition to the administrative efforts of Better Business Bureaus.[3]

While some large businessmen of the period (the "robber barons") were involved in bribery and other forms of political corruption, other large businessmen confined their abuses to unethical competitive practices. Standard Oil, for example, was certainly unethical in its treatment of competitors; but most of its practices did not involve political corruption, and there is no positive proof that John D. Rockefeller ever agreed to any corrupt transactions. Ida Tarbell does mention Standard Oil's control of the Pennsylvania legislature in 1887, in order to defeat a bill limiting charges for oil, transportation, and storage, but she admits that political corruption was not proved.[4]

Andrew Carnegie was another leading nineteenth-century industrialist against whom no charges of political corruption would seem to apply. Carnegie was capable of sharp business practices and was indirectly responsible for the bloody Homestead strike, but there is little evidence of his involvement in political corruption.[5]

"Robber barons" such as Jay Gould, Jim Fisk, Daniel Drew, Collis Huntington, David Colton, Thomas Scott, and H. O. Havemeyer, however, were actively engaged in many different corrupt activities. Gould, Fisk, and Drew bribed legislators, bought judges, and cooperated with Tammany Hall in order to further their objectives of plundering the Erie Railroad and of robbing the public. Huntington and Colton of the Central Pacific–Southern Pacific Railroad and Scott of the Pennsylvania and the Texas and Pacific Railroad bribed congressmen for preferential route legislation. H. O. Havemeyer, founder of the American Sugar Refining Company or the "Sugar Trust," was probably aware of his company's bribing American revenue officers to short-weight raw sugar, thus saving it from several million dollars of annual duties.[6]

Quite obviously, the railroads were a major source of political corruption as they expanded across the continent with government aid. The Credit Mobilier construction company of the Union Pacific distributed shares of stock to prominent congressmen in such a way that several political careers were abruptly ended when it was discovered. The Central Pacific-Southern Pacific Railroad system bribed or otherwise influenced important political figures in California for over 40 years and to a lesser extent influenced legislatures in Arizona and New Mexico. In attempting to secure monopolistic control of transportation in California, the Southern Pacific raised and lowered freight rates to obtain exorbitant profits. Much local opposition was aroused by these tactics, but the railroad used its political power freely, securing "the major share of the profit of virtually every business and industry on the coast."[7] In gathering a vote for the city of San Francisco to subscribe to the railroad, voters were reported to have been bribed in substantial numbers by Philip Stanford, brother of the governor and representative of the railroad. The Southern Pacific's domination of California political life finally ended in 1910 when Progressive Hiram Johnson was elected governor along with a reform legislature.

In an 1884-1885 trial regarding the treatment of a deceased official of the Central Pacific-Southern Pacific system, General David D. Colton, Mrs. Colton (who was the plaintiff) introduced a file of letters to Colton from Collis P. Huntington, one of the Central Pacific's "Big Four" owners, which revealed the railroad's dominance of California politics. In these letters, Huntington named many public officials who were taking instructions from the railroad. Those who voted against the railroad were retired to private life at the next election. The cost of legislation in Congress or the state legislature was categorized quite frankly as "the price of steel tracks."

Other railroads established similar relationships elsewhere. After securing government subscriptions for their financing, they became interested in avoiding regulation, or what they viewed as unduly severe regulation of their rates, heavy taxation of their physical assets, and the repayment of their government obligations. As railroad regulation increasingly shifted from municipal government to state and national government, however, the occasion for railroad corruption of public officials became less frequent.

A careful study of correspondence of railroad leaders from 1845 to 1890, by Thomas C. Cochran, portrays a point of view somewhat different from that of the Huntington letters. The railroad leaders seemed to recognize that they were in politics and must stay in politics, but several wished that they could get out of the system of distributing free passes to holders of public office. They generally assumed that federal and state legislators lacked understanding of railroad problems. Some of them believed that it was right to bribe a legislator for the sake of better railroad operation, but their remarks about bribery were more guarded than those of Collis Huntington.[8]

Municipal street traction companies also attempted to corrupt municipal and state government in order to secure franchises and to avoid tax payments.

Detroit in the 1890s, Chicago in the 1890s, and Cleveland in the 1900s are a few examples. In the public sector, the city-owned Philadelphia Gas Trust was a source of major political corruption.[9] Corruption in municipal transportation, however, began to decline sharply after 1917 when automobiles were increasingly being introduced on the road. Streetcar profits decreased; since then, the main difficulty has been to preserve municipal transportation as a form of urban travel.

Business Corruption of Government in the Twentieth Century

The selling of fraudulent securities in "bucket shops," which were named after stores that sold buckets of grain or flour to poorer customers, was a major area of political corruption in the early twentieth century. Arnold Rothstein developed and incorporated this activity into the network of organized crime which he established in New York City during the 1910s and 1920s. Bucket shops obtained protection from police action through bribery, often distributed through Rothstein to his Tammany Hall friends. Rothstein's rackets could be more appropriately classified as illicit activities seeking to protect themselves rather than "business" corrupting government. Like the transit companies, bucket shops chiefly corrupted local government.[10]

The Harding administration provided one of the more blatant examples of political corruption by a few individual businessmen. Secretary of the Interior Albert Fall was found to have accepted thinly disguised bribes from Harry Sinclair and Edward Doheny for oil field leases. Colonel Charles R. Forbes, director of the Veterans' Bureau, was later convicted of receiving kickbacks for selling government property to contractors and was sent to Leavenworth.

During the Great Depression, the public utilities industry was charged with corrupting government officials. Chief among those criticized was Samuel Insull of Chicago, former private secretary to Thomas A. Edison and a leading genius in the electrical utilities field. While Insull did not engage in bribery, his companies did contribute heavily to the campaign funds of candidates of both parties. A $100,000 contribution to the fund of Frank L. Smith, chairman of the Illinois state regulatory body and candidate for the U.S. Senate, was sharply criticized.[11] The Truman scandals involved both businessmen and business corporations in efforts to avoid taxes, to secure Reconstruction Finance Corporation loans, and to secure favors from the Federal Housing Agency.

More recently, American multinational corporations, such as International Telephone and Telegraph (ITT), Lockheed Aircraft Corporation, Gulf Oil Corporation, Exxon, and General Motors, were discovered to have made "illegal" payments to "representatives" of host governments.[12] While these payments, in the form of bribes, kickbacks, and campaign contributions, were illegal by American standards, many foreign countries regarded them as ordinary business transactions. The question arises of whether an American company is acting unethically when, because of corrupt officials or competitive pressures, it pays a foreign government in order to remain in operation.

It is not yet clear what form federal legislation will take, but there is little doubt that Congress will legislate against bribes to foreign officials or governments and that the United States will push vigorously toward international regulations against bribery of government officials by international business corporations. It is curious to have this push against international corruption come from a coountry which tolerates so much domestic corruption, but America has always had a startling contrast of idealism and grasping commercialism. If our idealistic thrust succeeds, it will help raise the level of international business and we will have real cause for pride in our country.

Business–Government Corruption as a Two-Way Relationship

In view of the widespread belief that business is the chief source of political corruption, it is worthwhile to examine some evidence regarding this theory. However, a fundamental question must be addressed: Which came first, the business bribe offer or the government extortion demand? Often the two propositions are merged so completely that an external observer cannot discern the answer.

Nineteenth-century examples clearly indicate a two-way movement, in which government was often the first to suggest illegal action. In Chapter 3, it was noted that the building inspector could ease or make more difficult the problem of a businessman. The Tweed Ring, not business, arranged the illegal use of enlarged municipal contracts. Abe Ruef secured his business clients in San Francisco at the suggestion of Mayor Schmitz. Business licenses in San Francisco were granted only after a retainer to Ruef or a bribe to the inspector. The Cox machine in Cincinnati required "donations" from city and county contractors, merchants, and saloonkeepers. There were, of course, exceptions; Jay Gould retained Tweed as legal advisor of the Erie Railroad.

In our chapter on state corruption, the "Black Horse Cavalry" of the New York legislature demanded $1000 per vote from Gould and Vanderbilt. The Black Horsemen frequently introduced strike bills to force business payments. In Pennsylvania the Quay machine insisted that banks which had public deposits should contribute the equivalent of the interest to the corrupt machine.

Lincoln Steffens, in his writings on the early 1900s, was initially inclined to blame most political corruption on business. Before he finished his writing of the muckraking era, however, he was admitting that perhaps management of a railroad requires corruption. In the same period, he was speculating that business had bosses just as politics did—a speculation which fits fairly well with a conclusion of this chapter that it is necessary to speak of the standards of all society, not of business alone or politics by itself.

In his later autobiography, first published in 1931, Steffens became even more tolerant of business. He repeats the thought that railroad management had to run the government. He was interested to learn that the Southern Pacific could not afford to control all California politics. He became interested in persuading business, government, and labor to work together. Perhaps he was at fault in not recognizing that there were Americas other than the corrupt one of 1890 to World War I which he knew so well, or that other democratic countries had learned to manage government and business together without corruption. But he did recognize the two-way relationship.

Several more modern examples indicate that political corruption frequently consists of both extortion and bribery with extortion in the lead. The 1972 report of the Knapp Commission on New York City police corruption revealed that police extortion was a common occurrence.[12] Investigators found that many bars doing a substantial volume of business made regular biweekly payments to the police in order to remain in operation. However, the Knapp Commission also found that the police department failed to take adequate measures against construction contractors who offered bribes to policemen. The most frequent form of misconduct was the acceptance by police officers of gratuities in the form of free meals, free goods, and cash payments. Virtually all policemen either solicited or accepted such favors. Officers also sold narcotics and extorted bribes from motorists and tow truck drivers. Drugs were frequently "planted" on suspects.

The Pennsylvania Crime Commission report on Philadelphia indicated that there were more "shakedowns" by police but also recorded "voluntary" contributions.[13] The commission concluded that systematic corruption resulted from the interaction of many factors, including the police department's attitude toward corruption, the vice enforcement policy of the department, various societal pressures on individual police officers and on other parts of the criminal justice system, and the public's tolerant reaction to corruption.

Some elements of the Watergate scandal demonstrated what can result from a mixed business-government relationship. While neither the "third-rate burglaries" nor their concealment was directly related to business, Watergate has often been interpreted as a result of excessive business involvement in politics. Common Cause, for example, contends that business contributions to the Committee to Re-elect the President (CREEP) were given so freely that some were used to conceal political misdeeds. While it is true that CREEP money was used for the legal defense of several Watergate offenders, it still cannot be cited as the "cause" of Watergate.

The special prosecuting staff working on Watergate did investigate several cases of illegal corporate contributions to campaign funds—to both Republican and Democratic candidates. Although a legal provision against corporate contributions to federal campaigns had been in effect for 70 years, it had not been previously enforced by either party. As a result of this failure, fines and jail sentences for individual defendants were light. In general, both the Republican and Democratic parties appear to have solicited money from business as much as business had approached them. While business may be rightly criticized for permitting unprincipled politicians to extort money, available evidence supports the view that business cannot be cited as the sole initial corrupter of government. Representatives of CREEP, for example, approached a number of corporations which had problems before federal agencies and asked for substantial contributions. Northrop Aircraft is a prominent example. While awaiting a decision on a government contract for airplanes, it was asked to contribute $100,000 to CREEP. The Northrop gift fell perilously close to becoming a bribe, but it should be noted that the political power initiated the contact with business.[14] In contrast, representatives of the Associated Milk Producers, Inc., apparently initiated contact with CREEP. This contact resulted in a $1 million contribution and a clear effect on the price of milk.[15] The milk producers had earlier made substantial contributions to Senator Humphrey's 1968 Presidential campaign, typifying the lack of partisan interest of contemporary corporate organizations.

International Telephone and Telegraph (ITT) was reported to have been ready to offer $400,000 in campaign contributions for the 1976 Republican Presidential Convention to be held in San Diego, ostensibly because the hotel ITT owned there would benefit but more probably because it desired a favorable decision from the Department of Justice and the Federal Trade Commission on its merger with Hartford Insurance Company.

After reviewing the above evidence, in addition to the mass of evidence elsewhere, one can clearly conclude that there was a two-way relationship between government and business corruption. Frequently it becomes a chicken-egg controversy as to whether the official or politician made the demand or a business representative offered the bribe first.

Business Sponsors Government Reform

The fact that many businessmen have opposed corruption also argues against the notion that business is solely responsible. American businessmen firmly supported the establishment of civil service reform organizations in the nineteenth century in order to reduce political corruption.[16] In 1967 the National Manufacturer's Association unanimously supported a congressional bill for that purpose, primarily to promote tax and revenue reform as well as greater economy in government. Businessmen interested in civil service reform were primarily smaller merchants rather than industrialists, latecomers rather than originators of the reform movement, and followers rather than leaders. They were generally hostile toward "monopolies," some of them arguing that so long as the civil service remained unreformed, legislation to curb the monopolists would be ineffective (since key government positions could be bought with campaign contributions). Business ideals pervaded the thinking of all reformers, even those who had little connection with businessmen, and reformers frequently called for "business methods" in government service.

From 1900 to 1977, American business ethics, prodded by national and some state governments and public opinion, have steadily improved in quality. The sharp competitive practices of Rockefeller disappeared; the rigging of stock prices by insiders like Daniel Drew would now be swiftly punished; the sale of near-fraudulent securities or nonexistent commodities by bucket shops has virtually been eradicated. The "blue sky" securities laws of the states were promoted by a "Truth in Advertising" campaign of businessmen. It should be noted that the National Association of Manufacturers and the chamber of commerce have been prominent in their support of legislation to promote more ethical government and business.

Other Ethical Questions about Business and Government

There are many unsolved questions of ethical relationships between business and government. If an aircraft company gives $100,000 to Republican officials just before a decision to buy a new light plane is made by the government, it is clearly a bribe. But is the gift a bribe if it is made to campaign funds during the campaign? If so, organized labor and farm groups as well as business have been bribing members of Congress and government officials. But is not government supposed to represent the various groups in our society?

Informational lobbying, in terms of representing a business view on administrative regulations or on legislation to political agencies, is generally regarded as both ethical and desirable. Frequently, lobbying can prod a government jurisdiction into taking an action it would not otherwise take. If a new tax is likely to discourage businesses from locating in an area or a new regulation might bankrupt a firm with many employees, then this information should be communicated to responsible government officials. Other forms of pressure, however, can enable an unethical business to transmit an undesirable position from business to government. These include the possibility of appointing government officials to an attractive business position or of making substantial campaign contributions in return for past or future favors. Such practices are common, and few efforts have been made to control them through legislation. While these activities have not corrupted entire governments, they do pose important ethical problems.

The profound effect that government policies can have on the condition of business firms or whole industries often stimulates heavy business involvement in politics. The 27 percent depletion allowance long allowed in certain extractive industries (such as petroleum) is an excellent example. The oil industry was involved in politics for many years in order to obtain and preserve this and similar tax advantages. As a result of such favors, Wilbur Mills, in 1976 Chairman of the Joint Ways and Means Committee, had little difficulty in securing contributions for his short Presidential campaign from firms which desired favors from his committee.

Ethical questions may also arise when prominent politicians or their relatives are connected with a business in private life. Much controversy surrounded the loan made to Donald Nixon, brother of President Nixon, by a Howard Hughes Company. Businesses which engaged President Nixon's law firm before his election had dealings with the government after his election. It is difficult to determine whether such connections establish undue influence on a political figure.

A more complex problem is posed by the substantial influence of organized crime on political life in America through campaign contributions and other means of political influence. Its methods and objectives undeniably are shocking and un-American. But what about a legitimate business which believes it must cooperate with organized crime to keep going? Is it responsible for the political evil caused by organized crime?

A related question arises about the corrupt political machine with which organized crime is so frequently associated. Is business wrong for paying bribes or rendering favors demanded by a governmental agency which can extinguish the business? The authors' inclination is to say that it is wrong, but that one could create a contrary argument of responsibility to corporate employees and shareholders.

This book does not have space to explore all the problems of public represenation of economic interests. It is likely that a form of public funding of parties will reduce some of the pressure. Presumably, maximum contributions will be set by statute, and unions will continue to receive special preference because the nature of their operations makes them an almost automatic political force. Political contributions which essentially appear to be bribes will probably continue.

Conclusions on Business–Government Relationships

The above evidence does not support the theory of business as the chief cause of political corruption. It does, however, leave blots on the escutcheons of both business and government. Neither was aware of the rules for conducting a modern industrialized society. Neither tried very hard to discover the necessary rules; nor did they secure much real help from church or educational leaders of American thought until the reform movement of the 1890s. The post-Civil

War period was a nadir of American political and business values. What should business have done, or what should business do today, to decrease the corruption of the American political process? The question was not easy for nineteenth-century business executives; it is easier today but still not child's play.

Professional groups are slowly beginning to recognize that it is unprofessional conduct to corrupt our government; state bars and organizations of CPAs currently put a colleague out of practice if he bribed a government official. It has been seriously suggested that engineering and architectural associations take a similar slant. Should not business groups take a similar attitude eliminating investment advisors from their professional association, or insurance advisors from theirs, as a penalty for corrupting or trying to corrupt officials? If these quasi-professional groups take this position, then comes the most difficult problem—what about corporate executives? Some boards of directors drop executives who are corrupt; others do not. Obviously, all should do so, but since the boards come from a miscellaneous background, would it be better to form associations of corporate executives who would eliminate members who corrupt their government? Would antitrust laws be violated by such eliminations? The problem needs further attention.

Another proposal involves few legal problems. Corporations, indeed all businesses, need to have constant programs of ethical education for their employees, at minimum a lesson or so a year on why the business wants highly ethical conduct from all employees in relation to each other, to the business, and to customers, suppliers, and finance sources. It would be appropriate to add ethical relations to the governments of which the business is a constituent member. The problem of business relations with employees raises the question to which the next section addresses itself, that is, the role of labor unions in corruption of government.

Organized Labor and Political Corruption

Labor unions have never, like business, been charged with being the chief source, or indeed a source, of political corruption. However, unions have been intimately tied to a substantial fraction of corrupt political machines and have themselves been the victims of corruption. In a few cases, the unions have themselves become a major corrupting force.

Union administration in the United States has been marred by a high degree of corruption. For several reasons, labor corruption is greater in America than in some other civilized countries.[17] The administration of union funds, particularly pension funds, has frequently been for the benefit of union executives, not of the average worker. However, many American unions have been administered quite honestly and have attempted to eliminate corrupt internal elements.

Political corruption unquestionably facilitates union corruption, particularly if municipal governments are corrupt, for if a local government will not enforce its laws, the opportunity for breeding corrupt unions is great. In the early 1900s, for example, the autocratic extortion practices of building trade leaders in New York City and Chicago were greatly aided by the political contacts of gangsters within the unions and by the delay of local governments in prosecuting them. During the 1930s, 28 different American Federation of Labor (AFL) unions in Chicago were dominated by vicious racketeers.[18]

Political corruption has also enabled organized crime to develop one of its major illicit activities in conjunction with unions—industrial racketeering.

A word should be said as to why some unions have become heavily entangled with organized crime—a plight into which the Teamster's Union is heavily entangled, the Longshoremen's East Coast union is involved, many building trades unions have been taken over, and a number of other unions have become victims. In some cases the union's national headquarters has not had sufficient strength to establish an honest union competitive with the unions riddled with organized crime. In some cases the union's national headquarters is itself under the influence of organized crime. In many cases corrupt local law enforcement officers are unwilling, or unable, to prosecute wrongdoers in the union.

A Brief History of Organized Labor and Political Corruption

New York City

The earliest examples of union corruption were in the New York City and the Chicago building trades, where labor leaders operated with the help of corrupt local governments. Walking delegates conducted union operations quite autocratically after the Haymarket bombing of 1886 brought discredit to the Knights of Labor. Professor Hutchinson, author of an authoritative volume frequently cited here, has maintained that these delegates needed authority to deal with employer antagonism against union organization. Unfortunately, however, the power of the delegates often resulted in their demanding graft from employers. By the 1890s, corruption in the building trades unions was quite prevalent, especially where circumstances favored the coercion of employers by delegates.

Labor leaders Sam Parks, originally in Chicago but after 1896 in New York City, and "Skinny" Madden in Chicago are two notable examples of corrupt building trades leaders. Parks exploited his Housesmith's Union for his own benefit, using union funds freely for himself and his wife. As president of the

New York City Board of Building Trades, he extorted money from employers until a reform district attorney, William Travers Jerome, obtained his conviction in 1902. The strength of Parks's political connections is illustrated by the fact that former Police Chief Bill Devery supplied his bail on one occasion. Devery later abandoned Parks when he began working with Devery's rival, Tammany Hall. Union control of politics was certainly not complete, however, since Parks and several of his associates received substantial prison sentences for extortion of funds from companies by strike threats.[19]

Robert P. Brindell, a more successful extortionist, eventually replaced Parks after becoming a business agent for the Independent Dock Union in 1912. Brindell was elected president of the New York Building Trades Council in 1919. New York State's Lockwood Commission vigorously criticized his methods of extorting funds from both employers and employees. Interestingly, the establishment of that commission was opposed by Tammany Hall, in which various building trades officials held high positions. Brindell was eventually convicted and imprisoned in Sing Sing where he received special treatment; he was later transferred to stricter Dannemora Prison, from which he was released in 1924. Brindell's release was another instance of corrupt political connections since it occurred without a consultation with the prosecuting officers. Joseph Fay of the Operating Engineers Union and James Bove of the Hod Carriers Union are examples of other extortionists who combined union and political power. In 1945 Bove was convicted of larceny from the union and income tax evasion.

Prohibition inspired the entrance of even more sinister elements into the labor unions. Gangs which had long existed in cities such as New York became racketeering groups for bootlegging and preying on bootleggers. With the repeal of Prohibition, they went heavily into the industrial relations field, selling their services to or forcing them on employers and unions. Municipal, state, and national commissions investigated such racketeering; all three concluded that politically controlled law enforcement furnished protection essential for racketeering. Samuel Seabury concluded that "The evidence before me compels the conclusion that the much heralded warfare on racketeers ended in complete and abject surrender by the law enforcing authorities in New York City."[20]

The needle trades in New York City especially suffered from gangsters like Buchalter and Shapiro to whom they paid large sums of tribute. Efforts to prosecute these gangs were usually unsuccessful; the labor policies of the New Deal reduced but did not eliminate gangsterism. The Communist-controlled fur workers' unions continued to hire gangs and to bribe police to beat up nonstrikers.[21]

Would the gangsters have been used if New York City had possessed an honest and effective government? The answer is probably not. Hundreds of low-paid needle workers were beaten up in strikes and in strikebreaking because New York City did not have honest and effective law enforcement.

Chicago

In the 1890s Chicago suffered from large-scale labor graft with strong political backing. Madden, the chief leader of Chicago organized labor, "enjoyed close relations with the city administration, ... with several building trade union officials being on the city payroll." Madden's puppet president of the Building Trades Council was also chairman of the Chicago Civil Service Board. In 1907 there was a great deal of labor graft, with employers claiming that the city police refused to protect nonstrikers. In 1921 a state Assembly committee reported that many important unions were controlled by convicts and other professional criminals. Many indictments resulted from this report, but few cases reached the courts and Governor Small (who was not removed from corruption himself) pardoned most of those who were convicted. In the 1920s and 1930s, unions were frequently taken over by gangsters, and many businesses used these unions to cripple competitors. These activities obviously required extensive cooperation from local government authorities. According to the president of the Chicago Crime Commission, at one time Al Capone offered to police Chicago in return for protection in the labor, liquor, and gambling rackets. As late as 1952, one Chicago local had enough influence with the police to enable it to force a restaurant to recognize a union without an election.[22]

Businesses can have a difficult time operating honorably if organized crime has political support, as in Chicago. Senator McClellan wrote that in the garment industry of the Northeastern states, it was difficult for a manufacturer to conduct business without trafficking with gangsters. The record shows that he dare not resist.[23]

Jersey City

Under the Hague machine in Jersey City in the 1920s, 1930s, and 1940s, Theodore Brandle became a powerful union leader in the milling industry and president of a major employers' association in the steel industry. Brandle helped engineer employer-union conspiracies, controlled public contracts, and procured various services from Jersey City police. He was eventually discredited by an unsuccessful strike.

New York Waterfront

The New York waterfront is one of the worst areas of union corruption in the world. The Longshoremen's Association, through a systematic reign of terror and murder, has exploited its members and the businesses using the New York docks.[24] The political organization of New York City has undoubtedly strengthened this kind of waterfront racketeering.

In the early 1900s, the Longshoremen's Union Protective Association (LUPA) came under the control of Richard Butler, a corrupt Democratic machine politician and longshoreman. In 1914 most of the LUPA became part of the International Longshoremen's Association (ILA), again under a combination of union and political leadership. The worst part of this corrupt regime began in 1927 when Joseph P. Ryan, a corrupt Tammany-trained longshoreman, assumed control of the ILA for the next quarter-century. Ryan's organization included an excessive number of local unions, some of which were "only paper organizations." Force was frequently employed, and some unions were prevented from voting. The "shape-up system" of hiring permitted arbitrary control of work opportunities by the dock boss, who demanded kickbacks from the already poorly paid workers. Theft of goods was well organized, payrolls were extensively padded, and men who revolted were murdered.

Yet the companies accepted this system, as did the union, and political support could always be relied upon. Indeed, ILA racketeers virtually became a part of the political system. Ryan was said to have packed some local union meetings with police plainclothesmen who voted as he wished.[25] Companies were forced to pay large sums to Ryan and his union.

The principal conclusion that can be drawn from corruption on the New York waterfront is that it probably would not have been as great if local government had tried more seriously to enforce the laws. Keating, in his exciting account of the trial of three waterfront gangsters, shows how men who revolted against the system were murdered with no fear of legal action against the murderer because of organized crime's reputation for intimidating or eliminating witnesses. Conviction of the three gangsters occurred only after constant delaying actions from some police officials and individuals in the New York County prosecutor's office. These officials were undoubtedly influenced by the fact that John Dunn, the chief murderer, had served on a Tammany Hall committee and had political influence as well as some business backing. Reform Mayor La Guardia, however, not only failed to endorse Dunn but was openly critical of the War Department for recommending Dunn's release because of presumed services to the military during World War II.[26]

Attempts at Union Reform

Trade union reaction to charges of corruption was quite slow and generally inadequate. The AFL passed resolutions against racketeering in the 1930s but took little action since its leaders regarded external criticism as a general attack on labor. As long as this defensive attitude prevailed, little could be expected from unions in terms of eliminating corrupt labor-political combinations. An exception was the American Labor party in New York City which endorsed

Thomas E. Dewey for reelection as district attorney. In the 1950s, the AFL assumed a slightly more aggressive stance, establishing a new longshoremen's union.[27]

The election of George Meany as president of the AFL in 1952 marked a turning point in the struggle against corruption. One of Meany's primary objectives was the elimination of corrupt and subversive elements within the partly corrupt AFL so that it could merge with the more honest Council for Industrial Organization (CIO). The AFL made an effort to replace the corrupt Longshoremen's Association, but gangster-connected James Hoffa of the Teamster's Union successfully prevented it. Undoubtedly, the election of prominent gangster Johnny Dio by the United Auto Workers (UAW), AFL, to the presidency of local 102 in New York City was an embarassment to Meany. Dio later led a Chicago local of the UAW-AFL.

After the merger in 1955, the AFL-CIO adopted a more active policy against labor corruption and actually suspended and expelled certain corrupt unions. The McClellan Committee hearings gave it more material to investigate, and action was subsequently taken. The corrupt Bakers' Union was suspended in 1957 and expelled in 1958; eventually, it was partially reformed. The Jewelry Workers' Union was put under a monitorship which was lifted in 1962 after the election of new officers. The powerful Teamster's Union was expelled in 1957 for continued corrupt practices, including organized crime control of several locals.

When efforts were made to clean up New York's waterfront through a bistate commission, the effort was weakened by the commission's appointment of political hacks and the union's assistance to racketeers attempting to retain their power. Unfortunately, the New York waterfront is still plagued by racketeers.

Professor John Hutchinson attempted to explain the corruption of American unions by citing the time-worn theme of social conditions, rather than individual ethical responsibility, as the principal reason for labor corruption. He stated that:

All were victims of a social condition. Crime is an expected feature of any new society, but it has shown a special strength and endurance in the United States. Far into the twentieth century, the heritage of frontier justice, the contempt of the pioneer for the law, a restless population, an individualistic culture, an entrenched philosophy of acquisition, an admiration for the sharp transaction, a tolerance of the fix, and a legacy of politics viewed as a business have brought to American criminal behavior a boldness and to law enforcement a capriciousness, foreign to most civilized societies.[28]

Hutchinson then proceeded to blame union ethical difficulties upon those of business.

Organized crime has increased its influence in government, business, and organized labor since Hutchinson wrote his book. Many unions have become the unwilling partners of organized crime. The building trades locals of various areas have been controlled by gangsters, chiefly through threats or violence. The Teamster's Union, the largest and wealthiest union, has become almost synonymous with organized crime. In the construction and longshoremen unions, employees have often been forced to pay kickbacks in order to obtain jobs. In the transportation industry, unions are often dominated by gangsters. Organized crime "services" are offered on job sites, docks, construction sites, and in the New York City garment district. Teamster and construction unions controlled by organized crime allocate their banking and other financial business on the advice of organized crime "consultants." Labor "mediators" are often gang members, and "sweetheart contracts" are frequently for the benefit of organized crime. Finally, loans are often arranged between criminal and labor organizations.

In the unions, as in municipal government, the presence of organized crime is likely to mean continuing corruption. Gangsters are less easy to eliminate than ordinary criminals since they can hire expensive attorneys, threaten opposition witnesses, and provide for gang stability through successive leadership. One authority estimates that there has been no real reduction in organized crime's infiltration of labor since 1950.[29] If this is true, the United States is likely to have organized crime in some unions for decades to come. This would naturally mean continued influence of organized crime on government.

The key to eliminating organized crime in the unions is labor reforms; yet several impediments hinder a thorough internal reform of the unions. First, the low educational level of union members has often kept them from appreciating the gravity of the misdeeds committed by union officials. Second, union members have lacked the money to pay lawyers to represent their cases against miscreant union executives, as a disgruntled but wealthy shareholder might press a case against bad corporate management. Third, the socioeconomic background of many union members has conditioned them against an attitude supportive of government intervention. Fourth, Seidman, author of *Labor Czars,* has indicated employer hostility to unionism may be responsible for a large amount of union corruption by forcing the unions to operate clandestinely.[30] Fifth, Lipset, author of *The First New Nation,* has suggested that the absence of clearly defined social and economic class lines in America may have meant that union officials regarded themselves more as individuals reaping whatever profit they could from union activities than as representatives of a suppressed working class who would always struggle for that group.[31]

Conclusions

The evidence indicates that an interrelationship exists between business, labor, and government in terms of political corruption. Chicago is an apt example of this interrelationship. The longevity of the Daley machine can be attributed to the support it has received from corrupt unions, organized crime, and the support of the business community. Union corruption from organized crime would not be as prevalent and damaging if organized crime had not been a major feature of the Daley machine. If business had been more selective in giving its support, corruption would probably have been less extensive.

The vicious circle of low individual ethical standards and poor law enforcement, from which political corruption springs, cannot be broken merely by reforming a single sector of political and economic life. Higher levels of individual ethical thought and more agreement on the need for law enforcement in business, labor, and government are necessary before Chicago can become a more honest city. Business or other reform groups may begin the process, but both must achieve a higher ethical level before genuine reform can occur. In New York City and Philadelphia, for example, reform movements have been relatively unsuccessful since they were only political and did not include efforts to improve the individual ethical standards of business and labor. Cities which have benefited from reform movements, such as Cincinnati, Dallas, and Los Angeles, have been led by business and professional reformers. An improvement in the ethical standards of local government has also resulted in a raising of union ethical standards.

American life undoubtedly offered economic opportunities for uneducated "natural" leaders of ethnic groups to progress up the political machine or union ladder too rapidly. Such individuals sometimes lacked adequate individual ethical standards or any sense of responsibility to their constituents. Hence, the methods which they developed in order to prosper were frequently illegal and unethical. Union racketeering of the Parks-Brindell type became, under Arnold Rothstein in the 1920s, a major technique of exploitation used by organized crime. Only the strict enforcement of the law could have prevented it, and this was obviously not available in machine-run cities. While political corruption was a source of union corruption, union corruption undoubtedly contributed to political corruption. The union member, the poorer citizen, the legitimate businessman, and the general public all suffered from the price raises caused by union extortion and the low level of city administration resulting from political corruption.

Business has made some contribution to ethical standards of government, but much more could be done. It has already assisted in a number of reforms in governmental procedures and financial operations—reforms which help force better ethical standards. Many business ethical codes today forbid bribery; all, of course, should do so. But business could also suggest standards of its own employees when they move over to government service, pointing out the desirability of no acceptance of favors. Business should also set higher standards about appointment of former government officials and immediate use of them as a pressure group against their former colleagues.

As Wraith and Simpkins have pointed out, business has major reasons for being ethical. Ethics can be good salesmanship.[32] But business cannot be ethical itself if it does not help to keep its regulating authorities ethical.

14 Improvement of Political Ethics

This chapter will comment on the problems of ethical education underlying political corruption in the United States. Loss of community and individual ethical standards is briefly discussed. Methods of ethical education, especially those of education in political-ethical problems in the schools, are reviewed. The failure of the church to develop a sense of political ethics in its membership is then reviewed. The important operations of the media both in achieving reform and at times ignoring corruption are discussed. The importance of professional attitudes and the highly significant role of citizen groups are reviewed.

Community Ethical Standards

In spite of America's humanitarianism and other great qualities, groups of Americans can easily be led astray in ethical matters. Chapter 7 notes the remarkable differences among states, even adjoining states, in ethical standards of public officials. There are also important local differences. Boston, a largely Catholic city which has not had unusually high crime rates, seemed to ignore all ethical standards in its frequent reelection of the colorful mayor James Michael Curley, who had a successful political career in spite of two jail sentences. A jury in the small town of Malone, New York, acquitted gangster Dutch Schultz against the evidence, shocking the judge and others, because Schultz had been spending and giving money freely in the town.[1] Several representatives (like Adam Clayton Powell) who were expelled from Congress were promptly reelected by electorates of questionable ethical standards. On a number of occasions, associations of police officers have bitterly fought investigations of corruption on the force. The "largest police funeral demonstration in New York" was at the funeral of a police captain who had committed suicide after being investigated for corrupt activity.[2] The problem of low community ethical standards goes back into the nineteenth century. Secretary of the Navy Gideon Welles recalled a comment of President Lincoln at the Cabinet meeting of January 16, 1865:

The president was happy. Says he is amused with the manners and views of some who address him, who tell him that he is now re-elected and can do just as he has a mind to, which means that he can do some unworthy thing that the person who addresses him has a mind to. There is very much of this.[3]

The above reactions are not invariable. Sometimes censored congressmen have been defeated. Sometimes investigations have been requested by honest police. Sometimes elections are won by the more honest candidates. But the number of large demonstrations against honesty in American public life needs explanation. It is often the case that the electorate or other group has been misinformed about breaches of standards. Partisan or job considerations may overcome normal ethical standards. *But one cannot review the number of these episodes in American life without wondering if they do not reflect inadequacy of basic ethical education.* Many Americans cannot seem to understand the reasons for civil service or other means of securing professional employees in government. Is it a surprise that they cannot understand the more complicated problem of maintaining ethical standards, if they lack adequate instruction in such standards?

Corrupt Educated Individuals

America has had so much corruption for so long that space does not permit listing individual leaders of corruption. This listing is confined to *educated* corrupt men, of whom there are enough to indicate that our political evils are not a result of lack of education.

Aaron Burr, who was first to use Tammany Hall for political purposes and urged it on to some of its less desirable techniques, was a graduate of Princeton (of which both his father and grandfather, the distinguished theologian Jonathan Edwards, had been president).

DeWitt Clinton, father of the New York spoils system, was a graduate of Columbia and a scholarly member of a leading New York family. In the original Tweed Ring in Tammany Hall, Oakey Hall, Sweeny, and Connolly were all well-educated attorneys. Oakey Hall, mayor under the Tweed Ring, was in some ways like Jimmy Walker. He had many talents, as playwright, lecturer, poet, journalist, lawyer, clubman, and humorist.[4]

Boies Penrose, long boss of Pennsylvania and of parts of Philadelphia, was a very able Harvard college graduate. "A taste for honest debauchery, a sense of humor and a natural cynicism drove Penrose from the ranks of the just into the arms of Matt Quay."[5] Boss Platt of New York was the son of a lawyer and a graduate of Yale. Mark Hanna was an educated, wealthy man. Abe Ruef, rapacious boss of San Francisco in the first decade of the century, graduated from the University of California at Berkeley with highest honors at age 18. At Hastings Law School, he was president of a municipal reform club.[6] The two Carter Harrisons worked closely with corrupt machine politicians in Chicago; both were well-educated men, the older being a Yale graduate.

President Richard Nixon is another example of the person who committed his misdeeds after he was estabished. He was a graduate of Whittier College and Duke University Law School. However, as President, he did conspire to conceal two breaking-and-entering cases.

Almost all the Watergate principals were graduates of good institutions of higher education, including excellent Catholic universities, liberal arts colleges, Ivy League schools, and state universities. Attorney General Mitchell had studied at Fordham University. Robert Haldeman and John Ehrlichman were graduates of the University of California at Los Angeles. E. Howard Hunt and Charles Colson were graduates of Brown University.

An outstanding example is that of one of the tried and convicted Watergate conspirators, Jeb Stuart Magruder. Magruder had studied ethics under William Sloan Coffin, then chaplain and professor at Williams College, later chaplain at Yale. Magruder testified on June 14, 1973, to the Senate Select Committee on Presidential Campaign Activities:

Now, I had gone to college, as an example, under Professor Coffin and had a course in ethics as an example under William Sloan Coffin, whom I respect greatly. I have great regard for him. He was quoted the other day as saying, well, I guess Mr. Magruder failed my course in ethics. And I think he is correct.

During this whole time we were in the White House and during this time we were directly employed with trying to succeed with the President's policies, we saw continuing violations of the law done by men like William Sloan Coffin. He tells me my ethics are bad. Yet he was indicted for criminal charges.

. . . So consequently, when these subjects came up, although I was aware they were illegal we had become somewhat inured to using some activities that would help us in accomplishing what we thought was a cause, a legitimate cause.

Magruder was probably suffering from the teaching of situation ethics—the theory that values are not general or absolute, so each individual must decide each ethical situation for himself.

A good many businessmen fall into the late-blooming corruption class. These are men who followed a fairly normal business practice of accepting small gifts or hospitality from suppliers or other commercial contracts. In business such gifts have often been forgiven, perhaps too readily, on the ground that they are too small to influence the recipient's business reaction to market decisions—a forgiveness which may be reasonable. Such gifts are, however, highly undesirable in government, where acceptance of any favors may influence a decision which is not governed by supply and demand. Sherman Adams and many other businessmen serving in government found the first blot on their record came from the acceptance of such gifts while in government service.

A case which deserves special notice is that of Senator Thomas J. Dodd who was censured by the Senate and defeated in the following primary because of frequent use of political contributions for personal purposes and acceptance of hospitality and lecture fees from organizations threatened with investigation by the Senate subcommittee of which he was chairman. Dodd was carefully reared as a Catholic, was a graduate of Providence College and Yale Law School, and was a "staunch moral absolutist." He had begun his political career primarily as a reformer.

Right and wrong are clearly demarcated he insisted, and could always be identified. When his son Nicholas was taught in catechism class that it was a less serious sin for a poor man than a rich man to steal $10, Dodd complained to me indignantly that the spurious doctrine of the relativists had invaded even the Catholic schools. He could see a moral issue in about every dispute and was exasperatingly pedantic about it.[7]

According to Boyd's account, Dodd was defended by many members of the Senate until frequent publication of his misdeeds forced the Senate to take action. Some of his associates in the Senate were not ethically sensitive, and the association undoubtedly had some effect on Dodd's lapses from his moral codes. Much of Dodd's difficulty came from too easy acceptance of the loose practices allowed by the U.S. Senate. Boyd comments:

Congressional ethics is an undefined and obscure area of human behavior. The point at which a Senator's small deceits, profiteering, misuse of public facilities, and acceptance of favors become culpable dishonesty is hard to know morally, and harder still to know legally.[8]

Chester A. Arthur, whose biographer called him a "gentleman boss," was a college graduate, a former school teacher, and a lawyer. His associations with Senator Roscoe Conkling and Republican "stalwarts" seem to have lowered his standards.[9]

Otto Kerner was the son of a lawyer and judge, a graduate of Brown University, a Presbyterian elder, governor of Illinois. Kerner is not known to have committed serious corrupt acts until his governorship, when he accepted a substantial bribe for securing certain racetrack privileges.

Most of these late-developing corrupt men seem to have been brought down at least in part by associates. A person of strong moral character may have resisted such associates, but American education does not emphasize such qualities of resistance. In *The Right and the Power* Leon Jaworski suggests that the principal vice of several of the Watergate conspirators was that they were followers of bad advice, not leaders.

Students of police corruption have observed that many men who had early records of honesty became corrupt after joining the police. Lecturers in the police academy talk of ethics but often to unlistening ears. After the new patrolman leaves the academy, he is assigned to work with an older member of the force. In some jurisdictions this older man may easily convert the newcomer to corruption. The special solidarity of policemen growing out of their uniforms and their habits of living often adds to the possibility of their being corrupted by associates.

Men Who Looked the Other Way

Leading political figures who looked the other way while subordinates or supporters performed corrupt actions are numerous in the annals of American political history. These men did not commit illegal actions; they often honestly believed that their acceptance of corrupt support was a necessary evil to help them accomplish major reforms. Nevertheless, their failure to insist on high ethical standards of staff and supporters is one of the main reasons for our relatively low level of political ethics.

A few examples are surprising. Franklin Roosevelt accepted major support for the 1932 nomination from Jimmy Hines, the Tammany district leader who succeeded Arnold Rothstein as liaison between Tammany Hall and the underworld. F.D.R.'s administration in its first year stopped prosecution of political gangsters in Missouri and Louisiana who happened to be Democrats. If Harding had brains enough to appoint Charles Evans Hughes and Herbert Hoover, he must have recognized the weakness of men like Daughterty, Fall, and Jess Smith. In 1947, Attorney General Tom Clark was talked into dropping charges against two evil gangsters.[10] President Harry Truman authorized appointment of men as Internal Revenue officials and supported them against criticism when he must have been aware of their lack of qualifications. Dwight Eisenhower may have been unaware of the character defects of Sherman Adams, Harold Talbott, and Richard Mack (all conflict-of-interest cases), but he was certainly remiss in not repeatedly letting them know that he wanted complete honesty in his administration.

Lyndon Johnson must have had some insight into the illegal maneuvers of Bobby Baker. Richard Nixon, himself a lawyer, should never have agreed to the Hoffa pardon or to the coverup of the break-ins. It is hard to believe that Martin Kennelly in 1949, after two years as mayor, did not know that Chicago had organized crime. Similar examples of governors, mayors, and many other public officials could be given. Most would respond to criticism with the comment that they had other more important things to worry about. The answer may be correct, but their lack of forceful ethical policies still keeps American politics at a lower level.

In *Resignation in Protest* (Penguin Books, 1976) Edward Weisband and Thomas M. Franck conclude that the ethics of American business and public service executives and lawyers require silence when persons resign because of disagreement with administrative policies. These authors regret that American political executives cannot follow the British practice of resigning with public protest, although they grant that administration would become impossible if *every* public servant decided to support his own judgment by resignation and public protest. Without necessarily agreeing with the examples chosen by Weisband and Franck, this writer is inclined to agree with them about the existence of attitudes against protesting resignations. Such attitudes probably make some contribution to the widespread existence of corruption in American political life.

After going through lists of communities and persons who become corrupt, and those who looked the other way, we must still face the fundamental question: Why? Could not a country with America's basic idealism and belief in democracy produce more reformers and fewer corrupt persons? America was producing educated, corrupt leaders such as Cameron, Penrose, Quay, Platt, and Conkling in the nineteenth century. Why did we continue to produce educated, corrupt men like Mayor Walker, Governor Kerner, Senator Dodd, Attorney General Daugherty, and the Watergate conspirators in the twentieth century? Why did so many men look the other way? The remainder of this chapter will look at ethical education of the schools, the churches, the media, the professions, and citizen reform groups.

Inadequate Ethical Education

The authors have elsewhere indicated their belief that ethical education in America is substantially below what is needed for our complex modern society. Professor Robert C. Brooks, at the end of the first decade and near the end of the national "reform" era in 1910, made similar judgments. As his title *Corruption in American Politics and Life* indicates, he thought corruption was general in the United States. Chapter 4 of his book is devoted to "Corruption in the Professions, Journalism, and the Higher Education." In another place he says, "We must develop a more robust virtue, capable of resisting the greater pressure that is brought [by modern society]." Elsewhere he expresses himself similarly on business ethics. The reader may remember that the late Profs. Paul Douglas and Leonard H. White, both distinguished academicians and public servants, had similar doubts about America's ethical level.

In nineteenth-century America, vigorous efforts were made to teach ethics. The International Sunday School Association had a text for every Sunday; liberal arts colleges had required courses in ethics in the senior year. Public school readers had many ethical references. These texts and courses were often unsuccessful; it may be that the failure of the ministers, professors, and teachers to understand the rules needed by a new, complex industrial society was the chief reason.

In the twentieth century, the failure of American churches, schools, and colleges to try to teach individual ethics is widespread. In any event, America teaches ethics less in its schools than any other modern democracy; the fact that our incidence of corruption is higher must be more than coincidental.

Civic Education and Corruption

Few Americans realize that instruction in indiviual ethical responsibility has been largely eliminated from the public school (and simultaneously from the Sunday Schools). DeCharms and Moeller found the number of pages in school readers (out of 25 pages) with moral teaching declining from 16 in 1810 to 0.06 in 1950. Margaret Foster found third-grade readers dropping from 100 percent of moral and religious content in 1776 to 1786 to only 5 percent in 1916 to 1920. Nietz and Mason found a drop from 60 percent to 10 percent in moral emphasis in civics books from 1814 to 1890, as noted later.[11] In sharp contrast to America, other modern democracies have been increasing their public school education in ethics.

American has recognized its problem of educating a heterogeneous group of persons to our democratic methods and has developed one of the most elaborate systems of civic education in the world. One estimate—perhaps too high—is that almost half the school time of fifth to twelfth graders is devoted to social and political education.[12] Gabriel Almond and Sidney Verba, in *The Civic Culture*, assign Americans' sense of participation in politics to our schooling civics—perhaps too optimistically.

However, little of this teaching is devoted to problems of political ethics. Most striking is the just-mentioned shift of civics books from a 60 percent emphasis on ethics prior to 1814 to less than 10 percent in the last half of the nineteenth century (and almost none today).[13] The lack of such materials is partly a result of the "value-free" posture of contemporary social scientists.

Ignoring the ethical problems of political corruption must make civic education meaningless to children in New York, Philadelphia, Boston, or Chicago, where any alert child must be aware of the presence of corruption. Professor Hess of Stanford has written: "It is the argument of this paper that the schools have contributed to divisions within society by teaching a view of the nation and its political processes which is incomplete and simplistic, stressing values and ideals but ignoring social realities."[14] The author disagrees with Hess's assertion that teaching stresses values and ideals but agree that civic texts ignore social realities.

Civic education could provide a great focus for ethical instruction in a country whose high corruption rates indicate the need for such instruction. Ethical instruction should, of course, appear in various parts of the curriculum, such as literature, history, and science; but there is also much to be said for "biting the bullet" in civic education. The costs and causes of political corruption are a meaningful part of American political life; any course which ignores corruption is weakened by this omission.

Ineffectiveness of Civic Education

The political socialization literature has some unhappy results to report. Langton, for example, reports that:

The results offer strikingly little support for the impact of the curriculum. . . . it is perfectly obvious from the size of the correlations that relationships are extremely weak, in most cases bordering on the trivial. . . . Furthermore, the impact of the history curriculum under the same control conditions is as low or lower than the civics curriculum.[15]

Langton's data were taken from a survey of 1669 high school seniors distributed among 97 public and independent schools. The results indicated that taking civics courses had little effect on whether the student is knowledgeable in politics, interested in politics, follows politics in the mass media, talks about politics, believes he might be effective in it, is interested in participating, and shows civic tolerance.

Little, in a study of three Boston-area communities, came to a similar conclusion: "Apparently attitudes toward political activity are so strongly channeled through other agencies in each community that the civic education program's efforts have little independent effect."[16]

Richard Merelman, in his study of two school districts, concludes "that teachers fail to socialize their students to partisanship."[17] He concluded that teachers were ignorant of the local politics of education.

Fred Greenstein concludes: "But there is little evidence that the educational programs explicitly directly toward citizenship, as presently constituted, have much of an impact upon political participation. As Mr. Dooley replied, when asked if education is responsible for the progress of the world, 'D'ye think 'tis th' mill that makes th' wather run?'"[18]

Can Civic Ethics Be Taught?

These negative reactions to civic education are discouraging. At least one commentator believes that the negative results suggest that teachers cannot convey the political norms of the nation. We are inclined to the theory that these results indicate the ineffectiveness of course materials which exclude vital ethical problems. Discussion of case studies with consideration of ethical problems would bring out a much higher degree of student interest, and possibly of student participation, in the political field.

We know from several studies of the advantage of discussion of cases in ethical problems; the new British moral education program relies on them, as does the elaborate testing of ethical levels designated by Prof. Lawrence

Kohlberg of the Harvard School of Education.[19] Discussion of cases could not fail to be more interesting than reading the descriptive civics texts which have come to the authors' attention. The emphasis on realism in case studies is likely to produce results. Children from poorer areas must resent the limited nature of the civics text. But would they not respond to something like the following paragraph?

Officer Callaghan, responding to a call for quieting a family row in a tenement house, discovers that the father is a drug pusher. There are three children, who clearly do not have adequate clothes and do not appear to have enough to eat. When Callaghan starts to arrest the drug dealing father, mother and the children begin to support father strenuously, pointing out that he is their only source of income. Father offers Officer Callaghan a $50 bribe to ignore the whole episode. What should Callaghan do?

A thoughtful teacher could pull out of a case like this lessons regarding the importance of the laws, the ways of enforcing them, and the importance of good family relationships.

In addition to case studies, civics texts could be helped by including historical episodes, which may themselves be the subject of class discussion. On the bad side could be presented the stories of Boss Tweed and his associates mulcting New York City, or of Abe Ruef and his supervisors dividing up bribe money in San Francisco, or of Tom Pendergast sponsoring organized crime in Kansas City. Why did they do it? How could it have been stopped? But Tweed and Ruef and Pendergast are significant parts of American history, as is the fact that all three went to jail.

On the cheerier side, some of the heroes of corruption fights could also be portrayed. Attorney Francis Heney, in San Francisco for no compensation, continued to prosecute the Ruef-Schmitz Ring until he was shot down in court. District Attorney Miles McDonald, backed by the ideals of St. Thomas More, continued to prosecute gangsters and corrupt police in Brooklyn, against full pressure from Mayor O'Dwyer and the Democratic machine which had nominated McDonald. Fiorello La Guardia and Tom Dewey both battled for honesty against difficult odds. Joseph W. Folk in St. Louis is another example of active rectitude. It took courage for Patrolman Serpico and Sergeant Durks to go to *The New York Times* with their criticisms after police executives and the mayor's office had ignored them. These and other constructive personalities could be presented to students.

The above suggestions on teaching political ethics have been made primarily for the public schools. But the teaching of political ethics should not be left to the schools alone. Several other groups which should help to carry this responsibility are suggested in the remainder of this chapter. Since most of these groups are not limited by the constitutional provisions, a variety of methods of teaching ethics may be suggested to them.

Through many centuries the Jews have had substantial success through teaching of the Mosaic law, discussing the provisions, interpreting them, codifying them. Other religious or nonreligious groups could use similar methods; their chief problem is to find a body of rules to start discussing.

Aristotle in his *Nicomachean Ethics,* St. Thomas Aquinas in his *Summa Theologica,* Castiglione in *The Courtier,* and Lord Chesterfield in his letters to his son have presented thoughts on individual values which could be related to the problems of contemporary political life. The comparative approach, emphasizing the similarity of ethical values of various religions and philosophies, has been suggested by C. S. Lewis in *The Abolition of Man.* Americans could benefit greatly by a study of ethical standards in the governments of other modern democracies. Jesus Christ in a series of remarkable parables secured attention to hidden ethical aspects of many problems. Biographical studies of men or women who helped the world forward ethically can also be taught. Plutarch's *Lives* is full of Greek and Roman examples of moral excellence. The lives of the Saints may be helpful to those who are religiously motivated. One, or two, or more of these or other methods of study of ethical problems could do much to help America. Use of these methods with particular reference to political ethics could go far toward helping America control political corruption.

As well as in the schools, ethical education is needed in colleges and universities. The liberal arts college, which should be a center for the instruction of ethical values, is often cynical and negativistic, viewpoints which hopefully can be overcome by rational consideration. Medical schools usually teach medical ethics (although the course is often largely medical economics). Law schools are now teaching legal ethics, although this instruction is largely confined to conflict-of-interest problems. Business schools are including some ethics in "business and society" courses. None of these courses are adequate, but they are all better than nothing.

Frank Goble of the Thomas Jefferson Research Center (Pasadena, California) has written *Beyond Failure* in which he describes several methods of teaching character education. Reports on each of these enterprises, all of which are based on increasing the student's or patient's sense of responsibility for his own actions, indicate a good degree of success.[20]

The Churches

Leonard D. White wrote that in the corrupt era of the late nineteenth century "the Churches did not waver in holding man's duty to his fellowman before him."[21] Certainly if religion stood for fairness of all men to one another, it should have opposed political corruption which is basically unfair, especially to the poor. Religions had been the matrix of most ethical studies prior to the Enlightenment; its help was needed on questions of political ethics.

There is much evidence to indicate that a respected former colleague, Professor White, was wrong, that the churches did waver and are still ineffective in holding man's duty to his fellowman before him. A few examples are illustrative. Griffith tells us that in the early 1900s Birmingham boasted record church and Sunday School attendance, but gave little support to a reform mayor's one-handed fight against graft.[22] Zink's study of 20 city bosses (mostly in the nineteenth century), most of whom were highly unethical and over half of whom had been indicted for a major crime, indicates that 10 were Catholics, 5 classified as "religious," 3 "regular" and 2 "indifferent," while the other 10 included 4 "indifferent" Protestants, 3 "casual" Methodists, 2 "healthy" Presbyterians, and one "indifferent" Jew. Catholicism seems to have failed to convince its "bosses" of the importance of ethics; Protestantism and Judaism were unsuccessful in holding their "bosses" at all.[23] When the prosecutions of the Ruef-Schmitz machine in San Francisco seemed to bog down in delay, people become divided on the question of whether the prosecutions should continue. Catholic, Jewish, and Protestant church leaders and members all shared this division.[24] In the early 1900s, the Catholic hierarchy of Milwaukee supported the flagrantly corrupt Mayor David Rose and opposed the German socialists with their municipal reform.[25]

More recently, several of the Watergate conspirators were devout churchmen. H. R. Haldeman and John Ehrlichman were strong Christian Scientists. Magruder was a good friend of an outstanding Protestant university chaplain. Mayor Daley was a very devout Catholic, presumably honest in his own personal finances, but held weak ethical standards for those whom he appointed to government positions. Did the weak standards of the Bridgeport group of Irish-American political leaders with whom he grew up defeat his Catholic religious training? The same question could be asked of many Catholic, Protestant, and Jewish bosses. Simple frontier religion seems to have failed in some cases. For example, Billy Sol Estes, major corrupter and fraudulent businessman, grew up in a devout Church of Christ family in Clyde, West Texas. Estes became a lay preacher, almost a zealot, and has returned to the church since his release from prison. The House Government Operations Committee commented that there must have been a number of persons and individuals dealing with the Estes empire who knew that it was fraudulent but did not report suspicions to the authorities.[26] In this sea of nonethics, Estes' early religious training helped him little.

Overall evidence indicates that the churches either have not tried very hard or were not very successful in efforts to control corruption. Corruption increased in the last half of the nineteenth century, when leading Protestant clergy were very important leaders of community but accomplished little against corruption. Indeed, one outstanding Protestant denomination named a theological seminary after a corrupt businessman who also corrupted politics as a sideline.

There is, however, some evidence of religious interest in political reform. A few clergymen, especially main-line Protestant ministers, did at times take a strong position against political corruption. Dr. Charles H. Parkhurst led a vigorous one-man fight against police corruption and its consequences in New York City in 1892, "securing the important result" of the Lexow investigation in 1894 and the Mazet committee of 1899. Catholic priests and Protestant ministers cooperated against the Boss Cox machine in Cincinnati.[28] Rabbi Mayerberg secured the cooperation of the Protestant ministerial association of Kansas City against the excesses of the Pendergast machine in the late 1930s.[29] In Pittsburgh a group of members of Calvary Church (Episcopal) took a leading role in forming the Voter's League, which was a strong reform organization.[30] The 1961 drive against organized crime in Newport, Kentucky, was aided by a movement begun in the Newport Ministerial Association in 1948.[31] The association, probably predominantly Protestant, supported a Catholic reform candidate. As already noted, Protestants, Catholics, and Jews were divided on continuing prosecution of the Ruef-Schmitz corruption in San Francisco.[32]

Apart from its failure to combat corruption, religion did contribute to American social ethics. Many churches and church leaders were active in the campaign against slavery, although Southern churches supported it and some Northern churches were inhospitable to abolitionists. Some church leaders fought actively for prison reform, against prostitution, against drunkenness, and for a variety of other real or presumed reforms. At the end of the century, the social gospel movement was turning needed attention to problems of the workingman, including wages, hours, and conditions of work. As late as the 1920s, the 12-hour workday in the steel industry was finally ended by pressure from the Federal Council of Churches and President Warren G. Harding. More recently churches, both white and black, made important and useful contributions to the civil rights movement.

Some writers wonder if America was truly religious in the nineteenth century when heavy corruption began. It has been suggested that the move of American Protestantism toward a militant emotional religion, often led by uneducated frontier preachers, made it less possible for ministers to appraise political ethical phenomena in a penetrating way. Other have said that the move toward "relativism" resulting from Darwin and "scientism" in the last half of the last century has removed belief in ethical values. Another writer believes that business values overwhelmed the ethics of civil religion. Many students believe that the variety of American denominations has weakened any effort at a religious stand for more political honesty. The Catholics, a religious group which places a salutary emphasis on ethics, may not have applied it to politics because many of their leading communicants were on the nonethical side of the political fence. Richard Niebuhr commented that the churches, established in European countries but forced to be competitive here, gained in personal immediacy of religion but lost in metaphysical and moral values.[33] Which of these reasons, or of any reasons, provides the most important explanation for American religion's failure to determine high ethical standards cannot be determined here.

But one statement can be made positively. The instruction given by most churches to youth involves almost nothing which would lead a young man or woman to avoid corrupt political action. The nineteenth-century teaching of Biblical texts opposed corruption only very indirectly; the twentieth-century teaching of a vague social ethics does not oppose individual bribery at all. Professor Clebsch, after noting that denominations have concerned themselves with their own ritual and dogma, queried: "What American denomination has developed moral norms that are at once realistic and genuinely religious to guide persons who are perplexed by a welter of new problems such as abortion, divorce, euthanasia, extra-marital sexual intercourse, financial manipulation, conscientious objection to military service in cases of intervention, ... ?" He might have added political corruption and ordinary crime as items that are ignored by American denominations.[34]

It is unlikely that American churches will make many contributions to reduction of political corruption. If they are to do so, two steps are necessary. First, the churches must learn to work together. In our pluralistic society, little can be achieved by any one denomination. But the combination of Protestants, Catholics, and Jews could become very meaningful in most communities. America still has the largest percentage of church attendance of any modern country; most priests, pastors, and rabbis are thoughtful, educated men. Their influence against corruption could be substantial.

Second, the churches must learn the costs of corruption and the rules needed to control corruption. If the clergy let themselves be confused by the social science literature in favor of corruption described in Chapter 10, they are not likely to help their communities forward toward more honest government. Also if the clergy confines itself to a brief review of the Mosaic law, intended for nomadic tribes of 4000 years ago, they will find themselves ill-equipped to fortify their younger members against the political and business corruption of today. All problems of corruption should be spelled out and positive rules laid down against them. In addition to "thou shalt not steal" and "thou shalt not bear false witness," rules against conflict of interest, against "honest" graft, against bribes and kickbacks, and for government for the public are needed.

The Press and Television

A very leading role in the control of corruption has been played by the press and other media. The most recent example is that of President Nixon being almost literally driven out of office by the *Washington Post, The New York Times,* and television.

Many times the media have been leaders for reform. *The New York Times* led the fight against the Tweed Ring. The *San Francisco Bulletin* was essential to the defeat of the Ruef machine. The *Kansas City Star* fought the Pendergast machine. The *Chicago Sun Times* in 1950 exposed Captain Gilbert's affluence and kept him out of the sheriff's office. In the reform period, the *St. Louis Post Dispatch,* the *Brooklyn Eagle,* the *Seattle Post Intelligence,* the *St. Paul Pioneer Press,* the *Omaha Bee,* and the *Chattanooga Times* were on the honor role of Dr. Ernest S. Griffith.[35] *The New York Times* finally turned David Burnham loose, and his writings had much to do with the investigation and partial reform of the New York City Police Department in the early 1970s.

The record is not universally good. The most avid newspaper reader would not have learned how often F.D.R. gave political support to bosses and gangsters in the 1930s. Even *The New York Times* delayed on publishing Serpico's story, after it had ignored an unhealthy situation in the New York Police Department. Most New York papers failed to publish articles on Robert Moses's mishandling of the Manhattan town development in 1957.[36] Few Chicago newspapermen have really shown the faults of Mayor Daley's government. Perhaps because of their larger size, perhaps because of their difficult competition with television, perhaps because their staff is so largely committed to one party, the press of today seems to have less of a crusading spirit.

It is hard to know why newspapers have lost their enthusiasm for reform. The loss may be in part a result of the decline in the number of metropolitan dailies. It may be fear of the hot breath of television competition, which emphasizes the latest of national and international news. It may be that advertising budgets tie newspapers more to the economic and political powers of the community. A different possibility is that the tone of cynicism which seems to pervade the newspaper community has killed off a desire for reform.[37] Perhaps this cynicism is a reflection of the many decades of corruption which reporters have seen; perhaps it is their version of a nationwide tendency to ignore ethics. Further ethical instruction of reporters and editors would help.

One hopeful aspect of the press needs commendation; this is the development of investigative reporters. In his thorough study *The Kefauver Commiteee and the Politics of Crime, 1950-1952,*[38] Moore lists several reporters who had much to do with the program of the committee, some in Chicago, in New York, and in California. Many of the books cited in this book have been written by investigative reporters.

Television is still an unknown quantity. More people learn news over television than via the press, but the limitations of time keep television from distributing a large part of the news; so thoughtful people continue to read newspapers. Television debates may have had a decisive effect in a few close contests, but a soon-to-be-published Rand study does not indicate that television is determining the outcome of national elections.

If television reporters continue to improve their professional standing, as have newspaper reporters in recent decades, their chance for selling the public on the need for reform is very great. But they still have the problem of paying enough time and attention to the news of local government, which is the place where reform is most needed. Like the newspaper reporters, the television news gatherers need ethical instruction.

Professions and Their Standards

Ethical standards have been important for professions such as medicine, dentistry, law, accounting, and other fields. The standards are frequently designed to attain personal advantages, but they have often represented distinct forward moves toward a more ethical America. Professional education offers an excellent opportunity to inculcate ethical standards. Usually these standards are supported by penalties, the strongest of which is the right, granted by some laws, to order an offender not to continue practice of his profession.

In recent years, it has been suggested that professional standards be broadened to help eliminate political corruption. Medical associations have frequently worked to ensure high standards of public health agencies. Bar associations have not tried to improve law enforcement agencies, but they have disbarred lawyers convicted of corrupt activities. They should do much more. A valuable study by The Center for Analysis of Public Issues[39] demonstrates how several corrupt machines in New Jersey used engineering firms as a vehicle for securing kickbacks. The fact that engineering or architectural firms are, for good reasons, chosen on a noncompetitive basis helped increase the use of such firms as a conduit for graft in New Jersey, Maryland, and elsewhere. The Center for Analysis of Public Issues studies the possibility that engineers should establish professional standards to exclude graft. If professional education generally made the ethical way of dealing with government synonymous with the professional way, the improvements in governmental honesty in states like New Jersey and Maryland would be tremendous.

Professionalization has been helpful within government. Ernest Griffith, in his *History of American City Government, 1870-1900* and *History of American City Government, 1900-1920*, provides examples of the development of professional standards in many municipal functions, including the meeting of associations of public officials and the occasional long tenure of a locally accepted professional leader. In some ways, the most interesting professional group is the International City Managers Association which, in addition to the customary association services, has a program for trying and dropping from membership any of its own member managers who are reported to have had unethical administration. Clearly a manager who is dropped from membership will find it hard to secure other managers' help in locating a new position. It may be that this internal check on the professional honesty of managers is one of the reasons for the spread of the manager plan.

Citizen Associations and Individual Reformers

At times in American history a small number of reform-minded people have made substantial progress against corruption. Professor George E. Mowrey estimates that less than 30 men organized and brought about the victory of the Progressive Movement in California in 1910, a victory which almost overnight transformed California from being one of the most corrupt to one of the least corrupt states in the Union (*The California Progressives,* Quadrangle Paperbacks, Chicago, 1963). In Cincinnati a club of young business and professional men of both parties started the reform of the early 1920s which catalyzed great improvements in Cincinnati's city government. The Dallas Council of a dozen more or less "liberal" businessmen took the steps to make Dallas a well-governed city. Several "fusionist" groups of both parties have at times helped New York City win better government.

Sometimes political leaders accomplish similar reforms. While Los Angeles reformers defeated that city's machine in the 1910s, the real drive to honesty came in the 1930s and 1940s from Mayor Fletcher Bowron and Chief of Police William Parker. Mayor Daniel Hoan in the 1920s and 1930s had much to do with building Milwaukee's great reputation. Robert M. La Follette laid the foundation in the early 1900s for the honest Wisconsin of today.

In the long run, reform citizen groups are important, not only to initiate reform but to protect the reform regime from political interference. New York's unhappy rotation from reform mayors back to Tammany is an example of what has happened in too many cities.

Who is needed in a reform group? Obviously, both sexes, leaders from all ethnic groups in which leaders can be found. It is better to have business, unions, professions, churches, and clubs represented. But most important is the ethical outlook and sincere public interest of the women and men who run the organization.

An appropriate reform group could probably move most of our cities and counties into honest government. Perhaps large cities like New York and Chicago or corrupt cities like Cicero and Revere are too much for one reform group. For such cities the suggestion in Chapter 12, that the federal and state governments require honesty as a condition to financial support, may be necessary. Such cities are also in sore need of a continuous fusion party or of nonpartisan elections so that those citizens from both parties who want honest government may have a choice.

The fact that graft has moved in the twentieth century from bribes and kickbacks toward more hidden forms of "honest" graft makes it especially important for reform groups to have some kind of staff to track down the misdeeds or corrupt officials. In Chicago a Better Government Association, which works with investigative reporters of several newspapers, has helped secure effective publicity pressure on the dominant machine. In some cities a Bureau of Governmental Research has maintained staff to expose some mistakes.

To the credit of Americans, frequently there have been individuals who stubbornly resisted corruption; some of these heroes of anticorruption fights will be listed here. Judge Allen C. Southern of Independence, Missouri, resisted gangster threats in the 1930s and ruled against the Pendergast machine.[40] Miles McDonald, prosecuting attorney of Brooklyn, resisted pressures from the machine which elected him, from the mayor of New York City, and from many others, and he proceeded to convict bookies and corrupt policemen.[41] Francis Heney received many threats and was actually shot in the courtroom in the prosecution of the bribers of the Ruef-Schmitz machine in San Francisco in the early 1900s. Such men are as much the heroes of modern America as are its military or political leaders.

In addition to such individuals, America has been fortunate in having many groups of reformers who have battled valiantly against corruption. Historians have given us a variety of interpretations of the social and economic groups from which the reformers come.

In Baltimore, according to historian James B. Crooks, the reformers were idealists: eight were sons of clergymen, three were sons of an earlier generation of Baltimore reformers, and eighteen were descended "from old Maryland families which had some tradition of *noblesse obligé*." Most were quite well educated. Many had maintained strong religious commitments.[42]

However, in Denver in 1911, "an assorted collection of political and social moralists, newcomers, anti-corporationists, middle level businessmen, and indignant men and women" turned out to become "a big business bunch of city pillagers."[43]

In an article on the adoption of the city manager plan in the United States, Don Price indicates that new councils elected to put the plan into effect were composed of "citizens who were neither employers nor labor-professional men, but salaried executives, small businessmen."[44] The American Federation of Labor as well as national business groups endorsed the city manager plan; however, Samuel Hays tells us that a series of studies made for Prof. Leonard D. White indicate that unions opposed the manager plan.

Samuel Hays has satisfied himself that the reform of municipal charters, which has usually included election of council members at large, was an effort by leading businessmen to secure direct control of city government and exclude the poorer candidates who were more likely to be chosen by ward (rather than citywide) elections.[45] Hays accepts the theory of business control of corruption as an antecedent step. It is difficult to accept Hays's conclusions for two reasons. He assumes a degree of business control, first of corruption and second of reform; neither contention is generally provable. Second, if businessmen thought election of the council at large would ensure their control in large cities, they were astonishingly naive.

Professor Ari Hoogenboom rightfully rejects Josephson's thesis that reformers were businessmen who wanted to eliminate graft in order to force politicians to be dependent on the businessmen for campaign funds. Hoogenboom adds thoughtfully that the reformer was out of step with his times. He wished to return to what has earlier been called the "golden age" "before Jacksonian democracy and the industrial revolution-days when men with their background, status and education were the unquestioned leaders of society."[46]

In contrast with the businessmen, there were also socialists among the reformers. Victor Berger and Dan Hoan in Milwaukee were examples. These men were only theoretical socialists, but they also had a practical regard for good government administration.

Lyle Dorsett tells us that several socially minded reformers—Samuel M. Jones in Toledo, Thomas L. Johnson in Cleveland, and Hazen S. Pingree in Detroit—built their own political machines, often using city officials as part of it.[47]

Professor Otis A. Pease's views coincide with the authors' acquaintance with early twentieth-century reformers. Pease believed that the heart of the reform movement lay with theorists and writers of "good government" who "believed that the high cost of public services was robbing the urban poor (as well as the middle class) of more than the urban poor was likely to gain from the charity of the political machine that profited from the high cost."[48] These men were concerned with the techniques and organizational methods that made government operate efficiently and effectively. They did not talk much about morality. Pease might have added that these men were fairly open-minded about how many services government should furnish. Their successors saw much good in both Herbert Hoover and Franklin Roosevelt. Their concern was to have government work well, almost the opposite of the corrupt machine.

In the twentieth century, there has been no reform movement like that of the 1880s to World War I period. Sporadic reforms are carried out in various cities and states, usually in the cities by business and professional groups and in the states by far-seeing political leaders (for example, a governor who wants to make a reputation). The process of reform continues but much more slowly than is desirable. Many more citizen reform groups are needed.

In the 1970s Common Cause has brought in a slightly different kind of reformer, the mildly left-of-center college graduate who is convinced that business control of the electoral and legislative process through bribes and legitimate contributions is the center of our troubles.

Summary and Conclusions

A few recommendations may be drawn from the preceding discussion. Clearly civic education should include material about political ethics. General education about ethics should be greatly strengthened in a number of courses in addition to civics. History, literature, even science are courses in which ethical education of various sorts can be introduced. Liberal arts colleges should shift from their somewhat negative attitude toward ethical standards.

The academic world could be of some help, although *it will do very little*. The academic world itself seems to be fairly honest, but it has little appreciation of the importance of honesty elsewhere. If professors who deal with governmental problems would come to appreciate the importance of governmental honesty, they could do much to help bring it about.

Professional education could greatly improve its ethical slant. More business ethics courses need to be designed by business schools. Law schools need to expand their ethics programs to discuss more than conflict-of-interest problems. The broader consequences of corruption should be clear to law students, since many of them will one day have top administrative and political responsibilities. The professions would help honest government substantially if their own membership requirements would forbid bribes, kickbacks, or other corrupt action.

Churches could perform much more effectively if they would revamp their sermons and Sunday School lessons to examine individual as well as social-ethical problems and solutions. It would also be helpful if churches would stop supporting corrupt members of their individual denominations.

The media of public information and entertainment could help raise standards of governmental ethics. Their attention must not be the cynical assumption that all government officials are corrupt. Instead they should present actual examples of the unfair and bad consequences of corruption and the advantage of honest government to an area.

The reformers themselves need to think more carefully about the ethics they are supporting. Business-supported reforms in municipal government have been helpful, but businesses need to do more to reform state and national governments. Common Cause seems to have assumed that business contributions to campaigns are a major part of the problem and needs to broaden its outlook. Undoubtedly there have been evils in such contributions, and Common Cause-sponsored legislation will probably help reduce those evils. But all the legislation sponsored by Common Cause to date will have little effect on the ongoing local government corruption by organized crime and by ward politicians, which constitutes the largest part of America's official lawlessness. Common Cause needs a broader, more realistic program.

15 The Way Out of Corruption

Professor Brooks, in his analysis of American corruption written almost 70 years ago, has a stimulating analysis of the importance of the subject.[1] He comments that universally triumphant corruption would destroy the body politic, and that corruption had a part in the decline of Greece and Rome, the Protestant Reformation, the overthrow of the Stuarts in England, the partition of Poland, and the French Revolution. If he had written a few decades later, he could have added the fall of czarist Russia and the collapse of Nationalist China. Aristotle gave us earlier examples in his *Politics*. Brooks also comments, quite correctly, that a nation may carry a certain proportion of corruption and still remain strong, as both America and England have done on occasions. It is clearly possible for a nation or organization to recover from corruption, as have the Roman Catholic Church from pre-Reformation excesses, the British from their eighteenth- and early nineteenth-century corruption, and Prussia from her losses in the Napoleonic wars. British history gives us an example of a slow development of ethical standards over centuries of time. Brooks believes that America has risen, that the crude stealing of the Tweed Ring could not have been repeated in 1910. He had not had an opportunity to become acquainted with organized crime and learn how vicious twentieth-century forms of corruption could be.

Today we know that nations have a way of changing their international standing very rapidly. Germany and Japan, after total defeat in World War II, are now respected, thriving nations. Britain, which led the world in the last century, is now politically and economically weak. Italy, which once dominated all the land around and some lands far from the Mediterranean and which produced great contributions to political and legal life, is now a weak country which has trouble governing itself.

Is America undergoing similar major changes? At the end of World War II, we were the predominant military power of the world. More importantly, we were also the predominant *moral* power which treated the conquered nations most constructively, started the United Nations, and launched the Marshall and other helpful foreign aid plans. One could easily be proud of American citizenship in that era.

Today Americans must have a more pessimistic outlook on their nation's position. In spite of our great wealth, our high per capita income, our high level of education, and our high church attendance, we are probably the worst of the modern democracies in amount of political corruption. This corruption damages our law enforcement and, since honest and capable law enforcement is one of the most effective methods of teaching people not to commit crimes, helps make us the worst of the modern democracies in rate of crimes of violence. Corruption also has some share of the blame for lowering the quality of American life. The quality of our unions has been lowered because of the failure of corrupt governments to protect honest union leaders. The urban poor suffer greatly from the constant fear of burglary or attack, the actual loss of assets, the fear of crime which makes schools into chalkboard jungles. Many of our racial and social disturbances are in part a result of corruption in our local governments. America's leadership in the world suffers when a President is forced out of office for major misdeeds, even if he was covering up minor offenses. Our information about bribery abroad by representation of a few big companies cannot enhance our reputation. The cost of living of all of us is affected adversely by corruption. Actual bribes may cost only a few score millions of dollars, but the weakening of law enforcement must be the cause of a substantial fraction of our total costs of crime and law enforcement—probably in the range of $100 billions.

The damaging effect of corruption on the psychology of public servants and citizens is hard to estimate. But it must have an impact on the quality of candidates for civil service jobs, the quality of candidates running for public office, and the citizen's interest in working with his government. Even our intelligentsia, whose cynical attitude toward ethics is one of the major causes of corruption, suffer from it. The plans that "liberal" professors urge on governments are not followed through by corrupt officials. The Prohibition which Protestant ministers supported so vigorously failed because of corrupt government. Well-intended social legislation is often made ineffective by corruption.

These evils do not grow out of some fundamental economic or social problem. Other modern democracies with per capita income below ours manage to enforce their laws and to administer their social and economic policies honestly. America's evils grow out of attitudes, of thoughtless or even jocose inattention to honesty in methods of doing things. At times, American lack of concern about the ethical way of doing things is backed up by traditional fears of "federal police" or attitudes of exaggerated concern for the rights of the guilty and neglect of individual responsibility for things which are done wrong.

No matter what balance of government and enterprise we may have in the future, continued corruption will be a severe handicap to our national goals. Far more effort and attention should be spent on eradicating corruption than has ever been needed before.

The last three chapters have indicated some of the things that must be done to help us reduce corruption to reasonable amounts. Law enforcement should become real and persistent, not something which individual prosecutors or judges or police chiefs or attorneys general turn on or off at will. Citizens should be given opportunities to learn how to cooperate more effectively with law enforcement.

American attitudes toward individual ethics must be turned around. We can no longer afford to take our cues from the relativist professor of sociology or political science who applauds corruption while ignoring its bad social and economic consequences. We should not be guided by the minister who believes that the divine spirit makes up for an individual responsibility to see that our governments treat our fellow citizens decently and honestly.

The changes proposed here are not radical. Compared to the changes of the New Deal, they are small in financial cost and in operation of the governmental structures. They are hardly as great as the changes of policy in any new presidential administration, but they can be of far greater significance for all of us.

Recommendations

What is needed to reduce corruption in American life? The following suggestions are made with no belief that they are the only answers; rather they are answers that are worth trying.

First, America needs better ethical instruction by various mechanisms of society. The present system of relying on parents for all ethical instruction is grossly inadequate, as the experiences of, for example, Watergate, Governor Kerner, Equity Funding, and large amounts of local corruption tell us.

The schools need to restore some study of the responsibility of the individual for honesty, truth, courage, and helping others in government as well as elsewhere in life. Case studies are probably the best means of teaching these qualities at the secondary level, but other methods should also be tried. The schools have not been successful in teaching civics, but this may be largely because textbooks have avoided the real ethical problems in government. Schoolwork in race relations has been better, but it, too, would probably be helped by more careful study of individual ethics.

The churches, like the schools, need to pay greater attention to instruction in individual ethics. Sunday School instruction could be greatly improved. Sermons should pay far more attention to the responsibilities of individuals to one another in the divine pattern of the universe.[2]

Television and the newspapers have great possibilities for curing political corruption if they would work on the problem. Television can still learn much from investigative reporters. The media need to concentrate more on the remedial ethical aspects of corruption.[3]

Second, we need an effort to establish enough central supervision of law enforcement machinery, probably through a grant-in-aid for law enforcement, so that no jurisdiction can continuously operate a corrupt regime. Grants-in-aid to local law-enforcing units should be made conditional on honest conduct of affairs. Only by continuous raising of the standards of law enforcement agencies can we help people learn to be law-abiding themselves.

State governments which create most of the laws that need enforcing have been particularly remiss in responsibility for the effectiveness and honesty of their creatures, local governments. States need to both write more enforceable laws and help local governments develop better-educated police, more professional prosecutors, and judges who have more sense of responsibility for making law enforcement work.

Notes

Introduction

1. Heidenheimer, *Political Corruption*, chap. 1.
2. Bayley, "The Effect of Corruption," in Heidenheimer, *Political Corruption*, section 53.
3. Payne, *The Corrupt Society*.
4. Kristol, "Post Watergate Morality," *The New York Times*, November 14, 1976.
5. Lasky, *It Didn't Start with Watergate*.

Chapter 1
The Nature of Corruption

1. de Tocqueville, *Democracy in America*, pp. 200, 226-7.
2. White, *The Federalists* and *the Jacksonians;* see also Griffith, Ernest; *Modern Development of City Government in the United States*.
3. Reiss, *The Police and the Public*, p. 156.
4. Reichley, "Getting at the Roots of Watergate," *Fortune*, July 1973, p. 91.
5. Friedrich, *The Pathology of Politics*, p. 136; Bailey, *British Parliamentary Democracy*, pp. 98-103, 166-72.
6. Stout, *British Government*, p. 278.
7. Schuster, "Graft Charges Rare in Western Europe's Judiciary," in *The New York Times*, October 8, 1972.
8. *The Nation*, March 9, 1974.
9. Huntford, *The New Totalitarians*, p. 129.
10. Heidenheimer, *The Governments of Germany*, pp. 210-16.
11. Rosenberg, *Bureaucracy, Aristocracy, and Autocracy*.
12. Brasy, "Administrative Corruption in Theory and Dutch Practice," in Heidenheimer (ed.), *Political Corruption*.
13. de Rougement, *La Suisse*, p. 120. See also Chevallez, *La Suisse ou Le Sommeil Du Juste*, chap. 12.
14. Shirer, *The Collapse of the Third Republic*, pp. 57 and 187.
15. Ministry of Justice, Government of Japan, *Summary of the White Paper on Crime, 1975*, p. 8.
16. *The Knapp Commission Report on Police Corruption*, New York, 1972. See also reports of the Pennsylvania Crime Commission.
17. Wraith and Simpkins, *Corruption in Developing Countries;* Andersen,

"Bureaucratic Institutionalization in Nineteenth Century Europe," in Heidenheimer, *Political Corruption,* p. 91 ff.

18. Hutchinson, *The Imperfect Union,* pp. 380-385.
19. Mosher, et al. *Watergate: Implications for Responsible Government,* pp. 9-10.
20. Cressey, *Theft of the Nation.*
21. Friedrich, *The Pathology of Politics.*
22. Amick, *American Way of Graft.*
23. Morris, *Let the Chips Fall.*
24. Riordon, *Plunkitt of Tammany Hall.*
25. Brooks, *Corruption in American Life and Politics,* p. 200.
26. Amick, *American Way of Graft,* chap. 5.
27. Costikyan, *Behind Closed Doors,* chap. 26.
28. Caro, *The Power Broker,* p. 718.
29. Amick, *American Way of Graft,* p. 15.
30. Ibid., pp. 34-41.
31. Ibid., p. 137.
32. *Fortune,* October 1973, Edsall, "Money and Morality in American Society," pp. 73-74.
33. Amick, *American Way of Graft,* pp. 104-105.
34. Key, "The Techniques of Political Graft in the United States," dissertation, University of Chicago, 1934, pp. 194-96.
35. Amick, *American Way of Graft,* pp. 113-15.
36. Key, "The Techniques of Political Graft," p. 146.
37. Crile, "A Tax Assessor Has Many Friends," *Harper's,* November 1972.
38. Amick, *American Way of Graft,* chap. 4.
39. Key, "The Techniques of Political Graft in the United States," chap. 8.
40. Boyarsky and Boyarsky, *Backroom Politics,* chap. 3.
41. Amick, *American Way of Graft,* pp. 168-9.
42. Key, "The Techniques of Political Graft," chap. 18.
43. Ibid., chap. 14.
44. Ibid. chap. 15.

Chapter 2
The Origin of Municipal Corruption

1. Bryce, *The American Commonwealth,* vol. 2, p. 641.
2. Griffith, *Modern Development of City Government,* vol. 1, pp. 10-11.
3. Trevelyan, *History of England,* vol. 2, p. 262.
4. Goodnow, "Historical Development," in Banfield, *Urban Government,* pp. 42-44.
5. Redlich and Hirst, *Local Government in England,* vol. 1, pp. 44-48.
6. Swart, *Sale of Offices in the Seventeenth Century,* pp. 62-63.

7. Barker, *Background of Revolution in Maryland*, pp. 124-6.
8. Griffith, *History of American City Government*, Vol. 1, pp. 384-5, 405.
9. Ibid., pp. 388-9, 393.
10. Swart, *Sales of Offices*, p. 65.
11. Skaggs, *Roots of Maryland Democracy*, pp. 113-35.
12. Fosdick, *American Police Systems*, p. 60.
13. Goodnow, F.J. "Historical Development", in Banfield, *Urban Government*, p. 47.
14. Griffith, *Modern Development*, pp. 16-17.
15. Klein, *Pennsylvania Politics*, p. 69.
16. U.S. Treasury, *Immigration into the United States*, pp. 4435-36.
17. Stewart, *A Half Century of Municipal Reform*, p. 6.
18. Connable and Silberfarb, *Tigers of Tammany*, p. 41.
19. Werner, *Tammany Hall*, p. 33.
20. Warner, *The Private City*, p. 80.
21. Laurie, "Fire Companies in Southwork," in Davis and Haller, *Peoples of Philadelphia*, p. 75.
22. Warner, *The Private City*, p. 93.
23. Clark, "The Philadelphia Irish," in Davis and Haller, *Peoples of Philadelphia*, p. 42.
24. U.S. Treasury, *Immigration into the United States*, p. 4338.
25. Taylor, *The Distant Magnet*, p. 176.
26. Schrirer, *Ireland and the American Emigration, 1850-1900*.
27. Walker, *Germany and the American Emigration, 1816-1885*, p. 47.
28. Ibid., p. 157.
29. Orth, *Our Foreigners*, p. 134.
30. Taylor, *The Distant Magnet*, pp. 31-32.
31. Hansen, *The Atlantic Migration*, pp. 274, 281, 287.
32. Godkin, in *The Nation*, October 18, 1866, p. 312.
33. Handlin, *The Uprooted*, pp. 209-210.
34. Wittke, *The Irish in America*, p. 103.
35. Shannon, *The American Irish*, p. 6.
36. Levine, *The Irish and Irish Politicians*, pp. 17, 47, 51, 20.
37. Ibid., p. 20.
38. Steffens, *Autobiography*, vol. 2, chap. 15; *The Struggle for Self-Government*, pp. 120-60.
39. Griffith, *A History of American City Government, 1870-1900*, p. 100.

Chapter 3
The Politics of Municipal Corruption

1. Bryce, *American Commonweath*, vol. 1, p. 642.

2. Griffith, *History of American City Government, 1870-1900*, pp. 68-69.
3. National Municipal League, *Proceedings of the Third National Conference for Good City Government*, 1896.
4. Zink, *City Bosses*, pp. 194-5.
5. Powell, "Municipal Conditions of Omaha," in *Proceedings of the Third National Conference on Good City Government*, pp. 419-420.
6. Wendt and Hogan, *Bosses in Lusty Chicago*, p. 19.
7. Miller, *Boss Cox's Cincinnati*.
8. Glabb and Brown, *A History of Urban America*, p. 200.
9. Fosdick, *American Policy Systems*, pp. 68-69.
10. Callow, *Tweed Ring*, p. 147.
11. Fosdick, *American Policy Systems*, p. 115.
12. O'Connor, *Hell's Kitchen*, p. 24.
13. Callow, *Tweed Ring*, p. 78.
14. Wingate, "An Episode in Municipal Government," *North American Review*, vol. CXIX, p. 407.
15. Zink, *City Bosses*, p. 107.
16. Wingate, "The Reign of the Ring", *North American Review*, vol. CXX, pp. 132-143.
17. Griffith, *American City Government, 1870-1900*, pp. 70-71.
18. Wingate, "The Ring Charter", *North American Review*, vol. CXXI, p. 114.
19. Callow, *Tweed Ring*, pp. 225, 229-30.
20. Ibid., pp. 229-230.
21. Wingate, "The Ring Charter", p. 137.
22. Werner, *Tammany Hall*, pp. 344, 422-3.
23. Lexow Committee Report quoted in Stead, *Satan's Invisible World*, p. 135.
24. O'Connor, *Hell's Kitchen*, pp. 125-6.
25. Werner, *Tammany Hall*, p. 577.
26. Zink, *City Bosses*, pp. 201-202.
27. Glaab and Brown, *History of Urban America*, p. 191.
28. Zink, *City Bosses*, p. 201.
29. Bryce, *American Commonwealth*, vol. 2, pp. 410-412.
30. Zink, *City Bosses*, pp. 20, 214-17.
31. Steffens, *Shame of the Cities*, pp. 139, 152-8.
32. Adrian and Griffith, *A History of American City Government*, pp. 89, 143.
33. Thomas, *A Debonair Scoundrel*, pp. 21-22, 23, 32.
34. Ibid., p. 83.
35. Peterson, *Barbarians in Our Midst*, pp. 20, 46, 27, 33, 90-91; Ginger, *Altgeld's America*.
36. Steffens, *Shame of the Cities*, p. 165.

37. Glaab and Brown, *History of Urban America*, pp. 192-3.
38. Callow, *Tweed Ring*, p. 153.
39. Griffith, *History of American City Government, 1870-1900*, p. 76.
40. Callow, *Tweed Ring*, p. 147.
41. National Municipal League, *Proceedings of National Conference on Good City Government, 1905*, p. 25.
42. Thomas, *Debonair Scoundrel*, p. 245.
43. Griffith, *A History of American City Government, 1870-1900*, pp. 81-82.
44. Ginger, *Altgeld's America*, p. 93.
45. Steffens, *Shame of the Cities*, p. 22.
46. Ibid., pp. 53, 72.
47. Werner, *Tammany Hall*, p. 428.
48. Adrian and Griffith, *History of American City Government, 1775-1870*, p. 92.
49. O'Connor, *Hell's Kitchen*, p. 22.
50. "The Bottom of the Great City Difficulty," in *The Nation*, September 1871, vol. 13, p. 157.
51. Hofstadter, *The Age of Reform;* Griffith, *The History of American City Government 1900-1920*, pp. 21-22.
52. Pease, "Urban Reformers in the Progressive Era," p. 53.
53. Tolman, *Municipal Reform Movements in the United States*, pp. 47-137; Stewart, *A Half Century of Municipal Reform*, p. 12.
54. Griffith, *The History of American City Government, 1900-1920*, pp. 106-107.
55. Stewart, *Half Century of Municipal Reform*, pp. 32-45, 53-60, 81.
56. Burnham, *Critical Elections and the Mainstream of American Politics*, p. 81.

Chapter 4
State Corruption in the Nineteenth Century

1. Steffens, *The Struggle for Self Government*, p. 43.
2. Fish, *Civil Service*, pp. 90-91.
3. Ellis et al., *History of New York State*, pp. 135, 145.
4. Ibid., p. 353.
5. Connable and Silberfarb, *Tigers of Tammany*, p. 156.
6. Ellis et al., *History of New York State*, p. 351.
7. Gosnell, *Boss Platt and His New York Machine*, pp. 262-5.
8. Ellis et al., *History of New York State*, p. 362.
9. Eaton, *The Spoils System and Civil Service Reform*, p. 85.
10. Gosnell, *Boss Platt and His New York Machine*, chaps. 7, 9.

11. Ellis et al., *History of New York State,* pp. 383.
12. Connable and Silberfarb, *Tigers of Tammany.*
13. Steffens, "Ohio, A Tale of Two Cities", in *Struggle for Self-Government.*
14. Warner, *Progressivism in Ohio* , pp. 10-14.
15. Jordan, "Ohio Comes of Age," in Wittke, *History of the State of Ohio.*
16. Nevins, Foreword to Walters, *Joseph Benson Foraker,* p. 8.
17. Jordan, "Ohio Comes of Age," p. 202.
18. Croly, *Marcus Alonzo Hanna,* pp. 75-77.
19. Jordan, "Ohio Comes of Age," p. 208.
20. Howe, *Confessions of a Reformer,* p. 153.
21. Walters, *Joseph Benson Foraker,* pp. 81-82.
22. Warner, *Progressivism in Ohio,* pp. 275-7.
23. Steffens, *Struggle for Self-Government,* p. 11.
24. Wetmer, *The Battle against Bribery,* p. 145.
25. McReynolds, *Oklahoma,* p. 296.
26. Hamilton, *From Wilderness to Statehood,* pp. 558-60; Connolly, "The Story of Montana," *McClure's Magazine,* September 1906.
27. Coulter, *The South during Reconstruction,* p. 148.
28. Currant, *Three Carpetbag Governors,* pp. 36-37.
29. Ibid., pp. 59-63.
30. Jackson (Miss.) *Weekly Clarion,* August 23, 1882, quoted in Woodward, *Origins of the New South,* p. 51.
31. Ibid., p. 52.
32. Ibid., pp. 369-73.
33. Sakolski, *The Great American Land Bubble,* p. 3.
34. Ibid., pp. 45, 56, 102.
35. Steffens, "Taming of the West," *American Magazine,* vol. 64, pp. 491-492.
36. Ibid., pp. 585-602.
37. Dagget, *Chapters on History of the Southern Pacific,* chap. 12.
38. *California State Administrations:* McDougal, vol. 4, pp. 71-73; Begler, vol. 4, pp. 146-8; Hittell, *History of California,* vol. 3, pp. 661-3.
39. Cleland, *A History of California,* pp. 405-406.
40. Callow, "Legislature," in *Southern California History Review,* vol. 39, December 1957, pp. 340-9.
41. Berge, *Free Pass Bribery System.*

Chapter 5
Federal Corruption in the Nineteenth Century

1. Woodward (ed.), *Responses of the Presidents,* p. xiv.

2. Randolph, *A Vindication of Mr. Randolph's Resignation.*
3. White, *Federalists,* pp. 170-1.
4. Woodward, *Responses of the President,* p. 35.
5. White, *Jeffersonians,* p. 319.
6. Fish, *Civil Service,* p. 103.
7. Jefferson, *Works* (Fed. ed.), pp. 175-7, November 29, 1820, quoted in Fish, *Civil Service,* p. 388.
8. *Benton's Report,* Sen. Doc. 88, 18th Cong., 1st Session, May 4, 1826, p. 7.
9. Fish, *Civil Service,* pp. 126.
10. Ibid., pp. 108-109.
11. Sakolski, *The Great American Land Bubble,* p. 233.
12. Schlesinger and Bruns, *Congress Investigates,* vol. 1, section on Sam Houston.
13. White, *Jacksonians,* p. 411.
14. Ibid., p. 413.
15. Report 353, 33d Cong, 1st Sess., August 3, 1854; and House Report 132, 2d Sess., February 23, 1855; House Report 243, 34th Cong., 3d Sess., February 19, 1857.
16. Senate Report 151, 23d Cong., 2d Sess., March 3, 1835; House Report 313, 25th Cong., 3d Sess., pp. 142-246, February 1839.
17. Woodward, *Responses of the Presidents,* pp. 73-74, 75-78, 81-83, 89-91.
18. Bruns, "The Covode Committee, 1860," pp. 1082-3, in Schlesinger and Bruns, *Congress Investigates,* vol. 2.
19. Woodward, *Responses of the Presidents,* pp. 93-96, 99-101.
20. Niven, *Connecticut for the Union,* pp. 365-7.
21. White, *The Republican Era,* p. 355.
22. Hesseltine, *Ulysses S. Grant, Politician,* pp. 309-12, 362-4.
23. White, *Republican Era,* pp. 372-3.
24. Fish, *Civil Service,* p. 213.
25. Woodward, *Origins of the New South,* p. 37 quotes letter.
26. Jordan, *Roscoe Conkling of New York,* p. 173.
27. Woodward, *Responses of the Presidents,* p. 31.
28. Fowler, *Cabinet Politician,* pp. 171-2.
29. Howe, *Chester A. Arthur,* pp. 178-83, 192.
30. Eaton, *The Spoils System in New York,* pp. 35, 71.
31. Reeves, *Gentleman Boss,* p. 140.
32. White, *Republican Era,* pp. 270-1.
33. Woodward, *Responses of the Presidents,* p. 203.
34. White, *Republican Era,* p. 272.
35. Walters, *Joseph Benson Foraker.*

Chapter 6
Local Corruption since World War I

1. Wolfinger, *The Politics of Progress,* chaps. 3 and 4.
2. Hanna, *Frank Costello,* p. 75; Kobler, *Capone,* p. 326.
3. Hanna, *Frank Costello,* p. 106.
4. Messick, *John Edgar Hoover,* p. 100.
5. Moynihan, "The Private Government of Crime," in Cohen, *Crime in America,* pp. 320-8.
6. Cressey, *Theft of the Nation,* pp. x, xi.
7. Messick, *The Silent Syndicate.*
8. Salerno and Tompkins, *Crime Confederation,* p. 325.
9. Katcher, *The Big Bankroll,* chaps. 12, 14, 17, 18.
10. Mitgang, *The Man Who Rode the Tiger,* chap. 10.
11. Moscow, *The Last of the Big Time Bosses,* p. 30.
12. Dewey, *Twenty against the Underworld,* ch. 8.
13. Hanna, *Frank Costello,* p. 117.
14. Garrett, *The La Guadia Years,* pp. 194-6.
15. Moscow, *The Last of the Big Time Bosses,* pp. 54-57.
16. Reid, *Grim Reapers,* p. 40.
17. Moscow, *The Last of the Big Time Bosses,* pp. 78-79.
18. Garrett, *The La Guardia Years,* pp. 305-306.
19. Moscow, *The Last of the Big Time Bosses,* pp. 202-203.
20. Reid, *Grim Reapers,* p. 44.
21. *U.S. News and World Report,* June 4, 1973.
22. *Newsweek,* October 20, 1972.
23. *Knapp Commission Report on Police Corruption,* pp. 3-4, 61.
24. Newfield and Du Brul, *The Abuse of Power,* Ch. 10.
25. Tarr, *A Study in Boss Politics,* pp. 74-75.
26. Haller, "Urban Crime and Criminal Justice," in *Journal of American History,* vol. 57, no. 3, December 1970.
27. Wendt and Hogan, *Big Bill of Chicago,* pp. 132, 239, 268.
28. Kobler, *Capone,* pp. 76, 104, 108, 119, 125, 166, 202, 288-9.
29. Gosnell, *Machine Politics,* p. 40.
30. O'Connor, *Clout,* p. 55.
31. Rayko, *Boss,* p. 55.
32. Demaris, *Captive City,* pp. 40, 122, 124, 125.
33. O'Connor, *Clout,* p. 56.
34. Demaris, *Captive City,* pp. 129, 134.
35. Meyerson and Banfield, "A Machine at Work," in *Politics, Planning and the Public Interest.*
36. Demaris, *Captive City,* pp. 148, 149, 197.
37. Royko, *Boss,* p. 70.

38. O'Connor, *Clout*, pp. 134, 151, 158-9.
39. Demaris, *Captive City*, pp. 153, 250-3.
40. Williams, *Vice Squad*, pp. 10, 31.
41. Los Angeles *Times*, December 31, 1976.
42. Reid, *Grim Reapers*, p. 254.
43. Salerno and Tompkins, *The Crime Confederation*, p. 251.
44. Royko, *Boss*, p. 174.
45. O'Connor, *Clout*, p. 174.
46. Los Angeles *Times*, November 11, 1975.
47. Royko, *Boss*, p. 101.
48. Rakove, *Don't Make No Waves*, p. 88.
49. Salter, *Boss Rule*, p. 211.
50. Zink, *City Bosses*, p. 201.
51. Patten, *The Battle for Municipal Reform*, pp. 203-11.
52. Salter, *Boss Rule*, pp. 48, 150, 155, 164, 170.
53. Reichley, *The Art of Government*.
54. Salter, *Boss Rule*.
55. Reichley, *Art of Government*, p. 11.
56. Petshek, *The Challenge of Urban Reform*.
57. Rubinstein, *City Police*.
58. Pennsylvania Crime Commission, *Report on Police Corruption*, March 1974.
59. Steinberg, *The Bosses*, pp. 319, 322, 324.
60. New York Times reporter in Steinberg *The Bosses*, p. 310.
61. Dorsett, *Pendergast Machine*, pp. 95-96; Beach, *The Mayor's Wife*, p. 14.
62. Steinberg, *The Bosses*, p. 341.
63. Peterson, *Barbarians in Our Midst*, p. 322.
64. Dorsett, *The Pendergast Machine*, p. 100.
65. Dorsett, *Pendergast Machine*, pp. 100, 107-11.
66. Kefauver, *Crime in America*, chap. 10.
67. Tyler, *Organized Crime in America*, pp. 296-8.
68. Mollenhoff, *Strike Force*, p. 148.
69. McNamara, "The Impact of Bureaucracy Dysfunctions on Attempts to Prevent Police Corruption," in the *Police Journal*, January-March 1975.
70. Caro, *The Power Broker*, pp. 718, 723-4, chap. 41, p. 104.
71. Sale, *Power Shift*.

Chapter 7
State Corruption since World War I

1. Steinberg, *The Bosses*.

2. Reichley, "Getting at the Roots of Watergate," *Fortune*, July 1973, p. 91.
3. Peirce, Los Angeles *Times*, January 9, 1977.
4. Ashman, *The Finest Judges Money Can Buy*.
5. Los Angeles *Times*, November 9, 1976.
6. Messick, *Syndicate in the Sun*; and Kefauver, *Crime in America*, chaps. 7, 8.
7. O'Leary, "Louisiana," in Allen (ed.) *Our Sovereign State*, p. 252.
8. Hagensick, "Flouting Their Own Law," *National Civic Review*, vol. 53, October 1964, pp. 479-82.
9. Cohen and Witcover, *A Heartbeat Away*, chap. 3.
10. Amick, *American Way of Graft*, pp. 223-4.
11. Dorman, *Payoff*, p. 137.
12. Shannon, "Massachusetts," in Allen (ed.) *Our Sovereign State*, p. 30.
13. Cook, *The Corrupted Land*, pp. 121-2.
14. Lockard, *New England State Politics*, p. 170.
15. *Harper's*, June 1946.
16. Litt, *Political Cultures of Massachusetts*, p. 85.
17. Levin, *The Compleat Politician*.
18. Litt, *Political Cultures of Massachusetts*.
19. Wheeler, *Yankee from the West*, pp. 79, 372.
20. Reid and Demaris, *The Green Felt Jungle*, pp. 120-48.
21. Reid, Grim Reapers, p. 229.
22. Dorman, *Payoff*, 144-57.
23. *Washington Post*, April 19, 1975.
24. Spivack, "New York," in Allen (ed.) *Our Sovereign State*.
25. Maker, "Ohio," in Allen (ed.) *Our Sovereign State*.
26. Goulden, *The Benchwarmers*, p. 245.
27. Ashman, *The Finest Judges*, pp. 59-65.
28. *Christian Science Monitor*, December 19, 1975.
29. *Time*, February 4, 1974, p. 79.
30. Ashman, *The Finest Judges*, pp. 174-6.
31. Loth, *Public Plunder*, p. 213.
32. Orth, *The Boss and the Machine*, p. 131.
33. McCullough, "Pennsylvania," in Alexander, *Campaign Money*.
34. Loth, *Public Plunder*, p. 286.
35. Van Devander, *The Big Bosses*, pp. 154-7.
36. Lowe, "Pennsylvania," in Allen (ed.) *Our Sovereign State*.
37. Ashman, *The Finest Judges*, p. 56.
38. Smith, *State Government in Transition*.
39. McCullough, *Pennsylvania in Alexander*, pp. 239-41.
40. Dorman, *Payoff*, pp. 121-3.
41. Loth, *Public Plunder*, pp. 283-4.

42. Stillwell, "Texas," in Allen (ed.) *Our Sovereign State*, p. 326.
43. Dorman, *Payoff*, p. 161.
44. Messick, *John Edgar Hoover*, p. 81.
45. Reichley, "The Texas Banker Who Bought Politicians," in *Fortune*, December 1971.
46. Ford, "Texas Big Money," in Alexander, *Campaign Money*.
47. Schendel, "Something Is Rotten in the State of Texas," *Colliers*.
48. Ashman, *The Finest Judges*, pp. 149-52.
49. Penn, "Telephone Tizzy," in *Wall Street Journal*, January 17, 1977.
50. Walton, "West Virginia," in Peters and Rothchild, *Inside the System*.
51. Smith, *The Tarnished Badge*.
52. Dorman, *Payoff*, pp. 20-22, 326.
53. Smith, *Tarnished Badge*, pp. 85-86.
54. Council of State Governments, "State Police," *Book of the States*.
55. *Washington Post*, April 19, 1975.
56. *Washington Post*, April 19, 1975.
57. Lawrence, "Nebraska," in Allen (ed.) *Our Sovereign State*.
58. Elazar, *American Federalism*; Mulcahy and Katz, *America Votes*, p. 101, chap. 6.
59. The Council of State Governments, *Ethics*, 1975.

Chapter 8
Federal Corruption from World War I to 1969

1. Beard and Horn, *Congressional Ethics*, p. 19.
2. Golden, *The Super Lawyers*, pp. 272, ff 286.
3. Getz, *Congressional Ethics*, p. 20.
4. Graham, *Mortality in American Politics*, pp. 80, 91.
5. Boyd, *Above the Law*.
6. Golden, *The Super Lawyers*.
7. Sheridan, "The Rise and Fall of Jimmy Hoffa," *Saturday Review Press*, p. 416.
8. Murray, *The Harding Era*, pp. 475-79.
9. Woodward, *Responses of the Presidents*, p. 293.
10. Ibid, p. 333.
11. Loth, *Public Plunder*, pp. 293-9.
12. Russell, *The Shadow of Blooming Grove*, p. 629.
13. Adams, *Incredible Era*, p. 235.
14. Murray, *The Harding Era*, pp. 403 ff.
15. Kobler, *Ardent Sprits*, p. 222.
16. Adams, *Incredible Era*, pp. 324-5.
17. Murray, *The Harding Era*, pp. 436-7.

18. Ibid, pp. 426-9, 432.
19. Adams, *Incredible Era*, pp. 233, 321, 418.
20. Woodward, *Responses of the Presidents*, pp. 236, 286, 294-5.
21. Ibid., 286; Abels, *The Truman Scandal*, p. 154.
22. Abels, *The Truman Scandal*, chap. 12, pp. 216-18, chap. 7, pp. 110-15, 286, 293-301, chap. 16.
23. Woodward, *Responses of the Presidents*, p. 295.
24. Frier, *Conflict of Interest*, pp. 3-4.
25. Ibid., p. 76.
26. Frier, *Conflict of Interest in the Eisenhower Administration*, pp. 3-4, 84-85, 100, 276, chap. 16.
27. Woodward, *Responses of the Presidents*, pp. 320-1.
28. Graham, *Morality in American Politics*, p. 167.
29. Gosh and Hammer, *The Last Testament of Lucky Luciano*, pp. 159-64.
30. Salerno and Tompkins, *Crime Confederation*, p. 249.
31. Steinberg, *The Bosses*, pp. 342, 344.
32. Messick, *The Silent Syndicate*, p. 234.
33. Salerno and Tompkins, *Crime Confederation*, p. 248.
34. Messick, *Secret File*, pp. 123-4, 321.
35. Salerno and Tompkins, *Crime Confederation*, pp. 206-307.
36. Dorman, *Payoff*, p. 36.
37. Salerno and Tompkins, *Crime Confederation*.
38. Frier, *Conflict of Interest*, chaps. 11, 12, p. 319.
39. Graham, *Morality in American Politics*, p. 196.
40. Pearson and Anderson, *The Case against Congress*, Ch. 7.
41. Mollenhoff, *Despoilers of Democracy*, p. 304.
42. Schwartz, *The Professor and the Commissions*.
43. Goulden, *The Benchwarmers*, chap. 3; Boyd, "Men of Distinction," in Heilbroner, *In the Name of Profit*.
44. Goulden, *Benchwarmers*, p. 333.

Chapter 9
Corruption in American Elections

1. Harris, *Registration of Votes in the U.S.*, p. 3.
2. Key, *Politics, Parties and Pressure Groups*, pp. 625, 636.
3. Wigmore, *The Australian Ballot System*; and Evans, *A History of the Australian Ballot System in the U.S.*
4. U.S. Commission on Civil Rights, *Voting*.
5. Strong, *Registration of Voters in Alabama*; Shadgett, *Voter Registration in Georgia*; and Key, *Southern Politics*.
6. Los Angeles *Times*, August 8, 1976, pp. 1, 24.

7. *The Philadelphia Inquirer*, November 1, 1956, p. 7.
8. Jonas, *Political Dynamiting*.
9. Heard, *The Costs of Democracy*, pp. 357-9.
10. Adamany and Agree, *Political Money*, pp. 4-40.
11. *Congressional Quarterly*, 1971, vol. 1, "Dallas Politics," pp. 17, 18.
12. Ibid., p. 88.
13. Berg, Hahn, and Schmidhauser, *Corruption in the American Political System*, pp. 88, 191, 195-201.

Chapter 10
Costs of Corruption

1. Brooks, *Corruption in American Life and Politics*.
2. Davenport, "Skinning the Tiger," *New York Affairs*, Fall 1975, p. 89.
3. Merton, *Social Theory and Social Structure*, p. 127.
4. Huntington, *Political Order in Changing Societies*, p. 68.
5. Warner, *The Urban Wilderness*, p. 176.
6. Smelser, "Stability, Instability, and Political Corruption," in Barber and Inkeles, *Stability and Social Change*, p. 11.
7. Tarr, *A Study in Boss Politics*.
8. Callow, *The City Boss in America*, p. 144.
9. *The Knapp Commission Report on Police Corruption*, pp. 89-90, 113.
10. Perambo, *No Cause for Indictment*, pp. 27-28; Tom Hayden, *Revolt in Newark*; John Gardiner, *The Politics of Corruption*, pp. 89-90.
11. Moscow, *The Last of the Big Time Bosses*, chap. 12.
12. Gosnell, *Machine Politics*, p. 7.
13. Gardiner, *The Politics of Corruption*, p. 88.
14. Draa, "Corruption and Dynasty."
15. Gardiner, "The Consequence of Corruption," in Gardiner and Olson, *Theft of the City*, p. 395.
16. Blanshard, *Investigation City Government in the La Guardia Administration*, pp. 8, 9-13, 18, 26, 57, 123-4.
17. Orth, *The Boss and the Machine*, p. 95.
18. Nelli, "John Powers and the Italians," in the *Journal of American History*, June 1970, pp. 57-80.
19. Harrison, *Stormy Years*, p. 237.
20. Holli, *Reform in Detroit*, pp. 24-29.
21. Crooks, *Politics and Progress*, pp. 20, 22, 214.
22. Gordon, *City Limits*, p. 70. State Crime Committee report is reprinted in Gardiner and Olson, *Theft of the City*, pp. 372-81.
23. Royko, *Boss*, pp. 104, 112, 117.
24. Garrett, *The La Guardia Years*.

25. Petshek, *The Challenge of Urban Reform*, p. 15.
26. Garrett, *The La Guardia Years*, p. 158.
27. Gardiner, *Politics of Corruption*, p. 97.
28. Benson and Engeman, *Amoral America*, chaps. 2, 3, and 4.
29. *Knapp Commission Report on Police Corruption*.
30. American Enterprise Institute, *The Economics of Crime and Punishment* and Wilson, *Thinking about Crime*, chap. 8.
31. Chevigny, *Police Power*, pp. 4, 39.
32. Astor, *The New York Cops*, p. 104.
33. Rubinstein, *City Police*, pp. 418-9.
34. Hughes, *The Story of Thomas E. Dewey*, pp. 209-10.
35. Chambers, *Samuel Seabury*, p. 232.
36. *The Knapp Commission Report on Police Corruption*, p. 97.
37. Williams, *Vice Squad*, p. 43.
38. Gambino, *Blood of My Blood*; and Mace, *The Crime Industry*.
39. Petersen, *Barbarians in Our Midst*, p. 324.
40. Salerno and Tompkins, *The Crime Confederation*, pp. 263-70.
41. Gardiner and Olson, *Theft of the City*, pp. 165 ff.
42. Lewis, *The Children of Sanchez*, p. 494.
43. Gans, *The Urban Villagers*.
44. Rudwick, *Race Riot*, chap. 7.
45. Cook, "Who Rules New Jersey," in Gardiner and Olson *Theft of the City*, p. 80.
46. Salerno and Tompkins, *Crime Confederation*, p. 360.
47. Rubinstein, *City Police*, p. 419.
48. Lindsay and Higgins, *The Beast*, p. 85.
49. Kobler, *Capone*, pp. 231, 235.
50. Osofsky, *Harlem*, p. 135 ff.
51. Ferber, *I Found Out*.
52. Salerno and Tompkins, *Crime Confederation*, pp. 201, 272 ff.
53. Keating and Carter, *The Man Who Rocked the Boat*.
54. Astor, *The New York Cops*, p. 162.
55. Williams, *Vice Squad*, pp. 202, 233.
56. Chambers, *Samuel Seabury*, chap. 17.
57. *The Knapp Commission Report on Police Corruption*, chap. 5.
58. Williams, *Vice Squad*, p. 43.
59. The New York State Joint Legislative Committee on Crime, 1969, pp. 108-13, in Gardiner and Olson, *Theft of the City*, pp. 372-81.
60. McClellan, *Crime without Punishment*, chap. 12.
61. Moynihan, "The Private Government of Crime," in Cohen, *Crime in America*, pp. 320-8.
62. Dewey; *Twenty Against the Underworld* pp. 18-181. See also Hughes, *The Story of Thomas E. Dewey*.

63. Hughes, *The Story of Thomas E. Dewey*, p. 76.
64. Mockridge and Pratt, *The Big Fix*, p. 318.
65. Fosdick, *Chronicle of a Generation*.
66. Huthmacher, *Wagner and the Rise of Urban Liberation*.
67. Hughes, *The Story of Thomas E. Dewey*, p. 341.
68. *The New York Times*, April 8, 1939, quoted in Milligan, *Missouri Waltz*, p. 4.

Chapter 11
Theories of Corruption

1. Calvert, "The Manifest Functions of the Machine," in Stave, *Urban Bosses*; Callow, *The City Boss in America*, p. 81; Merriam, "American Party System," in Werner, *Tammany Hall*; Reynolds, "Courtroom," *Popular Library*, 1950, pp. 159-66.
2. Merriam, "American Party System," in Werner, *Tammany Hall*.
3. Huntington, *Political Order in Changing Societies*, pp. 59, 66, 68-69.
4. Nye, "Corruption and Political Development," in *American Political Science Review*, June 1967, pp. 417-27.
5. Scott, "Corruption, Machine Politics and Political Change," in *American Political Science Review*, December 1969, pp. 1142-58.
6. Harrison, *Stormy Years*.
7. Mockridge and Pratt, *The Big Fix*, p. 283.
8. Mockridge and Pratt, *The Big Fix*, p. 328.
9. Lindsey and Higgins, *The Beast*.
10. Douglas, *Ethics in Government*.
11. Merton, *Social Theory and Social Structure*, chap. 3.
12. Smelser, "Stability, Instability, and the Analysis of Political Corruption," in Barber and Inkeles, *Stability and Social Change*.
13. Bracey, *A Functional Approach to Police Corruption*.
14. Griffith, *The Modern Development of City Government*, vol. 2, p. 614.
15. Huntington, *Political Order in Changing Societies*, p. 64.
16. Wilson, *Congress, Corruption and Compromise*; and Getz, *Congressional Ethics*.
17. Lipset, *Revolution and Counter-revolution*, title essay in book.
18. Steffens, *The Shame of the Cities*, p. 3.
19. White, *The Republican Era*, p. 366.
20. Ostrogorski, *Democracy and the Organization of Political Parties*..
21. Hoogenboom, *Outlawing the Spoils*.
22. Griffith, *The Modern Democracy of City Government*.
23. Banfield and Wilson, *Political Influence*, p. 126.
24. Ford, "Municipal Corruption," in *Political Science Quarterly*, December 19, 1904; and Bagehot, *The English Constitution*, p. 87.

25. Loth, *Public Plunder*, pp. 304-05.
26. Harrison, *Stormy Years*.
27. Wolfinger, *The Politics of Progress*, pp. 222-7.
28. Himmelfarb, *Lord Acton*, p. 161; Rogow and Lasswell, *Power Corruption and Rectitude*; Friedrich, *Pathology and Politics*, p. 129.
29. Berg, Hahn, Schmidhauser, *Corruption in the American Political System*.
30. Stoddard, *Master of Manhattan*, chap. 16; and Williams, *Vice Squad*, p. 222.
31. Maas, *Serpico*, pp. 31-32.
32. Williams, *Vice Squad*, p. 43.
33. Wilson, Moore, Wheat, "The Problems of Heroin," in *Public Interest*, Fall 1972, pp. 3-28.
34. Steffens, *The Shame of the Cities*, p. 2.
35. Wolfinger, *The Politics of Progress*, pp. 122-9.
36. The National Advisory Commission on Criminal Justice Standards and Goals, quoted in Gardiner and Olson, *Theft of the City*, p. 236.
37. Ostrogorski, *Democracy and the Organization of Political Parties*, vol. 2.
38. Douglas, *Ethics in Government*.
39. Friedrich, *The Pathology of Politics*; Huntington, *Political Order in Changing Societies*, p. 62.
40. Benson and Engeman, *Amoral America*.
41. Burnham, "How Police Corruption Is Built into the System," reprinted in Sherman, *Police Corruption*.
42. Bahn, *Police Socialization and the Psychosocial Costs of Police Corruption*.
43. Norwood, *About Paterson*, p. 196 ff.
44. Wilson, "Police Morale, Reform, and Citizen Respect," in Bordua, *The Police*.
45. Chambliss, "Vice Corruption, Bureaucracy, and Power," in *Wisconsin Law Review*, 1971, no. 4.

Chapter 12
Levels of Government and Corruption Control

1. Steinberg, *Bosses*, p. 59.
2. Rakove, *Don't Make No Waves*, p. 112.
3. Salerno and Tompkins, *The Crime Confederation*, p. 252.
4. Williams, *Huey Long*, pp. 193-755.
5. Holli, *Reform in Detroit*, p. 89.
6. Messick, *Syndicate in the Sun*.

313

7. Salerno and Tompkins, *The Crime Confederation*, pp. 270-1.
8. Dewey, *Twenty against the Underworld*; and Moellenhoff, *Strike Force*.
9. Gosch, and Hammer, *The Testament of Lucky Luciano*, p. 53.
10. Almond and Verba, *The Civic Culture*.
11. Benson, *The New Centralization*.
12. Messick, *Secret File*, p. 111.
13. Irey, *The Tax Dodgers*, chap. 4.
14. Salerno and Tompkins, *The Crime Confederation*, pp. 249-50.
15. Murphy, "Overhauling the Criminal Justice System," in *Criminal Justice Digest*, March 1976.
16. Fosdick, *American Police Systems*, chaps. 2 and 3.
17. Werner, *Tammany Hall*, pp. 85-87.
18. Holli, *Reform in Detroit*, pp. 40-41.
19. Steinberg, *The Bosses*, pp. 318, 328, 362.
20. Fosdick, *American Police Systems*, chap. 3.
21. *The Knapp Commission Report on Police Corruption*, p. 262.
22. *Royal Commission on Standards of Conduct in Public Life*, pp. 72-75.
23. Brown, *The New York City Police Department and Anti-Corruption Campaign*, p. 45.
24. Brown, *The New York City Police Dept. Anti-Corruption Campaign*, pp. 51.
25. Quote from Murphy in Daley, *Target Blue*, pp. 70, 137, 150, 399.
26. Peirce, *Washington Post*, April 19, 1975.
27. *Newsweek*, July 18, 1977, p. 21.
28. Salerno and Tompkins, *Crime Confederation*, p. 293.

Chapter 13
Business, Labor, and Political Corruption

1. Bradley, "Introduction," in Tocqueville, *Democracy in America*.
2. Brooks, *Corruption in American Politics and Life*, pp. 161-2.
3. Kenner, *The Fight for Truth in Advertising*.
4. Tarbell, *History of the Standard Oil Co.*, vol. 2.
5. Wall, *Andrew Carnegie*.
6. Fainsod and Gordon, *Government and the American Economy*, p. 442.
7. Lewis, *The Big Four*, p. 365.
8. Cochran, *Railroad Leaders*.
9. Bryce, *American Commonwealth*.
10. Katcher, *The Great Bankroll*.
11. McDonald, *Insull*, pp. 252-67.
12. *Knapp Commission Report*, pp. 65, 132, 136, 170.
13. Pennsylvania Crime Commission, *Report on Police Corruption*, pp. 14-17, 20.

14. *Senate Watergate Report*, pp. 57-58.
15. Ibid., pp. 181-386.
16. Hoogenboom, *Outlawing the Spoils*, p. 193.
17. Lipset, *The First New Nation*, p. 196.
18. Hutchinson, *The Imperfect Union*, pp. 116-7.
19. Seidman, *Labor Czars*, p. 22.
20. Hutchinson, *The Imperfect Union*, pp. 71-72.
21. Hutchinson, *Imperfect Union*, pp. 42, 45-46, 58.
22. Ibid., pp. 58, 60, 116, 206, chap. 6.
23. McClellan, *Crime without Punishment*, p. 118.
24. Hutchinson, *The Imperfect Union*, chap. 4; Keating with Carter, *The Man Who Rocked the Boat*.
25. Hutchinson, *Imperfect Union*, p. 100.
26. Keating and Carter, *Man Who Rocked the Boat*, pp. 76, 94.
27. Hutchinson, *The Imperfect Union*, chap. 23.
28. Hutchinson, *Imperfect Union*, pp. 291, 295, 312-16, 348, 382, 383.
29. Boehm, *Organized Crime and Organized Labor*, chap. 2.
30. Seidman, *Labor Czars*.
31. Lipset, *The First New Nation*.
32. Wraith and Simpkins, *Corruption in Developing Countries*, chap. 10.

Chapter 14
Improvement of Political Ethics

1. Dewey, *Twenty against the Underworld*, p. 272.
2. Arm, *Payoff*, p. 45.
3. *Diary of Gideon Welles*, p. 227.
4. Callow, *The Tweed Ring*, p. 34.
5. Loth, *Public Plunder*, p. 286.
6. Thomas, *A Debonair Scoundrel*, part I, chap. 1.
7. Boyd, *Above the Law*, pp. 59-60.
8. Boyd, *Above the Law*, p. 58.
9. Reeves, *Gentleman Boss*.
10. Peterson, *Barbarians in Our Own Midst*, pp. 235-6.
11. Benson and Engeman, *Amoral America*, pp. 22-23.
12. Bereday and Stretch, "Political Education in the USA and USSR," in *Comparative Education Review*, 1963; and Easton and Dennis, *Children in the Political System*, p. 406.
13. Nietz and Mason, "Early American Civil Government Textbooks," in *Social Education*, pp. 201-204.

14. Hess, *Harvard Educational Review*, pp. 528-36.
15. Langton, *Political Socialization*, pp. 97-98.
16. Litt, "Civic Education," *The American Sociological Review*, February 1963, pp. 69-75.
17. Merelman, *Political Socialization and Educational Climates*, p. 164.
18. Greenstein, *Children and Politics*, p. 178.
19. McPhail, *Moral Education in the Secondary School*; and Benson and Engeman, *Amoral America*, chaps. 9, 10.
20. Gable, *Beyond Failure*, chap. 13.
21. White, *The Republican Era*, p. 380.
22. Griffith, *A History of American City Government*, p. 49.
23. Zink, *City Bosses in the United States*, chap. 3.
24. Thomas, *A Debonair Scoundrel*, pp. 383-5.
25. Griffith, *American City Government*, p. 49.
26. Cook, *The Corrupted Land*, chap. 5, pp. 143-4.
27. Griffith, *A History of American City Government*, 1870-1900, p. 253.
28. Miller, *Boss Cox's Cincinnati*, pp. 143-80.
29. Reddy, *Tom's Town*, p. 247.
30. Harper, *Pittsburgh*, pp. 146-56.
31. Messick, *John Edgar Hoover*, p. 179.
32. Thomas, *The Debonair Scoundrel*, p. 384.
33. Niebuhr, *Social Sources of American Denominationalism*, p. 207.
34. Clebsch, *American Religion and the Care of Souls*.
35. Griffith, *American City Government*, p. 106.
36. Caro, *The Power Broker*, pp. 1006-23.
37. Hume, *Inside Story*, pp. 149, 161.
38. Moore, *The Kefauver Committee and the Politics of Crime*, pp. 39-41.
39. Kolesar, Harder, School, *Blueprint for Scandal*.
40. Redding, *Tom's Town*, p. 315.
41. Mockridge and Prall, *The Big Fix*.
42. Crooks, *Politics and Progress*.
43. Mitchell, "Boss Speer and City Functional," in *Pacific Northwest Quarterly*, October 1972, pp. 155-64.
44. Price, *The Promotion of the City Manager Plan*, pp. 563-78.
45. Hays, "The Politics of Reform in Municipal Government in the Progressive Era," in *Pacific Northwest Quarterly*, October 1964.
46. Hoogenboom, *Outlawing the Spoils*, p. 197.
47. Dorsett, "The City Boss and the Reformer," in *Pacific Northwest Quarterly*, October 1972, pp. 150-55.
48. Pease, "Urban Reformers in the Professive Era," *Pacific Northwest Quarterly*, April 1971, p. 53.

Chapter 15
The Way Out of Corruption

1. Brooks, *Corruption in American Politics and Life*, chap. 3.
2. Benson and Engeman, "Ethical Instruction and the Churches," in *Religious Education*, September-October 1974, pp. 568-78.
3. Boyarsky, *Bathroom Politics*, chap. 11.

Bibliography

Abels, Jules. *The Truman Scandal.* Chicago: Henry Regnery Company, 1956.
Adamany, David. "Public Financing: A Cure for the Curse of Slush Funds." *The Progressive.* October 1973.
Adamany, David, and G.E. Agree, *Political Money.* Baltimore: Johns Hopkins Univ. Press, 1975.
Adams, Samuel. *Incredible Era.* Boston: Houghton Mifflin, 1939.
Adrian, Charles, and Ernest, Griffith. *A History of American City Government, 1775-1780.* New York: Praeger, 1976.
Allen, Robert, ed. *Our Sovereign State.* New York: Vanguard Press, 1949.
Almond, Gabriel A., and Sidney Verba. *The Civic Culture.* Princeton: Princeton Univ. Press, 1963.
American Enterprise Institute. *The Economics of Crime and Punishment.* Washington D.C.: American Enterprise Institute, 1974.
Amick, George. *The American Way of Graft.* Princeton: Center for Analysis of Public Issues, 1976.
Arm, Walter. *Payoff.* New York: Appleton-Century-Crofts, 1951.
Ashman, Charles. *The Finest Judges Money Can Buy.* Los Angeles: Nash, 1973.
Astor, Gerald. *The New York Cops.* New York: Charles Scribner's, 1971.
Atkinson, C.R. "Recent Graft Exposures and Prosecutions." *National Municipal Review.* Vol. I. October 1912.
Bagehot, Walter. *The English Constitution.* New York: D. Appleton, 1908.
Bahn, Charles. *Police Socialization and the Psychosocial Costs of Police Corruption.* New York: Criminal Justice Center. John Jay College, 1976.
Bailey, Sidney. *British Parliamentary Democracy.* Boston: Houghton Mifflin, 1971.
Banfield, Edward C., and James Q. Wilson. *Political Influence.* New York: Vintage Books, 1963.
Barker, Charles. *The Background of Revolution in Maryland.* New Haven: Yale Univ. Press, 1940.
Bayley, David. "The Effect of Corruption in a Developing Nation." *Western Political Quarterly* 19, December 1966.
Beach, Marjorie M. *The Mayors Wife.* New York: Vantage Press, 1953.
Beard, Edmund, and Stephen Horn. *Congressional Ethics: The View from the House.* Washington, D.C.: Brookings Institution, 1975.
Benson, George C.S., and Thomas S. Engeman. *Amoral America.* Stanford: Hoover Institution Press, 1975.
Berg, Lang L., Harlan Hahn, and John R. Schmidhauser. *Corruption in the American Political System.* Morristown: General Learning Press, 1976.
Berge, George. *The Free Pass Bribery System.* Lincoln: Independent Publishing Company, 1905; reprint ed., New York: Arno Press, 1974.

Blanshard, Paul. *Investigating City Government in the La Guardia Administration. A Report of the Department of Investigation and Accounts 1934-1937.* New York City.

Boehm, Randolph. *Organized Crime and Organized Labor.* Arlington: The Foundation for the Advancement of the Public Trust, 1976.

Bordua, David J., ed. *The Police.* New York: Wiley, 1967.

"The Bottom of the Great City Difficulty". *The Nation* 13, September 7, 1971, p. 157.

Boyarsky, Bill, and Nancy Boyarsky. *Backroom Politics,* Los Angeles: J.P. Tarcher, 1974.

Boyd, James. *Above the Law.* New York: North American Library, 1968.

Bracey, Dorothy Heid. *A Functional Approach to Police Corruption.* New York: Criminal Justice Center, John Jay College of Criminology Ca. 1976.

Bradley, Phillips, ed. *Tocqueville: Democracy in America.* New York: Alfred Knapp, 1945.

Brasy, H.A. "Administrative Corruption in Theory and Dutch Practice." In Heidenheimer, ed., *Political Corruption.* New York: Holt, Rinehart and Winston, 1970.

Brooks, Robert. *Corruption in American Life and Politics.* New Jersey: Dodd, Mead, 1910; reprint ed., New York: Arno Press, 1974.

Brown, William. *The New York City Police Department Anti-Corruption Campaign,* October 1970-August 1972. State Univ. of New York at Albany, 1972.

Bruce, Laurie. "Fire Companies in Southward: The 1840's." Cited by Allen Davis and Mark Haller, eds., *People of Philadelphia: A History of Ethnic Groups and Lower Class Life, 1790-1940,* Philadelphia: Temple Univ. Press, 1973.

Bruns, Roger. *The Covode Committee, 1860.* Cited in Roger Bruns and Arthur Schlesinger, *Congress Investigates,* Vol II. New York: Chelsea House, 1975.

Bryce, James. *The American Commonwealth,* 2. New York: Macmillan, 1928.

Burnham, Walter Dean. *Critical Elections and the Mainsprings of American Politics.* New York: W.W. Norton, 1970.

Callow, Alexander. *The Tweed Ring.* London: Oxford Univ. Press, 1965.

_____. *The City Boss in America.* New York: Oxford Univ. Press, 1976.

Caro, Robert, *The Power Broker.* New York: Random House, 1975.

Chambers, Walter. *Samuel Seabury.* New York: Century, 1932.

Chambliss, William J. "Vice, Corruption, Bureaucracy and Power." In *Wisconsin Law Review,* 1971.

Chevallez, G.A. *La Suisse ou Le Sommeil Du Juste.* Lausanne: Payot, 1967.

Chevigny, Paul. *Police Power.* New York: Random House, 1969.

Clark, Dennis J. "The Philadelphia Irish; Persistent Presence." In Davis and Haller, *Peoples of Philadelphia.*

Cleland, Robert. *A History of California–The American Period.* New York: Macmillan, 1923.
Cochran, Thomas P. *Railroad Leaders, 1845-1890.* New York: Rusell and Russell, 1965.
Cohen, Bruce J., ed. *Crime in America: Perspectives on Criminal and Delinquent Behavior.* Itasca: F.E. Peacock, 1970.
Cohen, Richard, and Jules Witcover. *A Heartbeat Away.* New York: Viking Press, 1974.
Connable, Alfred, and Edward Silberfarb. *Tigers of Tammany.* New York: Holt, Rinehart and Winston, 1967.
Cook, Fred. *The Corrupted Land.* New York: Macmillan, 1966.
Costikyan, Edward. *Behind Closed Doors.* New York: Harcourt Brace, 1966.
E. Merton Coulter, *The South During Reconstruction,* Louisiana State University Press: 1947.
Council of State Governments. *Ethics, 1975.* Lexington, Ky.: 1975.
_____. "State Police." *Book of the States* 1974-1975.
Cressey, Donald. *Theft of the Nation.* New York: Harper and Row, 1969.
Crile, George. "A Tax Assessor Has Many Friends." *Harper's.* November 1972.
Croly, Herbert. *Marcus Alonzo Hanna, His Life and Works.* New York: Macmillan, 1923.
Crooks, James. *Politics and Progress.* Baton Rouge: Louisiana State Univ. Press, 1968.
Currant, Richard. *Three Carpetbag Governors.* Baton Rouge: Louisiana State Univ. Press, 1967.
Dagget, Stuart. *Chapters on History of the Southern Pacific.* New York: Augustum M. Kelly, 1966.
Daley, Robert. *Target Blue.* New York: Delacorte, 1971.
Davenport, John. "Skimming the Tiger". *New York Affairs* 3, Fall 1975.
Davis, Allen F., and Mark H. Haller. *Peoples of Philadelphia.* Philadelphia: Temple Univ. Press, 1973.
Demaris, Ovid. *Captive City.* New York: Lyle Stuart, 1969.
De Rougement, Denis. *La Suisse.* Paris: Hachette, 1965.
De Tocqueville, Alexis. *Democracy in America.* 2 Vol. New York: Alfred A. Knopf, 1946.
Dewey, Thomas E. *Twenty Against the Underworld.* New York: Doubleday, 1974.
Dorman, Michael. *Payoff.* New York: David McKay, 1972.
Dorsett, Lyle W. "The City Bosses and the Reformer". *Pacific Northwest Quarterly,* October 1972, pp. 150-155.
_____. *The Pendergast Machine.* New York: Oxford Univ. Press, 1972.
Douglas, Paul H. *Ethics in Government.* Connecticut: Greenwood, 1952.
Draa, Tyler G. "Corruption and Dynasty; An Analysis of the Chronology and Cohesion of Huey Long's Political Machine". Salvatori Center

Claremont Men's College, 1976.
Dunaway, Wayland. *A History of Pennsylvania.* New York: Prentice-Hall, 1948.
Easton, David, and Jack Dennis. *Children in the Political System.* New York: McGraw-Hill, 1969.
Eaton, Dorman B. *The Spoils System and Civil Service Reform,* originally published 1881. Reprinted Arno Press, New York, 1976.
____ . *The Spoils System in New York Civil Service Reform Association,* New York, 1881. Reprinted Arno Press, New York, 1974.
Elazar, Daniel. *American Federalism: A View from the States.* New York: Thomas Y. Crowell, 1966.
Ellis, David, James Frost, and Harold Syrett and Harry Carman. *A History of New York State.* Ithaca: Cornell Univ. Press, 1967.
Evans, E.C. *A History of the Australian Ballot System in the United States.* Chicago: Univ. of Chicago Press, 1917.
Evans, Frank. *Pennsylvania Politics, 1872-1877: A Study in Political Leadership.* Harrisburg: Pennsylvania History and Museum Commission 1966.
Fainsod, Merle, and Lincoln Gordon. *Government and the American Economy.* New York: Norton, 1941.
Ferber, Nat. *I Found Out.* New York: Dial, 1939.
Fish, Carl. *The Civil Service and the Patronage.* Cambridge: Harvard Univ. Press, 1920.
Ford, Henry James. "Municipal Corruption." *Political Science Quarterly,* December 19, 1904.
Ford, Jon. *Texas Big Money.* Cited in Hubert E. Alexander, ed. *Campaign Money.* New York: Free Press, 1976.
Fosdick, R.B. *American Police Systems.* Patterson Smith Paperback. Montclair, New Jersey. Reprinted in 1969, originally published in 1920.
____ . *Chronical of a Generation.* New York: Harper Bros., 1958.
Fowler, Dorothy. *The Cabinet Politician.* New York: Columbia Univ. Press, 1943.
Fowler, Gene. *Beau James.* New York: Viking Press, 1949.
Friedrich, Carl. J. *The Pathology of Politics.* New York: Harper and Row, 1972.
Frier, David A. *Conflict of Interest in the Eisenhower Administration.* Baltimore: Penguin Books, 1970.
Gambino, Richard. *Blood of My Blood.* New York: Doubleday Anchor Books, 1975.
Gans, Herbert. *The Urban Villagers.* Glencoe: Free Press, 1962.
Gardiner, John. *The Politics of Corruption.* New York: Russell Sage Foundation, 1970.
Gardiner, John, and David Olson. *Theft of the City.* Bloomington: Indiana Univ. Press, 1974.

Garrett, Charles. *The La Guardia Years.* New Brunswick: Rutgers Univ. Press, 1961.
Ginger, Ray. *Altgeld's America.* Chicago: Quadrangle Books, 1965.
Getz, Robert. *Congressional Ethics.* New York: Van Nostrand, 1966.
Glabb, Charles, and Theodore Brown. *A History of Urban American.* New York: Macmillan, 1976.
Goble, Frank. *Beyond Failure.* Ottawa, Illinois: Caroline House Books, 1977.
Golden, Joseph. *The Super Lawyers.* New York: Dell, 1971.
Goodnow, Frank J. "The Historical Development of the City's Position". Cited by Edward C. Banfield, ed. *Urban Government: A Reader in Politics and Administration.* New York: Free Press, 1961.
Gordon, Diana. *City Limits.* New York: Charterhouse, 1973.
Gosh, Martin, and Richard Hammer. *The Last Testament of Lucky Luciano.* Boston: Little, Brown, 1974.
Gosnell, Harold. *Machine Politics.* Chicago: Univ. of Chicago Press, 1968.
Goulden, Joseph. *The Benchwarmers.* New York: Ballantine Books, 1976.
_____. *Boss Platt and His New York Machine.* Chicago: Univ. of Chicago Press, 1924.
Government of Japan. *Summary of White Paper on Crime 1975.* Japan, 1975.
The Governors Select Commission on Civil Disorder. *Report for Action.* Trenton: 1968.
Graham, George. *Morality in American Politics.* New York: Random House, 1952.
Greenstein, Fred I. *Children and Politics.* New Haven: Yale Univ. Press, 1965.
Griffith, E.S. *A History of American City Government: 1900-1920.* New York: Praeger, 1974.
Griffith, Ernest. *Modern Development of City Government in the United Kingdom.* 2 Vol. London: Oxford Univ. Press, 1927.
_____. *Modern Development of City Government in the United States* 2 Vol. London: Oxford Univ. Press, 1927.
_____. *History of American City Government,* I. New York: Oxford Univ. Press, 1938.
_____. *A History of American City Government 1870-1900.* New York: Praeger, 1974.
_____. *History of American City Government: The Progressive Years, and Their Aftermath.* New York: Oxford Univ. Press, 1947.
Hagensick, A. Clarke. "Flouting Their Own Law". *National Civic Review* 53, October 1964.
Haller, Mark. "Urban Crime and Criminal Justice". *Journal of American History* LVII, December 1970.
Hamilton, James. *From Wilderness to Statehood, A History of Montana.* Portland: Brunsford Emort, 1957.

Hamilton, John. *The Dethronement of the City Boss.* New York: Funk and Wagnalls, 1910.
Handlin, Oscar. *The Uprooted.* New York: Little, Brown, 1951.
Hanna, David. *Frank Costello.* New York: Belmont Tower Books, 1974.
Hansen, Marcus L. *The Atlantic Migration.* New York: Harper, 1961.
Harris, J.P. *Registration of Votes in the United States.* Washington: Brookings Institution, 1929.
Harrison, Carter. *Stormy Years.* Indianapolis: Bobbs-Merrill, 1935.
Hayden, Tom. *Revolt in Newark.*
Hays, Samuel P. "The Politics of Reform in Municipal Government in the Progressive Era." *Pacific Northwest Quarterly,* October 1964.
Heard, Alexander. *Costs of Democracy.* Chapel Hill: Univ. of North Carolina Press, 1960.
Heidenheimer, Arnold. *Political Corruption.* New York: Holt, Rinehart, Winston, 1970.
_____. *The Governments of Germany.* New York: Thomas Y. Crowell, 1971.
Heilbroner, Robert L. *In the Name of Profit.* New York: Doubleday, 1972.
Hesseltine, William. *Ulysses S. Grant, Politician.* New York: Dodd, Mead, 1935.
Himmelfarb, Gertrude. *Lord Action.* Chicago: Univ. of Chicago Press, 1962.
Hittell, Theodore. *History of California,* III and IV. San Francisco: N.J. Stone, 1897.
Hofstadter, Richard. *The Age of Reform.* New York: Vintage Books, 1955.
Holden, Alice M. "The Graft Investigations of the Year." *National Municipal Review* 3, pp. 525-537.
Holli, Melvin. *Reform in Detroit: Hazen S. Pingree and Urban Politics.* New York: Oxford Univ. Press, 1969.
Hoogenboom, Ari. *Outlawing the Spoils.* Urbana: Univ. of Illinois Press, 1968.
Howe, George Frederick. *Chester A. Arthur: A Quarter Century of Machine Politics.* New York: Dodd, Mead, 1934.
Hughes, Rupert. *The Story of Thomas E. Dewey.* New York: Grosset and Dunlap, 1944.
Hume, Brit. *Inside Story.* New York: Doubleday, 1974.
Huntford, Roland. *The New Totalitarians.* New York: Stein and Day, 1972.
Huntington, Samuel. *Political Order in Changing Societies.* New Haven: Yale Univ. Press, 1968.
Hutchinson, John. *The Imperfect Union.* New York: Dutton, 1972.
Huthmacher, Joseph S. *Senator Robert F. Wagner and the Rise of Urban Liberation.* New York: Atheneum, 1968.
Irey, Elmer L. *The Tax Dodgers.* New York: Greenberg, 1948.
Jackson, Jay. *New Orleans in the Gilded Age.* Baton Rouge: Louisiana State Univ. Press, 1969.

Jaworski, Leon. *The Right and The Power.* New York: Thomas Y. Crowell, 1976.
Jonas, Frank H., ed., *Political Dynamiting,* Salt Lake City: Univ. of Utah Press, 1970.
Jordan, David. *Roscoe Conkling of New York.* Ithaca: Cornell Univ. Press, 1971.
Katcher, Leo. *The Big Bankroll.* New York: Harper and Bros., 1958.
Keating, William J., and Richard Carter. *The Man Who Rocked the Boat.* New York: Harper, 1956.
Kefauver, Estes. *Crime in America.* Garden City: Doubleday, 1951.
Kenner, H.J. *The Fight for Truth in Advertising.* Randtable Press, New York: 1936.
Key, V.O. *Southern Politics.* New York: Vintage Books, 1949.
_____ . "The Techniques of Political Graft in the United States." Dissertation, University of Chicago, 1934.
_____ . *Politics, Parties and Pressure Groups.* New York: Thomas Crowell, 1964.
Klein, Philip. *Pennsylvania Politics, 1817-1832: Games Without Rules.* Philadelphia: Historical Society of Pennsylvania, 1940.
Klein, Philip, and Ari Hoogenboom. *A History of Pennsylvania.* New York: McGraw-Hill, 1973.
Knapp Commission. *The Knapp Commission Report on Police Corruption.* New York: George Braziller, 1972.
Kobler, John. *Capone.* New York: G.P. Putnam's Sons, 1971.
_____ . *Ardent Spirits.* New York: G.P. Putnam's Sons, 1973.
Kristol, Irving. "Post Watergate Morality and To Good for our Good." *New York Times,* November 14, 1976.
LaFollette, Robert. *LaFollette's Autobiography.* Madison: Robert LaFollette, 1913.
Lait, Joel, and Lee Mortimer. *Chicago Confidential.* New York: Crown, 1950.
Langton, Kenneth P. *Political Socialization.* New York: Oxford Univ. Press, 1969.
Lasky, Victor. *It Didn't Start With Watergate.* New York: Dial Press, 1977.
Levin, Murray. *The Compleat Politician.* New York: Bobbs-Merrill.
Levine, Edward. *The Irish and Irish Politicians: A Study of Cultural and Social Alienation.* Notre Dame: Univ. of Notre Dame Press, 1966.
Lewis, Oscar. *The Big Four.* New York: Knopf, 1938.
_____ . *The Children of Sanchez.* New York: Random House, 1961.
Lindsay, Ben B., and Harvey J. O'Higgins. *The Beast.* New York: Doubleday, Page, 1910.
Lipset, Seymour Martin. *The First Nation.* New York: Doubleday Anchor Book, 1967.

_____. *Revolution and Counterrevolution.* New York: Basic Books, 1968.
Litt, Edgar. "Civic Education, Community Norms, and Political Indoctrination." *The American Sociological Review*, February 1963: 69-75.
_____. *Political Cultures of Massachusetts.* Cambridge, Massachusetts: Massachusetts Institute of Technology Press, 1965.
Lockard, Duane. *New England State Politics.* Princeton: Princeton Univ. Press, 1959.
Loth, David. *Public Plunder.* New York: Carrick and Evans, 1938.
Maas, Peter. *Serpico.* New York: Bantam Books, 1973.
Mace, John A. *The Crime Industry.* Lexington: Lexington Books, 1975.
"Machine Politics in Other Cities." *National Municipal Review*, October, 1915: 573-575.
McClellan, John L. *Crime without Punishment.* New York: Duell, Sloan and Pearce, 1962.
McCormick, R.P. *The History of Voting in New Jersey.* New Brunswick: Rutgers Univ. Press, 1953.
McCullough, Gerard. "Pennsylvania: The Failure of Campaign Reform." In *Campaign Money*, edited by Herbert Alexander. New York: Free Press, 1976.
McDonald, Forrest. *Insull.* Chicago: Univ. of Chicago Press, 1962.
McNamara, Joseph. "The Impact of Bureaucracy Dysfunctions on Attempts to Prevent Police Corruption." *Police Journal*, January-March, 1975.
McPhail et al. *Moral Education in the Secondary School.* London: Longman, 1972.
McReynolds, Edwin. *Oklahoma, A History of the Sooner State.* Oklahoma City: Univ. of Oklahoma Press, 1954.
Merelman, Richard M. *Political Socialization and Educational Climates.* New York: Holt, Rinehart, and Winston, 1971.
Merton, Robert K. *Social Theory and Social Structure.* New York: Free Press, 1968.
Messick, Hank. *The Silent Syndicate.* New York: Macmillan, 1961.
_____. *Secret File.* New York: G.P. Putnam's Sons, 1969.
_____. *John Edgar Hoover.* New York: David McKay, 1972.
_____. *Syndicate in the Sun.* New York: Macmillan, 1968.
Meyers, Gustavus. *History of Tammany Hall.* New York: Boni & Liveright, 1917.
Meyerson, Martin, and Edward Banfield. "A Machine at Work." First published in *Politics, Planning and the Public Interest.* New York: Free Press 1975; reprinted in Edward Banfield, ed., *Urban Government.* New York: Free Press, 1961.
Miller, Zane. *Boss Cox's Cincinnati.* New York: Oxford Univ. Press, 1968.
Milligan, Maurice M. *Missouri Waltz.* New York: Charles Scribner's Sons, 1949.

Mitchell, J. Paul. "Boss Speer and the City Functional." *Pacific Northwest Quarterly*, October 1972: 155-164.

Mitgang, Herbert. *The Man Who Rode the Tiger*. New York: J.P. Lippincott, 1963.

Mockridge, Norton, and Robert H. Pratt. *The Big Fix*. New York: Holt, 1954.

Mollenhoff, Clark. *Despoilers of Democracy*. Garden City: Doubleday, 1965.

_____. *Strike Force*. Englewood Cliffs: Prentice-Hall, 1972.

Moore, William H. *The Kefauver Committee and the Politics of Crime, 1950-1952*. Columbia: Univ. of Missouri Press, 1974.

Morris, Newbold. *Let the Chips Fall*. New York: Appleton-Century-Crofts, 1955.

Moscow, Warren. *The Last of the Big Time Bosses*. New York: Stein and Day, 1971.

Mosher, Frederick, et al. *Watergate: Implications for Responsible Government*. New York: Basic Books, 1974.

Moynihan, Daniel. "The Private Government of Crime." *The Reporter* 25, July 6, 1961; reprinted in Bruce J. Cohen, ed., *Crime in America*. Ithasca: Peacock, 1970.

Mulcahy, Kevin, and Richard Katz. *America Votes*. New Jersey: Prentice-Hall, 1976.

Murphy, Patrick V. "Overhauling the Criminal Justice System." *Criminal Justice Digest*, March 1976.

Murray, Robert. *The Harding Era*. Minneapolis: Univ. of Press, 1969.

National Municipal League. Proceedings of the Third, Sixth, Eighth, and Twelfth Annual Meetings. New York City, 1900, 1902, 1906, 1894, 1896.

Nelli, Humbert. "John Powers and the Italians; Politics in a Chicago Ward, 1896-1921." *Journal of American History*, 57, June 1970.

Nevins, Allan. *Study in Power I*. New York: Charles Scribner's Sons, 1953.

Newfield, Jack, and Paul DuBrul. *The Abuse of Power*. New York: Viking Press, 1977.

Niebuhr, Richard. *Social Sources of American Denominationalism*. New York: Meridan Brooks, 1972.

Nietz, John A., and Wayne E. Mason. "Early American Civil Government Textbooks." *Social Education*, May 1950.

Niven, John. *Connecticut for the Union*. New Haven: Yale Univ. Press, 1965.

Norwood, Christopher. *About Paterson: The Making and Unmaking of an American City*. New York: Harper and Row, 1974.

Nye, J.S. "Corruption and Political Development: A Cost Benefit Analysis." *American Political Science Review*, June 1967: 417-427.

O'Connor, Len. *Clout*. New York: Avon, 1975.

O'Connor, Richard. *Hell's Kitchen*. Philadelphia: J.P. Lippencott, 1958.

Orth, Samuel. *Our Foreigners: A Chronicle of Americans in the Making*. New

Haven: Yale Univ. Press, 1920.

———. *The Boss and the Machine*. New Haven: Yale Univ. Press, 1919.

Osofsky, Gilbert. *Harlem: The Making of a Ghetto*. New York: Harper and Row, 1971.

Ostrogorski, M. *Democracy and the Organization of Political Parties*, Vol. 2. New York: Haskell House, 1970.

Patten, Clifford. *The Battle for Municipal Reform*. Washington, D.C.: American Council on Public Affairs, 1940.

Payne, Robert. *The Corrupt Society*. New York: Praeger, 1975.

Pearson, Drew, and Jack Anderson. *The Case Against Congress*. New York: Simon and Schuster, 1968.

Pease, Otis A. "Urban Reformers in the Progressive Era." *Pacific Northwest Quarterly*, April 1971:53.

Pennsylvania Crime Commission. Harrisburg, Pennsylvania.

———. *Report on Police Corruption and the Quality of Law Enforcement in Philadelphia*. Harrisburg: Department of Justice, 1974.

Perambo, Ron. *No Cause for Indictment* Holt, Rinehart, and Winston, New York, 1971.

Peterson, Virgil. *Barbarians in Our Midst*. Boston: Little, Brown, 1952.

Petshek, Kirk. *The Challenge of Urban Reform*. Philadelphia: Temple Univ. Press, 1973.

Price, Don. "The Promotion of the City Manager Plan." *Public Opinion Quarterly*, Winter 1941:563-578.

Rakove, Milton. *Don't Make No Waves, Don't Back No Losers*. London: Indiana Univ. Press, 1975.

Randolph, Edmund. *A Vindication of Mr. Randolph's Resignation*. Philadelphia: Samuel H. Smith, 1800.

Reddig, William M. *Tom's Town*. Philadelphia: Lippincott, 1947.

Redlich, Josef, and Francis Hirst. *Local Government in England*, Vol. 2. London: Macmillan, 1903.

Reeves, Thomas C. *Gentleman Boss*. New York: Knapf, 1975.

Reichley, A. James. "Getting at the Roots of Watergate." *Fortune*, July 1973.

———. "The Texas Banker Who Bought Politicians." *Fortune*, December 1971.

———. *The Art of Government: Reform and Organization Politics in Philadelphia*. Santa Barbara: The Fund for the Republic, 1959.

Reid, Ed. *The Grim Reapers*. Chicago: Henry Regency, 1969.

Reid, Ed, and Ovid Demaris. *The Green Felt Jungle*. New York: Trident Press, 1963.

Reiss, J. Albert. *The Police and the Public*. New Haven: Yale Univ. Press, 1971.

Riordon, William. *Plunkitt of Tammany Hall*. New York: E.P. Dutton, 1963.

Rogow, Arnold A., and Harold D. Lasswell. *Power Corruption and Rectitude*. New Jersey: Prentice-Hall, 1963.

Rosenberg, Hans. *Bureaucracy, Aristocracy, and Autocracy.* Boston: Beacon Press, 1958.
Royal Commission on Standards of Conduct in Public Life. London: Stationary Office, 1976.
Royko, Mike. *Boss.* New York: Signet, 1971.
Rubinstein, Jonathan. *City Police.* New York: Farrar, Straus, Giroux, 1973.
Rudwick, Elliott M. *Race Riot at East St. Louis.* Cleveland: World, 1966.
Russell, Francis. *The Shadow of Blooming Grove.* New York: McGraw-Hill, 1968.
Sakolski, A.M. *The Great American Land Bubble.* New York: Harper and Row, 1932.
Sale, Kirkpatrick. *Power Shift.* New York: Random House, 1975.
Salerno, Ralph, and John Tompkins. *The Crime Confederation.* Garden City: Doubleday, 1969.
Salter, J.F. *Boss Rule.* New York: McGraw-Hill, 1934.
Sampson, Anthony. *The Arms Bazaar.* New York: Viking Press, 1977.
Schendel, Gordon. "Something is Rotten in the State of Texas." *Colliers*, June 5, 1971.
Schlesinger, Arthur Jr. and Roger Bruns. *Congress Investigates*, Vol. I. New York: Chelsea House, 1975.
Schrirer, Arnold. *Ireland and the American Emigration 1850-1900.* New York: Russell and Russell 1958.
Schuster, Alvin. "Graft Charges Rare in Western Europe's Judiciary." *New York Times*, October 8, 1972.
Schwartz, Bernard. *The Professor and the Commissions.* New York: Alfred A. Knopf, 1959.
Sciacoa, Tony. *Lucky Luciano.* New York: Pinnacle Books, 1975.
Scott, James C. "Corruption, Machine Politics and Political Charge." *American Political Science Review*, December 1969:1142-1158.
Seidman, Harold. *Labor Czars.* New York: Livenright, 1938.
Shadgett, O.H. *Voter Registration in Georgia.* Athens: Univ. of Georgia, 1955.
Shannon, William V. *The American Irish.* New York: Collier Books, Macmillan, 1963.
Sheridan, Walter. "The Rise and Fall of Jimmy Hoffa." *Saturday Review Press*, 1972.
Sherman, Lawrence W., ed. *Police Corruption.* New York: Doubleday Anchor, 1974.
Shirer, William. *The Collapse of the Third Republic.* New York: Pocket Books, 1971.
Skaggs, David. *The Roots of Maryland Democracy, 1753-1776.* Westport: Greenwood Press, 1973.
Smith, Ralph. *The Tarnished Badge.* New York: Thomas Y. Crowell, 1965.

Smith, Reed. *State Government in Transition.* Philadelphia: Univ. of Pennsylvania Press, 1961.
Stave, Bruce. *Urban Bosses, Machines and Progressive Reformers.* Lexington: D.C. Heath and Company, 1972.
Stead, William T. *Satan's Invisible World Displayed*, Arno Press, New York, 1974 p. 135.
Steffens, Lincoln. *The Shame of the Cities.* McClure, Phillips, 1904. Reprinted by Hill and Wang, New York, 1960.
_____. *The Struggle for Self-Government.* New York: McLane, Phillips, 1906.
_____. "The Taming of the West: Discovery of the Land Fraud System." *American Magazine* 64, May-October 1907.
_____. "The Taming of the West: Henry Grapples the Oregon Land-Graft." *American Magazine* 4, May-October 1907.
_____. *Autobiography.* New York: Harcourt, Brace and World, 1931, 1958.
Steinberg, Alfred. *The Bosses.* New York: Macmillan, 1972.
Stephenson, Wendell Holmes, ed. *A History of The South*, Vol. 8. E. Martin Coulter, *The South During Reconstruction, 1865-1877.* Baton Rouge: Louisiana State Univ. Press, 1947.
Stewart, Frank. *A Half Century of Municipal Reform: The History of the National Municipal League.* Berkeley: Univ. of California Press, 1950.
Stoddard, Lothrop. *Master of Manhattan.* New York: Longman, Green, 1931.
Stout, Hiram. *British Government.* New York: Oxford Univ. Press, 1953.
Strong, Donald. *Registration of Voters in Alabama.* Bureau of Public Administration, 1956.
Swart, Koenrad. *Sales of Offices in the Seventeenth Century.* 5'Gavenhage: Martinus Nijhoff, 1949.
Tarbell, Ida. *History of Standard Oil Company*, Vol. 2. New York: McClure, Phillips, 1904.
Tarr, Joel. *A Study in Boss Politics.* Urbana: Univ. of Illinois Press, 1971.
Taylor, Philip. *The Distant Magnet: European Emigration to the U.S.A.* New York: Harper and Row, 1971.
Thayer, George. *Who Shakes the Money Tree.* New York: Simon and Schuster, 1973.
Theresa, Vincent. *My Life in the Mafia.* Garden City: Doubleday, 1973.
Thomas, Lately. *A Debonair Scoundrel: An Episode in the Moral History of San Francisco.* New York: Holt, Rinehart, 1962.
Tolman, William. *Municipal Reform Movements in the United States.* New York: Revell, 1895.
Trevelyan, J.M. *History of England.* Vol II. New York: Doubleday Anchor Books, 1952.
Tyler, Gus. *Organized Crime in America.* Ann Arbor: Univ. of Michigan Press, 1973.

U.S. Commission on Civil Rights. *Voting.* Washington, D.C.: Government Printing Office, 1961.

U.S. Treasury Department. *Immigration into the United States from 1820-1903.* Washington, D.C.: Government Printing Office, 1903.

Van Devander, Charles W. *The Big Bosses.* New York: Arno Press, 1974.

Walker, Mack. *Germany and the Emigration 1816-1885.* Cambridge: Harvard Univ. Press, 1964.

Wall, Joseph Frazier. *Andrew Carnegie.* New York: Oxford Univ. Press, 1970.

Walters, Everett. *Joseph Benson Foraker.* Columbus: Ohio History Press, 1948.

Walton, Mary. *West Virginia: The Governor Taketh.* Reprinted in Charles Peters and John Rothchild, *Inside the System.* New York: Praeger, 1973.

Warner, Hoyt. *Progressivism in Ohio 1897-1971.* Ohio: Ohio State Univ. Press, 1964.

Warner, Sam. *The Private City: Philadelphia in Three Periods of Growth.* Philadelphia: Univ. of Pennsylvania Press, 1968.

_____. *The Urban Wilderness.* New York: Harper and Row. 1972.

Weisband, Edward, and Thomas M. Frank. *Resignation in Protest.* New York: Penguin, 1975.

Welles, Gideon. *Diary of Gideon Welles.* Boston: Houghton Mifflin, 1911.

Wendt, Lloyd, and Herman Hogan. *Bosses in Lusty Chicago: The Story of Bathhouse John and Hinky Dink.* Bloomington: Indiana Univ. Press, 1943.

_____. *Big Bill of Chicago.* Indianapolis: Bobbs-Merrill, 1953.

Werner, M.R. *Tammany Hall.* Garden City: Doubleday and Doran, 1928.

Wetmer, Claude. *The Battle Against Bribery.* St. Louis: Pan-American Press, 1904.

Wheeler, Burton. *Yankee from the West.* Garden City: Doubleday, 1962.

White, Leonard D. *The Federalists, The Republican Era.* New York: Macmillan, 1958.

_____. *The Jeffersonians: A Study in Administrative History 1801-1829.* New York: Macmillan, 1951.

_____. *The Jacksonians: A Study in Administrative History 1828-1861.* New York: Macmillan, 1954.

Wigmore, John. *The Australian Ballot System.* Boston: Boston Book Company. 1889.

Williams, Henry T. *Huey Long.* New York: Bantam Books, 1970.

Williams, Robert. *Vice Squad.* New York: Pinnacle Books, 1974.

Wilson H.R. *Congress, Corruption and Compromise.* New York: Rinehart, 1951.

Wilson, James Q. *Thinking About Crime.* New York: Basic Books, 1975.

Wingate, Charles. "The Judiciary of New York City." *North American Review*, July 1867. Vol. CV, 148-177. *North American Review*, October 1874. Vol. CXIX, 378-408, Vol. CXXI, July 1875, 113-155, Vol. CXX, January 1875, 120-174, Vol. CXXIII, October 1876, 362-425.

Wittke, Carl, ed. *History of the State of Ohio.* Columbus: Ohio State Archaeological and Historical Society, 1943.

———. *The Irish in America.* Baton Rouge: Louisiana State Univ. Press, 1956.

Wolfinger, Raymond. *The Politics of Progress.* Englewood Cliffs: Prentice-Hall, 1974.

Woodward, C. Vann, ed. *Responses of the Presidents to Charges of Misconduct.* New York: Dell, 1974.

———. *Origins of the New South 1877-1913.* Louisiana: Louisiana State Univ. Press, 1951.

Wraith, Ronald, and Edgar Simpkins. *Corruption in Developing Countries.* Lonton: George Allen and Unwin, 1963.

Zink, Harold. *City Bosses in the United States.* Durham: Univ. of North Carolina Press, 1930.

Index

Index

Acton, Lord, 226
Adams, John Q.: administration of, 74
Adams, Sherman, 164
Agnew, Spiro, 8, 120, 180
Ahmanson, Howard, 181
Alaska, 123
Albany Regency, 58
Almond, Gabriel, and Verba, Sidney, 279
American Bridge Company, 13
American Federation of Labor, 166
Anaconda Copper, 125
Aquinas, St. Thomas, 282
Aristotle, 282
Arthur, Chester, 61, 83–84, 276
Ashbridge, Samuel H., 44
Australian Ballot, 170

Bahn, Charles, 234–235
Baker, Bobby, 141, 158
Balk, Alfred, 13
Baltimore, 193–194
Banfield, Edward, 231
Barron, Governor William Wallace, 129
Bayley, David H., xiii
Beard, Edmund, and Horn, Stephen, 138
Behrman, Major Martin, 121, 124
Benson, George C. S., 196, 233, 279, 281, 295
Berg, Hahn, and Schmidhauser, xvi, 184, 227
Bernard, Prince, 3
Bilbo, Senator Theodore G., 140
Black Horse Cavalry, 59, 260
Blaine, James G., 178
Boston, 2, 14
Boylan, James, 153
Bracey, Dorothy Heid, 216–217
Bradley, Phillips, 256
Brandle, Theodore, 268
Brayton, General, 13
Brewster, Daniel, 2, 121
Bricker, Senator John W., 138
Brindell, Robert P., 267

Brody, Thomas, 84
Brooks, Robert C., 8, 187, 256, 278, 293
Brown, William, 247–249
Bryce, James, 17, 33
Buchanan, President James, 1, 78–79
Burnham, David, 234
Burr, Aaron, 22, 274
Butler, Edward "Colonel", 50
Byrd, Machine, xiv, 132

Cahill, Governor William, 2, 121
California, 70–71, 115, 134
Callow, Alexander B., Jr., 134, 188–189, 211
Cameron, Donald, 126–127
Cameron, Simon, 79, 126
Campaigns, tactics ("dirty tricks"), 174–175; contributions to, 182
Capone, Al, 99–100, 242, 268
Carnegie, Andrew, 257
Caro, Robert, 9
Carter, President Jimmy, 251
Caudle, Theron L., 152
Cermak, Anton J., 100–101
Chambliss, William J., 236
Chandler, Judge Stephen S., 126
Chevigny, Paul, 196
Chicago, 12, 46–47, 99–106
Citizen participation in government, community action programs, 206–207; community control of schools, 207; decentralization, 207; neighborhood development corporation, 207
City government, 93–117, 120–121; city offices, 33; colonial traditions of, 17–19, origins of corruption 19–22
Civil Service, 223–224
Civil War, 79–80
Clark, William A., 66
Cleveland, President Grover, 61
Clinton, De Witt, 58, 274

333

Cochran, Thomas C., 258
Colton, David D., 258
Committee to Re-elect the President, 183, 261-262
Commodity Credit Corporation, 153
Common Cause, xiv, 14, 134, 139, 227, 256, 261, 291
Congress, 137-145; conflict of interest in, 138-139; disclosure of income and property, 139; low moral standard, 141
Congressional investigations, 142-145
Conkling, Roscoe, 61
Connolly, Richard, 38
Cook County, 179
Coolidge, President Calvin, 147, 151
Corruption, political. See Political Corruption
Costello, Frank, 14, 91
Costikyan, Edward N., 9
Coughlin, "Bathhouse John", 46, 103
Covode Committee, 79
Cox, Representative Eugene, 140
Cox, George B., 64-65
Credit Mobilier, 81, 87, 258
Cressey, Donald R., 92, 198
Croker, Richard, 42-43
Crooks, James B., 289
Curley, Mayor James M., 272
Currant, Richard, 67

Daley, Mayor Richard J., 8, 102-103, 194-195, 240
Daley, Robert, 249
Daugherty, Harry, 143, 148, 150
Davenport, John F., 187
Demaris, Ovid, 104 ff
Democratic Party, 24, 39, 59
Denby, Edwin, 148
Denver, 200
Detroit, 50
De Sapio, Carmine, 9, 96-97, 190-191
Dewey, Thomas E., 95, 161, 203-204
Di Grazia, Robert, 230
Dixon-Yates affair, 155
Dodd, Senator Thomas J., 140, 275-276
Dorman, Michael, 130-163, 198
Doublas, Paul, 215, 233
Draa, Tyler, 191-192
Duffy, Patrick, 49
Durham "Judge" Israel, 44-45

East St. Louis, 199
Eaton, Dorman B., 60, 84
Eisenhower, President Dwight, 277
Elazar, Daniel, 132-133
Elections, administration of, 169-174; Federal Corrupt Practices Act, 178, 182; Federal Election Campaign Act, 178-179; Hatch Act, 178; money in, 177-181; Macing, 177; public employee contributions to, 177-179;
Elk Hills, 143
Engeman, Thomas S., 196, 233, 279, 281, 295
Erie Canal, 60
Erwin, Senator Sam, 145
Estes, Billie Sol, 157, 283
Ethics legislation, 139

Fall, Albert, 146, 150, 259
Federal Bureau of Investigation (F. B. I.), 15, 241
Federal government, corruption from World War I to 1969, 137-166; role in nineteenth century, 73-86
Federal Housing Agency, 153
Federalists and Jeffersonians, 73
Fenton, Reuben, 59
Ferguson, Governor James, 128
Fishbourne, Mayor, 19
Florida, 11, 123
Flynn, Edward J., 191
Folk, Joseph W., 281
Foraker, Joseph B., 64-65, 86
Forbes, Charles R., 143, 146, 150, 259
Ford, Henry J., 224
Fosdick, Raymond, 204
Friedrich, Carl J., 213, 226-227, 233
Frier, David A., 155

Gambino, Richard, 198
Gardiner, John A., 190, 195
Garfield, James A., 83, 177
Gas Ring (Philadelphia), 54, 193
Giancana, Sam "MONO", 102
Ginger, Ray, 50
Goble, Frank, 282
Godkin, E. L., 26-27
Goldfine, Bernard, 155
Gordon, Diana, 194
Gosnell, Harold, 61, 191
Gould, Jay, 257, 260
Grant, President Ulysses S., 1-2, 80-82
Green, Governor Dwight, 123
Greenstein, Fred, 280
Gremillion, Jack, 2
Griffith, Ernest S., 17, 218, 224, 283, 287
Gross, Harry, 214-215

Hague, Mayor Frank, 125, 211, 240
Halfen, Jack, 128
Hall, Governor David, 126
Hall, Oakey A., 274
Handlin, Oscar, 28
Hanna, Marcus, 64-65, 85, 126, 274
Harding, President Warren G., xv, 2, 145-147, 277, 284
Harlem, 200-201
Harris, Joseph P., 169
Harrison, Carter, 46
Hayes, President Rutherford B., 83-84
Haynes, Roy A., 146
Hays, Samuel, 289
Havemeyer, H. O., 257
Hearst, William R., 86
Heidenheimer, Arnold, xiii, 3
Heney, Francis, 281, 289
Hines, Jimmy, 277
Hoffa, James R., 102, 270
Hoffman, John, 60
Hoogenboom, Ari, 289-290
Hoover, President Herbert, 252
Hughes, Governor Charles E., 131
Huntford, Roland, 3
Huntington, Collis P., 83, 257-258

Huntington, Samuel P., 188, 212-216, 218, 222, 233
Hutchinson, John, 266, 271

Illinois, 11-12, 14-15, 123-124, 129-130
Immigration, 22-25, 90; influence of, 72; role in urban machine, 24-32
India, 5
Indiana, 12, 133
Insull, Samuel, 259
Internal Revenue Service, corruption in, 152
International City Managers Association, 287
International Sunday School Association, 278
International Telephone and Telegraph Company, (ITT), 262
Iroquois, Theatre, 193

Jackson, President Andrew, 1, 22, 75-77, 219
James II, 18
Jaworski, Leon, 276
Jay Commission, 84
Jefferson, President Thomas, 74
Jerome, William T., 267
Jersey City, 10, 179, 240, 268
Johnson, Judge Albert W., 127
Johnson, Hiram, 258
Johnson, President Lyndon, 128, 141, 162, 277
Jones, Governor Sam, 124, 132
Judiciary, 123, 165-166
Justice Department, 250

Kalmbach, Herbert, 179
Kansas City, 110-113, 170, 244
Keane, Thomas E., 8, 12
Keating, William J., 269
Kefauver Committee, 101, 112
Kelly, "honest John", 177
Kelly, Clarence, 112
Kenna, "hinky dink", 46, 103
Kennedy, Robert, 16, 163

Kennelly, Martin, 277
Kerner, Otto, 2, 12, 276
Key, V. O., 11-12, 15, 169
King, Representative Cecil R., 144
Knapp Commission Report on Police Corruption, 97-98, 190, 197, 202, 215-216, 236, 246, 261
Kobler, John, 104
Kohlberg, Lawrence, 280-281
Korth, Fred, 145, 157
Kristol, Irving, xv
Kuehnle, Boss, 15, 86

La Follette, Robert M., 2, 71, 131
La Guardia, Fiorello, 94-95, 247, 269
Lait, Jack, 105
Land corruption, 68-71
Langton, Kenneth P., 280
Lasky, Victor, xvi
Las Vegas, 7, 125, 241
Law Enforcement Assistance Administration (LEAA), 251
Laxalt, Paul, 241
Lazia, Johnny, 111, 162
Leader, Governor George, 127
Levin, Murray, 125
Lewis, C. S., 282
Lexow Committee Report, 42, 196
Libonati, Roland, 102
Lincoln, President Abraham, 79-80
Lindsey, Judge Ben, 200, 215
Lindsey, John, 2, 97, 194, 235
Lipset, Seymour M., 219, 271
Lobbying, congressional, 138-140
Local government, 18, 120; influence of state, 72; land use, 13
Lockheed Corporation, 4
Long, Senator Edward D., 140
Long, Governor Huey, 124, 151, 243
Longshoremen Union, 266, 268-269
Los Angeles, 13, 114-115, 172
Louisiana, 124, 131, 133, 136
Lowden, Governor Frank, 123, 132
Luciano, Lucky, 242

MacDonald, Mike "King", 46, 48
McCarthy, Senator Joseph R., 140, 142
McClelland, John L., 15, 104, 203, 268
McCormack, Speaker John W., 141
McDonald, Miles, 281, 289
McGovern, Senator George, 182
McGrath, Howard, 152
Machine, political. See Political machine
Mackin, Joseph, 35
McKinley, William, 85-86
McLean, John, 63, 75
McLaughlin, Hugh, 59
McManes, James "King", 44, 106
Madden, Skinny, 268
Madison, James, 74
Mafia. See Organized Crime
Magruder, Jeb Stuart, 275
Mandel, Governor Marvin, 122
Marcello, Carlos, 124
Marcus, James, 10, 97
Maryland, 8, 11, 13, 124
Massachusetts, 124-125
May, Representative Andrew Jackson, 140, 144
Means, Gaston B., 150
Meany, George, 270
Merelman, Richard, 280
Merriam, Charles E., 212
Merton, Robert K., 188, 216, 218
Messick, Hank, 92
Michigan, 11, 131, 133
Miller, Thomas W., 148, 150
Mob. See Organized Crime
Montana, 121, 122, 125, 133
Montana Power and Light, 121
Moore, Governor Arch A., 129
Morgenthau, Henry, 243
Morris, Newbold, 7
Mortimer, Lee, 105
Moscow, Warren, 190
Moses, Robert, 9
Mowrey, George E., 288
Moynihan, Daniel P., 92, 203, 242
Mulcahy, Kevin, 132-133
Municipal reform, 50-54; Civil Service, 54, 96-97; reform charters, 53

Murphy, Charles F., 93–94
Murphy, Patrick V., 233–234, 247–249
Mutscher, Gus, 2, 121, 128

National Association of Manufacturers, 262–263
Nevada, 7, 125, 229
Newfield, and Du Brul, 90
New Jersey, 125, 126, 130, 133
New Orleans, 113, 124
New York City, 22, 38, 93–99, 222, 239; waterfront, 268–269
New York state, 21–22, 37, 126, 222; corrupt government, 58–65; Tammany Hall, 50
Niven, John, 80
Nixon, President Richard M., xv, 2, 115, 179, 264, 274–275, 277
North Carolina, 19, 133
Norwood, Christopher, 235
Nunan, Joseph D., 152
Nye, J. S., 213

O'Dwyer, William, 96
Ogilvie, Richard B., 102–104
Ohio, 63–65, 126
Oklahoma, 66, 126, 180
Oliphant, Herman, 152
O'Neill, Representative Thomas P., 182
Organized Crime, 90–94, 96, 98–106, 108–109, 111–113, 115, 117, 122, 124, 126, 128, 140, 151, 200–201, 228–229, 236–237
Osofsky, Gilbert, 200–201
Ostrogorski, M., 221, 233

Parkhurst, Charles H., 284
Parks, Sam, 266–267
Parr, George B., 128
Paterson, New Jersey, 235
Patriarca, Raymond, 124
Payne, Robert, xiii
Pease, Otis A., 290
Peirce, Neal R., 122, 132–133, 250
Pendergast, Thomas J., 110–113, 205, 240

Pendleton Act, 85
Penrose, Boies, 127, 274
Pennsylvania, 11, 20, 126–127, 179
Pennsylvania Crime Commission, 109, 202, 235, 261
Petersen, Virgil, 198
Petshek, Kirk R., 109
Philadelphia, 22–24, 89; Judge Israel Durham, 44; Republican machine, 43–44
Philadelphia Gas Ring, 43–44
Pingree, Mayor Hazen S., 193, 214, 244
Plunkitt, George Washington, 8, 187–188
Police, state control of, 244; reform of, 247–249
Political corruption and civic education, 279–282; and the churches, 282–285; common cause, xiv; Cuban Post Office, 85; definition of, xiii, xiv; effects of, xvii, xviii, 189, 204; in England, 3–5; exaggerated corruption, xv, xvi; fighting anti-corruption measures, 15; foreign, 3–5; in France, 3; in Holland, 3; importance of, 5; increase of, 100–101; in Japan, 4; machine politics, xiv, xv; non-machine, 49–50; and organized labor, 265–271; patronage, 222–223; police, xvi, 14; post office, 85–86; and professional standards, 287; in Sweden, 3; in Switzerland, 3; techniques of, 5–9; theories of, 211–237; T.V. and the press, 285–287; in West Germany, 3; Western and Southern states, 65–68; zoning and land use, 13
Political machine, xiv, xv, 48–49; immigration, 27–31; state and federal government, 24–25; machine control, 34
Polk, President James K., 78
Powell, Representative Adam Clay-

ton, 140
Powell, Paul, 123
Prohibition, 94, 99

Quay, Matthew S., 11, 127

Railroad corruption, 81, 257-258
Randolph, Edmund, 74
Reading, Pennsylvania, 190, 192, 239
Reconstruction Finance Corporation, 153
Reform, 2, 54; in Britain, 4-5; citizen associations and individual reformers, 288-290; Clark-Dilworth in Philadelphia, 108; municipal, 51
Registration of Blacks, 171
Reichley, A. J., 2, 121
Remus, George, 147-148
"Repeaters," 171
Republican Party, 21, 23-24, 59
Rhode Island, 13, 133
Richardson, William, 81
Robber Barons, 257
Ronan, William M., 187-188
Roosevelt, Franklin D., 92, 112, 151, 243, 277
Roosevelt, Theodore, 85
Rosenberg, Hans, 3
Ross, Robert Tripp, 157
Rothstein, Arnold, 94, 259
Royko, Mike, 105, 194-195
Rubinstein, Jonathon, 196, 200, 235
Ruef, Abe, 6, 45-46, 49, 260, 274
Ryan, Joseph P., 269

Sale, Kirkpatrick, 115
Salerno, Ralph, 198-199, 241, 252
Salinger, Pierre, 181
Salter, J. T., 106
Sanborn Contracts, 81
San Francisco, 45-46, 49
Schmitz, Eugene, 6, 45-46, 49, 260
Scott, James C., 213
Seabury, Judge Samuel, 95, 196-197
Serpico, Frank, 281
Sharp, Frank W., 128

Sheppard, Senator Morris, 143
Simpkins, Edgar, 4, 272
Small, Governor Len, 11, 268
Smathers, Senator George, 138
Smelser, Neil J., 188, 216, 218
Smith, Alfred E., 149
Smith, Senator "Cotton Ed", 138
Smith, Frank L., 259
Smith, Jess, 148, 149
Smith, Ralph Lee, 129
South Carolina, 66, 133
Southern Pacific Railroad, 15, 70-71, 87, 258
Spencer, Judge, 58
State governments, effect of separation of powers, 119; failure to set standards for local government, 120; "individualistic, moralistic, traditionalist," 132-133; reform of, 130-131; role in corruption, 119-120; politics of, 120; law enforcement, 244
State Police, 129-130
Stead, William T., 47
Steffens, Lincoln, 50, 64, 217, 231, 255-256, 261-262
Stout, Hiram, 3
"Street money", 172
Strobel, Peter, 156
Sulzer, Governor William, 62-63
Sutherland, Joel B., 23
Sweeny, Peter, 38-39
Swartwout, Samuel, 22

Tammany Hall, 8, 22-23, 37-38, 42-43, 50, 62, 91, 93-94; Organized Crime, 96; political connections, 49
Talbot, Harold, 156
Tarr, Joel A., 188, 211
Tasmanian, Dodge, 172
Teamsters Union, 102, 266, 270-271
Teapot Dome, 12, 143, 146
Texas, 11, 127-128
Thomas, Lately, 49
Thompson, Governor James R., 123, 250

Thompson, William "Big Bill", 99–100
De Tocqueville, Alexis, 1
Tolchin, Martin and Susan, 222–223
Triangle shirtwaist fire, 204
Truman, President Harry, xv, 2, 7, 145, 151–153, 160, 277
Tweed Ring, 8, 12, 15, 35–37, 40–41, 48–49, 114, 116, 213, 225, 260
Tweed, William Marcy, 35, 37–41

Union Pacific Railroad, 81
Unruh, Jess, 180
Utah, 131, 133

Vare Brothers, 106
Vare, Edwin, 45
Van Buren, Martin, 58–59
Vaughan, Harry H., 144
Virginia, 68, 131–133
Voloshen, Nathaniel, 141

Walsh, Senator Thomas J., 143
Warren, Earl, 197, 228
War of 1812, misconduct, 74
Warmoth, Henry Clay Governor, 67
Warner, Sam Bass, Jr., 188
Washington, President George, 73–74
Washington state, 133
Watergate, Omission of, xiii, xv, xvi
Watkins, Tobias, 74
Weccacoe Engine Company, 23
Weisband, Edward and Homas M. Frank, 277–278

Welles, Gideon, 273
Wenzell, Adolphe, 155–156
Wesley, John, 4
West Virginia, 10, 129, 133
Wetmer, Claude, 66
Wever, Max, 209
Wheeler, Senator Burton K., 142
Whig Party, administration of President Zachary Taylor, 78
Whiskey Ring, 81–82
White, Leonard D., 1, 76, 221, 233, 282–283
Wickersham Commission, 147
Wilkinson, General James, 74
Williams, Senator John J., 144
Williams, Robert H., xv, xvi, 228–229
Wilson, James Q., 229, 231, 235
Wilson, Orlando W., 198
Wilson, President Woodrow, 146
Winter-Berger, Robert N., 141
Wisconsin, 123, 130, 131, 133
Wolfinger, Raymond E., 90, 209, 212, 225–226, 231
Wood, Fernando Mayor, 170
Works Progress Administration, 151
Wraith, Ronald, 4, 272

Yazoo land frauds, 69
Yerkes, Charles T., 47
Young, Merle, 153

Zink, Harold, 283

About the Authors

George C. S. Benson received the B.A. in 1928 from Pomona College, the M.A. in 1929 from the University of Illinois and the M.A. in 1930 from Harvard University. He also received the Ph.D. from Harvard University and has several honorary degrees. He has had a distinguished career of lecturing and teaching positions at several major universities, as well as a positon as Deputy Assistant Secretary of Defense (Education) from 1969-72. Dr. Benson is currently President Emeritus, Claremont Men's College and director of the Salvatori Center for the Study of Individual Freedom in the Modern World. In addition, he has held numerous consulting and public service positions with many organizations including Governor of California's Coordinating Council on Higher Education (1967-69), president, Western College Association (1958-62), and the Board of Foreign Scholarships, U.S. Department of State (1956-60). Along with many articles on political science and ethical matters, Dr. Benson has published several books—*Amoral America* (1975), *The Politics of Urbanism* (1972), *The New Centralization* (1941), *Civil Service in Massachusetts,* and *Financial Control and Integration* (1933).

Steven A. Maaranen received the B.A. in political science from Claremont Men's College and the M.A. and the Ph.D. from Claremont Graduate School. Dr. Maaranen has been a research associate at the Salvatori Center for the Study of Individual Freedom in the Modern World from 1975 to 1976, and an area analyst-Middle East, for the U.S. Army from May 1972 to October 1973. His research interests include political philosophy, nineteenth century American politics, the political machine and political corruption, and British politics and foreign policy in the interwar years. He is currently assistant professor of political science at Claremont Men's College, where he teaches american government, ancient and medieval political philosophy, and modern political philosophy. He has just published an article on Leo Strauss in *Modern Age.*

Alan Heslop received the B.A. and M.A. from Oxford University, and the Ph.D. in political science from the University of Texas, Austin. He has been associate professor and chairman of the Department of Political Science at Clarement Men's College and the Don H. and Edessa Rose Associate Professor of State and Local Government at Claremont Graduate School. He was recently dean of faculty at Claremont Men's College. Dr. Heslop has been a legislative aide to U.S. Senators Hugh Scott and Richard Schweiker and has served as a consultant to various state and national legislative committees. He has been executive director of the California Congressional Recognition Plan and has been active as a consultant in senatorial and presidential election campaigns. Dr. Heslop is the author of "Design and Implementation of a Computerized Redistricting System for California: Consulting Papers for the California Assembly and Compass Systems, Inc." and has special expertise in campaign expenditures, redistricting of legislative seats, and welfare problems.